ESSAYS DIVINE AND HUMAN

Sri Aurobindo

Essays Divine and Human

with
Thoughts and Aphorisms

SRI AUROBINDO ASHRAM
PONDICHERRY

First edition 1994
Second edition 1997
Second impression 2009

Rs 185
ISBN 978-81-7058-891-7

© Sri Aurobindo Ashram Trust 1994, 1997
Published by Sri Aurobindo Ashram Publication Department
Pondicherry 605 002
Web http://www.sabda.in

Lotus Press
PO Box 325
Twin Lakes, WI 53181 USA
www.lotuspress.com
lotuspress@lotuspress.com

Publisher's Note

Essays Divine and Human consists of short prose pieces written by Sri Aurobindo after his arrival in Pondicherry in 1910 but not published before his passing in 1950. Short prose works written during the same period and published during his lifetime appear in *Essays in Philosophy and Yoga*, volume 13 of THE COMPLETE WORKS OF SRI AUROBINDO.

There are indications in Sri Aurobindo's Pondicherry notebooks that he intended to bring out a collection of essays on yoga and other subjects. The headings written above two pieces, "Essays Divine and Human" and "Essays — Human and Divine", seem to have been intended as possible titles for this proposed book. The editors have chosen the first of these to be the title of the present volume.

The material has been arranged in four parts:
  I. *Essays Divine and Human* — complete essays on yoga and related subjects, arranged in five chronological sections.
  II. *From Man to Superman: Notes and Fragments on Philosophy, Psychology and Yoga*, arranged in three thematic sections.
  III. *Notes and Fragments on Various Subjects*, arranged in five thematic sections.
  IV. *Thoughts and Aphorisms*, as arranged by the author in three sections, with a section of additional aphorisms.

All the writings in this book have been reproduced from Sri Aurobindo's manuscripts. He did not prepare any of them for publication and left many in an unfinished state. Simple editorial problems arising from illegibility, incomplete revision, etc. are indicated by means of the system explained in the Guide to Editorial Notation on the next page. More complex problems are discussed in the reference volume.

Guide to Editorial Notation

The contents of this volume were never prepared by Sri Aurobindo for publication. They have been transcribed from manuscripts that present a variety of textual difficulties. As far as possible the editors have indicated these problems by means of the notation shown below.

Notation	Textual Problem
[?word]	Doubtful reading
[...]	Illegible word(s), one group of three spaced dots for each presumed word
[.......]	Word(s) lost by mutilation of the manuscript (at the beginning of a piece, indicates that a page or pages of the manuscript have been lost)
[word]	Word(s) omitted by the author or lost through damage to the manuscript that are required by grammar or sense, and that could be supplied by the editors
[?]	Word(s) omitted by the author that could not be supplied by the editors
[ ]	Blank left by the author to be filled in later but left unfilled, which the editors were not able to fill
[*note*]	Situations requiring textual explication; all such information is printed in italics

Some textual situations requiring editorial intervention could not be handled by the above system. Such cases are discussed or tabulated in the reference volume (volume 35).

CONTENTS

Part One
Essays Divine and Human

Section One (circa 1911)
Certitudes	5
Moksha	6
Man	7
Philosophy	8
The Siddhis	14
The Psychology of Yoga	18

Section Two (1910–1913)
Na Kinchidapi Chintayet	23
The Sources of Poetry	28
The Interpretation of Scripture	33
On Original Thinking	38
The Balance of Justice	46
Social Reform	50
Hinduism and the Mission of India	59
The Psychology of Yoga	64
The Claims of Theosophy	67
Science & Religion in Theosophy	72
Sat	75
Sachchidananda	84
The Silence behind Life	88

Section Three (circa 1913)
The Psychology of Yoga	
Initial Definitions and Descriptions	93
The Object of Our Yoga	96
Purna Yoga	
I. The Entire Purpose of Yoga	98
II. Parabrahman, Mukti & Human Thought-Systems	103
III. Parabrahman and Parapurusha	107

CONTENTS

Natural and Supernatural Man
    The Evolutionary Aim in Yoga   108
    The Fullness of Yoga — In Condition   115
    Nature   122
    Maya   133

Section Four (1914–1919)
    The Beginning and the End   141
    The Hour of God   146
    Beyond Good and Evil   148
    The Divine Superman   150

Section Five (1927 and after)
    The Law of the Way   155
    Man and the Supermind   157
    The Involved and Evolving Godhead   161
    The Evolution of Consciousness   165
    The Path   169

Part Two
From Man to Superman: Notes and Fragments on Philosophy, Psychology and Yoga

Section One. Philosophy: God, Nature and Man
    God: The One Reality   177
    Nature: The World-Manifestation   193
    Man and Superman   221

Section Two. Psychology: The Science of Consciousness
    The Problem of Consciousness   271
    Consciousness and the Inconscient   290
    The Science of Consciousness   302

Section Three. Yoga: Change of Consciousness and Transformation of Nature
    The Way of Yoga   327
    Partial Systems of Yoga   344
    Integral Yoga   356

CONTENTS

Part Three
Notes and Fragments on Various Subjects

Section One. The Human Being in Time
The Marbles of Time	379
A Theory of the Human Being	380
A Cyclical Theory of Evolution	382

Section Two. The East and the West
A Misunderstanding of Continents	389
Towards Unification	391
China, Japan and India	394

Section Three. India
Renascent India	397
Where We Stand in Literature	398

Section Four. Genius, Poetry, Beauty
The Origin of Genius	403
Poetic Genius	404
The Voices of the Poets	405
Pensées	407
A Dream	409
The Beauty of a Crow's Wings	410

Section Five. Science, Religion, Reason, Justice
Science	413
Religion	414
Reason and Society	415
Justice	418

Part Four
Thoughts and Aphorisms

Jnana	423
Karma	453
Bhakti	481
Additional Aphorisms	500

Part One

Essays Divine and Human

The essays in this part have been arranged chronologically in five sections. The contents of several of the sections or subsections seem to have been intended by Sri Aurobindo to be published as series or collections of essays.

Section One

Circa 1911

Certitudes

In the deep there is a greater deep, in the heights a greater height. Sooner shall man arrive at the borders of infinity than at the fulness of his own being. For that being is infinity, is God —
   I aspire to infinite force, infinite knowledge, infinite bliss. Can I attain it? Yes, but the nature of infinity is that it has no end. Say not therefore that I attain it. I become it. Only so can man attain God by becoming God.
   But before attaining he can enter into relations with him. To enter into relations with God is Yoga, the highest rapture & the noblest utility. There are relations within the compass of the humanity we have developed. These are called prayer, worship, adoration, sacrifice, thought, faith, science, philosophy. There are other relations beyond our developed capacity, but within the compass of the humanity we have yet to develop. Those are the relations that are attained by the various practices we usually call Yoga.
   We may not know him as God, we may know him as Nature, our Higher Self, Infinity, some ineffable goal. It was so that Buddha approached Him; so approaches him the rigid Adwaitin. He is accessible even to the Atheist. To the materialist He disguises Himself in matter. For the Nihilist he waits ambushed in the bosom of Annihilation.

ये यथा मां प्रपद्यन्ते तांस्तथैव भजाम्यहम् ।

Moksha

The pessimists have made moksha synonymous with annihilation or dissolution, but its true meaning is freedom. He who is free from bondage, is free, is mukta. But the last bondage is the passion for liberation itself which must be renounced before the soul can be perfectly free, and the last knowledge is the realisation that there is none bound, none desirous of freedom, but the soul is for ever and perfectly free, that bondage is an illusion and the liberation from bondage is an illusion. Not only are we bound but in play, the mimic knots are of such a nature that we ourselves can at our pleasure undo them.

Nevertheless the bonds are many and intricate. The most difficult of all their knots is egoism, the delusion that we have an individual existence sufficient in itself, separate from the universal and only being, ekamevadwitiyam, who is one not only beyond Time, Space and Causality. Not only are we all Brahman in our nature and being, waves of one sea, but we are each of us Brahman in His entirety, for that which differentiates and limits us, nama and rupa, exists only in play and for the sake of the world-drama.

Whence then comes this delusion of egoism, if there is no separate existence and only Brahman is? We answer that there is separate existence but only in manifestation not in reality. It is as if one actor could play different parts not in succession but at one and the same moment; each part is He Himself, one and indivisible, but each part is different from the other. Brahman extends Himself in Time, Space & Causality which do not condition Him but exist in Him and can at any time be changed or abolished, and in Time, Space & Causality He attaches Himself to many namarupas which are merely existences in His universal being. They are real in manifestation, unreal outside manifestation.

Man

The Shastras use the same word for man and the one divine and universal Being — Purusha — as if to lay stress upon the oneness of humanity with God. Nara and Narayana are the eternal couple, who, though they are two, are one, eternally different, eternally the same. Narayana, say the scholiasts, is he who dwells in the waters, but I rather think it means he who is the essence and sum of all humanity. Wherever there is a man, there there is Narayana; for the two cannot be separated. I think sometimes that when Christ spoke of himself as the Son of Man, he really meant the son of the Purusha, and almost find myself imagining that *anthropos* is only the clumsy Greek equivalent, the literal and ignorant translation of some Syrian word which corresponded to our Purusha.

Be that as it may, there can be no doubt that man is full of divine possibilities — he is not merely a term in physical evolution, but himself the field of a spiritual evolution which with him began and in him will end. It was only when man was made, that the gods were satisfied — they who had rejected the animal forms, — and cried सुकृतमेव, "Man indeed is well and wonderfully made; the higher evolution can now begin." He is like God, the sum of all other types and creatures from the animal to the god, infinitely variable where they are fixed, dynamic where they, even the highest, are static, and, therefore, although in the present and in his attainment a little lower than the angels, yet in the eventuality and in his culmination considerably higher than the gods. The other or fixed types, animals, gods, giants, Titans, demigods, can rise to a higher development than their own, but they must use the human body and the terrestrial birth to effect the transition.

Philosophy

The knowledge which the man of pure intellect prefers to a more active and mundane curiosity, has in its surroundings a certain loftiness and serene detachment that cannot fail in their charm. To withdraw from contact with emotion and life and weave a luminous colourless shadowless web of thought, alone and far away in the infinite azure empyrean of pure ideas, can be an enthralling pastime fit for Titans or even for Gods. The ideas so found have always their value and it is no objection to their truth that, when tested by the rude ordeal of life and experience, they go to pieces. All that inopportune disaster proves is that they are no fit guides to ordinary human conduct; for material life which is the field of conduct is only intellectual on its mountaintops; in the plains and valleys ideas must undergo limitation by unideal conditions and withstand the shock of crude sub-ideal forces.

Nevertheless conduct is a great part of our existence and the mere metaphysical, logical or scientific knowledge that either does not help me to act or even limits my self-manifestation through action, cannot be my only concern. For God has not set me here merely to think, to philosophise, to weave metaphysical systems, to play with words and syllogisms, but to act, love and know. I must act divinely so that I may become divine in being and deed; I must learn to love God not only in Himself but in all beings, appearances, objects, enjoyments, events, whether men call them good or bad, real or mythical, fortunate or calamitous; and I must know Him with the same divine impartiality and completeness in order that I may come to be like Him, perfect, pure and unlimited — that which all sons of Man must one day be. This, I cannot help thinking, is the meaning and purpose of the Lila. It is not true that because I think, I am; but rather because I think, feel and act, and even while I am doing any or all of these things, can transcend the thought, feeling and action, therefore I am. Because I manifest, I am, and because I transcend manifestation, I am. The formula is not so clear and catching as the Cartesian, but there is a fuller truth in its greater comprehensiveness.

The man of unalloyed intellect has a very high and difficult function; it is his function to teach men to think clearly and purely. In order to effect that for mankind, to carry reason as far as that somewhat stumbling and hesitating Pegasus will go, he sacrifices all the bypaths of mental enjoyment, the shady alleys and the moonlit gardens of the soul, in order that he may walk in rare air and a cold sunlight, living highly and austerely on the peaks of his mind and seeking God severely through knowledge. He treads down his emotions, because emotion distorts reason and replaces it by passions, desires, preferences, prejudices, prejudgments. He avoids life, because life awakes all his sensational being and puts his reason at the mercy of egoism, of sensational reactions of anger, fear, hope, hunger, ambition, instead of allowing it to act justly and do disinterested work. It becomes merely the paid pleader of a party, a cause, a creed, a dogma, an intellectual faction. Passion and eagerness, even intellectual eagerness, so disfigure the greatest minds that even Shankara becomes a sophist and a word-twister, and even Buddha argues in a circle. The philosopher wishes above all to preserve his intellectual righteousness; he is or should be as careful of his mental rectitude as the saint of his moral stainlessness. Therefore he avoids, as far as the world will let him, the conditions which disturb. But in this way he cuts himself off from experience and only the gods can know without experience. Sieyès said that politics was a subject of which he had made a science. He had, but the pity was that though he knew the science of politics perfectly, he did not know politics itself in the least and when he did enter political life, he had formed too rigidly the logical habit to replace it in any degree by the practical. If he had reversed the order or at least coordinated experiment with his theories before they were formed, he might have succeeded better. His readymade Constitutions are monuments of logical perfection and practical ineffectiveness. They have the weakness of all logic; — granting your premises, your conclusion is all-triumphant; but then who is going to grant you your premises? There is nothing Fact and Destiny delight in so much as upsetting the logician's major and minor.

The logician thinks he has ensured himself against error when he has made a classification of particular fallacies; but he forgets the supreme and general fallacy, the fallacy of thinking that logic can, as a rule, prove anything but particular and partial propositions dealing with a fragmentary and one-sided truth. Logic? But Truth is not logical; it contains logic, but is not contained by it. A particular syllogism may be true, so far as it goes, covering a sharply limited set of facts, but even a set of syllogisms cannot exhaust truth on a general subject, for the simple reason that they necessarily ignore a number of equally valid premises, facts or possibilities which support a modified or contrary view. If one could arrive first at a conclusion, then at its exact opposite and, finally, harmonise the contradiction, one might arrive at some approach to the truth. But this is a process logic abhors. Its fundamental conception is that two contradictory statements cannot be true at the same time and place & in the same circumstances. Now, Fact and Nature and God laugh aloud when they hear the logician state his fundamental conception. For the universe is based on the simultaneous existence of contradictions covering the same time, place and circumstances. The elementary conception that God is at once One and Many, Finite & Infinite, Formed and Formless and that each attribute is the condition of the existence of its opposite, is a thing metaphysical logic has been boggling over ever since the reign of reason began.

The metaphysician thinks that he has got over the difficulty about the validity of premises by getting to the tattwas, the ideal truths of universal existence. Afterwards, he thinks, there can be no fear of confusion or error and by understanding and fixing them we shall be able to proceed from a sound basis to the rest of our task. He fashions his critique of reason, his system of pramanas, and launches himself into the wide inane. Alas, the tattwas are the very foundation, support and initial reason of this worldwide contradiction and logically impossible conciliation of opposites in which God has shadowed out some few rays of His luminous & infinite reality, — impossible to bind with the narrow links of a logical chain precisely because it is infinite. As for the pramanas, their manipulation is the instrument of all difference of opinion and the accompaniment to an unending jangle of debate.

Both the logician and the philosopher are apt to forget that they are dealing with words and words divorced from experience can be the most terrible misleaders in the world. Precisely because they are capable of giving us so much light, they are also capable of lighting us into impenetrable darkness. Tato bhuya iva te tamo ya u vidyayam ratah; "Deeper is the darkness into which they enter who are addicted to knowledge alone." This sort of word worship and its resultant luminous darkness is very common in India and nowhere more than in the intellectualities of religion, so that when a man talks to me about the One and Maya and the Absolute, I am tempted to ask him, "My friend, how much have you experienced of these things in which you instruct me or how much are you telling me out of a vacuum or merely from intellectual appreciation? If you have merely ideas and no experience, you are no authority for me and your logic is to me but the clashing of cymbals good to deafen an opponent into silence, but of no use for knowledge. If you say you have experienced, then I have to ask you, 'Are you sure you have measured all possible experience?' If you have not, then how can you be sure that my contradictory experience is not equally true? If you say you have, then I know you to be deluded or a pretender, one who has experienced a fragment or nothing; for God in His entire being is unknowable, avijnatam vijanatam."

The scientist thinks he has corrected the mistakes of the metaphysician because he refuses to deal with anything but a narrow and limited circle of facts and condemns everything else as hallucination, imposture and imagination. His parti pris, his fierce and settled prejudgments, his determined begging of the question are too obvious and well known to need particular illustration. He forgets that all experiences are facts, that ideas are facts, that subjective knowledge is the one fact of which he can be decently sure and that he knows nothing even of the material world by his senses but only by the use his subjective knowledge makes of the senses. Many a materialist will tell you that only those facts can be accepted as a basis to knowledge which the senses supply, — a position which no man can substantiate and which his science daily denies in practice. These reasoners consent to trust to their sovereign subjective instrument when it settles for them the truths about this world visible to their lower instruments, but the same sovereign instrument is condemned as wholly fallacious and insane when it deals in precisely the same way with another field of perceptions and experiences. When my subjective experience tells him, "I am hungry", he consents; "Of course, you must be since you say so." But let it tell him, "I am full of bliss from an immaterial source"; or "By certain higher instruments repeatedly tested I know that I have wandered in regions illuminated by no material sun," and he answers, "You are only fit for the gaol or the lunatic asylum." No one has seen the earth whirling round the sun, indeed we see daily the opposite, yet he holds the first opinion obstinately, but if you say "Although God is not seen of men, yet He exists," he turns from you angrily and stalks into his laboratory.

The practical man avoids error by refusing to think at all. His method at least cannot be right. It is not right even for the practical uses he prefers exclusively to all others. You see him stumbling into some pit because he refuses to walk with a light and then accusing adverse circumstances or his evil fortune, or he shouts, elbows, jostles, tumbles and stumbles himself into a final success and departs at last, satisfied; leaving behind a name in history and a legacy of falsehood, evil and suffering to unborn generations. The method of the practical man is the shortest and most facile, but the least admirable of all.

Truth is an infinitely complex reality and he has the best chance of arriving nearest to it who most recognises but is not daunted by its infinite complexity. We must look at the whole thought-tangle, fact, emotion, idea, truth beyond idea, conclusion, contradiction, modification, ideal, practice, possibility, impossibility (which must be yet attempted,) and keeping the soul calm and the eye clear in this mighty flux and gurge of the world, seek everywhere for some word of harmony, not forgetting immediate in ultimate truth, nor ultimate in immediate, but giving each its due place and portion in the Infinite Purpose. Some minds, like Plato, like Vivekananda, feel more than others this mighty complexity and give voice to it. They pour out thought in torrents or in rich and majestic streams. They are not logically careful of consistency, they cannot build up any coherent, yet comprehensive systems, but they quicken men's minds and liberate them from religious, philosophic and scientific dogma and tradition. They leave the world not surer, but freer than when they entered it.

Some men seek to find the truth by imaginative perception. It is a good instrument like logic, but like logic it breaks down before it reaches the goal. Neither ought to be allowed to do more than take us some way and then leave us. Others think that a fine judgment can arrive at the true balance. It does, for a time; but the next generation upsets that fine balancing, consenting to a coarser test or demanding a finer. The religious prefer inspiration, but inspiration is like the lightning, brilliantly illuminating only a given reach of country and leaving the rest in darkness intensified by the sharpness of that light. Vast is our error if we mistake that bit of country for the whole universe. Is there then no instrument of knowledge that can give us the heart of truth and provide us with the key word of existence? I think there is, but the evolution of mankind at large yet falls far short of it; their highest tread only on the border of that illumination. After all pure intellect carries us very high. But neither the scorner of pure intellectual ideation, nor its fanatic and devotee can attain to the knowledge in which not only the senses reflect or the mind thinks about things, but the ideal faculty directly knows them.

The Siddhis

Some men sneer at the Siddhis because they do not believe in them, others because they think it is noble and spiritual to despise them. Both attitudes proceed from ignorance. It is true that to some natures the rule of omne ignotum pro magnifico holds and everything that is beyond their knowledge is readily accepted as true marvel and miracle, and of such a temper are the credulous made, it is also true that to others it is omne ignotum pro falso and they cannot forbear ridiculing as fraud or pitiable superstition everything that is outside the reach of their philosophy. This is the temper of the incredulous. But the true temper is to be neither credulous nor incredulous, but calmly and patiently to inquire. Let the inquiry be scrupulous, but also scrupulously fair on both sides. Some think it shows superior rationality, even when they inquire, to be severe, and by that they mean to seize every opportunity of disproving the phenomenon offered to their attention. Such an attitude is good rather for limiting knowledge than increasing it. If it saves us from some errors of assertion, it betrays us into many errors of negation and postpones developments of the utmost importance to our human advance.

I do not wish to argue the question of the existence or nonexistence of Yogic siddhis; for it is not with me a question of debate, or of belief and disbelief, since I know by daily experience that they exist. I am concerned rather with their exact nature and utility. And here one is met by the now fashionable habit, among people presuming to be Vedantic and spiritual, of a denunciation and holy horror of the Yogic siddhis. They are, it seems, Tantric, dangerous, immoral, delusive as conjuring tricks, a stumbling block in the path of the soul's liberation. Swami Vivekananda did much to encourage this attitude by his eagerness to avoid all mention of them at the outset of his mission in order not to startle the incredulity of the Europeans. "These things are true" he said, "but let them lie hidden." And now many who have not the motives of Vivekananda, think that they can ape his spiritual greatness by imitating his limitations.

There was no such weakness in the robust temperament of our forefathers. Our great Rishis of old did not cry out upon Siddhis, but recognised them as a part, though not the most important part of Yogic accomplishment, and used them with an abundant and unhesitating vigour. They are recognised in our sacred books, formally included in Yoga by so devotional a Purana as the Bhagawat, noted and some of their processes carefully tabled by Patanjali. Even in the midnight of the Kali great Siddhas and saints have used them more sparingly, but with power and effectiveness. It would be difficult for many of them to do otherwise than use the siddhis since by the very fact of their spiritual elevation, these powers have become not exceptional movements, but the ordinary processes of their thought and action. It is by the use of the siddhis that the Siddhas sitting on the mountains help the world out of the heart of their solitude and silence. Jesus Christ made the use of the siddhis a prominent feature of his pure, noble and spiritual life, nor did he hesitate to communicate them to his disciples — the laying of hands, the healing of the sick, the ashirvada, the abhishap, the speaking with many tongues were all given to them. The day of Pentecost is still kept holy by the Christian Church. Joan of Arc used her siddhis to liberate France. Socrates had his siddhis, some of them of a very material nature. Men of great genius are usually born with some of them and use them unconsciously. Even in natures far below the power and clarity of genius we see their occasional or irregular operation. The West, always avid of knowledge, is struggling, sadly hampered by misuse and imposture, to develop them and gropes roughly for the truth about them in the phenomena of hypnotism, clairvoyance, telepathy, vouched for by men and women of great intellectuality and sincerity. Returning Eastwards, where only their right practice has been understood, the lives of our saints northern and southern are full of the record of Siddhis. Sri Ramakrishna, whose authority is quoted against them, not only made inward use of them but manifested them with no inconsiderable frequency in His lila. I see nothing in this long record immoral, dangerous or frivolous. But because Europe looks with scorn and incredulity on these "miracles" and this "magic", we too must needs be ashamed of them, hustle them into the background and plead that only a few charlatans and followers of false paths profess their use. But as for us, we are men of intellect and spirituality, ascetics, devotees, self-deniers, Vedantins; for these things we are too high and we leave them to Theosophists, immoral Tantrics and deluded pseudo-Yogins.

Let us have done with cant and pretension in all matters. There are no such things as miracles in this world of divine processes, for either there is no such thing as a miracle or, if we consider more closely, everything in this world is a miracle. A miracle is, literally, a marvel, a thing to be wondered at — so long as the process is [not] known. Wireless telegraphy is a great marvel, the speechless passage of a thought from brain to brain is a yet greater, yet it happens daily even in the most commonplace minds and existences. But when the process is known, nothing is left to be wondered at except the admirable greatness of wisdom, width & variety of conception & subtlety & minuteness in execution with which this universe is managed. And even that wonder ceases when we know God and realise that the most wonderful movements of the cosmos are but trifles and "conjuring-tricks" compared with His infinite Reality. And as it is with this siddhi of science which we call wireless telegraphy and with this other siddhi of nature which is exampled in the momentary or rapid spread of a single thought or emotion in a mob, a nation, an army, so it is with the Yogic siddhis. Explain & master their processes, put them in their proper relation to the rest of the economy of the universe and we shall find that they are neither miraculous nor marvellous nor supernatural. They are supernormal only in the way in which aviation is supernormal or motoring or the Chinese alphabet. Nor is there anything magical in them except in so far as magic, the science of the Persian Magi, means originally & properly the operations of superior power or superior knowledge. And in that sense the occultism of the present day is magic precisely in the same sense as the scientific experiments of Roger Bacon or Paracelsus. There is a good deal of fraud and error and self-deception mixed up with it, but so there was with the earliest efforts of the European scientists. The defects of Western practitioners or Eastern quacks do not get rid of our true & ancient Yoga.

The Psychology of Yoga

Yoga is not a modern invention of the human mind, but our ancient and prehistoric possession. The Veda is our oldest extant human document and the Veda, from one point of view, is a great compilation of practical hints about Yoga. All religion is a flower of which Yoga is the root; all philosophy, poetry & the works of genius use it, consciously or unconsciously, as an instrument. We believe that God created the world by Yoga and by Yoga He will draw it into Himself again. Yogah prabhavapyayau, Yoga is the birth and passing away of things. When Srikrishna reveals to Arjuna the greatness of His creation and the manner in which He has built it out of His being by a reconciliation of logical opposites, he says "Pasya me yogam aishwaram", Behold my divine Yoga. We usually attach a more limited sense to the word; when we use or hear it, we think of the details of Patanjali's system, of rhythmic breathing, of peculiar ways of sitting, of concentration of mind, of the trance of the adept. But these are merely details of particular systems. The systems are not the thing itself, any more than the water of an irrigation canal is the river Ganges. Yoga may be done without the least thought for the breathing, in any posture or no posture, without any insistence on concentration, in the full waking condition, while walking, working, eating, drinking, talking with others, in any occupation, in sleep, in dream, in states of unconsciousness, semiconsciousness, double-consciousness. It is no nostrum or system or fixed practice, but an eternal fact of process based on the very nature of the Universe.

Nevertheless in practice the name may be limited to certain applications of this general process for specific and definite ends. Yoga stands essentially on the fact that in this world we are everywhere one, yet divided; one yet divided in our being, one with yet divided from our fellow creatures of all kinds, one with yet divided from the infinite existence which we call God, Nature or Brahman. Yoga, generally, is the power which the soul in one body has of entering into effective relation with other souls, with parts of itself which are behind the waking consciousness, with forces of Nature and objects in Nature, with the Supreme Intelligence, Power & Bliss which governs the world either for the sake of that union in itself or for the purpose of increasing or modifying our manifest being, knowledge, faculty, force or delight. Any system which organises our inner being & our outer frame for these ends may be called a system of Yoga.

Section Two

1910–1913

Section Two

1910–1943

Na Kinchidapi Chintayet

The cessation of thought is the one thing which the believer in intellect as the highest term of our evolution cannot contemplate with equanimity. To master the fleeting randomness of thought by regulating the intellectual powers and thinking consecutively and clearly is an ideal he can understand. But to still this higher development of thought seems to him the negation of human activity, a reversion to the condition of the stone. Yet it is certain that it is only by the stilling of the lower that the higher gets full play. So long as the body and the vital desires are active the mind is necessarily distracted and it is only when the body is forgotten and the vital part consents to quietude that a man can concentrate himself in thought and follow undisturbed the consecutive development whether of a train of reasoning or a train of inspiration. Not only is this so, but the higher faculties of the mind can only work at their best when the lower are quieted. If the accumulations in the chitta, the recording part of the mind, are continually active, full as it is of preconceived ideas, prejudices, predilections, the great mass of previous *sanskaras*, the reflective mind which is ordinarily called the reason is obstructed in its work and comes to false conclusions. It is essential for the faculties of the reason to be freed as far as may be from this ever increasing accumulation of thought-sensations good and bad, false and true which we call mind — manas. It is this freedom which is called the scientific spirit. To form no conclusions which are not justified by observation and reasoning, to doubt everything until it is proved but to deny nothing until it is disproved, to be always ready to reconsider old conclusions in the light of new facts, to give a candid consideration to every new idea or old idea revived if it deserves a hearing, no matter how contradictory it may be of previously ascertained experience or previously formed conclusion, is the sceptical temper, the temper of the inquirer, the true scientist, the untrammelled thinker. The interference of prejudgment and predilection means bondage and until the higher mind has shaken off these fetters, it is not free; it works in chains, it sees in blinkers. This is as true of the materialist refusing to consider spiritualism and occultism as it is of the religionist refusing to consider Science. Freedom is the first requisite of full working power, the freedom of the higher from the lower. The mind must be free from the body if it is to be purified from the grossness which clogs its motions, the heart must be free from the obsessions of the body if love and high aspiration are to increase, the reason must be free from the heart and the lower mind if it is to reflect perfectly, — for the heart can inspire, it cannot think, it is a vehicle of direct knowledge coloured by emotion, not of ratiocination. By [a] similar process if there is anything higher than the reason it can only be set free to work by the stillness of the whole mind not excluding the reflective faculties. This is a conclusion from analogy, indeed, and not entirely binding until confirmed by experience and observation. But we have given reason in past articles for supposing that there is a higher force than the logical reason — and the experience and observation of Yoga confirm the inference from analogy that the stillness of the mind is the first requisite for discovering, distinguishing and perfecting the action of this higher element in the psychology of man.

The stillness of the mind is prepared by the process of concentration. In the science of Rajayoga after the heart has been stilled and the mind prepared, the next step is to subjugate the body by means of *asan* or the fixed and motionless seat. The aim of this fixity is twofold, first the stillness of the body and secondly the forgetfulness of the body. When one can sit still and utterly forget the body for a long period of time, then the asan is said to have been mastered. In ordinary concentration when the body is only comparatively still it is not noticed, but there is an undercurrent of physical consciousness which may surge up at any moment into the upper current of thought and disturb it. The Yogin seeks to make the forgetfulness perfect. In the higher processes of concentration this forgetfulness reaches such a point that the bodily consciousness is annulled and in the acme of the *samadhi* a man can be cut or burned without being aware of the physical suffering. Even before the concentration is begun the forgetfulness acquired is sufficient to prevent any intrusion upon the mind except under a more than ordinarily powerful physical stimulus. After this point has been reached the Yoga proceeds to the processes of pranayam by which the whole system is cleared of impurities and the *pranasakti*, the great cosmic energy which lies behind all processes of Nature, fills the body and the brain and becomes sufficient for any work of which man is actually or potentially capable. This is followed by concentration. The first process is to withdraw the senses into the mind. This is partly done in the ordinary process of absorption of which every thinking man is capable. To concentrate upon the work in hand whether it be a manual process, a train of thought, a scientific experiment or a train of inspiration, is the first condition of complete capacity and it is the process by which mankind has been preparing itself for Yoga. To concentrate means to be absorbed; but absorption may be more or less complete. When it is so complete that for all practical purposes the knowledge of outward things ceases, then the first step has been taken towards Yogic absorption. We need not go into the stages of that absorption rising from pratyahar to samadhi and from the lower samadhi to the higher. The principle is to intensify absorption. It is intensified in quality by the entire cessation of outward knowledge, the senses are withdrawn into the mind, the mind into the buddhi or supermind, the supermind into Knowledge, Vijnana, Mahat, out of which all things proceed and in which all things exist. It is intensified in quantity or content; instead of absorption in a set of thoughts or a train of intuitions, the Yogin concentrates his absorption on a single thought, a single image, a single piece of knowledge, and it is his experience that whatever he thus concentrates on, he masters, — he becomes its lord and does with it what he wills. By knowledge he attains to mastery of the world. The final goal of Rajayoga is the annulment of separate consciousness and complete communion with that which alone is whether we call Him Parabrahman or Parameshwara,

Existence in the Highest or Will in the Highest, the Ultimate or God.

In the Gita we have a process which is not the process of Raja-Yoga. It seeks a short cut to the common aim and goes straight to the stillness of the mind. After putting away desire and fear the Yogin sits down and performs upon his thoughts a process of reining in by which they get accustomed to an inward motion. Instead of allowing the mind to flow outward, he compels it to rise and fall within, and if he sees, hears, feels or smells outward objects he pays no attention to them and draws the mind always inward. This process he pursues until the mind ceases to send up thoughts connected with outward things. The result is that fresh thoughts do not accumulate in the chitta at the time of meditation, but only the old ones rise. If the process be farther pursued by rejecting these thoughts as they rise in the mind, in other words by dissociating the thinker from the mind, the operator from the machine and refusing to sanction the continuance of the machine's activity, the result is perfect stillness. This can be done if the thinker whose interest is necessary to the mind, refuses to be interested and becomes passive. The mind goes on for a while by its own impetus just as a locomotive does when the steam is shut off, but a time must come when it will slow down and stop altogether. This is the moment towards which the process moves. Na kinchid api chintayet: — the Yogin should not think of anything at all. Blank cessation of mental activity is aimed at leaving only the sakshi, the witness watching for results. If at this moment the Yogin entrusts himself to the guidance of the universal Teacher within himself, Yoga will fulfil itself without any farther effort on his part. The passivity will be confirmed, the higher faculties will awake and the cosmic Force passing down from the vijnana through the supermind will take charge of the whole machine and direct its workings as the Infinite Lord of All may choose.

Whichever of the two methods be chosen, the result is the same. The mind is stilled, the higher faculties awakened. This stillness of the mind is not altogether a new idea or peculiar to India. The old Highland poets had the secret. When they wished to compose poetry, they first stilled the mind, became entirely passive and waited for the inspiration to flow into them. This habit of yogic passivity, a relic doubtless of the discipline of the Druids, was the source of those faculties of second sight and other psychic powers which are so much more common in this Celtic race than in the other peoples of Europe. The phenomena of inspiration are directly connected with these higher faculties of which we find rudiments or sporadic traces in the past history of human experience.

The Sources of Poetry

The swiftness of the muse has been embodied in the image of Pegasus, the heavenly horse of Greek legend; it was from the rapid beat of his hoofs on the rock that Hippocrene flowed. The waters of Poetry flow in a current or a torrent; where there is a pause or a denial, it is a sign of obstruction in the stream or of imperfection in the mind which the waters have chosen for their bed and continent. In India we have the same idea; Saraswati is for us the goddess of poetry, and her name means the stream or "she who has flowing motion". But even Saraswati is only an intermediary. Ganga is the real mother of inspiration, she who flows impetuously down from the head of Mahadev, God highseated, over the Himalay of the mind to the homes and cities of men. All poetry is an inspiration, a thing breathed into the thinking organ from above; it is recorded in the mind, but is born in the higher principle of direct knowledge or ideal vision which surpasses mind. It is in reality a revelation. The prophetic or revealing power sees the substance; the inspiration perceives the right expression. Neither is manufactured; nor is poetry really a poiesis or composition, nor even a creation, but rather the revelation of something that eternally exists. The ancients knew this truth and used the same word for poet and prophet, creator and seer, *sophos, vates, kavi*.

But there are differences in the manifestation. The greatest motion of poetry comes when the mind is still and the ideal principle works above and outside the brain, above even the hundred petalled lotus of the ideal mind, in its proper empire; for then it is Veda that is revealed, the perfect substance and expression of eternal truth. This higher ideation transcends genius just as genius transcends ordinary intellect and perception. But that great faculty is still beyond the normal level of our evolution. Usually we see the action of the revelation and inspiration reproduced by a secondary, diluted and uncertain process in the mind. But even this secondary and inferior action is so great that it can give us Shakespeare, Homer and Valmekie. There is also a tertiary and yet more common action of the inspiration. For of our three mental instruments of knowledge, — the heart or emotionally realising mind, the observing and reasoning intellect with its aids, fancy and memory, and the intuitive intellect, — it is into the last and highest that the ideal principle transmits its inspirations when the greatest poetry writes itself out through the medium of the poet. But if the intuitive intellect is not strong enough to act habitually, it is better for the poetry to descend into the heart and return to the intellect suffused and coloured with passion and emotion than to be formed directly in the observing intellect.

Poetry written from the reasoning intellect is apt to be full of ingenious conceits, logic, argumentation, rhetorical turns, ornamental fancies, echoes learned and imitative rather than uplifted and transformed. This is what is sometimes called classical poetry, the vigorous and excellent but unemotional and unuplifted poetry of Pope and Dryden. It has its inspiration, its truth and value; it is admirable in its way, but it is only great when it is lifted out of itself into intuitive writing or else invaded by the heart. For everything that needs fire rather than light, driving-force rather than clearness, enthusiasm rather than correctness, the heart is obviously the more potent instrument. Now, poetry to be great must have either enthusiasm or ecstasy.

Yet the poetry that rises up from the heart is usually a turbid stream; our own restless ideas and imaginations mix with the pure inrush from above a turbulent uprush from below, our excited emotions seek an exaggerated expression, our aesthetic habits and predilections busy themselves to demand a satisfaction greatly beyond their due. Such poetry may be inspired, but it is not always suitable or inevitable. There is often a double inspiration, the higher or ecstatic and the lower or emotional, and the lower disturbs and drags down the higher. This is the birth of romantic or excessively exuberant poetry, too rich in expression, too abundant and redundant in substance. The best poetry coming straight from the right centres may be bare and strong, unadorned and lofty, or it may be rich and splendid; it may be at will romantic or classical; but it will always be felt to be the right thing for its purpose; it is always nobly or rapturously inevitable.

But even in the higher centres of the intuitive intellect there may be defects in the inspiration. There is a kind of false fluency which misses the true language of poetry from dulness of perception. Under the impression that it is true and inspired writing it flows with an imperturbable flatness, saying the thing that should be said but not in the way that it should be said, without force and felicity. This is the tamasic or clouded stimulus, active, but full of unenlightenment and self-ignorance. The thing seen is right and good; accompanied with the inspired expression it would make very noble poetry. Instead, it becomes prose rendered unnatural and difficult to tolerate by being cut up into lengths. Wordsworth is the most characteristic and interesting victim of tamasic stimulus. Other great poets fall a prey to it, but that superb and imperturbable self-satisfaction under the infliction is his alone. There is another species of tamasic stimulus which transmits an inspired and faultless expression, but the substance is neither interesting to man nor pleasing to the gods. A good deal of Milton comes under this category. In both cases what has happened is that either the inspiration or the revelation has been active, but its companion activity has refused to associate itself in the work.

It is when the mind works at the form and substance of poetry without either the revelation or the inspiration from above that respectable or minor poetry is produced. Judgment, memory and imagination may work, command of language may be there, but without that secondary action of a higher than intellectual force, it is labour wasted, work that earns respect but not immortality. Doggerel and bastard poetry take their rise not even in the observing intellect but from the sensational mind or the passive memory guided only by the mere physical pleasure of sound and emotion. It is bold, blatant, external, imitative, vulgar; its range of intellectuality and imaginativeness cannot go beyond the vital impulse and the vital delight. But even in the sensational mind there is the possibility of a remote action from the ideal self; for even to the animals who think sensationally only, God has given revelations and inspirations which we call instincts. Under such circumstances even bastard poetry may have a kind of worth, a kind of inevitability. The poet in the sensational man may be entirely satisfied and delighted, and even in the more developed human being the sensational element may find a poetical satisfaction not of the highest. The best ballad poetry and Macaulay's lays are instances in point. Scott is a sort of link between sensational and intellectual poetry. While there are men mainly sensational, secondarily intellectual and not at all ideal, he will always be admired.

Another kind of false inspiration is the rajasic or fiery stimulus. It is not flat and unprofitable like the tamasic, but hasty, impatient and vain. It is eager to avoid labour by catching at the second best expression or the incomplete vision of the idea, insufficiently jealous to secure the best form, the most satisfying substance. Rajasic poets, even when they feel the defect in what they have written, hesitate to sacrifice it because they also feel and are attached either to what in it is valuable or to the memory of their delight when it was first written. If they get a better expression or a fuller sight, they often prefer to reiterate rather than strike out inferior stuff with which they are in love. Sometimes, drifting or struggling helplessly along that shallow and vehement current, they vary one idea or harp on the same imagination without any final success in expressing it inevitably. Examples of the rajasic stimulus are commonest in Shelley and Spenser, but few English poets are free from it. This is the rajasic fault in expression. But the fiery stimulus also perverts or hampers the substance. An absence of self-restraint, an unwillingness to restrict and limit the ideas and imaginations is a sure sign of a rajasic ideality. There is an attempt to exhaust all the possibilities of the subject, to expand and multiply thoughts and imaginative visions beyond the bounds of the right and permissible. Or else the true idea is rejected or fatally anticipated by another which is or seems to be more catching and boldly effective. Keats is the principle exemplar of the first tendency, the Elizabethans of the second. The earlier work of Shakespeare abounds with classical instances. As distinguished from the Greek, English is a pronouncedly rajasic literature and, though there is much in it that is more splendid than almost anything done by the Greeks, — more splendid, not better, — a great deal even of its admired portions are rather rich or meretricious than great and true.

The perfect inspiration in the intuitive intellect is the sattwic or luminous inspiration, which is disinterested, self-contained, yet at will noble, rich or vigorous, having its eye only on the right thing to be said and the right way to say it. It does not allow its perfection to be interfered with by emotion or eagerness, but this does not shut it out from ecstasy and exaltation. On the contrary, its delight of self-enjoyment is a purer and more exquisite enthusiasm than that which attends any other inspiration. It commands and uses emotion without enslaving itself to it. There is indeed a sattwic stimulus which is attached to its own luminosity, limpidity and steadiness, and avoids richness, force or emotion of a poignant character even when these are needed and appropriate. The poetry of Matthew Arnold is often though not always of this character. But this is a limited inspiration. Sattwic as well as rajasic poetry may be written from the uninspired intellect, but the sensational mind never gives birth to sattwic poetry.

One thing has to be added. A poet need not be a reflective critic; he need not have the reasoning and analysing intellect and dissect his own poetry. But two things he must have in some measure to be perfect, the intuitive judgment which shows him at a glance whether he has got the best or the second-best idea, the perfect or the imperfect expression and rhythm, and the intuitive reason which shows him without analysis why or wherein it is best or second-best, perfect or imperfect. These four faculties, revelation or prophecy, inspiration, intuitive judgment and intuitive reason, are the perfect equipment of genius doing the works of interpretative & creative knowledge.

The Interpretation of Scripture

The spirit who lies concealed behind the material world, has given us, through the inspiration of great seers, the Scriptures as helpers and guides to unapparent truth, lamps of great power that send their rays into the darkness of the unknown beyond which He dwells, *tamasah parastat*. They are guides to knowledge, brief indications to enlighten us on our path, not substitutes for thought and experience. They are *shabdam Brahma*, the Word, the oral expression of God, not the thing to be known itself nor the knowledge of Him. *Shabdam* has three elements, the word, the meaning and the spirit. The word is a symbol, *vak* or *nama*; we have to find the *artha*, the meaning or form of thought which the symbol indicates. But the meaning itself is only the indication of something deeper which the thought seeks to convey to the intellectual conception. For not only words, but ideas also are eventually no more than symbols of a knowledge which is beyond ideas and words. Therefore it comes that no idea by itself is wholly true. There is indeed a *rupa*, some concrete or abstract form of knowledge, answering to every name, and it is that which the meaning must present to the intellect. We say a form of knowledge, because according to our philosophy, all things are forms of an essentially unknowable existence which reveals them as forms of knowledge to the essential awareness in its Self, its Atman or Spirit, the Chit in the Sat. But beyond *nama* and *rupa* is *swarupa*, the essential figure of Truth, which we cannot know with the intellect, but only with a higher faculty. And every *swarupa* is itself only a symbol of the one essential existence which can only be known by its symbols because in its ultimate reality it defies logic and exceeds perception, — God.

Since the knowledge the Scripture conveys is so deep, difficult and subtle, — if it were easy what would be the need of the Scripture? — the interpreter cannot be too careful or too perfectly trained. He must not be one who will rest content in the thought-symbol or in the logical implications of the idea; he must hunger and thirst for what is beyond. The interpreter who stops short with the letter, is the slave of a symbol and convicted of error. The interpreter who cannot go beyond the external meaning, is the prisoner of his thought and rests in a partial and incomplete knowledge. One must transgress limits & penetrate to the knowledge behind, which must be experienced before it can be known; for the ear hears it, the intellect observes it, but the spirit alone can possess it. Realisation in the self of things is the only knowledge; all else is mere idea or opinion.

The interpretation of the Veda is hampered by many human irrelevancies. Men set up an authority and put it between themselves and knowledge. The orthodox are indignant that a mere modern should presume to differ from Shankara in interpreting the Vedanta or from Sayana in interpreting the Veda. They forget that Shankara and Sayana are themselves moderns, separated from ourselves by some hundreds of years only, but the Vedas are many thousands of years old. The commentator ought to be studied, but instead we put him in place of the text. Good commentaries are always helpful even when they are wrong, but the best cannot be allowed to fetter inquiry. Sayana's commentary on the Veda helps me by showing what a man of great erudition some hundreds of years ago thought to be the sense of the Scripture. But I cannot forget that even at the time of the Brahmanas the meaning of the Veda had become dark to the men of that prehistoric age. Shankara's commentary on the Upanishads helps me by showing what a man of immense metaphysical genius and rare logical force after arriving at some fundamental realisations thought to be the sense of the Vedanta. But it is evident that he is often at a loss and always prepossessed by the necessity of justifying his philosophy. I find that Shankara had grasped much of Vedantic truth, but that much was dark to him. I am bound to admit what he realised; I am not bound to exclude what he failed to realise. *Aptavakyam*, authority, is one kind of proof; it is not the only kind: *pratyaksha* is more important.

The heterodox on the other hand swear by Max Muller and the Europeans. It is enough for them that Max Muller should have found henotheism in the Vedas for the Vedas to be henotheistic. The Europeans have seen in our Veda only the rude chants of an antique and primitive pastoral race sung in honour of the forces of Nature, and for many their opinion is conclusive of the significance of the *mantras*. All other interpretation is to them superstitious. But to me the ingenious guesses of foreign grammarians are of no more authority than the ingenious guesses of Sayana. It is irrelevant to me what Max Muller thinks of the Veda or what Sayana thinks of the Veda. I should prefer to know what the Veda has to say for itself and, if there is any light there on the unknown or on the infinite, to follow the ray till I come face to face with that which it illumines.

There are those who follow neither Sayana and Shankara nor the Europeans, but interpret Veda and Vedanta for themselves, yet permit themselves to be the slaves of another kind of irrelevancy. They come to the Veda with a preconceived and established opinion and seek in it a support for some trifling polemic; they degrade it to the position of a backer in an intellectual prizefight. Opinions are not knowledge, they are only sidelights on knowledge. Most often they are illegitimate extensions of an imperfect knowledge. A man has perhaps travelled to England and seen Cumberland and the lakes; he comes back and imagines England ever after as a country full of verdant mountains, faery woodlands, peaceful and enchanted waters. Another has been to the manufacturing centres; he imagines England as a great roaring workshop, crammed with furnaces and the hum of machinery and the smell of metal. Another has sojourned in the quiet country-side and to him England is all hedges and lanes and the daisy-sprinkled meadow and the well-tilled field. All have realised a little, but none have realised England. Then there is the man who has only read about the country or heard descriptions from others and thinks he knows it better than the men who have been there. They may all admit that what they have seen need not be the whole, but each has his little ineffaceable picture which, because it is all he has realised, persists in standing for the whole. There is no harm in that, no harm whatever in limitation if you understand and admit the limitation. But if all the four begin quarrelling, what an aimless confusion will arise! That is what has happened in India because of the excessive logicality and too robust opinionativeness of Southern metaphysicians. We should come back to a more flexible and rational spirit of inquiry.

What then are the standards of truth in the interpretation of the Scripture? The standards are three, the knower, knowledge and the known.

The known is the text itself that we seek to interpret. We must be sure we have the right word, not an emendation to suit the exigency of some individual or sectarian opinion; the right etymology and shade of meaning, not one that is traditional or forced to serve the ends of a commentator; the right spirit in the sense, not an imported or too narrow or too elastic spirit.

The knower is the original *drashta* or seer of the *mantra*, with whom we ought to be in spiritual contact. If knowledge is indeed a perishable thing in a perishable instrument, such contact is impossible; but in that case the Scripture itself must be false and not worth considering. If there is any truth in what the Scripture says, knowledge is eternal and inherent in all of us and what another saw I can see, what another realised I can realise. The *drashta* was a soul in relation with the infinite Spirit, I am also a soul in relation with the infinite Spirit. We have a meeting-place, a possibility of communion.

Knowledge is the eternal truth, part of which the *drashta* expresses to us. Through the part he shows us, we must travel to the whole, otherwise we shall be subject to the errors incidental to an imperfect knowledge. If even the part is to be rightly understood, it must be viewed in the terms of the whole, not the whole in the terms of the part. I am not limited by the Scriptures; on the contrary I must exceed them in order to be master of their knowledge. It is true that we are usually the slaves of our individual and limited outlook, but our capacity is unlimited, and, if we can get rid of *ahankara*, if we can put ourselves at the service of the Infinite without any reservation of predilection

The Interpretation of Scripture

or opinion, there is no reason why our realisation should be limited. *Tasmin vijnate sarvam vijnatam.* He being known, all can be known. To understand Scripture, it is not enough to be a scholar, one must be a soul. To know what the *drashta* saw one must oneself have *drishti*, sight, and be a student if not a master of the knowledge. *Atha para yaya tad aksharam adhigamyate.* Grammar, etymology, prosody, astronomy, metaphysics, logic, all that is good; but afterwards there is still needed the higher knowledge by which the Immutable is known.

On Original Thinking

The attitude of mankind towards originality of opinion is marked by a natural hesitation and inconsistency. Admired for its rarity, brilliancy and potency, yet in practice and for the same qualities it is more generally dreaded, ridiculed or feared. There is no doubt that it tends to disturb what is established. Therefore tamasic men and tamasic states of society take especial pains to discourage independence of opinion. Their watchword is authority. Few societies have been so tamasic, so full of inertia and contentment in increasing narrowness as Indian society in later times; few have been so eager to preserve themselves in inertia. Few therefore have attached so great an importance to authority. Every detail of our life has been fixed for us by Shastra and custom, every detail of our thought by Scripture and its commentators, — but much oftener by the commentators than by Scripture. Only in one field, that of individual spiritual experience, have we cherished the ancient freedom and originality out of which our past greatness sprang; it is from some new movement in this inexhaustible source that every fresh impulse and rejuvenated strength has arisen. Otherwise we should long ago have been in the grave where dead nations lie, with Greece and Rome of the Caesars, with Esarhaddon and the Chosroes. You will often hear it said that it was the forms of Hinduism which have given us so much national vitality. I think rather it was its spirit. I am inclined to give more credit for the secular miracle of our national survival to Shankara, Ramanuja, Nanak & Kabir, Guru Govind, Chaitanya, Ramdas & Tukaram than to Raghunandan and the Pandits of Nadiya & Bhatpara.

The result of this well-meaning bondage has been an increasing impoverishment of the Indian intellect, once the most gigantic and original in the world. Hence a certain incapacity, atrophy, impotence have marked our later activities even at their best. The most striking instance is our continued helplessness in the face of the new conditions and new knowledge imposed on us by recent European contact. We have tried to assimilate, we have tried to reject, we have tried to select; but we have not been able to do any of these things successfully. Successful assimilation depends on mastery; but we have not mastered European conditions and knowledge, rather we have been seized, subjected and enslaved by them. Successful rejection is possible only if we have intelligent possession of that which we wish to keep. Our rejection too must be an intelligent rejection; we must reject because we have understood, not because we have failed to understand. But our Hinduism, our old culture are precisely the possessions we have cherished with the least intelligence; throughout the whole range of our life we do things without knowing why we do them, we believe things without knowing why we believe them, we assert things without knowing what right we have to assert them, — or, at most, it is because some book or some Brahmin enjoins it, because Shankara thinks it, or because someone has so interpreted something that he asserts to be a fundamental Scripture of our religion. Nothing is our own, nothing native to our intelligence, all is derived. As little have we understood the new knowledge; we have only understood what the Europeans want us to think about themselves and their modern civilisation. Our English culture — if culture it can be called — has increased tenfold the evil of our dependence instead of remedying it.

More even than the other two processes successful selection requires the independent play of intellect. If we merely receive new ideas and institutions in the light in which they are presented to us, we shall, instead of selecting, imitate — blindly, foolishly and inappropriately. If we receive them in the light given by our previous knowledge, which was on so many points nil, we shall as blindly and foolishly reject. Selection demands that we should see things not as the foreigner sees them or as the orthodox Pandit sees them, but as they are in themselves. But we have selected at random, we have rejected at random, we have not known how to assimilate or choose. In the upshot we have merely suffered the European impact, overborne at points, crassly resisting at others, and, altogether, miserable, enslaved by our environments, able neither to perish nor to survive. We preserve indeed a certain ingenuity and subtlety; we can imitate with an appearance of brightness; we can play plausibly, even brilliantly with the minutiae of a subject; but we fail to think usefully, we fail to master the life and heart of things. Yet it is only by mastering the life and heart of things that we can hope, as a nation, to survive.

How shall we recover our lost intellectual freedom and elasticity? By reversing, for a time at least, the process by which we lost it, by liberating our minds in all subjects from the thraldom to authority. That is not what reformers and the Anglicised require of us. They ask us, indeed, to abandon authority, to revolt against custom and superstition, to have free and enlightened minds. But they mean by these sounding recommendations that we should renounce the authority of Sayana for the authority of Max Muller, the Monism of Shankara for the Monism of Haeckel, the written Shastra for the unwritten law of European social opinion, the dogmatism of Brahmin Pandits for the dogmatism of European scientists, thinkers and scholars. Such a foolish exchange of servitude can receive the assent of no self-respecting mind. Let us break our chains, venerable as they are, but let it be in order to be free, — in the name of truth, not in the name of Europe. It would be a poor bargain to exchange our old Indian illuminations, however dark they may have grown to us, for a derivative European enlightenment or replace the superstitions of popular Hinduism by the superstitions of materialistic Science.

Our first necessity, if India is to survive and do her appointed work in the world, is that the youth of India should learn to think, — to think on all subjects, to think independently, fruitfully, going to the heart of things, not stopped by their surface, free of prejudgments, shearing sophism and prejudice asunder as with a sharp sword, smiting down obscurantism of all kinds as with the mace of Bhima. Let our brains no longer, like European infants, be swathed with swaddling clothes; let them recover the free and unbound motion of the gods; let them have not only the minuteness but the wide mastery and sovereignty natural to the intellect of Bharata and easily recoverable by it if it once accustoms itself to feel its own power and be convinced of its own worth. If it cannot entirely shake off past shackles, let it at least arise like the infant Krishna bound to the wain, and move forward dragging with it wain and all and shattering in its progress the twin trees, the twin obstacles to self-fulfilment, blind mediaeval prejudice and arrogant modern dogmatism. The old fixed foundations have been broken up, we are tossing in the waters of a great upheaval and change. It is no use clinging to the old ice-floes of the past, they will soon melt and leave their refugees struggling in perilous waters. It is no use landing ourselves in the infirm bog, neither sea nor good dry land, of a secondhand Europeanism. We shall only die there a miserable and unclean death. No, we must learn to swim and use that power to reach the good vessel of unchanging truth; we must land again on the eternal rock of ages.

Let us not, either, select at random, make a nameless hotchpotch and then triumphantly call it the assimilation of East and West. We must begin by accepting nothing on trust from any source whatsoever, by questioning everything and forming our own conclusions. We need not fear that we shall by that process cease to be Indians or fall into the danger of abandoning Hinduism. India can never cease to be India or Hinduism to be Hinduism, if we really think for ourselves. It is only if we allow Europe to think for us that India is in danger of becoming an ill-executed and foolish copy of Europe. We must not begin by becoming partisans but know before we take our line. Our first business as original thinkers will be to accept nothing, to question everything. That means to get rid of all unexamined opinions old or new, all mere habitual sanskaras in the mind, to have no preconceived judgments. Anityah sarvasanskarah, said the Buddha. I do not know that I quite agree. There are certain sanskaras that seem to me as eternal as things can be. What is the Atman itself but an eternal and fundamental way of looking at things, the essentiality of all being in itself unknowable, neti, neti. Therefore the later Buddhists declared that the Atman itself did not exist and arrived at ultimate nothingness, a barren and foolish conclusion, since Nothingness itself is only a sanskara. Nevertheless it is certain that the great mass of our habitual conceptions are not only temporary, but imperfect and misleading. We must escape from these imperfections and take our stand on that which is true and lasting. But in order to find out what in our conceptions is true and lasting, we must question all alike rigorously and impartially. The necessity of such a process not for India, but for all humanity has been recognised by leading European thinkers. It was what Carlyle meant when he spoke of swallowing all formulas. It was the process by which Goethe helped to reinvigorate European thinking. But in Europe the stream is running dry before it has reached its sea. Europe has for some time ceased to produce original thinkers, though it still produces original mechanicians. Science preserves her freedom of inquiry in details, in the mint and anise and cummin of the world's processes, but, bound hand & foot in the formulas of the past, she is growing helpless for great ideas and sound generalisations. She sits contented with her treasuries; she has combed all the pebbles on the seashore and examined the shoreward gulfs and bays; of the oceans beyond and their undiscovered continents she cries scornfully "They are a dream; there is nothing there but mists mistaken for land or a waste of the same waters that we have already here examined." Europe is becoming stereotyped and unprogressive; she is fruitful only of new & ever multiplying luxuries and of feverish, fiery & ineffective changes in her political and social machinery. China, Japan and the Mussulman States are sliding into a blind European imitativeness. In India alone there is self-contained, dormant, the energy and the invincible spiritual individuality which can yet arise and break her own and the world's fetters.

It is true that original thinking makes for original acting, and therefore a caution is necessary. We must be careful that our thinking is not only original but thorough before we even initiate action. To run away with an isolated original idea, or charmed with its newness and vigour, to ride it into the field of action is to make of ourselves cranks and eccentrics. This world, this society, these nations and their civilisations are not simple existences, but complex & intricate, the result of a great organic growth in many centuries, sometimes in many millenniums. We should not deal with them after snatching at a few hurried generalisations or in the gust and fury of a stiff fanaticism. We must first be sure that our new thought is wide and strong-winged enough, our thoughts large enough, our natures mighty enough to deal with those vastnesses. We must be careful, too, to comprehend what we destroy. And destroy we must not unless we have a greater and more perfect thing to put in the place even of a crumbling and mouldering antiquity. To tear down Hindu society in the spirit of the social reformers or European society in the spirit of the philosophical or unphilosophical Anarchists would be to destroy order and substitute a licentious confusion. If we carefully remember these cautions, there is no harm in original thinking even of the boldest and most merciless novelty. I may, for example, attack unsparingly the prevailing system of justice and punishment as extraordinarily senseless and evil, even if I have no new system ready-made to put in as its successor; but I must have no wish to destroy it, senseless & evil though it be, until our new system is ready. For it fills a place the vacancy of which the Spirit that uplifts & supports our human welfare, would greatly abhor. I may expose, too, the weaknesses and narrownesses of an existing form of religion, even if I have no new & better form to preach of my own, but I must not so rage against those weaknesses as to destroy all religious faith and I should remember before the end of my criticism that even a bad religion is better than no religion, — that it is wiser to worship energy in my surroundings with the African savage than to be dead to all faith and all spirituality like the drunkards of a little knowledge — for even in that animal and unintelligent worship there is a spark of the divine fire which keeps humanity living, while the cultured imperial Roman or the luxurious modern wealth-gatherer and body worshipper drags his kind into a straight

& well built road which is so broad only to lead more easily to a mighty perdition — *na ched ihavedin mahati vinashtih*. Otherwise there is no harm in spreading dissatisfaction with fetish worship or refusing praise to an ancient and cruel folly. We need not be troubled if our thinking is condemned as too radical or even as reckless & revolutionary, — for the success of revolutionary thought always means that Nature has need of one of her cataclysms; even otherwise, she will make of it whatever modified use is best for our present humanity. In thought as in deeds, to the thinking we have a right, the result belongs to the wise & active Power of God that stands over us & in us originating, cherishing, indefatigably dissolving & remoulding man and spirit in the progressive harmonies of His universe. Let us only strive that our light should be clear, diffused & steady, not either darkness or a narrow glare and merely violent lustre. And if we cannot compass that ideal, still it is better to think than to cease from thinking. For even out of darkness the day is born and lightning has its uses!

[Draft opening of another version]

We have had recently in India a great abundance of speculations on the real causes of that gradual decline and final arrest which Indian civilisation no less than European suffered during the Middle Ages. The arrest was neither so sudden as in Europe nor so complete; but its effect on our nation, like the undermining activity of a slow poison, was all the more profoundly destructive, pervasive, hard to remedy, difficult to expel. At a certain period we entered into a decline, splendid at first like a long and gorgeous sunset, afterwards more & more sombre, till the darkness closed in, and if our sky was strewn with stars of a great number & brilliance, it was only a vast decay, confusion and inertia that they lighted and emphasised with their rays. We have, most of us, our chosen explanation of this dolorous phenomenon. The patriot attributes our decline to the ravages of foreign invasion and the benumbing influences of foreign rule; the disciple of European materialism finds out the enemy, the evil, the fount and origin of all our ills, in our religion and its time-honoured social self-expression. Such explanations, like most human thoughts, have their bright side of truth as well as their obscure side of error; but they are not, in any case, the result of impartial thinking. Man may be, as he has been defined, a reasoning animal, but it is necessary to add that he is, for the most part, a very badly-reasoning animal. He does not ordinarily think for the sake of finding out the truth, but much more for the satisfaction of his mental preferences and emotional tendencies; his conclusions spring from his preferences, prejudices and passions; and his reasoning & logic paraded to justify them are only a specious process or a formal mask for his covert approach to an upshot previously necessitated by his heart or by his temperament. When we are awakened from our modern illusions, as we have been awakened from our mediaeval superstitions, we shall find that the intellectual conclusions of the rationalist for all their [...] pomp & profuse apparatus of scrupulous enquiry were as much dogmas as those former dicta of Pope & theologian, which confessed without shame their simple basis in the negation of reason. Much more do all those current opinions demand scrutiny & modification, which express our personal view of things and rest patently on a partial and partisan view or have been justified by preferential selection of the few data that suited our foregone & desired conclusion. It is always best, therefore, to scrutinise very narrowly those bare, trenchant explanations which so easily satisfy the pugnacious animal in our intellects; when we have admitted that small part of the truth on which they seize, we should always look for the large part which they have missed. Especially is it right, when there are subjective movements & causes of a considerable extent and complexity behind the phenomena we have to observe, to distrust facile, simple and rapid solutions.

The Balance of Justice

The European Court of Justice is a curious and instructive institution. Europe, even while vaunting a monopoly of civilisation, cherishes and preens herself in some remarkable relics of barbarism. In mediaeval times, with the scientific thoroughness and efficiency which she shares with the Mongolian, she organised torture as the most reliable source of evidence and the ordeal of battle as the surest guide to judicial truth. Both ideas were characteristically European. A later age may seem to have got rid of these luminous methods, but it is not so in reality. In place of the rack the French have invented the investigating judge and the Americans some remarkable processes, which I think they call questioning (the old name for torture) in the first, second and up to the fifth degree if not to higher stages of excellence. The torture is sometimes of the mind not of the body; it is less intense, more lingering, but it leads to the same result in the end. When the tortured wretch, after protecting with lies for as long as may be his guilt or his innocence, escapes from his furious and pitiless persecutor by a true or false confession, preferring jail or the gallows to this prolongation of tense misery, the French call it delicately "entering into the way of avowals". The Holy Office in Seville could not have invented a more Christian and gentlemanly euphemism. The American system, is in the fifth degree, I think, to keep the miserable accused fasting and sleepless and ply him with a ceaseless assault of torturing questions and suggestions until the brain reels, the body sinks, the heart is sick and hopeless and the man is ready to say anything his torturers believe or want to be the truth. It is a true Inquisition; the mediaeval name fits these modern refinements.

The English people have often been accused as a brutal or a stupid nation; but they have a rugged humanity when their interests are not touched and enjoy glimpses of a rough common sense. They have besides an honourable love of publicity and do not like, for themselves at least, secret police methods. They have rejected the investigating judge and torture in the fifth degree. But their courts resemble the European. Under a civilised disguise these Courts are really the mediaeval ordeal by battle; only in place of the swords and lances of military combatants we have the tongues and technicalities of lawyers and the mutually tilting imaginations of witnesses. The victory is to the skilfullest liar and the most plausible workman in falsehoods and insincerities. It is largely an elaborate pitch and toss, an exhilarating gamble, a very Monte Carlo of surprising chances. But there is skill in it, too; it satisfies the intellect as well as the sensations. One should rather call it a game of human Bridge which admirably combines luck and skill, or consider it as an intellectual gladiatorial show. In big cases the stake is worthy of the play and the excitement, a man's property or his life. But woe to the beaten! In a criminal case, the tortures of the jail or the terrifying drop from the gallows are in prospect, and it is rather the hardihood of guilt than the trembling consciousness of innocence that shall best help him. Woe to him if he is innocent! As he stands there, — for to add to the pleasurableness of his condition, the physical ache of hours of standing is considerately added to the cruel strain on his emotions, — he looks eagerly not to the truth or falsehood of the evidence for or against him, but to the skill with which this or that counsel handles the web of skilfully mixed truth and lies and the impression he is making on the judge or the jury. A true witness breaking down under a confusing cross-examination or a false witness mended by a judicious reexamination may be of much better service to him than the Truth, which, our Scriptures tell us, shall prevail and not falsehood, — eventually perhaps and in the things of the truth, but not in the things of falsehood, not in a court of Justice, not in the witness box. There the last thing the innocent man against whom circumstances have turned, dare tell is the truth; it would either damn him completely by fatally helping the prosecution or it is so simple and innocent as to convince the infallible human reason of its pitiful falsity. The truth! Has not the Law expressly built up a hedge of technicalities to keep out the truth?

As one looks on, one begins to understand the passion of the Roman poet's eulogy of the defence counsel, *praesidium maestis reis*, the bulwark of the sorrowful accused. For in this strange civilised gambling with human dice where it is so often impossible to be certain about guilt or innocence, one's sympathies naturally go to the sufferer, the scapegoat of a callous society, who may be moving to a long period of torturing and unmerited slavery or an undeserved death on the gallows. But if one could eliminate this element of human pity, it would be a real intellectual pleasure to watch the queer barbarous battle, appraise the methods of the chief players, admire, in whatever climes, the elusiveness and fine casualness of Indian perjury or the robust manly cheery downrightness of Saxon cross-swearing. If the Courts convince us of our common humanity by making all men liars, they yet preserve a relishable unlikeness in likeness. And I think that even theology or metaphysics does not give such admirable chances for subtlety as the Law, nor even Asiatic Research or ethnology favour so much the growth of that admirable scientific faculty which deduces a whole animal out of some other animal's bone. If the thing proved is generally wrong, it is always ingenious; and after all in all these five sciences, or are they not rather arts? — it is not the thing that is true but the thing that is desired which must be established. This is perhaps why the Europeans think the system civilised, but as a semi-civilised Oriental, one would prefer less room for subtlety and more for truth.

On the whole, if anyone were to complain that modern civilisation eliminates danger and excitement out of human life, we could well answer the morbid grumbler, "Come into our Courts and see!" Still, praise must be given where praise is due, and let the English system once more be lauded for not normally exposing the accused to the torture of savage pursuit by a prosecuting judge or the singular revival in modern dress of the ancient "question" by the American police. Where political or other passions are not roused and bribery does not enter, the poor muddled magistrate does his honest best, and where there is a system of trial by jury, the blunders, whims and passions of twelve men may decide your fate less insanely than the caprices of a Kazi, — though even that is hardly certain. At any rate, if the dice are apt to be loaded, it is, with the exceptions noted, not on one but on both sides of the gamble.

Social Reform

Reform is not an excellent thing in itself as many Europeanised intellects imagine; neither is it always safe and good to stand unmoved in the ancient paths as the orthodox obstinately believe. Reform is sometimes the first step to the abyss, but immobility is the most perfect way to stagnate and to putrefy. Neither is moderation always the wisest counsel: the mean is not always golden. It is often an euphemism for purblindness, for a tepid indifference or for a cowardly inefficiency. Men call themselves moderates, conservatives or extremists and manage their conduct and opinions in accordance with a formula. We like to think by systems and parties and forget that truth is the only standard. Systems are merely convenient cases for keeping arranged knowledge, parties a useful machinery for combined action; but we make of them an excuse for avoiding the trouble of thought.

One is astonished at the position of the orthodox. They labour to deify everything that exists. Hindu society has certain arrangements and habits which are merely customary. There is no proof that they existed in ancient times nor any reason why they should last into the future. It has other arrangements and habits for which textual authority can be quoted, but it is oftener the text of the modern Smritikaras than of Parasara and Manu. Our authority for them goes back to the last five hundred years. I do not understand the logic which argues that because a thing has lasted for five hundred years it must be perpetuated through the aeons. Neither antiquity nor modernity can be the test of truth or the test of usefulness. All the Rishis do not belong to the past; the Avatars still come; revelation still continues.

Some claim that we must at any rate adhere to Manu and the Puranas, whether because they are sacred or because they are national. Well, but, if they are sacred, you must keep to the whole and not cherish isolated texts while disregarding the body of your authority. You cannot pick and choose; you cannot say "This is sacred and I will keep to it, that is less sacred and I will leave it alone." When you so treat your sacred authority, you are proving that to you it has no sacredness. You are juggling with truth; for you are pretending to consult Manu when you are really consulting your own opinions, preferences or interests. To recreate Manu entire in modern society is to ask Ganges to flow back to the Himalayas. Manu is no doubt national, but so is the animal sacrifice and the burnt offering. Because a thing is national of the past, it need not follow that it must be national of the future. It is stupid not to recognise altered conditions.

We have similar apologies for the unintelligent preservation of mere customs; but, various as are the lines of defence, I do not know any that is imperiously conclusive. Custom is *shishtachar*, decorum, that which all well-bred and respectable people observe. But so were the customs of the far past that have been discontinued and, if now revived, would be severely discountenanced and, in many cases, penalised; so too are the customs of the future that are now being resisted or discouraged, — even, I am prepared to believe, the future no less than the past prepares for us new modes of living which in the present would not escape the censure of the law. It is the *achar* that makes the *shishta*, not the *shishta* who makes the *achar*. The *achar* is made by the rebel, the innovator, the man who is regarded in his own time as eccentric, disreputable or immoral, as was Sri Krishna by Bhurisrava because he upset the old ways and the old standards. Custom may be better defended as ancestral and therefore cherishable. But if our ancestors had persistently held that view, our so cherished customs would never have come into being. Or, more rationally, custom must be preserved because its long utility in the past argues a sovereign virtue for the preservation of society. But to all things there is a date and a limit. All long-continued customs have been sovereignly useful in their time, even totemism and polyandry. We must not ignore the usefulness of the past, but we seek in preference a present and a future utility.

Custom and Law may then be altered. For each age its shastra. But we cannot argue straight off that it must be altered, or even if alteration is necessary, that it must be altered in a given direction. One is repelled by the ignorant enthusiasm of social reformers. Their minds are usually a strange jumble of ill-digested European notions. Very few of them know anything about Europe, and even those who have visited it know it badly. But they will not allow things or ideas contrary to European notions to be anything but superstitious, barbarous, harmful and benighted, they will not suffer what is praised and practised in Europe to be anything but rational and enlightened. They are more appreciative than Occidentals themselves of the strength, knowledge and enjoyment of Europe; they are blinder than the blindest and most self-sufficient Anglo-Saxon to its weakness, ignorance and misery. They are charmed by the fair front Europe presents to herself and the world; they are unwilling to discern any disease in the entrails, any foulness in the rear. For the Europeans are as careful to conceal their social as their physical bodies and shrink with more horror from nakedness and indecorum than from the reality of evil. If they see the latter in themselves, they avert their eyes, crying, "It is nothing or it is little; we are healthy, we are perfect, we are immortal." But the face and hands cannot always be covered, and we see blotches.

The social reformer repeats certain stock arguments like shibboleths. For these antiquities he is a fanatic or a crusader. Usually he does not act up to his ideas, but in all sincerity he loves them and fights for them. He pursues his nostrums as panaceas; it would be infidelity to question or examine their efficacy. His European doctors have told him that early marriage injures the physique of a nation, and that to him is the gospel. It is not convenient to remember that physical deterioration is a modern phenomenon in India and that our grandparents were strong, vigorous and beautiful. He hastens to abolish the already disappearing nautchgirl, but it does not seem to concern him that the prostitute multiplies. Possibly some may think it a gain that the European form of the malady is replacing the Indian! He tends towards shattering our cooperative system of society and does not see that Europe is striding Titanically towards Socialism.

Orthodox and reformer alike lose themselves in details; but it is principles that determine details. Almost every point that the social reformers raise could be settled one way or the other without effecting the permanent good of society. It is pitiful to see men labouring the point of marriage between subcastes and triumphing over an isolated instance. Whether the spirit as well as the body of caste should remain, is the modern question. Let Hindus remember that caste as it stands is merely *jat*, the trade guild sanctified but no longer working, it is not the eternal religion, it is not *chaturvarnya*. I do not care whether widows marry or remain single; but it is of infinite importance to consider how women shall be legally and socially related to man, as his inferior, equal or superior; for even the relation of superiority is no more impossible in the future than it was in the far-distant past. And the most important question of all is whether society shall be competitive or cooperative, individualistic or communistic. That we should talk so little about these things and be stormy over insignificant details, shows painfully the impoverishment of the average Indian intellect. If these greater things are decided, as they must be, the smaller will arrange themselves.

There are standards that are universal and there are standards that are particular. At the present moment all societies are in need of reform, the Parsi, Mahomedan and Christian not a whit less than the Hindu which alone seems to feel the need of radical reformation. In the changes of the future the Hindu society must take the lead towards the establishment of a new universal standard. Yet being Hindus we must seek it through that which is particular to ourselves. We have one standard that is at once universal and particular, the eternal religion, which is the basis, permanent and always inherent in India, of the shifting, mutable and multiform thing we call Hinduism. Sticking fast where you are like a limpet is not the dharma, neither is leaping without looking the dharma. The eternal religion is to realise God in our inner life and our outer existence, in society not less than in the individual. *Esha dharmah sanatanah*. God is not antiquity nor novelty: He is not the Manava Dharmashastra, nor Vidyaranya, nor Raghunandan; neither is He an European. God who is essentially Sacchidananda, is in manifestation *Satyam, Prema, Shakti*, — Truth, Strength and Love. Whatever is consistent with the truth and principle of things, whatever increases love among men, whatever makes for the strength of the individual, the nation and the race, is divine, it is the law of Vaivaswata Manu, it is the *sanatana dharma* and the Hindu shastra. Only, God is the triple harmony, He is not one-sided. Our love must not make us weak, blind or unwise; our strength must not make us hard and furious; our principles must not make us fanatical or sentimental. Let us think calmly, patiently, impartially; let us love wholly and intensely but wisely; let us act with strength, nobility and force. If even then we make mistakes, yet God makes none. We decide and act; He determines the fruit, and whatever He determines is good.

He is already determining it. Men have long been troubling themselves about social reform and blameless orthodoxy, and orthodoxy has crumbled without social reform being effected. But all the time God has been going about India getting His work done in spite of the talking. Unknown to men the social revolution prepares itself, and it is not in the direction they think, for it embraces the world, not India only. Whether we like it or not, He will sweep out the refuse of the Indian past and the European present. But the broom is not always sufficient; sometimes He uses the sword in preference. It seems probable that it will be used, for the world does not mend itself quickly, and therefore it will have violently to be mended.

But this is a general principle; how shall we determine the principles that are particular to the nature of the community and the nature of the Age? There is such a thing as yugadharma, the right institutions & modes of action for the age in which we live. For action depends indeed on the force of knowledge or will that is to be used, but it depends, too, on the time, the place & the vessel. Institutions that are right in one age are not right in another. Replacing social system by social system, religion by religion, civilisation by civilisation God is perpetually leading man onwards to loftier & more embracing manifestations of our human perfectibility. When in His cosmic circling movement He establishes some stable worldwide harmony, that is man's Satya Yuga. When harmony falters, is maintained with difficulty, not in the nature of men, but by an accepted force or political instrument, that is his Treta. When the faltering becomes stumbling and the harmony has to be maintained at every step by a careful & laborious regulation, that is his Dwapara. When there is disintegration, & all descends in collapse and ruin, nothing can stay farther the cataclysm that is his Kali. This is the natural law of progress of all human ideas & institutions. It applies always in the mass, continually though less perfectly in the detail. One may almost say that each human religion, society, civilisation has its four Ages. For this movement is not only the most natural, but the most salutary. It is not a justification of pessimism nor a gospel of dumb fate & sorrowful annihilation. It is not, as we too often think in our attachment to the form, a melancholy law of decline & the vanity of all human achievements. If each Satya has its Kali, equally does each Kali prepare its Satya. That destruction was necessary for this creation, and the new harmony, when it is perfected, will be better than the old. But there is the weakness, there is the half success turning to failure, there is the discouragement, there is the loss of energy & faith which clouds our periods of disintegration, the apparent war, violence, ragging, tumult & trample to and fro which attends our periods of gradual creation and half-perfection. Therefore men cry out dismally & lament that all is perishing. But if they trusted in God's Love & Wisdom, not preferring to it their conservative & narrow notions, they would rather cry out that all is being reborn.

So much depends on Time & God's immediate purpose that it is more important to seek out His purpose than to attach ourselves to our own nostrums. The Kala Purusha, Zeitgeist & Death Spirit, has risen to his dreadful work — lokakshayakritpravriddhas — increasing to destroy a world, — and who shall stay the terror & mightiness & irresistibility of Him? But He is not only destroying the world that was, He is creating the world that shall be; it is therefore more profitable for us to discover & help what He is building than to lament & hug in our arms what He is destroying. But it is not easy to discover His drift, & we often admire too much temporary erections which are merely tents for the warriors in this Kurukshetra and take them for the permanent buildings of the future.

The Pandits are therefore right when they make a difference between the practice of the Satya & the practice of the Kali. But in their application of this knowledge, they do not seem to me to be always wise or learned. They forget or do not know that Kali is the age for a destruction & rebirth, not for a desperate clinging to the old that can no longer be saved. They entrench themselves in the system of Kalivarjya, but forget that it is not the weaknesses but the strengths of the old harmony that are being subjected to varjanam, abandonment. That which is saved is merely a temporary platform which we have erected on the banks of the sea of change awaiting a more stable habitation; and it too must one day break down under the crash of the waves, must disappear into the engulfing waters. Has the time arrived for that destruction? We think that it has. Listen to the crash of those waters, — more formidable than the noise of assault, mark that slow, sullen, remorseless sapping, — watch pile after pile of our patched incoherent ramshackle structure corroding, creaking, shaking with the blows, breaking, sinking silently or with a splash, suddenly or little by little into the yeast of those billows. Has the time arrived for a new construction? We say it has. Mark the activity, eagerness and hurrying to and fro of mankind, the rapid prospecting, seeking, digging, founding — see the Avatars & great vibhutis coming, arising thickly, treading each close behind the other. Are not these the signs and do they not tell us that the great Avatar of all arrives to establish the first Satya Yuga of the Kali?

For in the Kali too, say the secret & ancient traditions of the Yogins, there is a perpetual minor repetition of Satya-Treta-Dwapara-Kali subcycles, the subSatya a temporary & imperfect harmony which in the subTreta & subDwapara breaks down and disappears in the subKali. The process then begins over again [............................] for each new temporary harmony is fairer and more perfect than its preceding harmony, each new temporary collapse more resounding & terrible than its anterior dissolution. Already ended are the first five thousand years of the Kali which were necessary to prepare for final destruction the relics of the ancient Satya. Weakness & violence, error and ignorance and oblivion rushing with an increasing speed & rhythm over the whole earth have done for us that work. The morning of the first Kali-Satya is ready to break, the first few streaks dimly visible. So runs the not incredible tradition.

Yes. A new harmony, but not the scrannel pipes of European materialism, not an Occidental foundation upon half truths & whole falsehoods. When there is destruction it is the form that perishes, not the spirit — for the world and its ways are forms of one Truth which appears in this material world in ever new bodies and constantly varied apparel — the inward Eternal taking the joy of outward Mutability. The truth of the old Satya that is dead was not different from the Truth of the new Satya that is to be born, for it is Truth that restores itself always and persists. In India, the chosen land, it is preserved; in the soul of India it sleeps, expectant of that soul's awakening, the soul of India leonine, luminous, locked in the closed petals of the ancient lotus of strength and wisdom, not in her weak, sordid, transient & miserable externals. India alone can build the future of mankind; in India alone can the effective Avatar appear to the nations. And until He appears, it is for India to gather herself up out of her dust & degradation, — symbol of the shattered Satyayuga — commune with her soul by Yoga and to know her past & her future. I have not here speculated on what we should build, what we should break, nor shall I now define my detailed opinions — but whatever it be, we must do it in the light and in the spirit of that triple principle of the divine nature; we must act in the reflection of God's Love, Strength & Wisdom.

We are Hindus seeking to re-Hinduise society, not to Europeanise it. But what is Hinduism? Or what is its social principle?

One thing at least is certain about Hinduism religious or social, that its whole outlook is Godward, its whole search and business is the discovery of God and our fulfilment in God. But God is everywhere and universal. Where did Hinduism seek Him? Ancient or preBuddhistic Hinduism sought him both in the world and outside it; it took its stand on the strength & beauty & joy of the Veda, unlike modern or postBuddhistic Hinduism which is oppressed with Buddha's sense of universal sorrow and Shankara's sense of universal illusion, — Shankara who was the better able to destroy Buddhism because he was himself half a Buddhist. Ancient Hinduism aimed socially at our fulfilment in God in life, modern Hinduism at the escape from life to God. The more modern ideal is fruitful of a noble and ascetic spirituality, but has a chilling and hostile effect on social soundness and development, social life under its shadow stagnates for want of belief and delight, sraddha and ananda. If we are to make our society perfect and the nation is to live again, then we must revert to the earlier and fuller truth. We must not make life a waiting for renunciation, but renunciation a preparation for life; instead of running from God in the town to God in the forest, we must rather plunge into the mountain solitude in our own souls for knowledge & joy & spiritual energy to sustain any part that may be given to us by the master of the Lila. If we get that strength, any society we build up must be full of the instinct of immortal life and move inevitably towards perfection. As to the precise way in which society will be reconstructed, we have hardly yet knowledge enough to solve the problem. We ought to know before we act, but we are rather eager to act violently in the light of any dim ray of knowledge that may surprise our unreflecting intellects, and although God often uses our haste for great and beneficial purposes, yet that way of doing things is not the best either for a man or a nation. One thing seems to me clear that the future will deny that principle of individual selfishness and collective self-interest on which European society has hitherto been based and our renovated systems will be based on the renunciation of individual selfishness and the organisation of brotherhood, — principles common to Christianity, Mahomedanism and Hinduism.

Hinduism and the Mission of India

[.....] [That] which is permanent in the Hindu religion, must form the basis on which the world will increasingly take its stand in dealing with spiritual experience and religious truth. Hinduism, in my sense of the word, is not modern Brahmanism. Modern Brahmanism developed into existence at a definite period in history. It is now developing out of existence; its mission is done, its capacities exhausted, the Truth which, like other religions, it defended, honoured, preserved, cherished, misused and disfigured, is about to take to itself new forms and dispense with all other screens or defender than its own immortal beauty, grandeur, truth and effectiveness. It is this unchanging undying Truth which has to be discovered and placed in its native light before humanity. Tad etat satyam.

There are many defenders and discoverers of truth now active among us. They are all busy defending, modifying, attacking, sapping or bolstering current Hinduism. I am not eager to disparage but neither do I find myself satisfied with any of them. If I were, there would be no need for any speculation of my own. There are the orthodox who are busy recovering and applying old texts or any interpretations, new or old, of these texts, which will support the existing order, — and ignoring all that go against it. Their learning is praiseworthy and useful; it brings to notice many great and helpful things which were in danger of being misprized, lost or flung away as worthless; but they do not seem to me to go to the heart of the matter. There are the heterodox who are busy giving new interpretations to old texts and institutions in order to get rid of all such features as the modern world finds it hard to assimilate. Their brainwork can hardly be too highly praised; it is bringing to light or to a half light many luminous realities and possibilities which, if they cannot all be accepted, yet invigorate and sharpen the habit of original thinking and help to remove that blind adherence to traditions which is truth's greatest obstacle. Still they too do not seem to me to have the right grasp and discernment. Then there are the ascetics mystical or rationalistic who call men to disgust with the world and point to the temple, the monastery or the mountaintop as the best, if not the only place for finding God, and most of whom, in order to honour the Maker slight and denounce His works. Their position and temperament is so lofty and noble and their solvent force on the gross impurities of a materialised humanity has been so invaluable that it is with some reluctance one finds oneself obliged to put them on one side and pass onward. But it seems to me that we must pass onward if we would know and possess God in His entirety and not merely in a side or aspect. There is a story in the Jewish Scriptures which relates that when God wished to show himself to Moses, he could only, owing to the spiritual imperfections of the Jewish prophet, reveal safely to him His hinder parts. Moses would have died if he had seen the front of God; he had not the dharanam, the soul-power to support that tremendous vision. The story well illuminates the character of materialism generally and to its aggressive modern form, European thought & civilisation, it applies with a quite overwhelming appositeness. But it seems to me that the average Vedantist, too, has only seen, for his part, the crown of the Lord's head and the average bhakta only the Kaustubh-stone over His heart or the Srivatsa mark upon it. On the other hand, there are those rationalists who are by no means ascetical in their views or temperament and their name is legion; they insist on our putting religion and God aside or keeping Him only for ornamental uses in spare moments, leave that, they say, & devote yourselves to practical work for mankind. That rationalism is necessary too if only to balance the error of the ascetics who would make of God's world a mistake and of its Maker an Almighty blunderer or an inscrutable eccentric or an indefinable Something inhabiting a chaos or a mirage. Nevertheless, from materialism least of all, however philanthropic or patriotic, can our future salvation be expected. Finally, there are the mystics who are not ascetics, —

the Theosophists. From one point of view I cannot find praise warm enough to do justice to the work of Theosophy; from another I cannot find condemnation strong enough to denounce it. It has forced on the notice of an unwilling world truths to which orthodoxy is blind and of which heterodoxy is afraid or incredulous. It has shown a colossal courage in facing ridicule, trampling on prejudice and slander, persisting in faith in spite of disillusionment, scandal and a continual shifting of knowledge. They have kept the flag of a past & future science flying against enormous difficulties. On the other hand by bringing to the investigation of that science — not its discovery, for to the Hindu Yogin it is known already — the traditional European methods, the methods of the market-place and the forum, it has brought on the truths themselves much doubt and discredit, and by importing into them the forms, jugglery and jargon of European mystics, their romanticism, their unbridled imagination, their galloping impatience, their haste, bragging and loudness, their susceptibility to dupery, trickery, obstinate error and greedy self-deception, Theosophists have strengthened doubt and discredit and driven many an earnest seeker to bewilderment, to angry suspicion or to final renunciation of the search for truth. They have scattered the path of the conscientious investigators, the severe scientists of Yoga who must appear in the future, with the thorns and sharp flints of a well-justified incredulity and suspicion. I admit the truths that Theosophy seeks to unveil; but I do not think they can be reached if we fall into bondage even to the most inspiring table talk of Mahatmas or to the confused anathemas and vaticinations hurled from their platform tripods by modern Pythonesses of the type of Mrs Annie Besant, that great, capacious but bewildered and darkened intellect, now stumbling with a loud and confident blindness through those worlds of twilight and glamour, of distorted inspirations, perverted communications and misunderstood or half-understood perceptions which are so painfully familiar to the student and seeker.

    If these things do not satisfy me, what then do I seek? I seek a light that shall be new, yet old, the oldest indeed of all lights.

I seek an authority that accepting, illuminating and reconciling all human truth, shall yet reject and get rid of by explaining it all mere human error. I seek a text and a Shastra that is not subject to interpolation, modification and replacement, that moth and white ant cannot destroy, that the earth cannot bury nor Time mutilate. I seek an asceticism that shall give me purity and deliverance from self and from ignorance without stultifying God and His universe. I seek a scepticism that shall question everything but shall have the patience to deny nothing that may possibly be true. I seek a rationalism not proceeding on the untenable supposition that all the centuries of man's history except the nineteenth were centuries of folly and superstition, but bent on discovering truth instead of limiting inquiry by a new dogmatism, obscurantism and furious intolerance which it chooses to call common sense and enlightenment; I seek a materialism that shall recognise matter and use it without being its slave. I seek an occultism that shall bring out all its processes and proofs into the light of day, without mystery, without jugglery, without the old stupid call to humanity, "Be blind, O man, and see!" In short, I seek not science, not religion, not Theosophy, but Veda — the truth about Brahman, not only about His essentiality, but about His manifestation, not a lamp on the way to the forest, but a light and a guide to joy and action in the world, the truth which is beyond opinion, the knowledge which all thought strives after — yasmin vijnate sarvam vijnatam. I believe that Veda to be the foundation of the Sanatan Dharma; I believe it to be the concealed divinity within Hinduism, — but a veil has to be drawn aside, a curtain has to be lifted. I believe it to be knowable and discoverable. I believe the future of India and the world to depend on its discovery and on its application, not to the renunciation of life, but to life in the world and among men.

In these articles I shall not try to announce truth, but merely to inquire what are those things in Hinduism by following which we may arrive at the truth. I shall try to indicate some of my reasons — as far as within these limits it can be done — for my faith in my guides and the manner in which I think they should be followed. I am impelled to this labour by the necessity of turning the mind of young India to our true riches, our real source of power, purification and hope for the future and of safeguarding it in the course of its search both from false lights and from the raucous challenges and confident discouragements cast at us by the frail modern spirit of denial. I write, not for the orthodox, nor for those who have discovered a new orthodoxy, Samaj or Panth, nor for the unbeliever; I write for those who acknowledge reason but do not identify reason with Western materialism; who are sceptics but not unbelievers; who, admitting the claims of modern thought, still believe in India, her mission and her gospel, her immortal life and her eternal rebirth.

The Psychology of Yoga

As the Indian mind, emerging from its narrow mediaeval entrenchments, advances westward towards inevitable conquest, it must inevitably carry with it Yoga & Vedanta for its banners wherever it goes. Brahmajnana, Yoga & Dharma are the three essentialities of Hinduism; wherever it travels & find harbourage & resting place, these three must spread. All else may help or hinder. Shankara's philosophy may compel the homage of the intellectual, Sankhya attract the admiration of the analytical mind, Buddha capture the rationalist in search of a less material synthesis than the modern scientist's continual Annam Brahma Pranam Brahma, but these are only grandiose intellectualities. The world at large does not live by the pure intellect, concrete itself it stands by things concrete or practical, although, immaterial in its origin, it bases practicality upon abstractions. A goal of life, a practice of perfection and a rational, yet binding law of conduct, — these are man's continual quest, and in none of these demands is modern Science able to satisfy humanity. In reply to all such wants Science can only cry, Society and again Society and always Society. But the nature of man knows that Society is not the whole of life. With the eye of the soul it sees that Society is only a means, not an end, a passing & changing outward phenomenon, not that fixed, clear & eternal inward standard & goal which we seek. Of Society as of all things Yajnavalkya's universal dictum stands; a man loves & serves Society for the sake of the Self & not for the sake of Society. That is his nature & whatever Rationalism may teach, to his nature he must always return. What Science could not provide India offers, Brahman for the eternal goal, Yoga for the means of perfection, dharma (swabhavaniyatam karma) for the rational yet binding law of conduct. Therefore, because it has something by which humanity can be satisfied & on which it can found itself, the victory of the Indian mind is assured.

But in order that the victory may not be slow & stumbling in its progress and imperfect in its fulfilment, it is necessary that whatever India has to offer should be stated to the West in language that the West can understand and through a principle of knowledge which it has made its own. Europe will accept nothing which is not scientific, nothing, that is to say which does not take up its stand on an assured, well-ordered and verifiable knowledge. Undoubtedly, for practical purposes the West is right; since only by establishing ourselves on such an assured foundation can we work with the utmost effectiveness and make the most of what we know. For shastra is the true basis of all perfect action & shastra means the full and careful teaching of the principles, relations and processes of every branch of knowledge, action or conduct with which the mind concerns itself. Indian knowledge possesses such a scientific basis, but, in these greater matters, unexpressed or expressed only in broad principles, compact aphorisms, implied logical connections not minutely treated in detail, fully, with a patient logical order & development in the way to which the occidental intellect is now accustomed and which it has become its second nature to demand. The aphoristic method has great advantages. It prevents the mind from getting encrusted in details and fossilising there; it leaves a wide room & great latitude for originality & the delicate play of individuality in the details. It allows a science to remain elastic and full of ever new potentialities for the discoverer. No doubt, it has disadvantages. It leaves much room for inaccuracy, for individual error, for the violences of the ill-trained & the freaks of the inefficient. For this, among other more important reasons, the Indian mind has thought it wise to give a firm & absolute authority to the guru & to insist that the disciple shall by precept & practice make his own all that the master has to teach him & so form & train his mind before it is allowed to play freely with his subject. In Europe the manual replaces the guru; the mind of the learner is not less rigidly bound & dominated but it is by the written rule

& detail not by the more adaptable & flexible word of the guru.

Still, the age has its own demands, and it is becoming imperatively necessary that Indian knowledge should reveal in the Western way its scientific foundations. For if we do not do it ourselves, the Europeans will do it for us and do it badly, discrediting the knowledge in the process. The phenomenon of the Theosophical Society is a warning to us of a pressing urgency. It will never do to allow the science of Indian knowledge to be represented to the West through this strange & distorting medium. For this society of European & European-led inquirers arose from an impulse on which the Time-Spirit itself insists; their object, vaguely grasped at by them, was at bottom the systematic coordination, explanation & practice of Oriental religion & Oriental mental & spiritual discipline. Unfortunately, as always happens to a great effort in unfit hands, it stumbled at the outset & went into strange bypaths. It fell into the mediaeval snare of Gnostic mysticism, Masonic secrecy & Rosicrucian jargon. The little science it attempted has been rightly stigmatised as pseudo-science. A vain attempt to thrust in modern physical science into the explanation of psychical movements, — to explain for instance pranayam in the terms of oxygen & hydrogen! — to accept uncritically every experience & every random idea about an experience as it occurred to the mind & set it up as a revealed truth & almost a semi-divine communication, to make a hopeless amalgam & jumble of science, religion & philosophy all expressed in the terms of the imagination — this has been the scientific method of Theosophy. The result is that it lays its hands on truth & muddles it so badly that it comes out to the world as an untruth. And there now abound other misstatements of Indian truth, less elaborate but almost as wild & wide as Theosophy's. From this growing confusion we must deliver the future of humanity.

The Claims of Theosophy

I wish to write in no narrow and intolerant spirit about Theosophy. There can be nothing more contemptibly ignorant than the vulgar prejudice which ridicules Theosophy because it concerns itself with marvels. From that point of view the whole world is a marvel; every operation of thought, speech or action is a miracle, a thing wonderful, obscure, occult and unknown. Even the sneer on the lips of the derider of occultism has to pass through a number of ill-understood processes before it can manifest itself on his face, yet the thing itself is the work of a second. That sneer is a much greater and more occult miracle than the precipitation of letters or the reading of the Akashic records. If Science is true, what more absurd, paradoxical and Rabelaisian miracle can there be than this, that a republic of small animalcules forming a mass of grey matter planned Austerlitz, wrote Hamlet or formulated the Vedanta philosophy? If I believed that strange dogma, I should no longer hold myself entitled to disbelieve anything. Materialism seems to me the most daring of occultisms, the most reckless and presumptuous exploiter of the principle, *Credo quia impossibile*, I believe it because it is impossible. If these minute cells can invent wireless telegraphy, why should it be impossible for them to precipitate letters or divine the past and the future? Until one can say of investigation "It is finished" and of knowledge "There is nothing beyond", no one has a right to set down men as charlatans because they profess to be the pioneers of a new kind of Science.

Neither, I hope, shall I be inclined to reject or criticise adversely because Theosophy has a foreign origin. There is no law of Nature by which spiritual knowledge is confined to the East or must bear the stamp of an Indian manufacture before it can receive the imprimatur of the All-Wise. He has made man in his own image everywhere, in the image of the Satyam Jnanam

Anantam, the divine Truth-Knowledge-Infinity, and from wheresoever true knowledge comes, it must be welcomed.

Nevertheless if men claim to be the pioneers of a new kind of Science, they must substantiate their claims. And if foreigners come to the people of India and demand to be accepted as instructors in our own special department of knowledge, they must prove that they have a prodigious superiority. Has the claim been substantiated? Has the superiority been proved?

What Indians see is a body which is professedly and hospitably open to all enquiry at the base but entrenches itself in a Papal or mystic infallibility at the top. To be admitted into the society it is enough to believe in the freest investigation and the brotherhood of mankind, but everyone who is admitted must feel, if he is honest with himself, that he is joining a body which stands for certain well-known dogmas, a definite and very elaborate cosmogony and philosophy and a peculiar organisation, the spirit, if not the open practice in which seems to be theocratic rather than liberal. One feels that the liberality of the outer rings is only a wisely politic device for attracting a wider circle of sympathisers from whom numerous converts to the inner can be recruited. It is the dogmas, the cosmogony, the philosophy, the theocratic organisation which the world understands by Theosophy and which one strengthens by adhesion to the society; free inquiry and the brotherhood of man benefit to a very slight degree.

One sees also a steady avoidance of the demand for substantiation, a withdrawal into mystic secrecy, a continual reference to the infallible knowledge of the male & female Popes of Theosophy or, when that seems to need bolstering, to the divine authority of invisible and inaccessible Mahatmas. We in India admit the Guru and accept the Avatar. But still the Guru is only a vessel of the infinite Knowledge, the Avatar is only a particular manifestation of the Divine Personality. It is shocking to our spiritual notions to find cosmic Demiurges of a vague semi-divine character put between us and the All-Powerful and All-Loving and Kutthumi and Maurya taking the place of God.

One sees, finally, a new Theocracy claiming the place of the old, and that Theocracy is dominantly European. Indians figure numerously as prominent subordinates, just as in the British system of government Indians are indispensable and sometimes valued assistants. Or they obtain eminence on the side of pure spirituality and knowledge, just as Indians could rise to the highest places in the judicial service or in advisory posts, but not in the executive administration. But if the smaller hierophants are sometimes and rarely Indians, the theocrats and the bulk of the prophets are Russian, American or English. An Indian here and there may quicken the illumination of the Theosophist, but it is Madame Blavatsky or Mrs Besant, Sinnett or Leadbeater who lays down the commandments and the Law. It is strange to see the present political condition of India reproducing itself in a spiritual organisation; it illustrates perhaps the subtle interconnection and interdependence of all individual and communal activities in the human being. But the political subordination finds its justification in the physical fact of the British rule. It is argued plausibly, and perhaps correctly, that without this subordination British supremacy could have no sure foundation. But where is the justification for the foreign spiritual control? The argument of native incapacity may be alleged. But I do not find this hypothesis of superiority supported by the facts. I do not see that Mrs Besant has a more powerful and perfect intellectuality, eloquence, personality or religious force than had Swami Vivekananda or that a single Theosophist has yet showed him or herself to be as mighty and pure a spirit as the Paramhansa Ramakrishna. There are Indian Yogins who have a finer and more accurate psychical knowledge than the best that can be found in the books of the Theosophists. Some even of the less advanced have given me proofs of far better-developed occult powers than any Theosophist I have yet known. The only member of the Theosophical Society who could give me any spiritual help I could not better by my unaided faculties, was one excluded from the esoteric section because his rare and potent experiences were unintelligible to the Theosophic guides; nor were his knowledge and powers gained by Theosophic methods but by following the path of our Yoga and the impulse of an

Indian guru, one who meddled not in organisations and election cabals but lived like a madman, *unmattavat*.

These peculiarities of the Theosophical movement have begun to tell and the better mind of India revolts against Theosophy. The young who are the future, are not for the new doctrine. Yet only through India can Theosophy hope to survive. It may attract a certain number of European adherents, but cannot hope to control the thought and life of the West. Its secretive and Papal tendency is a fatal bar. Europe has done definitely with all knowledge that will not submit itself to scrutiny; it is finishing with the usurpations of theocracy in things spiritual as it has finished with them in things temporal. Even devout Catholics writhe uneasily under the shower of Papal encyclicals and feel what an embarrassment it is to have modern knowledge forbidden by a revenant from the Middle Ages or opinion fixed by a Council of priests no more spiritual, wise or illustrious than the minds they coerce with their irrational authority. Europe is certainly not going to exchange a Catholic for a Theosophical Pope, the Council of Cardinals for the Esoteric Section, or the Gospel and the Athanasian Creed for *Ancient Wisdom* and *Isis Unveiled*.

Will India long keep the temper that submits to unexamined authority and blinds itself with a name? I believe not. We shall more and more return to the habit of going to the root of things, of seeking knowledge not from outside but from the Self who knows and reveals. We must more and more begin to feel that to believe a thing because somebody has heard from somebody else that Mrs Besant heard it from a Mahatma, is a little unsafe and indefinite. Even if the assurance is given direct, we shall learn to ask for the proofs. Even if Kutthumi himself comes and tells me, I shall certainly respect his statement, but also I shall judge it and seek its verification. The greatest Mahatma is only a servant of the Most High and I must see his *chapras* before I admit his plenary authority. The world is putting off its blinkers; it is feeling once more the divine impulse to see.

It is not that Theosophy is false; it is that Theosophists are weak and human. I am glad to believe that there is much truth in Theosophy. There are also considerable errors. Many of the things they say which seem strange and incredible to those who decline the experiment, agree with the general experience of Yogins; there are other statements which our experience appears to contradict or to which it gives a different interpretation. Mahatmas exist, but they are not omnipotent or infallible. Rebirth is a fact and the memory of our past lives is possible; but the rigid rules of time and of Karmic reaction laid down dogmatically by the Theosophist hierophants are certainly erroneous. Especially is the hotchpotch of Hindu and Buddhist mythology and Theosophic prediction served up to us by Mrs Besant confusing and misleading. At any rate it does not agree with the insight of much greater Yogins than herself. Like most Theosophists she seems to ignore the numerous sources and possibilities of error which assail the Yogin before his intellect is perfectly purified and he has his perfection in the higher and superintellectual faculties of the mind. Until then the best have to remember that the mind even of the fairly advanced is not yet divine and that it is the nature of the old unchastened human element to leap at misunderstandings, follow the lure of predilections and take premature conclusions for established truths. We must accept the Theosophists as enquirers; as hierophants and theocrats I think we must reject them.

If Theosophy is to survive, it must first change itself. It must learn that mental rectitude to which it is now a stranger and improve its moral basis. It must become clear, straightforward, rigidly self-searching, sceptical in the nobler sense of the word. It must keep the Mahatmas in the background and put God and Truth in the front. Its Popes must dethrone themselves and enthrone the intellectual conscience of mankind. If they wish to be mystic and secret like our Yogins, then they must like our Yogins assert only to the initiate and the trained; but if they come out into the world to proclaim their mystic truths aloud and seek power, credit and influence on the strength of their assertions, then they must prove. It need not and ought not to be suddenly or by miracles; but there must be a scientific development, we must be able to lay hold on the rationale and watch the process of the truths they proclaim.

Science & Religion in Theosophy

I have said that I wish to write of Theosophy in no strain of unreasoning hostility or spirit of vulgar ridicule; yet these essays will be found to be much occupied with criticisms and often unsparing criticisms of the spirit and methods of Theosophists. There is, however, this difference between my criticisms and much that I have seen written in dispraise of the movement, that I censure not as an enemy but as an impartial critic, not as a hostile and incredulous outsider but as an earnest and careful inquirer and practical experimentalist in those fields which Theosophy seeks to make her own. Theosophy was not born with Madame Blavatsky, nor invented by the Mahatmas in the latter end of the nineteenth century. It is an ancient and venerable branch of knowledge, which unfortunately has never, in historical times, been brought out into the open and subjected to clear, firm and luminous tests. The imaginations of the cultured and the superstitions of the vulgar played havoc with its truths and vitiated its practice. It degenerated into the extravagances of the Gnostics & Rosicrucians and the charlatanism of magic and sorcery. The Theosophical Society was the first body of inquirers which started with the set & clear profession of bringing out this great mass of ancient truth into public notice and establishing it in public belief. The profession has not been sustained in practice. Instead of bringing them out into public notice they have withdrawn them into the shrouded secrecy of the Esoteric society; instead of establishing them to public belief, they have hampered the true development of Theosophy & injured its credit by allowing promise to dwarf performance and by a readiness to assert which was far beyond their power to verify. I do not deny that the Theosophical Society increases in its numbers, but it increases as a mystic sect and not in the strength of its true calling. I do not deny that it has done valuable service in appealing to the imaginations of men both in India & Europe; but it has appealed to their imaginations & has not convinced their reason. When there is so serious a failure in a strong and earnest endeavour, we must look for the cause in some defect which lies at the very roots of its action. And it is just there at the very roots of its active life that we find the vital defect of modern Theosophy. We find a speculative confusion which fatally ignores the true objects and the proper field of such a movement and a practical confusion which fatally ignores the right and necessary conditions of its success. They have failed to see what Theosophy rightly is and what it is not; they have failed to understand that error and the sources of error must be weeded out before the good corn of truth can grow. They have fallen into the snare of Gnostic jargon and Rosicrucian mummery and have been busy with a nebulous chase after Mahatmas, White Lodges and Lords of the Flame when they should have been experimenting earnestly and patiently, testing their results severely and arriving at sound and incontestable conclusions which they could present, rationally founded, first to all enquirers and then to the world at large.

Mrs Besant would have us believe that Theosophy is Brahmavidya. The Greek Theosophia and the Sanscrit Brahmavidya, she tells us in all good faith, are identical words and identical things. Even with Mrs Besant's authority, I cannot accept this extraordinary identification. It can only have arisen either from her ignorance of Sanscrit or from that pervading confusion of thought and inability to perceive clear and trenchant distinctions which is the bane of Theosophical inquiry & Theosophical pronouncements. Vidya may be represented, though not perfectly represented by sophia; but Brahman is not Theos and cannot be Theos, as even the veriest tyro in philosophy, one would think, ought to know. We all know what Brahmavidya is, — the knowledge of the One both in Itself and in its ultimate and fundamental relations to the world which appears in It whether as illusion or as manifestation, whether as Maya or as Lila. Does Theosophy answer to this description? Everyone knows that it does not and cannot. The modern Theosophist tells us much about Mahatmas, Kamaloka, Devachan, people on Mars, people on the Moon, astral bodies, precipitated letters, Akashic records and a deal of other matters, of high value if true and of great interest whether true or not. But what on earth, I should like to know, has all this to do with Brahmavidya? One might just as well describe botany, zoology & entomology or for that matter, music or painting or the binomial theory or quadratic equations as Brahmavidya. In a sense they are so since everything is Brahman, — sarvam khalvidam Brahma. But language has its distinctions on which clear thinking depends, & we must insist on their being observed. All this matter of Theosophy is not Brahmavidya, but Devavidya. Devavidya is the true equivalent, so far as there can be an equivalent, of Theosophy.

I am aware that Theosophy speaks of the Logos or of several Logoi and the government of the world — not so much by any Logos as by the Mahatmas. Still, I say, that all this does not constitute Theosophy into Brahmavidya, but leaves it what it was, Devavidya. It is still not the knowledge of the One, not the knowledge that leads to salvation, but the knowledge of the Many, — of our bondage & not of our freedom, Avidya & not Vidya. I do not decry it for that reason, but it is necessary that it should be put in its right place and not blot out for us the diviner knowledge of our forefathers. Theosophy is or should be a wider & profounder Science, a knowledge that deals with other levels & movements of consciousness, planes if you like so to call them, phenomena depending on the activity of consciousness on those levels, worlds & beings formed by the activity of consciousness on those levels, — for what is a world but the synthesis in Space & Time of a particular level of consciousness, — forming a field of consciousness with which material Science, the Science of this immediately visible world, cannot yet deal, and for the most part, not believing in it as fact, refuses to deal. Theosophy is, therefore, properly speaking, a high scientific enquiry. It is not or ought not to be a system of metaphysics or a new religion.

Sat

What is Truth? said Pilate confronted with a mighty messenger of the truth, not jesting surely, not in a spirit of shallow lightness, but turning away from the Christ with the impatience of the disillusioned soul for those who still use high words that have lost their meaning and believe in great ideals which the test of the event has proved to be fallacious. What is truth, — this phantom so long pursued, so impossible to grasp firmly, — that a man young, beautiful, gifted, eloquent and admired should consent to be crucified for its sake? Have not circumstance and event justified the half-pitying, half-sorrowful question of the Roman governor? The Messenger suffered on the cross, and what happened to the truth that was his message? As Christ himself foresaw, it has never been understood even by its professors. For five hundred years it was a glorious mirage for which thousands of men and women willingly underwent imprisonment, torture and death in order that Christ's kingdom might come on earth & felicity possess the nations. But the kingdom that came was not Christ's; it was Constantine's, it was Hildebrand's, it was Alexander Borgia's. For another thirteen centuries the message was — what? Has it not been the chief support of fanaticism, falsehood, cruelty and hypocrisy, the purveyor of selfish power, the keystone of a society that was everything Christ had denounced? Jesus died on the cross, for the benefit, it would seem, of those who united to slay him, the Sadducee, atheist & high priest, the Pharisee, zealot, hypocrite & persecutor and the brutal, self-seeking, callous military Roman. Now in its last state, after such a lamentable career, Christ's truth stands finally rejected by the world's recent enlightenment as a hallucination or a superstition which sometimes helpfully, sometimes harmfully amused the infancy of the human intellect. This history is written in too pronounced characters to be the exact type of all messages that the world has received, but is it not in some sort a type of the fate of all truth? What idea has stood successfully the test of a prolonged & pitiless inquiry? what ideal has stood successfully the test of time? Has not mankind been busy for the last fifty years and more denying almost all that it had formerly affirmed? And now that under the name of rationalism or materialism the denial has shaped itself into some form of workably practical affirmation, mankind is again at its work of denying its denial and rearranging — but this time doubtingly — its old affirmations. The scepticism of Pilate would therefore seem to have some excuse in a recurrent human experience. Is there, indeed, such a thing as truth, — beyond of course that practical truth of persistent material appearances by which we govern our lives, the truth of death, birth, hunger, sexuality, pain, pleasure, commerce, money making, ease, discomfort, ambition, failure and success? Has not indeed the loftiest of our philosophical systems declared all things here to be Maya? And if Maya is illusion, a deceit of the thinking consciousness, then indeed there can be no truth anywhere in the world except that indefinable Existence which we cannot comprehend and which, after all, Buddhism, not without logic and plausibility, setting it down as another & more generalised sanskara, a false sensation of consciousness in the eternal Void, denies. And yet man is so constituted that he must follow after truth whether it is attained or not; something in him secret, masterful, essential to his existence, forbids him to be satisfied with a falsehood; the moment it is perceived or even believed to be a falsehood, he rejects it and the thing begins to crumble. If he persists in his rejection, it cannot last. Yesterday it was, today we see it tottering, tomorrow we shall look for it and find that it is no longer. It has passed back into Prakriti; it has dissolved into that of which it was made. For sraddha is the condition of all existence in consciousness and that to which sraddha is denied, ceases to have existence whether here or elsewhere, na caivamutra no iha. It is not, neither in this world nor in another. We may not unreasonably infer from this importance and this imperative necessity that Truth does really exist and everything is not illusion. If then Truth is always escaping our hold and leaving us to disillusionment and derision, it may be because we have neither formed any clear conception of what Truth itself is nor taken hold of the right means by which it can be grasped. Let us leave aside, for a while, Buddha's world of sanskaras; let us put aside, packed away in an accessible corner of the brain, Shankara's gospel of Maya, and start instead from the old Vedantic beginnings OM Tat Sat, That (Brahman) is the thing that Is, and Sarvam khalvidam Brahma, Verily, *all this*, everything of which we are aware, is Brahman. It is at least possible that we may return from this inquiry with a deeper idea both of sanskaras and of Maya and may find that we have answered Pilate's question by discovering the nature and conditions of Truth.

I am speaking of the fundamental truth, the truth of things and not merely the fact about particulars or of particulars only as their knowledge forms a basis or a help to the discovery of fundamental truth. The fact that a particular sort of contact makes me uncomfortable is nothing in itself except in so far as it throws light upon the general causes of pain; the nature, origin and purpose of pain is the fundamental truth that I seek about the sensational reaction to contact. This law of pain, moreover, is not so fundamental as the truth about the nature, origin and purpose of sensation and contact themselves, of which pain is a particularity, an example or a modification. This more fundamental truth becomes again itself particular when compared with the truth about the nature, origin and purpose of existence of which sensation and contact are only particular circumstances. In this we arrive at the one fundamental truth of all, and a little consideration will show that if we really & rightly know that, the rest ought and probably will reveal themselves at once and fall into their places. Tasmin vijnate sarvam vijnatam, That being known, all is known. Our ancestors perceived this truth of the fundamental unity of knowledge and sought to know Sat first, confident that Sat being known, the different tattwas, laws, details & particulars of Sat would more readily yield up their secret. The moderns follow another thought, which, also, has a truth of its own. They think that since being is one the knowledge of the particulars must lead to the knowledge of the fundamental unity and they begin therefore at the bottom and climb upwards — a slow but, one might imagine, a safe method of procession. "Little flower in the crannies" cries Tennyson addressing a pretty blossom in the wall in lines which make good thought, but execrable poetry, "if I could but know what you are, I should know what God and man is." Undoubtedly; the question is whether, without knowing God, we can really know the flower, — know *it*, and not merely its name and form or all the details of its name and form. Rupa we can know & analyse by the aid of science, nama by the aid of philosophy; but swarupa? It would seem that some third instrument is needed for that consummation of knowledge. The senses & reason, even though aided by microscope and telescope, cannot show it to us. Na sandrishe tisthati rupam asya. The form of That stands not in the ken of sight. Mind and speech are not permitted to lead us to it, na vag gacchati na mano. Even the metaphysical logic of a Shankara stops short of that final victory. Naisha tarkena matir apaneya. This realisation in thought is not to be obtained by logic. All these various disabilities are due to one compelling cause; they are, because Sat, the truth of existence, Brahman, the reality of things which fills & supports their idea and form, is beyond the recognisable & analysable elements of idea and form. Anor aniyan atarkyam anupramanat. It is subtler even than elemental subtlety and therefore not to be deduced, induced, inferred or discovered by a reasoning which proceeds from a consideration of the elements of name and form and makes that its standard. This is a truth which even the greatest philosophers, Vedantic or unVedantic, are apt to forget; but the Sruti insists on it always.

    Nevertheless mankind has for some thousands of years been attempting obstinately & with passion to discover that Truth by the very means which the Sruti has forbidden. Such error is natural and inevitable to the human consciousness. For the Angel in man is one who has descended out of light & bliss into the darkness, twilight and half light here, the darkness of matter, the twilight of vital consciousness, the broken half lights of the mind, and the master impulse of his nature is to yearn passionately towards the light from which [he] has fallen. Unable to find it at once, too little *dhira* (calm & discerning) to perfect himself patiently, it is natural that he in his eagerness should grasp at other instruments meant for a limited utility and straining them beyond their capacity compel them to serve this his supreme object — which is always to recover the perfect light and by that recovery to recover also what dwells only in the perfect light, — the perfect & unfailing bliss. From this abuse of his parts of knowledge have resulted three illegitimate human activities, of which Philosophy, Religion & Science have severally made themselves guilty, the disputatious metaphysical philosophy of the schools, the theology of the Churches and the scientific philosophy of the laboratories. Philosophy, Religion & Science have each their appointed field and dominion; each can help man in his great preoccupation, the attempt to know all that he can about Sat, about Brahman. The business of Philosophy is to arrange logically the general modes of Sat, the business of Religion is to arrange practically & vitally the personal relations of Sat, the business of Science is to arrange observantly & analytically the particular forms & movements of Sat. They are really necessary to and ought to lean on each other; and, if all recognised proper limitations and boundary marks, could by their joint activity help man to his present attainable fullness; but by a sort of intellectual land hunger they are perpetual invaders of each other's dominion, deny each other's positions and therefore remain unprofitably at war through the human ages. Finally, all three after illegitimately occupying each other's fields insist on snatching at a knowledge of which they are all equally incapable — the essential nature of the world, the secret reality of Sat, the uttamam rahasyam of the Brahman. This error, this confusion, this sankara or illegitimate mixing of different nature and function is the curse of the Kali and from it arises much, if not most, of the difficulty we experience as a race in escaping from this misery & darkness into bliss and light. It is part and a great part of Kali Kalila, the chaos of the Kali.

India has always attempted, though not, since the confusion of Buddhism, with any success, if not to keep the three to their proper division of labour — which, with the general growth of ignorance became impossible — at least, always to maintain or reestablish, if disturbed, some harmony between them. Of this attempt the Gita is the standing monument and the most perfect example. To see the confusion working in its untrammelled force, — and it is only so, by isolating the disease from the modification of curative forces, that we can observe, diagnose and afterwards find its remedy — we must go to the intellectual history of the European continent. There have been, properly speaking, two critical periods in this history, the Graeco-Roman era of philosophic illumination previous to Christianity and the era of modern scientific illumination which is still unexhausted. In the first we see the revolt of Philosophy (with Science concealed in her protective embrace) against the usurpation of religion. We find it, after achieving liberation, in its turn denying religion and usurping her sacred prerogative. In the modern era we see Science this time emerged and adult, keeping Philosophy behind her, in revolt against religion, first liberate herself, then deny religion & usurp her prerogatives, then, or as part of this final process of conquest, turn, deny & strike down her lofty ally and usurp also her ancient territory. For if Science has scorned & denied religion, she has equally scorned & denied Metaphysics. If she has declared God to be a barbarous myth, a fiction of dreams and terrors and longings and denied us the right of communion with the infinite, equally has she declared metaphysics to be an aberration of the ideative faculty, a false extension of logic and denied our right to recognise any metaphysical existence or anything at all which cannot be judged by or inferred from the results of the test tube, the scalpel, the microscope & the telescope. Neither, however, has she herself hesitated to dogmatise about the essential nature of existence and the mutual relations of its general modes, matter, life, mind and spirit. But for our immediate purpose it is only necessary to note the result in either of these eras of these tremendous usurpations. The result of the usurpations of philosophy was that mankind flung itself with an infinite sincerity, with a passionate sense of relief into the religion of an obscure Jewish sect and consented for a length of time which amazes us to every theological absurdity, even the most monstrous, so that it might once more be permitted to believe in something greater than earth & to have relations with God. The old philosophical spirit was torn to pieces with Hypatia in the bloodstained streets of Alexandria. Theology usurped her place and discoursed blindly & foolishly on transubstantiation and consubstantiality and one knows not what other barren mysteries. So far as philosophy was allowed an independent existence, she was compelled to do not her own work but the work of science; so we find the schoolmen elaborately determining by logic and a priori word fencing questions which could only be properly determined by observation and analysis. For Theology, for Mediaeval Religion herself did not care for this field of knowledge; she had no need for scientific truths just as the Jacobin Republic had "no need of chemists"; in fact she guillotined Science wherever its presence attracted her attention. But all injustice — and that means at bottom all denial of truth, of the satyam and ritam — brings about its own punishment or, as Religion would put it, God's visitation & vengeance. Science liberated, given in her strenuous emergence the strength of the Titans, avenges herself today on her old oppressors, on Religion, on Philosophy, breaks their temples, scorns their gods & prophets & seeks to deprive them even of the right to existence. That was the result of the Graeco-Roman illumination. And what will be the result of the scientific illumination, the modern enlightenment, the fiery triumph and ardent intellectual bigotry of the materialist? It is too early to foresee the final denouement, but unformed lines of it show themselves, obscure masses arise. Mysticism is growing obscurely in strength, as Science grew obscurely in strength in the Middle Ages. We see Titanic & mystic figures striding out of the East, building themselves fortresses & points of departure, spreading among the half-intellectual, capturing even the intellectual — vague figures of Theosophy, Spiritualism, Mental Science, Psychical Research, Neo-Hinduism, Neo-Buddhism,

Neo-Mahomedanism, Neo-Christianity. The priests of Isis, the adepts & illuminati of Gnosticism, denied their triumph by the intervention of St Paul & the Pope, reborn into this latter age, claim now their satisfaction. Already some outworks of materialism are giving way, the attack grows more insistent, the defence more uncertain, less proudly self-confident, though not less angry, contemptuous, bitter & intolerant; the invaders increase their adherents, extend the number of their strongholds. If no wider & higher truth intervenes, it would almost seem as if the old confusion in a new form might replace the new. Perhaps an Esoteric Society or a Spiritualist Circle of High Mediums will in a few centuries be laying down for us what we shall think about this world & the next, what particular relations with Gods will be permitted us, what Influences or Initiates we shall worship. Who knows? The fires of Smithfield may yet reblaze to save heretics from the perdition which an illustrious voice has declared to us to be the destined doom of all who do not acknowledge Maurya & Kutthumi.

These are not mere fantastic speculations. The history of humanity & the peculiar capacities of that apparently incalculable & erratic thing, human nature, ought to warn us of their possibility — or at least that they are not entirely impossible, in spite of the printing press, in spite of the clarities of Science. No doubt the old philosophers [thought] that with so many Stoas & Academies, such spread of education, never again would enlightenment be dimmed and the worship of gods & ghosts would in the end amuse none but the vulgar. We must accept these things as possible & examine why they are possible. This reaction is inevitable because Philosophy, though exceedingly high & luminous, tends to be exclusive & narrow and Science, though exceedingly patient, accurate & minute, tends to be limited, dry & purblind. They are both apt to be as dogmatic & intolerant in their own high way or in their own clear, dry way as Religion in her way which is not high, but intense, not clear but enthusiastic; and they live on a plane of mentality on which humanity at large does not yet find itself at perfect ease, cannot live without a struggle and a difficulty in breathing. They both demand from man that he shall sacrifice his heart & his imagination to his intellect, shall deny his full human nature and live coldly & dryly. You might just as well ask him to live without free breathing. The mental world in which we are asked to live, resembles what the life of humanity would be if the warmth of the sun had diminished, the earth were growing chill and its atmosphere were already too rarefied for our comfort. It is no use saying that he ought to live in such an atmosphere, that it will improve his mental health & vigour. Perhaps he ought, though I do not think so, but he cannot. Or rather the individual may, — everything is possible to individual man, — but the race cannot. The demand can never be allowed; for it is a denial of Nature, a violation of the great Mother, a displacement of her eternal facts by the aridities of logic; it is a refusal of the Truth of things, of the Satyam, Ritam, and if it is persisted in, it will bring its own revenges. Philosophy & Science, if they are to help mankind without hurting it and themselves, must recognise that mankind is a complex being and his nature demands that every part of that complexity shall have its field of activity & every essential aspiration in him must be satisfied. It is his nature & his destiny to be aptakama, satisfied in his desires, in the individual & in the race — though always in accordance with the satyam, the ritam, which is also the sukham & sundaram, not lawlessly & according to aberrations & caprices. It was the great virtue of the ancient Hinduism, before Buddhism upset its balance & other aberrations followed, that it recognised in principle at least this fundamental verity, did not deny what God insists upon but strove, it does not matter whether perfectly or imperfectly, to put everything in its place & create a natural harmony.

Sachchidananda

The Vedanta, that solemn affirmation of the ultimate truths beyond which no human thinking has ever proceeded or can proceed, looking deep into the last recesses where existence takes refuge from the scrutiny of the Mind, affirms there as the beginning and the end of all possible description of the infinite Knowable-Unknowable three terms, Being, Comprehension and Delight. They are the initial & final trinity of existence. From them all phenomena proceed, to them all phenomena seek to return. This personality envisaged as myself, has come out of infinite being, lives in infinite being; emmeshed in the limitations of form & idea it seeks laboriously to recover itself as the infinite being. This Awareness in me which centralised in my personality suffers and examines all impressions that reach me out of the infinite existence, is a selection from an infinite Awareness contemplating itself in its whole & its parts; localised & limited, involved at first in this form it has created, it emerges out of its creation and seeks first to comprehend that and then to comprehend itself; master in some sort of its surroundings, it seeks to become master of itself; enlarging always from the factor to the sum, from the particular to the general, from the form to the essence it seeks to recover itself as the infinite self-comprehension. This Will to be & know in myself is essentially the joy of being & the joy of comprehending — Ananda, Delight; and the particular delight in me is but a spark, a wave, a foam-crest of an infinite delight; fastened at first on partial, limited & transient pleasures, it seeks always to enlarge them, to combine, to intensify; it goes out seeking for new forms of happiness; it goes in turning from the vital joy to sense-delights, from sense-delights to pleasures of emotion, from pleasures of emotion to intellectual satisfaction, from intellectual satisfaction to the self-existent bliss of the spirit which depends on no object or circumstance; in all these motions it is seeking to recover itself as infinite Delight. In this way the final perceptions of Vedanta explain the whole process & labour of consciousness in the world.

These three, Sat, Chit and Ananda are one Trinity, Sachchidananda. They are not three different factors making a single sum, neither are any two of them merely attributes, even inseparable & invariable attributes, of the third. No doubt, they are always coexistent. Where there is no delight, latent or developed, there can be no existence; where there is no awareness self-absorbed or manifest, there can be no existence. Follow existence into utter & blind inertia, consciousness sits secret in that night; follow consciousness into the abyss of desolation, joy sits self-stunned in the mask of that misery. But their coexistence is only an exterior sign of their essential unity. They do not exist separately, because they are not different from each other, — all three are one thing-in-itself seen diversely; seen sensationally, touching the fibres of conscious life in us it is delight; seen mentally, touching the fibres of living consciousness, it is comprehension; seen spiritually, touching the very core of this living & conscious I, it is being. But the thing-in-itself is one; it is Brahman. Go behind the Trinity and you can say nothing of it but this, Tat, anirdeshyam, the indefinable, That which transcends all words & thoughts; seek to know & define it, you come back to the universal & mysterious Trinity, Sachchidananda, being, comprehension & delight. This is all that you can know fundamentally about yourself; you are That which Is, which, being, comprehends Its own existence, which, comprehending, has in its silence of being or in its play of comprehension a self-existent delight. It is all we can know fundamentally & all we need to know, for, this once grasped & pursued in knowledge, the whole of life begins to unroll itself in its secret motion & purpose to our gaze.

Against this sublime Trinity of the Vedanta, this penetrating analysis of the reality of things, this discovery of the real existence of God in the world, the appearances of that world seem to protest and militate. That which strikes us most saliently & leaps on us fiercely at every turn, is grief & pain, not delight; that which besieges our eyes always & everywhere is not conscious awareness, but the inertia or the brute movement of unconscious Matter. Existence we cannot deny; the voice of the mighty Life in us rejects always the systems of Nihilism & leaves them to the enjoyment of a few curious & subtle metaphysicians; nothing either in science or in experience supports the purely metaphysical idea of Nullity. But this undeniable existence stands before us rather as an inextricable confusion of pleasure & pain than as synonymous with delight; in its vast fields sown with worlds we find instead of an omnipresent consciousness rather an omnipresent non-consciousness in which tongues of consciousness flame like little points & tongues of fire on a huge inert pyre of various timber. Be not deceived, answers the Vedantin; appearances can never be trusted till the secrets behind them are fathomed. To the eye's unvarying experience the sun is a globe of fire that voyages round its worshipped earth; generations so conceived it & would have mocked at the truth; these solid appearances are an assemblage of gases; the colour of a rose is a brilliant deceit of the vision. Interrogate consciousness to find what it is or holds & unconsciousness to discover its secrets. Interrogate not only the state of waking but the states of dream & sleep. You will find at the end of long, patient & searching experiments that the confused consciousness of dream was confused only in the receiving parts of the material waking mind and behind it was a state of awareness even more perfect & orderly than the awareness of our waking life. You will find that the consciousness in abeyance of dreamless sleep was in abeyance only in the overpowered & cessant parts of the same material waking mind and behind it was a most exalted & perfect state of awareness which stands near the threshold of the House of God in which we really dwell; for here we are only labourers or overseers in His outer farms. It is admitted that when we are in sound sleep we dream; we are conscious, when we are swooned or stunned only a part of our consciousness, the outward, the here active is withdrawn. When you have interrogated unconsciousness in yourself, interrogate it in the tree & the clod. You will find, for by that time you will have entered into the kingdoms within & learned to command a self-exceeding experience of being, that in the tree & the rock there is the same being, the same consciousness, the same principle of Will to live, of delight, in a word, that is [in] yourself. The unconsciousness of the tree & the rock is the same unconsciousness as that which occupies your body when mind is withdrawn from the observation of its working. It is the sleep, the universal trance of Matter. And that means, eventually, the trance of consciousness forgetting itself in its own symbol or form. Consciousness in this its outer shell has become to the appearance something else which seems not to have any resemblance to conscious being, as gas becoming water is to appearance something else which has no remotest gaseous semblance. The truth sits veiled behind the appearance, self-absorbed; there is in all things, without exception, "That which is conscious in these conscious & unconscious existences, that which is awake in these who sleep."

The Silence behind Life

There is a silence behind life as well as within it and it is only in this more secret, sustaining silence that we can hear clearly the voice of God. In the noise of the world we hear only altered & disturbed echoes of it; for the Voice comes always — who else speaks to us on our journey? — but the gods of the heart, the gods of the mind, the gods of desire, the gods of sense take up the divine cry, intercept it and alter it for their purposes. Krishna calls to us, but the first note, even the opening power or sweetness, awakes a very brouhaha of these echoes. It is not the fault of these poor gods. The accent of power is so desirable, the note of sweetness is so captivating that they must seize it, they would be dull & soulless, there would be no hope of their redemption if they did not at once leap at it and make it their own. But in becoming their own, it ceases to be entirely his. How many who have the religious faith and the religious temperament, are following the impulses of their heart, the cravings of their desire, the urgency of their senses, the dictates of their opinion when they fully imagine that their God is leading them! And they do well, for God is leading them. It is the way He has chosen for them, & since He has chosen it, it is the best & wisest & most fruitful way for them. Still it is their God — not one they have made in their own image as the Atheist believes, but One who makes Himself in the image that they prefer, the image that best suits with their nature or their development. "In whatever way men come to me, in that way I love & cleave to them." It is a saying of fathomless depth which contains the seed of the whole truth about God & religion. After all it is only in this way that the conditioned can meet the Absolute, that which has a nature or dharma of its own with that which is beyond all limit of nature or dharma. After the meeting of the soul with God, — well, that is a different matter. The secrets of His nuptial chamber cannot all be spoken.

Nevertheless, there is a higher way of meeting him than that which leads us through subjection to the Gods. By perfect Love, by perfect Joy, by perfect Satisfaction, by perfected mind one can hear what the Voice truly says if not the Voice itself, — catch the kernel of the message with a sort of ecstatic perfection, even if afterwards the Gods dilate on it & by attempting to amplify & complete, load it with false corollaries or prevent some greater fullness of truth from arriving to us. Therefore this way also, though it is high, cannot be the highest.

Section Three

Circa 1913

THE PSYCHOLOGY OF YOGA
Initial Definitions and Descriptions

Yoga has four powers and objects, purity, liberty, beatitude and perfection. Whosoever has consummated these four mightinesses in the being of the transcendental, universal, lilamaya and individual God is the complete and absolute Yogin.

All manifestations of God are manifestations of the absolute Parabrahman.

The Absolute Parabrahman is unknowable to us, not because It is the nothingness of all that we are, for rather whatever we are in truth or in seeming is nothing but Parabrahman, but because It is pre-existent & supra-existent to even the highest & purest methods and the most potent & illimitable instruments of which soul in the body is capable.

In Parabrahman knowledge ceases to be knowledge and becomes an inexpressible identity. Become Parabrahman, if thou wilt and if That will suffer thee, but strive not to know It; for thou shalt not succeed with these instruments and in this body.

In reality thou art Parabrahman already and ever wast and ever will be. To become Parabrahman in any other sense, thou must depart utterly out of world manifestation and out even of world transcendence.

Why shouldst thou hunger after departure from manifestation as if the world were an evil? Has not That manifested itself in thee & in the world and art thou wiser & purer & better than the Absolute, O mind-deceived soul in the mortal? When That withdraws thee, then thy going hence is inevitable; until Its force is laid on thee, thy going is impossible, cry thy mind never so fiercely & wailingly for departure. Therefore neither desire nor shun the world, but seek the bliss & purity & freedom & greatness of God in whatsoever state or experience or environment.

So long as thou hast any desire, be it the desire of non-birth or the desire of liberation, thou canst not attain to Parabrahman. For That has no desires, neither of birth nor of non-birth, nor of world, nor of departure from world. The Absolute is unlimited by thy desire as It is inaccessible to thy knowledge.

If thou wouldst know Paratpara brahman, then know It as It chooses to manifest Itself in world and transcending it — for transcendence also is a relation to world & not the sheer Absolute, — since otherwise It is unknowable. This is the simultaneous knowing & not knowing spoken of in the Vedanta.

Of Parabrahman we should not say that "It" is world-transcendent or world-immanent or related or non-related to the world; for all these ideas of world and not-world, of transcendence and immanence and relation are expressions of thought by which mind puts its own values on the self-manifestation of Parabrahman to Its own principle of knowledge and we cannot assert any, even the highest of them to be the real reality of that which is at once all and beyond all, nothing and beyond nothing. A profound and unthinking silence is the only attitude which the soul manifested in world should adopt towards the Absolute.

We know of Parabrahman that It Is, in a way in which no object is and no state in the world, because whenever & in whatever direction we go to the farthest limits of soul-experience or thought-experience or body-experience or any essential experience whatsoever, we come to the brink of That and perceive It to be, unknowably, without any capacity of experiencing about it any farther truth whatsoever.

When thy soul retiring within from depth to depth & widening without from vastness to vastness stands in the silence of its being before an unknown & unknowable from which & towards which world is seen to exist as a thing neither materially real nor mentally real and yet not to be described as a dream or a falsehood, then know that thou art standing in the Holy of Holies, before the Veil that shall not be rent. In this mortal body thou canst not rend it, nor in any other body; nor in the state of self in body nor in the state of pure self, nor in waking nor in sleep nor in trance, nor in any state or circumstances whatsoever for thou must be beyond state before thou canst enter into the Paratpara brahman.

That is the unknown God to whom no altar can be raised and no worship offered; universe is His only altar, existence is His only worship. That we are, feel, think, act or are but do not feel, do not think, do not act is for That enough. To That, the saint is equal with the sinner, activity with inactivity, man with the mollusc, since all are equally Its manifestations. These things at least are true of the Parabrahman & Para Purusha, which is the Highest that we know & the nearest to the Absolute. But what That is behind the veil or how behind the veil It regards Itself and its manifestations is a thing no mind can assume to tell or know; and he is equally ignorant and presumptuous who raises & inscribes to It an altar or who pretends to declare the Unknown to those who know that they can know It not. Confuse not thought, bewilder not the soul of man in its forward march, but turn to the Universe & know That in this, Tad va etat, for so only & in these terms It has set itself out to be known to those who are in the universe. Be not deceived by Ignorance, be not deceived by knowledge; there is none bound & none free & none seeking freedom but only God playing at these things in the extended might of His self-conscious being, para maya, mahimanam asya, which we call the universe.

The Object of Our Yoga

The object of our Yoga is self-perfection, not self-annulment.

There are two paths set for the feet of the Yogin, withdrawal from the universe and perfection in the Universe; the first comes by asceticism, the second is effected by tapasya; the first receives us when we lose God in Existence, the second is attained when we fulfil existence in God. Let ours be the path of perfection, not of abandonment; let our aim be victory in the battle, not the escape from all conflict.

Buddha and Shankara supposed the world to be radically false and miserable; therefore escape from the world was to them the only wisdom. But this world is Brahman, the world is God, the world is Satyam, the world is Ananda; it is our misreading of the world through mental egoism that is a falsehood and our wrong relation with God in the world that is a misery. There is no other falsity and no other cause of sorrow.

God created the world in Himself through Maya; but the Vedic meaning of Maya is not illusion, it is wisdom, knowledge, capacity, wide extension in consciousness. Prajna prasrita purani. Omnipotent Wisdom created the world, it is not the organised blunder of some Infinite Dreamer; omniscient Power manifests or conceals it in Itself or Its own delight, it is not a bondage imposed by His own ignorance on the free and absolute Brahman.

If the world were Brahman's self-imposed nightmare, to awake from it would be the natural and only goal of our supreme endeavour; or if life in the world were irrevocably bound to misery, a means of escape from this bondage would be the sole secret worth discovering. But perfect truth in world-existence is possible, for God here sees all things with the eye of truth; and perfect bliss in the world is possible, for God enjoys all things with the sense of unalloyed freedom. We also can enjoy this truth and bliss, called by the Veda amritam, Immortality, if by casting away our egoistic existence into perfect unity with His being we consent to receive the divine perception and the divine freedom.

The world is a movement of God in His own being; we are the centres and knots of divine consciousness which sum up and support the processes of His movement. The world is His play with His own self-conscious delight, He who alone exists, infinite, free and perfect; we are the self-multiplications of that conscious delight, thrown out into being to be His playmates. The world is a formula, a rhythm, a symbol-system expressing God to Himself in His own consciousness, — it has no material existence but exists only in His consciousness and self-expression; we, like God, are in our inward being That which is expressed, but in our outward being terms of that formula, notes of that rhythm, symbols of that system. Let us lead forward God's movement, play out His play, work out His formula, execute His harmony, express Him through ourselves in His system. This is our joy and our self-fulfilment; to this end we who transcend & exceed the universe, have entered into universe-existence.

Perfection has to be worked out, harmony has to be accomplished. Imperfection, limitation, death, grief, ignorance, matter, are only the first terms of the formula — unintelligible till we have worked out the wider terms and reinterpreted the formulary; they are the initial discords of the musician's tuning. Out of imperfection we have to construct perfection, out of limitation to discover infinity, out of death to find immortality, out of grief to recover divine bliss, out of ignorance to rescue divine self-knowledge, out of matter to reveal Spirit. To work out this end for ourselves and for humanity is the object of our Yogic practice.

PURNA YOGA

I

The Entire Purpose of Yoga

By Yoga we can rise out of falsehood into truth, out of weakness into force, out of pain and grief into bliss, out of bondage into freedom, out of death into immortality, out of darkness into light, out of confusion into purity, out of imperfection into perfection, out of self-division into unity, out of Maya into God. All other utilisation of Yoga is for special and fragmentary advantages not always worth pursuing. Only that which aims at possessing the fullness of God is purna Yoga; the sadhaka of the Divine Perfection is the purna Yogin.

Our aim must be to be perfect as God in His being and bliss is perfect, pure as He is pure, blissful as He is blissful, and, when we are ourselves siddha in the purna Yoga, to bring all mankind to the same divine perfection. It does not matter if for the present we fall short of our aim, so long as we give ourselves whole-heartedly to the attempt and by living constantly in it and for it move forward even two inches upon the road; even that will help to lead humanity out of the struggle and twilight in which it now dwells into the luminous joy which God intends for us. But whatever our immediate success, our unvarying aim must be to perform the whole journey and not lie down content in any wayside stage or imperfect resting place.

All Yoga which takes you entirely away from the world, is a high but narrow specialisation of divine tapasya. God in His perfection embraces everything; you also must become all-embracing.

God in His ultimate existence beyond all manifestation and all knowledge, is the Absolute Parabrahman; in relation to the world He is that which transcends all universal existence while regarding it or in turning away from it; He is that which contains and upholds the universe, He is that which becomes the universe and He is the universe & everything which it contains.

He is also Absolute and Supreme Personality playing in the universe and as the universe; in the universe He appears to be its Soul & Lord, as the universe He appears to be the motion or process of the Will of the Lord and to become all the subjective and objective results of the motion. All the states of the Brahman, the transcendent, the continent, the universal, the individual are informed & sustained by the divine Personality. He is both the Existent & the state of existence. We call the state of existence the Impersonal Brahman, the Existent the Personal Brahman. There is no difference between them except to the play of our consciousness; for every impersonal state depends upon a manifest or secret Personality and can reveal the Personality which it holds and veils and every Personality attaches to itself and can plunge itself into an impersonal existence. This they can do because Personality & Impersonality are merely different states of self-consciousness in one Absolute Being.

Philosophies & religions dispute about the priority of different aspects of God & different Yogins, Rishis & Saints have preferred this or that philosophy or religion. Our business is not to dispute about any of them, but to realise & become all of them, not to follow after any aspect to the exclusion of the rest, but to embrace God in all His aspects and beyond aspect.

God descending into world in various forms has consummated on this earth the mental and bodily form which we call humanity.

He has manifested in the world through the play of all-governing Soul with its own formative Will or Shakti a rhythm of existence of which Matter is the lowest term and pure being the highest. Mind & Life stand upon Matter (Manas & Prana on Annam) and make the lower half of world-existence (aparardha); pure consciousness and pure bliss proceed out of pure Being (Chit and Ananda out of Sat) and make the upper half of world-existence. Pure idea (vijnana) stands as the link between the two. These seven principles or terms of existence are the basis of the sevenfold world of the Puranas (Satyaloka, Tapas, Jana, Mahar, Swar, Bhuvar & Bhur).

The lower hemisphere in this arrangement of consciousness consists of the three vyahritis of the Veda, "Bhur, Bhuvah, Swar"; they are states of consciousness in which the principles of the upper world are expressed or try to express themselves under different conditions. Pure in their own homes, they are in this foreign country subject to perverse, impure & disturbing combinations & workings. The ultimate object of life is to get rid of the perversity, impurity & disturbance & express them perfectly in these other conditions. Your life on this earth is a divine poem that you are translating into earthly language or a strain of music which you are rendering into words.

Being in Sat is one in multiplicity, one that regards its multiplicity without being lost or confused in it and multiplicity that knows itself as one without losing the power of multiple play in the universe. Under the conditions of mind, life & body, ahankara is born, the subjective or objective form of consciousness is falsely taken for self-existent being, the body for an independent reality & the ego for an independent personality; the one loses itself in us in its multiplicity & when it recovers its unity, finds it difficult, owing to the nature of mind, to preserve its play of multiplicity. Therefore when we are absorbed in world, we miss God in Himself; when we seek God, we miss Him in the world. Our business is to break down & dissolve the mental ego & get back to our divine unity without losing our power of individual & multiple existence in the universe.

Consciousness in Chit is luminous, free, illimitable & effective; that which it is aware of as Chit (Jnanashakti) it fulfils infallibly as Tapas (Kriyashakti); for Jnanashakti is only the stable & comprehensive, Kriyashakti only the motional and intensive form of one self-luminous Conscious Being. They are one power of conscious force of God (Chit-Shakti of Sat-Purusha). But in the lower hemisphere, under the conditions of mind, life & body, the luminousness becomes divided & broken up into uneven rays, the freedom trammelled by egoism and unequal forms, the effectiveness veiled by the uneven play of forces. We

The Entire Purpose of Yoga

have, therefore, states of consciousness, non-consciousness & false consciousness, knowledge & ignorance & false knowledge, effective force & inertia and ineffective force. Our business is by renouncing our divided & unequal individual force of action & thought into the one, undivided universal Chitshakti of Kali to replace our egoistic activities by the play in our body of the universal Kali and thus exchange blindness & ignorance for knowledge and ineffective human strength for the divine effective Force.

Delight in Ananda is pure, unmixed, one & yet multitudinous. Under the conditions of mind, life & body it becomes divided, limited, confused & misdirected and owing to shocks of unequal forces & uneven distribution of Ananda subject to the duality of positive & negative movements, grief & joy, pain & pleasure. Our business is to dissolve these dualities by breaking down their cause & plunge ourselves into the ocean of divine bliss, one, multitudinous, evenly distributed (sama), which takes delight from all things & recoils painfully from none.

In brief, we have to replace dualities by unity, egoism by divine consciousness, ignorance by divine wisdom, thought by divine knowledge, weakness, struggle & effort by self-contented divine force, pain & false pleasure by divine bliss. This is called in the language of Christ bringing down the kingdom of heaven on earth, or in modern language, realising & effectuating God in the world.

Humanity is, upon earth, the form of life chosen for this human aspiration & divine accomplishment; all other forms of life either do not need it or are ordinarily incapable of it unless they change into humanity. The divine fullness is therefore the sole real aim of humanity. It has to be effected in the individual in order that it may be effected in the race.

Humanity is a mental existence in a living body; its basis is matter, its centre & instrument mind & its medium life. This is the condition of average or natural humanity.

In every human being there is concealed (avyakta) the four higher principles. Mahas, pure ideality in vijnana, is not a vyahriti but the source of the vyahritis, the bank upon which mental, vital and bodily action draw & turn its large & infinite wealth into small coin of the lower existence. Vijnana being the link between the divine state & the human animal is the door of escape for man into the supernatural or divine humanity.

Inferior mankind gravitates downward from mind towards life & body; average mankind dwells constant in mind limited by & looking towards life & body; superior mankind levitates upward either to idealised mentality or to pure idea, direct truth of knowledge & spontaneous truth of existence; supreme mankind rises to divine beatitude & from that level either goes upward to pure Sat & Parabrahman or remains to beatify its lower members & raise to divinity in itself & others this human existence.

The man who dwells in the higher or divine & now hidden hemisphere of his consciousness, having rent the veil, is the true superman and the last product of that progressive self-manifestation of God in world, Spirit out of matter, which is now called the principle of evolution.

To rise into divine existence, force, light & bliss and recast in that mould all mundane existence is the supreme aspiration of religion & the complete practical aim of Yoga. The aim is to realise God in the universe, but it cannot be done without realising God transcendent of the Universe.

II

Parabrahman, Mukti & Human Thought-Systems

Parabrahman is the Absolute, & because It is the Absolute, it cannot be reduced into terms of knowledge. You can know the Infinite in a way, but you cannot know the Absolute.

All things in existence or non-existence are symbols of the Absolute created in self-consciousness (Chid-Atman); by Its symbols the Absolute can be known so far as the symbols reveal or hint at it, but even the knowledge of the whole sum of symbols does not amount to real knowledge of the Absolute. You can become Parabrahman; you cannot know Parabrahman. Becoming Parabrahman means going back through self-consciousness into Parabrahman, for you already are That, only you have projected yourself forward in self-consciousness into its terms or symbols, Purusha & Prakriti through which you uphold the universe. Therefore, to become Parabrahman void of terms or symbols you must cease out of the universe.

By becoming Parabrahman void of Its self-symbols you do not become anything you are not already, nor does the universe cease to operate. It only means that God throws back out of the ocean of manifest consciousness one stream or movement of Himself into that from which all consciousness proceeded.

All who go out of universe-consciousness, do not necessarily go into Parabrahman. Some go into undifferentiated Nature (Avyakrita Prakriti), some lose themselves in God, some pass into a dark state of non-recognition of universe, (Asat, Shunya), some into a luminous state of non-recognition of universe — Pure Undifferentiated Atman, Pure Sat or Existence-Basis of Universe, — some into a temporary state of deep sleep (sushupti) in the impersonal principles of Ananda, Chit or Sat. All these are forms of release & the ego gets from God by His Maya or Prakriti the impulse towards any one of them to which the supreme Purusha chooses to direct him. Those whom He wishes to liberate, yet keep in the world, He makes jivanmuktas or sends them out again as His vibhutis, they consenting to wear for the divine purposes a temporary veil of Avidya, which does not at all bind them and which they can rend or throw off very easily. Therefore to lust after becoming Parabrahman is a sort of luminous illusion or sattwic play of Maya; for in reality there is none bound & none free & none needing to be freed and all is only God's Lila, Parabrahman's play of manifestation. God uses this sattwic Maya in certain egos in order to draw them upwards in the line of His special purpose & for these egos it is the only right and possible path.

But the aim of our Yoga is Jivanmukti in the universe; not because we need to be freed or for any other reason, but because that is God's will in us, we have to live released in the world, not released out of the world.

The Jivanmukta has, for perfect knowledge & self-fulfilment to stand on the threshold of Parabrahman, but not to cross the threshold.

The statement he brings back from the threshold is that That is & we are That, but what That is or is not, words cannot describe, nor mind discriminate.

Parabrahman being the Absolute is indescribable by any name or definite conception. It is not Being or Non-Being, but something of which Being & Non-Being are primary symbols; not Atman or unAtman or Maya; not Personality or Impersonality; not Quality or Non-Quality; not Consciousness or Non-Consciousness; not Bliss or Non-Bliss; not Purusha or Prakriti; not god nor man nor animal; not release nor bondage; but something of which all these are primary or derivative, general or particular symbols. Still, when we say Parabrahman is not this or that, we mean that It cannot in its essentiality be limited to this or that symbol or any sum of symbols; in a sense Parabrahman is all this & all this is Parabrahman. There is nothing else which all this can be.

Parabrahman being Absolute is not subject to logic, for logic applies only to the determinate. We talk confusion if we say that the Absolute cannot manifest the determinate & therefore the universe is false or non-existent. The very nature of the Absolute is that we do not know what it is or is not, what it can do or cannot do; we have no reason to suppose that there is anything it cannot do or that its Absoluteness is limited by any kind of impotency. We experience spiritually that when we go beyond everything else we come to something Absolute; we experience spiritually that the universe is in the nature of a manifestation proceeding, as it were, from the Absolute; but all these words & phrases are merely intellectual terms trying to express the inexpressible. We must state what we see as best we can, but need not dispute what others see or state; rather we must accept & in our own system locate & account for what they have seen & stated. Our only dispute is with those who deny credit to the vision or freedom & value to the statements of others; not with those who are content with stating their own vision. A philosophical or religious system is only a statement of that arrangement of existence in universe which God has revealed to us as our status of being. It is given in order that the mind may have something to stand upon while we act in Prakriti. But our vision need not be precisely the same in arrangement as the vision of others, nor is the form of thought that suits our mentality bound to suit a mentality differently constituted. Firmness, without dogmatism, in our own system, toleration, without weakness, of all other systems should therefore be our intellectual outlook.

You will find disputants questioning your system on the ground that it is not consistent with this or that Shastra or this or that great authority, whether philosopher, saint or Avatar. Remember then that realisation & experience are alone of essential importance. What Shankara argued or Vivekananda conceived intellectually about existence or even what Ramakrishna stated from his multitudinous and varied realisation, is only of value to you so far as you [are] moved by God to accept and renew it in your own experience. The opinions of thinkers & saints

& Avatars should be accepted as hints but not as fetters. What matters to you is what you have seen or what God in His universal personality or impersonally or again personally in some teacher, guru or pathfinder undertakes to show to you in the path of Yoga.

III

Parabrahman and Parapurusha

God or Para Purusha is Parabrahman unmanifest & inexpressible turned towards a certain kind of manifestation or expression, of which the two eternal terms are Atman and Jagati, Self and Universe. Atman becomes in self-symbol all existences in the universe; so too, the universe when known, resolves all its symbols into Atman. God being Parabrahman is Himself Absolute, neither Atman nor Maya nor unAtman; neither Being nor Not-Being (Sat, Asat); neither Becoming nor non-Becoming (Sambhuti, Asambhuti); neither Quality nor non-Quality (Saguna, Nirguna); neither Consciousness nor non-consciousness, (Chaitanya, Jada); neither Soul nor Nature (Purusha, Prakriti); neither Bliss nor non-Bliss; neither man nor god nor animal; He is beyond all these things, He maintains & contains all these things; in Himself as world He is & becomes all these things.

The only difference between Parabrahman & Parapurusha is that we think of the first as something beyond our universe-existence, expressed here indeed, but still inexpressible, and of the second as something approaching our universe-existence, inexpressible indeed, but still here expressed. It is as if, in reading a translation of the Ramayan or Homer's Iliad, we were to look at the unapproachable something no translator can seize and say "This is not the Ramayan", "This is not the Iliad" and yet, looking at the comparative adequacy of the expressions which do succeed in catching something of the original spirit and intention, were at the same time to say "This is Homer", "This is Valmekie." There is no other difference except this of standpoint. The Upanishads speak of the Absolute Parabrahman as Tat; they say Sa when they speak of the Absolute Parapurusha.

NATURAL AND SUPERNATURAL MAN
The Evolutionary Aim in Yoga

In the Katha Upanishad there occurs one of those powerful and pregnant phrases, containing a world of meaning in a point of verbal space, with which the Upanishads are thickly sown. Yogo hi prabhavapyayau. For Yoga is the beginning & ending of things. In the Puranas the meaning of the phrase is underlined & developed. By Yoga God made the world, by Yoga He will draw it into Himself in the end. But not only the original creation & final dissolution of the universe, all great changes of things, creations, evolutions, destructions are effected by the essential process of Yoga, tapasya. In this ancient view Yoga presents itself as the effective, perhaps the essential & real executive movement of Nature herself in all her processes. If this is so in the general workings of Nature, if that is to say, a divine Knowledge and a divine Will in things by putting itself into relation with objects is the true cause of all force & effectuality, the same rule should hold good in human activities. It should hold good especially of all conscious & willed processes of psychological discipline, — Yogic systems, as we call them; Yoga can really be nothing but a consummate & self-conscious natural process intended to effect rapidly objects which the ordinary natural movement works out slowly, in the tardy pace of a secular or even millennial evolution.

There is an apparent difference. The aim put before us in Yoga is God; the aim of Nature is to effect supernature; but these two aims are of one piece & intention. God & supernature are only one the real & the other the formal aspect of the one unattainable fulfilment towards which our human march is in its ascent directed. Yoga for man is the upward working of Nature liberated from slow evolution and long relapses and self-conscious in divine or human knowledge.

God is That which is the All and yet exceeds and transcends the All; there is nothing in existence which is not God, but

God is neither the sum of existence nor anything in that sum, except symbolically, in image to His own consciousness. In other words, everything that exists, separately, is a particular symbol and the whole sum of existence is a general symbol which tries to translate the untranslatable existence, God, into the terms of world-consciousness. It is intended to try, it is not intended to succeed; for the moment it succeeds, it ceases to be itself and becomes that untranslatable something from which it started, God. No symbol is intended to express God perfectly, not even the highest; but it is the privilege of the highest symbols to lose in Him their separate definiteness, cease to be symbols and become in consciousness that which is symbolised. Humanity is such a symbol or eidolon of God; we are made, to use the Biblical phrase, in His image; and by that is meant not a formal image, but the image of His being and personality; we are of the essence of His divinity and of the quality of His divinity; we are formed in the mould and bear the stamp of a divine being and a divine knowledge.

In everything that exists phenomenally, or, as I shall prefer to say, going deeper into the nature of things, symbolically, there are two parts of being, thing in itself and symbol, Self and Nature, res (thing that is) and factum (thing that is done or made), immutable being and mutable becoming, that which is supernatural to it and that which is natural. Every state of existence has some force in it which drives it to transcend itself. Matter moves towards becoming life, Life travails towards becoming Mind, Mind aspires towards becoming ideal Truth, Truth rises towards becoming divine and infinite Spirit. The reason is that every symbol, being a partial expression of God, reaches out to and seeks to become its own entire reality; it aspires to become its real self by transcending its apparent self. Thing that is made, is attracted towards thing that is, becoming towards being, the natural towards the supernatural, symbol towards thing-in-itself, Nature towards God.

The upward movement is, then, the means towards self-fulfilment in this world; but it is not imperative on all objects. For there are three conditions for all changeable existences, the upward ascension, the arrested status and the downward lapse. Nature in its lower states moves upward indeed in the mass, but seeks the final salvation for only a limited number of its individuals. It is not every form of matter that organises life although every form of matter teems with the spirit of life and is full of its urgent demand for release & self-manifestation. Not every form of life organises mind, although in all forms of life mind is there, insistent, seeking for its escape and self-expression. Nor is every mental being fitted to organise the life of ideal truth, although in every mental being, in dog & ape & worm no less than in man, the imprisoned spirit of truth & knowledge seeks for its escape and self-expression. Nature in each realised state of her building seeks first to assure the natural existence of her creatures in that state; only after this primary aim is accomplished does she seek through the best fitted of them to escape from her works, to break down what she has built and arrive at something beyond. It is not till she reaches man that she arrives at a type of being of which every individual is essentially capable of realising not only the natural but the supernatural within it; and even this is true with modifications, with qualifications. But of this it will be better to speak at greater length in another connection.

Nevertheless, it remains true that the upward movement is the master movement of Nature; arrested status is a lower fulfilment, & if perfect, a transient perfection. It is a perfection in the realms of struggle and in the style of passing forms, a fulfilment in the kingdoms of Ashanaya Mrityu, Hunger who is death, Hunger that creates & feeds upon its creations; the upward movement is that which leads up through death to immortality & realises in this earth of the body the blissful and luminous kingdom of heaven; the downward lapse is destruction, Hell, a great perdition, mahati vinashtih. These are the three gatis or final states of becoming indicated in the Gita, uttama, madhyama & adhama, highest, middle and lowest, offered to the choice of humanity. It is for each individual of us to choose. For as we choose, God shall fulfil Himself in us, towards a transient human satisfaction, a divine perfection or a decomposition of our humanity into the fruitful waste-matter of Nature.

Every nature, then, is a step towards some super-nature, — towards something natural to itself, but supernatural to that which is below. Life is supernatural to Matter, Mind supernatural to Life, Ideal Being supernatural to Mind, the Infinite Spirit supernatural to ideal being. We must, therefore, accept the supernatural as our goal; for the tendency of our nature to the super-nature just above it is a command of the World Power to be obeyed and not rebelled against & distrusted. It is here that Faith has its importance & Religion, when uncorrupted, its incalculable utility; for our natural mind seeks to dwell in its nature & is sceptical of supernature. Faith & religion were provisions of the All Wise Energy to accustom the natural & merely mental man to the promptings of the ideal soul in him which seeks even now to escape out of twilight into light, out of groping into truth, out of the senses & reasoning into vision & direct experience. The upward tendency is imposed on us & we cannot permanently resist it; at some time or another God will lay his hands on us and force us up that steep incline so difficult to our unregenerate treading. For as surely as the animal develops towards humanity & in its most flexible types attains a kind of humanity, as surely as the ape and the ant having once appeared, man was bound to follow, so surely man develops towards godhead & in his more capable types approaches nearer & nearer towards godhead, attains a kind of deity, & so surely the genius & the saint having appeared man is bound to develop in himself & out of himself the superman, the siddha purusha. For this conclusion no prophetic power or revelation is needed; it is the inevitable corollary from the previous demonstrations worked out for us in the vast laboratory of Nature.

We have to transcend Nature, to become super-Nature, but it follows from what I have said that it is by taking advantage of something still imprisoned in Nature itself, by following some line which Nature is trying to open to us that we ought to proceed. By yielding to our ordinary nature we fall away both from Nature itself and from God; by transcending Nature we at once satisfy her strongest impulse, fulfil all her possibilities and rise towards God. The human first touches the divine and then becomes the divine. But there are those who seek to kill Nature in order to become the Self. Shall we follow them? No, however great & lofty be their path, however awful & dazzling their aspiration, because it is not God's intention in humanity & therefore not our proper dharma. Let any say, if he will, that we have made the lower choice. We answer in the language of the Gita, Sreyan swadharmo viguno, Better is the law of our own being though inferior, too perilous the superior law of another's being. To obey God's will in us, is certainly more blissful, perhaps even more divine than to rise to the austere heights of the Adwaitin & the ineffable self-extinction in an indefinable Existence. For us the embrace of Krishna is enough and the glory of the all-puissant bosom of Kali. We have to transcend & possess Nature, not to kill her.

In any case, whatever may be the choice for exceptional individuals, it is a general path of supreme attainment for humanity that we are seeking, — for I am not proposing to you in Yoga an individual path unconcerned with the rest of mankind, — and here there can be no doubt or hesitation. Neither the exaggerations of spirituality nor the exaggerations of materialism are our true path. Every general movement of our humanity which seeks to deny Nature, however religious, lofty or austere, of whatever dazzling purity or ethereality, has been & will always be doomed to failure, sick disappointment, disillusionment or perversion, because it is in its nature for the mass of humanity a transient impulse of exaggeration, because it contradicts God's condition for us who set Nature there as an indispensable term for His self-fulfilment in the universe and ourselves as the supreme instruments & helpers on this earth of that divine self-fulfilment. Every movement of humanity which bids us be satisfied with our ordinary Nature, dwell upon the earth, cease to aspire to the empyrean within us and choose rather to live like the animals looking to our mortal future before us & downwards at the earth we till, not upwards to God & our ungrasped perfection, has been & will always be doomed to weariness, petrifaction & cessation or to a quick & violent supernaturalistic reaction, because this also is for the mass of men a transient impulse of exaggeration & because it contradicts God's intention in us who has entered in and dwells secret in our Nature compelling us towards Him by an obscure, instinctive & overmastering attraction. Materialistic movements are more unnatural and abnormal than ascetic and negative religions & philosophies; for these lead us upward at least, though they go too furiously fast & far for our humanity, but the materialist under the pretence of bringing us back to Nature, takes us away from her entirely. He forgets or does not see that Nature is only phenomenally Nature, but in reality she is God. The divine element in her is that which she most purely & really is; the rest is only term and condition, process and stage in her whole progressively developed revelation of the secret divinity. He forgets too that Nature is evolving not evolved & what we are now can never be the term of what we shall be hereafter. The supernatural must be by the very logic of things the end & goal of her movement.

Therefore, not to be ensnared, emmeshed and bound by Nature, and not, on the other hand, to be furious with her & destroy her, is the first thing we must learn if we are to be complete Yogins and proceed surely towards our divine perfection. All beings, even the sages, follow after their nature and what shall coercion and torture of it, avail them? Prakritim yanti bhutani, nigrahah kim karishyati? And it is all so useless! Do you feel yourself bound by her and pant for release? In her hand alone is the key which shall unlock your fetters. Does she stand between you & the Lord? She is Sita; pray to her, she will stand aside & show Him to you; but presume not to separate Sita & Rama, to cast her out into some distant Lanca under the guard of giant self-tortures so that you may have Rama to yourself in Ayodhya. Wrestle with Kali, if you will, she loves a good wrestler; but wrestle not with her unlovingly, or in mere disgust & hate; for her displeasure is terrible and though she loves the Asuras, she destroys them. Rather go through her & under her protection, go with a right understanding of her and with a true & unfaltering Will; she will lead you on with whatever circlings, yet surely & in the wisest way, to the All-Blissful Personality & the Ineffable Presence. Nature is the Power of God Himself, leading these multitudes of beings, through the night & the desert & the tracts of the foeman to their secret & promised heritage.

Supernature, then, is in every way our aim in Yoga; being still natural to the world, to transcend Nature internally so that both internally and externally we may possess and enjoy her as free & lord, swarat and samrat; being still the symbol in a world of symbol-beings, to reach through it to that which is symbolised, to realise the symbol; being still a figure of humanity, a man among men, a living body among living bodies, manus, mental beings housed in that living matter among other embodied mental beings; being & remaining in our outward parts all this that we are apparently, yet to exceed it and become in the body what we are really in the secret self, — God, spirit, supreme & infinite being, pure Bliss of divine joy, pure Force of divine action, pure Light of divine knowledge. Our whole apparent life has only a symbolic value & is good & necessary as a becoming; but all becoming has being for its goal & fulfilment & God is the only being. To become divine in the nature of the world and in the symbol of humanity is the perfection for which we were created.

The Fullness of Yoga — In Condition

We are to exceed our human stature and become divine; but if we are to do this, we must first get God; for the human ego is the lower imperfect term of our being, God is the higher perfect term. He is the possessor of our supernature and without His permission there can be no effectual rising. The finite cannot become infinite unless it perceives its own secret infinity and is drawn by it or towards it; nor can the symbol-being, unless it glimpses, loves and pursues the Real-being in itself, overcome by its own strength the limits of its apparent nature. It is a particular becoming & is fixed in the nature of the symbol that it has become; only the touch of that which is all becomings and exceeds all becomings, can liberate it from the bondage to its own limited Nature. God is That which is the All and which exceeds the All. It is therefore only the knowledge, love and possession of God that can make us free. He who is transcendent, can alone enable us to transcend ourselves; He who is universal can alone enlarge us from our limited particular existence.

In this necessity is the justification of that great & imperishable force of Nature, which Rationalism has unjustly & irrationally despised, Religion. I speak of religion, — not of a creed, church or theology, for all these things are rather forms of religiosity than essence or even always action of religion, — but of that personal and intimate religion, a thing of temper and spirit and life, not of views & formal actions, which draws a man passionately and absorbingly to his own vision of the Supreme or his own idea of something higher than himself which he must follow or become. Without a fervent worship of the Supreme in the heart, a strong aspiration upwards to It in the will or a vehement thirst for it in the temperament, we cannot have the impulse to be other than ourselves or the force to do anything so difficult as the transcending of our own ingrained and possessing human nature. The prophets have spoken & the Avatars have descended always for the one purpose, to call us to God, to inspire us to this great call on our upward straining energies or else to prepare something in the world which will help to bring humanity nearer to the goal of its difficult ascending journey.

It may seem at first sight that there is no need for these religious terms or this religious spirit. If the aim is to become something superior to man, to evolve a superman out of ourselves, as man has been evolved out of the ape, — if that statement of the progression be indeed the truth, — the ape out of inferior animal forms, they again out of mollusc & protoplasm, jellyfish or vegetable animals, & so to the end of the series, then what need is there of anything but the training, preferably the most intelligent & scientific training of our mental, moral and physical energies till they reach a point when they are transmuted by the psychical chemistry of Nature into the coming superior type? But the problem is not so simple, in reality. There are three errors hidden at the basis of this sceptical question. We mistake the nature of the operation to be effected, we mistake the nature of the power & process that works it out, we mistake the nature of the thing that uses the power & works out the process.

Nature does not propose to man to work out a higher mental, moral and physical variation-type in the mould of the present human being, — the symbol we are; it proposes to break that general type altogether in order to advance to a new symbol-being which shall be supernatural to present man as present man is to the animal below him. It is doubtful whether in the pure human mould Nature can go much farther than she has gone at present; that she can for instance produce a higher mental type than Newton, Shakespeare, Caesar or Napoleon, a higher moral type than Buddha, Christ or St Francis, a higher physical type than the Greek athlete or to give modern examples, a Sandow or a Ramamurti. She may seek to bring about a better combination of mental & moral, or of moral, mental & physical energies; but is she likely to produce anything much above the level of Confucius or Socrates? It is more probable & seems to be true that Nature seeks in this field to generalise a higher level and a better combination. Neither need we believe that, even here, her object is to bring all men to the same level; for that can only be done by levelling downwards. Nothing in Nature is free from inequalities except the forms that are the lowest and least developed. The higher the effort accomplished, the more richly endowed the organism of the species, the greater the chances of inequality. In so high and developed a natural movement as Man, equality of individual opportunity is conceivable, equality of natural powers and accomplishment is a chimera. Nor will the generalisation of powers or the increase of material make any difference to the level of natural attainment. All the accumulated discoveries & varied information of the modern scientist will not make him mentally the superior of Aristotle or Socrates; he is neither an acuter mind nor a greater mental force. All the varied activities of modern philanthropy will not produce a greater moral type than Buddha or St Francis. The invention of the motor car will not make up for the lost swiftness & endurance nor gymnastics restore the physical capacity of the Negro or the American Indian. We see therefore the limits of Nature's possibilities in the human symbol, fixed by the character of the symbol itself and recognised by her in her strivings.

It is still a question whether in these limits the chief preoccupation of Nature is the exhaustion of the possibilities of the human symbol. That is rather man's preoccupation and therefore the direction she takes when human intellect interferes with her normal progression. Left to herself & even utilising human interferences, she seems bent rather on breaking the mould, than on perfecting it, — only indeed in her more advanced individuals & more daring movements and with due regard to the safety of the general human type, but this is always her method when she wishes to advance to a fresh symbol without destroying the anterior species. The more civilised man becomes, the more she plagues him with moral abnormalities, excesses of vice & virtue and confusions of the very type of vice & virtue; the more he intellectualises, the more he insists on rationality as his utmost bourne, the more she becomes dissatisfied and clamours to him to develop rather his instincts & his intuitions; the more he strives after health & hygiene, the more she multiplies diseases & insanities of mind and body. He has triumphed over supernaturalism, he has chained her down to the material, human & rational; immediately she breaks out fiercely into unthought-of revivals and gigantic supernaturalisms. Whatever work she is intent on, she will not be baulked in that work by the limited human reason. Through all her vast being she feels the pulsation of a supernatural power, the workings & strivings of a knowledge superior to material reason. She breaks out, therefore, she compels, she insists. Everywhere we see her striving to break the mental, moral & physical type she has created & to get beyond it to some new processes as yet not clearly discerned. She attacks deliberately the sound healthfulness & equilibrium of our normal type of intellectuality, morality & physical being. She is stricken also with a mania of colossalism; colossal structures, colossal combinations, colossal heights & speeds, colossal dreams & ambitions outline themselves everywhere more or less clearly, more or less dimly. Unable as yet to do her will in the individual, she works with masses; unable in the mind, with material forms & inventions; unable in actualities, with hopes & dreams; unable to reproduce or produce Napoleons & super-Napoleons, she generalises a greater reach of human capacity from which they may hereafter emerge more easily, & meanwhile she creates instead Dreadnoughts & Super-dreadnoughts, Trusts & mammoth combines, teems with distance destroying inventions & seems eager & furious to trample to pieces the limitations of space & time she herself has created.

As if to point her finger to the thing she intends, she has accumulated the signs of this process of breaking & rebuilding in the phenomena of genius. It is now common knowledge that genius hardly appears in the human species unattended, unprepared or unaccompanied by abnormalities in the individual body, vitality & mind which contains it, — degeneration, insanity or freak in the heredity which produces it and even disturbance & supranormality in the human environment in which it occurs. The haste of a brilliant generalisation establishes on this basis the paradox that genius itself is a morbid phenomenon of insanity or degeneration. The true explanation is sufficiently clear. In order to establish genius in the human system, Nature is compelled to disturb & partially break the normality of that system, because she is introducing into it an element that is alien as it is superior to the type which it enriches. Genius is not the perfect evolution of that new & divine element; it is only a beginning or at the highest an approximation in certain directions. It works fitfully & uncertainly in the midst of an enormous mass of somewhat disordered human mentality, vital nervosity, physical animality. The thing itself is divine, it is only the undivine mould in which it works that is to a lesser or greater extent broken & ploughed up by the unassimilated force that works in it. Sometimes there is an element in the divine intruder which lays its hand on the mould & sustains it, so that it does not break at all, nor is flawed; or if there is a disturbance, it is slight and negligible. Such an element there was in Caesar, in Shakespeare, in Goethe. Sometimes also a force appears to which we can no longer apply the description of genius without being hopelessly inadequate in our terminology. Then those who have eyes to see, bow down and confess the Avatar. For it is often the work of the Avatar to typify already, partly or on the whole, what Nature has not yet effected in the mass or even in the individual, so that his passing may stamp it on the material ether in which we live.

But what is this type of which the great Mother is in labour? What birth will emerge from the cries & throes of this prolonged & mighty pregnancy? A greater type of humanity, it may be said. But in order to understand what we are saying, we must first see clearly what the humanity is which she seeks to surpass. This human symbol, this type we now are is a mental being with a mental ego, working in a vital case by mind always, but upon matter, in matter & through matter. It is limited in its higher workings by its lower instruments. Its basis of mind is egoistic, sensational & determined by experience & environment, its knowledge therefore pursues wider or narrower circles in a fixed and meagre range. Its moral temperament & action is similarly egoistic, sensational, experiential and determined by environment; for this reason it is bound equally to sin & virtue and all attempts radically to moralise the race within the limits of its egoistic nature have been & must necessarily, in spite of particular modifications, end in general failure. It is not only a mixed but a confused type, body & vitality interfering with mind & mind both hampered by & hampering body & vitality. Its search for knowledge, founded on sense contact, is a groping like that of a man finding his way in a forest at night; it makes acquaintance with its surroundings by touching, dashing on or stumbling over them; and, although it has an uncertain light of reason given it which partially corrects this disability, yet since reason has also to start from the senses which are consistent falsifiers of values, rational knowledge is not only restricted but pursued by vast dimnesses & uncertainties even in that which it seems to itself to have grasped. It secures a few flowers of truth by rummaging in a thorny hedge of doubts & errors. The actions of the type also are a breaking through thickets, a sanguine yet tormented stumbling forward through eager failures to partial and temporary successes. Immensely superior to all else that Nature had yet effected, this type is yet so burdened with disabilities, that, if it were impossible to break its mould and go forward, there would be much justification for those pessimistic philosophies which despair of Life & see in the Will not to Live humanity's only door of escape admitting to it no other salvation. But Nature is the will of the all-Wise God and she is not working out a reduction of the world to absurdity. She knows her goal, she knows that man as he is at present is only a transitional type; and so far as she can consistently with the survival of the type, she presses forward to what she has seen in God's eternal knowledge as standing beyond. From this ego, she moves towards a universal consciousness, from this limitation to a free movement in infinity, from this twilit & groping mind to the direct sunlit vision of things, from this conflict without issue between vice & virtue to a walking that keeps spontaneously to a God-appointed path, from this broken & grief-besieged action to a joyous & free activity, from this confused strife of our members to a purified, unentangled and harmonious combination, from this materialised mentality to an idealised

& illuminated life, body & mind, from the symbol to reality, from man separated from God to man in God & God in man. In brief, as she has aspired successfully from matter to life, from life to mind & mental ego, so she aspires & with a fated success to an element beyond mind, the vijnana of the Hindus, the self-luminous idea or Truth-self now concealed & superconscious in man and the world, as life was always concealed in matter and mind in life. What this vijnana is, we have yet to see, but through it she knows she can lay firm hold on that highest term of all which is the reality of all symbols, in Spirit, in Sachchidananda.

The aim of Nature is also the aim of Yoga. Yoga, like Nature at its summit, seeks to break this mould of ego, this mould of mentalised life body and materialised mind, in order to achieve ideal action, ideal truth and infinite freedom in our spiritual being. To effect so enormous an end great and dangerous processes have to be used. Those who have been eager on this road or have opened up new paths towards the goal, have had to affront as a possibility frequently realised loss of reason, loss of life & health or dissolution of the moral being. They are not to be pitied or scorned even when they succumb; rather are they martyrs for humanity's progress, far more than the lost navigator or the scientist slain by the dangers of his investigation. They prepare consciently the highest possible achievement towards which the rest of humanity instinctively & unconsciously moves. We may even say that Yoga is the appointed means Nature holds in reserve for the accomplishment of her end, when she has finished her long labour of evolving at least a part of humanity temperamentally equal to the effort and intellectually, morally & physically prepared for success. Nature moves toward supernature, Yoga moves towards God; the world-impulse & the human aspiration are one movement and the same journey.

Nature

If this is the nature of the operation to be effected, not a perfection of the present human mould but a breaking of it to proceed to a higher type, what then is the power & process that works it out? What is this Nature of which we speak so fluently?[1] We habitually talk of it as if it were something mighty & conscious that lives and plans; we credit it with an aim, with wisdom to pursue that aim and with power to effect what it pursues. Are we justified in our language by the actualities of the universe or is this merely our inveterate habit of applying human figures to non-human things and the workings of intelligence to non-intelligent processes which come right because they must and not because they will and produce this magnificent ordered universe by some dumb blind and brute necessity inconceivable in its origin & nature to intelligent beings? If so, this blind brute force has produced something higher than itself, something which did not exist preconceived in its bosom or in any way belong to it. We cannot understand what being & Nature are, not because we are as yet too small and limited, but because we are too much above being & Nature. Our intelligence is a luminous freak in a darkness from which it was impossibly produced, since nothing in that darkness justified itself as a cause of its creation. Unless mind was inherent in brute matter, — & in that case matter is only apparently brute, — it was impossible for matter to produce mind. But since this leads us to an impossibility, it cannot be the truth. We must suppose then, if matter is brute, that mind is also brute. Intelligence is an illusion; there is nothing but a shock of

---

[1] *The following sentence was written at the beginning of this essay during revision. It was not worked into the text, and so is given here as a footnote:*
    Nature is Force of Consciousness in infinite Being. The opinion that sees a mechanical world in which consciousness is only an exceptional figure of things, is a hasty conclusion drawn from imperfect data.

material impacts creating vibrations & reactions of matter which translate themselves into the phenomena of intelligence. Knowledge is only a relation of matter with matter, and is intrinsically neither different nor superior to the hurtling of atoms against each other or the physical collision of two bulls in a meadow. The material agents involved & phenomenon produced are different & therefore we do not call the recoil of one horned forehead from another an act of knowledge or intelligence, but the thing that has happened is intrinsically the same. Intelligence is itself inert & mechanical & merely the physiological result of a physiological movement & has nothing in it psychical or mental in the time-honoured sense of the words soul and mind. This is the view of modern scientific rationalism, — put indeed in other language than the scientist's, put so as to bring out its logical consequences & implications, but still effectively the modern account of the universe.

In that account the nature of a thing consists of its composition, the properties contained in that composition and the laws of working determined by those properties; as for [example] iron is composed of certain elementary substances, possesses as a consequence of its composition certain properties, such as hardness etc. and under given circumstances will act in a given manner as the result of its properties. Applying this analysis on a larger scale we see the universe as the composition of certain brute forces working in certain material substances, possessed in itself and in those substances of certain primary & secondary, general & particular properties and working as a result by certain invariable tendencies & fixed processes which we call by a human figure Nature's Laws. This is Nature. When searchingly analysed she is found to be a play of two entities, Force & Matter; but these two, if the unitarian view of the universe is correct, will some day be proved to be only one entity, either only Matter or only Force.

Even if we accept this modern view of the universe, which, it is not at all dangerous to prophesy, will have disappeared in the course of a century into a larger synthesis, there is still something to be said about the presence or absence of intelligence in Nature. In what after all does intelligence consist, what are its composition, properties, laws? What in its circumstances is human intelligence, the only kind of intelligence which we are in a position to study from within & therefore understand? It is marked by three qualities or processes, the power & process of adaptation towards an end, the power & process of discrimination between the impacts on its senses & the power & process of mentally conscious comprehension. Human intelligence is, to put it briefly, teleological, discriminative and mentally conscious. About other than human beings, about animals, trees, metals, forces, we can say nothing from inside, we can only infer the absence or presence of these elements of consciousness from the evidence collected by an external observation. We cannot positively say, having no internal evidence, that the tree is not a mind imprisoned in matter and unable to express itself in the media it has at its disposal; we cannot say that it does not suffer the reactions of pleasure and pain; but from the external evidence we infer to the contrary. Our negative conclusion is probable, it is not certain. It may be itself negatived in the future march of knowledge. But still, taking the evidence as it stands, what are the facts we actually arrive at in this comparison of intelligent & non-intelligent Nature?

First, Nature possesses in a far higher degree than man the teleological faculty & process. To place an aim before one, to combine, adapt, modify, unify, vary means & processes in order to attain that end, to struggle against and overcome difficulties, to devise means to circumvent difficulties when they cannot be overcome, this is one of the noblest & divinest parts of human intelligence. But its action in man is only a speciality of its universal action in Nature. She works it out in man partly through the reason, in animals with very little & rudimentary reason, mainly through instinct, memory, impulse & sensation, in plants & other objects with very little & rudimentary reason, mainly through impulse & mechanical or, as we call it, involuntary action. But throughout there is the end & the adaptation to the end, & throughout the same basic means are used; for in man also it is only for a selection of his ends & processes that the reason is used; for the greater part she uses the animal means, memory, impulse, sensation, instinct, — instincts differently directed, less decisive & more general than the animal instincts but still in the end & for their purpose as sure; & for yet another part she uses the same merely mechanical impulse & involuntary action precisely as in her mistermed inanimate forms of existence. Let us not say that the prodigality of Nature, her squandering of materials, her frequent failure, her apparent freaks and gambollings are signs of purposelessness and absence of intelligence. Man with his reason is guilty of the same laches and wanderings. But neither Man nor Nature is therefore purposeless or unintelligent. It is Nature who compels Man himself to be other than too strenuously utilitarian, for she knows better than the economist & the utilitarian philosopher. She is an universal intelligence & she has to attend, not only in the sum, but in each detail, to the universal as well as to the particular effect; she has to work out each detail with her eye on the group and not only on the group but the whole kind & not only on the whole kind but the whole world of species. Man, a particular intelligence limited by his reason, is incapable of this largeness; he puts his particular ends in the forefront and neither sees where absorption in them hurts his general well being nor can divine where they clash with the universal purpose. Her failures have an utility — we shall see before long how great an utility; her freaks have a hidden seriousness. And yet above all she remembers that beyond all formal ends, her one great object is the working out of universal delight founded on arrangement as a means, but exceeding its means. Towards that she moves; she takes delight on the way, she takes delight in the work, she takes delight, too, beyond the work.

But in all this we anticipate, we speak as if Nature were self-conscious; what we have arrived at is that Nature is teleological, more widely than man, more perfectly than man, & man himself is only teleological because of that in Nature & by the same elementary means & processes as the animal & the plant, though with additions of fresh means peculiar to mind. This, it may be said, does not constitute Intelligence, — for intelligence is not only teleological, but discriminative & mentally conscious. Mechanical discrimination, Nature certainly possesses in the highest degree; without it her teleological processes would be impossible. The tendril growing straight through the air comes into contact with a rope, a stick, the stalk of a plant; immediately it seizes it as with a finger, changes its straight growth for a curled & compressive movement, & winds itself round & round the support. What induces the change? what makes it discriminate the presence of a support & the possibility of this new movement? It is the instinct of the tendril and differs in no way, intrinsically, from the instinct of the newborn pup seizing at once on its mother's teats or the instinct of a man in his more mechanical needs & actions. We see the moon-lotus open its petals to the moon, close them to the touch of the day. In what does this discriminative movement differ from the motion of the hand leaping back from the touch of a flame, or from the recoiling movement of disgust & displeasure in the nerves from an abhorrent sight or from the recoiling movement of denial & uncongeniality in the mind from a distasteful idea or opinion? Intrinsically, there seems to be no difference; but there is a difference in circumstance. One is not attended with mental self-consciousness, the others are attended with this supremely important element. We think falsely that there is no will in the action of the tendril and the lotus, and no discrimination. There is a will, but not mentalised will; there is discrimination but not mentalised discrimination. It is mechanical, we say, — but do we understand what we mean when we say it, — & we give other names, calling will force, discrimination a natural reaction or an organic tendency. These names are only various masks concealing an intrinsic identity.

Even if we could go no farther, we should have gained an enormous step; for we have already the conception of the thing we call Nature as possessing, containing or identical with a great Force of Will placing before itself a vast end & a million complexly related incidental ends, working them out by contrivance, adaptation, arrangement, device, using an unfailing discrimination & vastly fulfilling its complex work. Of this great

Force human intelligence would only be a limited and inferior movement, guided and used by it, serving its ends even when it seems to combat its ends. We may deny Intelligence to such a Power, because it does not give signs of mental consciousness & does not in every part of its works use a human or mental intelligence; but our objection is only a metaphysical distinction. Practically, looking out on life & not in upon abstract thought, we can, if we admit this conception, rely on it that the workings of this unintelligent discrimination will be the same as if they were the workings of a universal Intelligence & the aim & means of the mechanical will the aims & means which would be chosen by an Almighty Wisdom. But if we arrive at this certainty, does not Reason itself demand of us that we should admit in Nature or behind it a universal Intelligence and an Almighty Wisdom? If the results are such as these powers would create, must we not admit the presence of these powers as the cause? Which is the truer Rationalism, to admit that the works of Intelligence are produced by Intelligence or to assert that they are produced by a blind Machine unconsciously working out perfection? to admit that the emergence of overt intelligence in humanity is due to the specialised function of a secret intelligence in the universe or to assert that it is the product of a Force to which the very principle of Intelligence is absent? To justify the paradox by saying that things are worked out in a particular way because it is their nature to be worked out in that way, is to play the fool with reason; for it does not carry us an inch beyond the mere fact that they are so worked out, one knows not why.

The true reason for the modern reluctance to admit that Nature has intelligence & wisdom or is intelligence & wisdom, is the constant association in the human mind of these things with mentally self-conscious personality. Intelligence, we think, presupposes someone who is intelligent, an ego who possesses & uses this intelligence. An examination of human consciousness shows that this association is an error. Intelligence possesses us, not we intelligence; intelligence uses us, not we intelligence. The mental ego in man is a creation & instrument of intelligence and intelligence itself is a force of Nature manifesting itself in a rudimentary or advanced state in all animal life. This objection, therefore, vanishes. Not only so, but Science herself by putting the ego in its right place as a product of mind has shown that Intelligence is not a human possession but a force of Nature & therefore an attribute of Nature, a manifestation of the universal Force.

The question remains, is it a fundamental & omnipresent attribute or only a development manifested in a select minority of her works? Here again, the difficulty is that we associate intelligence with an organised mental consciousness. But let us look at & interrogate the facts which Science has brought into our ken. We will glance at only one of them, the fly catching plant of America. Here is a vegetable organism which has hunger, — shall we say, an unconscious hunger, which needs animal food, which sets a trap for it, as the spider sets it, which feels the moment the victim touches the trap, which immediately closes & seizes the prey, eats & digests it & lies in wait for more. These motions are exactly the motions of the spider's mental intelligence altered & conditioned only by the comparative immobility of the plant & confined only, so far as we can observe, to the management of this supreme vital need & its satisfaction. Why should we attribute mental intelligence to the spider & none to the plant? Granted that it is rudimentary, organised only for special purposes, still it would seem to be the same natural Force at work in the spider & plant, intelligently devising means to an end & superintending the conduct of the device. If there is no mind in the plant, then, irresistibly, mental intelligence & mechanical intelligence are one & the same thing in essence, & the tendril embracing its prop, the plant catching its prey & the spider seizing its victim are all forms of one Force of action, which we may decline to call Intelligence if we will, but which is obviously the same thing as Intelligence. The difference is between Intelligence organised as mind, & Intelligence not organised but working with a broad elementary purity more unerring, in a way, than the action of mind. In the light of these facts the conception of Nature as infinite teleological & discriminative Force of Intelligence unorganised & impersonal because superior to organisation & personality becomes the supreme probability, the mechanical theory is only a possibility. In the absence of certainties Reason demands that we should accept the probable in preference to the possible and a harmonious & natural in preference to a violent and paradoxical explanation.

But is it certain that in this Intelligence & its works Mind is a speciality and Personality — as distinguished from mental ego — is entirely absent except as an efflorescence & convenience of Mind? We think so, because we suppose that where there are no animal signs of consciousness, there consciousness cannot and does not exist. This also may be an assumption. We must remember that we know nothing of the tree & the stone except its exterior signs of life or quiescence; our internal knowledge is confined to the phenomena of human psychology. But even in this limited sphere there is much that should make us think very deeply and pause very long before we hasten to rash negative assertions. A man sleeps, dreamlessly, he thinks; but we know that all the time consciousness is at work within him, dreaming, always dreaming; of his body & its surroundings he knows nothing, yet that body is of itself conducting all the necessary operations of life. In the man stunned or in trance there is the same phenomenon of a divided being, consciousness mentally active within apart from the body which is mentally even as the tree & the stone, but vitally active & functioning like the tree. Catalepsy presents a still more curious phenomenon of a body dead & inert like the stone, not even vitally active like the tree, but a mind perfectly aware of itself, its medium & its surroundings, though no longer in active possession of the medium and therefore no longer able to act materially on its surroundings. In face of these examples how can we assert that there is no life in the stone, no mind in stone or tree? The premise of the syllogism by which science denies mind to the tree or life to the stone, viz that where there is no outward sign of life or conscious mentality, life & mentality do not exist, is proven to be false. The possibility, even a certain probability presents itself, — in view of the unity of Nature & the omnipresent intelligence in her works, that the tree & the stone are in their totality just such a divided being, a form not yet penetrated & possessed by conscious mind, a conscious intelligence within dreaming in itself or, like the cataleptic, aware of its surroundings, but because not yet possessed of its medium (the intelligence in the cataleptic is temporarily dispossessed) unable to show any sign of life or of mentality or to act aggressively on its surroundings.

We do not need to stop at this imperfect probability, for the latest researches of psychology make it almost overwhelming in its insistence & next door to the actual proof. We now know that within men there is a dream self or sleep self other than the waking consciousness, active in the stunned, the drugged, the hypnotised, the sleeping, which knows what the waking mind does not know, understands what the waking mind does not understand, remembers accurately what the waking mind has not even taken the trouble to notice. Who is this apparent sleeper in the waking, this waker in the sleeping in comparison with whose comprehensive attentiveness & perfect observation, memory and intelligence our waking consciousness is only a fragmentary & hasty dream? Mark this capital point that this more perfect consciousness within us is not the product of evolution, — nowhere in the evolved & waking world is there such a being who remembers & repeats automatically the sounds of a foreign language which is unnoticed jabbering to the instructed mind, solves spontaneously problems from which the instructed mind has retired baffled & weary, notices everything, understands everything, recalls everything. Therefore this consciousness within is independent of evolution and, consequently, we may presume, anterior to evolution. Esha supteshu jagarti, says the Katha Upanishad, This is the Waker in all who sleep.

This new psychological research is only in its infancy & cannot tell us what this secret consciousness is, but the knowledge gained by Yoga enables us to assert positively that this is the complete mental being within who guides life & body, manomayah pranashariraneta. He it is who conducts our evolution & awakes mind out of life & is more & more getting possession of this vitalised human body, his medium & instrument, so that it may become what it is not now, a perfect instrument of mentality. In the stone he also is and in the tree, in those sleepers also there is one who wakes; but he has not in those forms got possession yet of the instrument for the purposes of mind; he can only use them for the purposes of vitality in its growth or in its active functioning.

We see, therefore, modern psychology, although it still gets away from the only rational & logical conclusion possible on its data, marching inevitably & under the sheer compulsion of facts to the very truths arrived at thousands of years ago by the ancient Rishis. How did they arrive at them? Not by speculation, as the scholars vainly imagine, but by Yoga. For the great stumbling block that has stood in the way of Science is its inability to get inside its object, the necessity under which it labours of building on inferences from external study, — & all its desperate & cruel attempts to make up the deficiency by vivisection or other ruthless experiments cannot remedy the defect. Yoga enables us to get inside the object by dissolving the artificial barriers of the bodily experience & the mental ego-sense in the observer. It takes us out of the little hold of personal experience and casts us into the great universal currents; takes us out of the personal mind sheath & makes [us] one with universal self and universal mind. Therefore were the ancient Rishis able to see what now we are beginning again to glimpse dimly that not only is Nature herself an infinite teleological and discriminative impersonal Force of Intelligence or Consciousness, prajna prasrita purani,[2] but that God dwells within & over Nature as infinite universal Personality, universal in the universe, individualised as well as universal in the particular form, or self-consciousness who perceives, enjoys & conducts to their end its vast & complex workings. Not only is there Prakriti; there is also Purusha.

So far, then, we succeed in forming some idea of the great force which is to work out our emergence from our nature to our

---

[2] Intelligent Consciousness that went forth in the beginning. Swetaswatara Upanishad.

supernature. It is a force of Conscious Being manifesting itself in forms & movements & working out exactly as it is guided, from stage to stage, the predetermined progress of our becoming & the Will of God in the world.

Maya

The world exists as symbol of Brahman; but the mind creates or accepts false values of things and takes symbol for essential reality. This is ignorance or cosmic illusion, the mistake of the mind & senses, from which the Magician Himself, Master of the Illusion, is calling on us to escape. This false valuation of the world is the Maya of the Gita and can be surmounted without abandoning either action or world-existence. But in addition, the whole of universal existence is in this sense an illusion of Maya that it is not an unchanging transcendent and final reality of things but only a symbolical reality; it is a valuation of the reality of Brahman in the terms of cosmic consciousness. All these objects we see or are mentally aware of as objectively existing, are only forms of consciousness. They are the thing-in-itself turned first into terms & ideas born of a movement or rhythmic process of consciousness and then objectivised, in consciousness itself and not really external to it. They have therefore a fixed conventional reality, but not an eternally durable essential reality; they are symbols, not altogether the thing symbolised, means of knowledge, not altogether the thing known. To look at it from another point of view Existence or Brahman has two fundamental states of consciousness, cosmic consciousness and transcendental consciousness. To cosmic consciousness the world is real as a direct first term expressing the inexpressible; to transcendental consciousness the world is only a secondary & indirect term expressing the inexpressible. When I have the cosmic consciousness, I see the world as my Self manifested; in transcendental consciousness I see the world not as the manifestation of my Self but as a manifestation of something I choose to be to my Self-consciousness. It is a conventional term expressing me which does not bind me; I could dissolve it and express myself otherwise. It is a vocable of a particular language expressing something in speech or writing which could be equally well expressed by quite another vocable in another language. I say tiger in English; I might equally have spoken Sanscrit & used the word shardula; it would have made no difference to the tiger or to myself, but only to my play with the symbols of speech and thought. So it is with Brahman & the universe, the Thing in itself and its symbols with their fixed conventional values, some of which are relative to the general consciousness & some to the individual consciousness of the symbol-being. Matter, Mind, Life for instance are general symbols with a fixed general value to God in His cosmic consciousness; but they have a different individual value, make a different impression or represent themselves differently, as we say, to myself, to the ant or to the god and angel. This perception of the purely conventional value of form & name in the Universe is expressed in metaphysics by the formula that the world is a creation of Para Maya or supreme Cosmic Illusion.

It does not follow that the world is unreal or has no existence worth the name. None of the ancient Scriptures of Hinduism affirms the unreality of the world, nor is it a logical consequence of the great but remote and difficult truth words are so inadequate to express. We must remember that all these terms, Maya, illusion, dream, unreality, relative reality, conventional value, are merely verbal figures and must not be pressed with a too literal scholastic or logical insistence. They are like the paint-brush hurled by the painter at his picture in desperation at not arriving at the effect he wanted; they are stones thrown at the truth, not the truth itself. We shall see this clearly enough when we come to look at the Cosmos from quite another standpoint, — the standpoint not of Maya, but Lila.[1] But certain great metaphysical minds, not perceiving sufficiently that words like everything else have only conventional values and are symbols of a truth which is in itself inexpressible, have drawn from the

---

[1] Illusion is itself an illusion. That which seems to the soul escaping from ignorance to be Maya, an illusion or dream, is seen by the soul already free to be Lila of God and the spirit's play.

ideas suggested by these words, the most rigorous and concrete conclusions. They have condemned the whole world as a miserable & lying dream, all the more hateful & profitless for a certain element of ineffugable reality which the more clearsighted part of their minds was compelled to realise & partially to admit. The truth in their premises has made their doctrines a mighty instrument for the liberation of great & austere souls, the error in their conclusion has afflicted humanity with the vain & barren gospel of the vanity not only of false mundane existence, but of all mundane existence. In the extreme forms of this view both nature & supernature, man & God are lies of consciousness, myths of a cosmic dream & not worth accepting. Amelioration is a chimera, divinity a lure and only absorption in a transmundane impersonal existence worth pursuing. The worshippers of God, the seekers after human perfection, those who would raise humanity from nature to supernature, find in their path two great stumbling blocks, on one side, the lower trend of Nature to persist in its past gains which represents itself in the besotted naturalism of the practical man & the worldling and on the other, this grand overshooting of the mark represented not only by the world-fleeing ascetic, who is after all, within his rights, but by the depressing pessimism of the ignorant who mean neither to flee the world, nor, if they did, could rise to the real grandeur of asceticism, but are still imbued intellectually & overshadowed in temperament by these high & fatal doctrines. A better day will dawn for India when the shadow is lifted and the Indian mental consciousness without renouncing the truth of Maya, perceives that it is only a partial explanation of existence. Mundane existence is not indispensable either to God's being or to God's bliss, but it is not therefore a vanity; nor is a liberated mundane existence — liberated in God — either a vain or a false existence.

The ordinary doctrine of Maya is not a simple truth, but proceeds upon three distinct spiritual perceptions. The first & highest is this supreme perception that the world is a mass of consciousness-symbols, having a conventional value, beings exist only in Brahman's self-consciousness & individual personality & ego-sense are only symbols & terms in the universal symbol-existence. We have said that & we shall see that we are not compelled by this perception to set down the world as a myth or a valueless convention. Nor would the Mayavadin himself have been brought to this extreme conclusion if he had not brought into the purity of this highest soul-experience his two other perceptions. The second of these, the lowest, is the perception of the lower or Apara Maya which I have indicated in the opening of this essay — the perception of the system of false values put by mind & sense on the symbol facts of the universe. At a certain stage of our mental culture it is easy to see that the senses are deceiving guides, all mental opinions & judgments uncertain, partial & haunted & pursued by doubt, the world not a reality in the sense in which the mind takes it for a reality, in the sense in which the senses only occupied by & only careful of the practical values of things, their vyavaharic artha, deal with it as a reality. Reaching this stage the mind arrives at this perception that all its values for the world being false, perhaps it is because there is no true value or only a true value not conceivable to the mind, and from this idea it is easy for our impatient human nature to stride to the conclusion that so it is & all existence or all world-existence at least is illusory, a sensation born of nothingness, a play of zeros. Hence Buddhism, the sensational Agnostic philosophies, Mayavada. Again, it is easy at a certain stage of moral culture to perceive that the moral values put by the emotions, passions and aspirations on actions & experiences are false values, that the objects of our sins are not worth sinning for & even that our principles & values do not stand in the shock of the world's actualities, but are, they too, conventional values which we do not find to be binding on the great march of Nature. From this it is natural & right to come to vairagya or dissatisfaction with a life of false valuations and very easy to stride forward, again in the impatience of our imperfect human nature, to the consummation of an entire vairagya, not only dissatisfaction with a false moral life, but disgust with life of any sort & the conclusion of the vanity of world-existence. We have a mental vairagya, a moral vairagya and to these powerful motives is added in the greater types the most powerful of all, spiritual vairagya. For at a certain stage of spiritual culture we come to the perception of the world as a system of mere consciousness values in Parabrahman or to a middle term, the experience, which was probably the decisive factor in the minds of great spiritual seekers like Shankara, of the pure & bright impersonal Sachchidananda beyond, unaffected by & apparently remote from all cosmic existence. Observing intellectually through the mind this great experience, the conclusion is natural & almost inevitable that this Pure & Bright One regards the universe as a mirage, an unreality, a dream. But these are only the terms, the word-values & conventional idea-values into which mind then translates this fact of unaffected transcendence; & it so translates it because these are the terms it is itself accustomed to apply to anything which is beyond it, remote from it, not practically affecting it in tangible relations. The mind engrossed in matter at first accepts only an objective reality; everything not objectivised or apparently capable of some objective expression it calls a lie, a mirage, a dream, an unreality or, if it is favourably disposed an ideal. When, afterwards, it corrects its views, the first thing it does is to reverse its values; coming into a region & level where life in the material world seems remote, unspiritual or apparently not capable of spiritual realisation, it immediately applies here its old expressions dream, mirage, lie, unreality or mere false idea and transfers from object to spirit its exclusive & intolerant use of the word-symbol reality. Add to this mental translation into its own conventional word-values of the fact of unaffected transcendence the intellectual conclusions & temperamental repulsions of mental & moral vairagya, both together affecting & disfiguring the idea of the world as a system of consciousness values and we have Mayavada.

Section Four

1914–1919

The Beginning and the End

Who knows the beginning of things or what mind has ever embraced their end? When we have said a beginning, do we not behold spreading out beyond it all the eternity of Time when that which has begun was not? So also when we imagine an end our vision becomes wise of endless Space stretching out beyond the terminus we have fixed. Do even forms begin and end? Or does eternal Form only disappear from one of its canvases?

*
* *

The experiment of human life on an earth is not now for the first time enacted. It has been conducted a million times before and the long drama will again a million times be repeated. In all that we do now, our dreams, our discoveries, our swift or difficult attainments we profit subconsciously by the experience of innumerable precursors and our labour will be fecund in planets unknown to us and in worlds yet uncreated. The plan, the peripeties, the denouement differ continually, yet are always governed by the conventions of an eternal Art. God, Man, Nature are the three perpetual symbols.

The idea of eternal recurrence affects with a shudder of alarm the mind entrenched in the minute, the hour, the years, the centuries, all the finite's unreal defences. But the strong soul conscious of its own immortal stuff and the inexhaustible ocean of its ever-flowing energies is seized by it with the thrill of an inconceivable rapture. It hears behind the thought the childlike laughter and ecstasy of the Infinite.

God, Man, Nature, what are these three? Whence flow their divergences? To what ineffable union advances the ever-increasing sum of their contacts? Let us look beyond the hours and moments; let us tear down the hedge of the years and the concept-wall of centuries and millenniums and break out beyond the limits of our prison-house. For all things seek to concentrate our view on the temporal interests, conceptions and realisations of our humanity. We have to look beyond them to know that which they serve and represent. Nothing in the world can be understood by itself, but only by that which is beyond it. If we would know all, we must turn our gaze to that which is beyond all. That being known all else is comprehended.

* * *

A beginningless and endless eternity and infinity in which divisible Time and Space manage to subsist is the mould of existence. They succeed in subsisting because they are upheld by God's view of Himself in things.

God is all existence. Existence is a representation of ineffable Being. Being is neither eternal nor temporary, neither infinite nor limited, neither one nor many; it is nothing that any word of our speech can describe nor any thought of our mentality can conceive. The word existence unduly limits it; eternity & infinity are too petty conceptions; the term Being is an x representing not an unknown but an unknowable value. All values proceed from the Brahman, but it is itself beyond all values.

This existence is an incalculable Fact in which all possible opposites meet; its opposites are in truth identities.

It is neither one nor many and yet both one and many. Numberlessness increases in it and extends till it reaches unity; unity broken cannot stop short of numberlessness.

It is neither personal nor impersonal and yet at once personal and impersonal. Personality is a fiction of the impersonal; impersonality the mask of a Person. That impersonal Brahman was all the time a world-transcendent Personality and universal Person, is the truth of things as it is represented by life and consciousness. "I am" is the eternal assertion. Analytic thought gets rid of the I, but the Am remains and brings it back. Materialism changes "I am" into "It is", and when it has done so, has changed nothing. The Nihilist gets rid of both Am and Is only to find them waiting for him beyond on either side of his negation.

When we examine the Infinite and the Finite, Form and the Formless, the Silence and the Activity, our oppositions are equally baffled. Try however hard we will, God will not allow us to exclude any of them from His fathomless universality. He carries all Himself with Him into every transcendence.

*
* *

All this is Infinity grasped by the Finite and the Finite lived by the Infinite.

The finite is a transience or a recurrence in the infinite, therefore Infinity alone is utterly real. But since that Real casts always this shadow of itself and since it is by the finite that its reality becomes conceivable, we must suppose that the phenomenon also is not a fiction.

The Infinite defines itself in the finite, the finite conceives itself in the Infinite. Each is necessary to the other's complete joy of being.

The Infinite pauses always in the finite; the finite arrives always in the Infinite. This is the wheel that circles forever through Time and Eternity.

If there were nothing to be transcended, the Transcendent would be incomplete in its own conception.

What is the value of the Formless unless it has stooped to Form? And on the other hand what truth or value has any form except to represent as in a mask the Indefinable and Invisible?

From what background have all these numberless forms started out, if not from the termless profundities of the Incommensurable? He who has not lost his knowledge in the Unknowable, knows nothing. Even the world he studies so sapiently, cheats and laughs at him.

When we have entered into the Unknowable, then all this other knowledge becomes valid. When we have sacrificed all forms into the Formless, then all forms become at once negligible and infinitely precious.

For the rest, that is true of all things. What we have not renounced, has no worth. Sacrifice is the great revealer of values.

* * *

As all words come out of the Silence, so all forms come out of the Infinite.

When the word goes back into the silence is it extinct for ever or does it dwell in the eternal harmony? When a soul goes back to God is it blotted out from existence or does it know and enjoy that into which it enters?

Does universe ever end? Does it not exist eternally in God's total idea of His own being?

Unless the Eternal is tired out by Time as by a load, unless God suffers loss of memory, how can universe cease from being?

Neither for soul nor universe is extinction the goal, but for one it is infinite self-possessing and for the other the endless pursuit of its own immutably mutable rhythms.

* * *

Existence, not annihilation is the whole aim and pursuit of existence.

If Nothing were the beginning Nothing also would be the end; but in that case Nothing also would be the middle.

If indiscriminable unity were the beginning it would also be the end. But then what middle term could there be except indiscriminable unity?

There is a logic in existence from which our Thought tries to escape by twisting and turning against its own ultimate necessity, as if a snake were to try to get away from itself by coiling round its own body. Let it cease coiling and go straight to the root of the whole matter, that there is no first nor last, no beginning nor ending, but only a representation of successions and dependences.

Succession and dependence are laws of perspective; they cannot be made a true measure of that which they represent.

Precisely because God is one, indefinable and beyond form, therefore He is capable of infinite definition and quality, realisation in numberless forms and the joy of endless self-multiplication. These two things go together and they cannot really be divided.

*
* *

The Hour of God

There are moments when the Spirit moves among men and the breath of the Lord is abroad upon the waters of our being; there are others when it retires and men are left to act in the strength or the weakness of their own egoism. The first are periods when even a little effort produces great results and changes destiny; the second are spaces of time when much labour goes to the making of a little result. It is true that the latter may prepare the former, may be the little smoke of sacrifice going up to heaven which calls down the rain of God's bounty. Unhappy is the man or the nation which, when the divine moment arrives, is found sleeping or unprepared to use it, because the lamp has not been kept trimmed for the welcome and the ears are sealed to the call. But thrice woe to them who are strong and ready, yet waste the force or misuse the moment; for them is irreparable loss or a great destruction.

In the hour of God cleanse thy soul of all self-deceit and hypocrisy and vain self-flattering that thou mayst look straight into thy spirit and hear that which summons it. All insincerity of nature, once thy defence against the eye of the Master and the light of the ideal, becomes now a gap in thy armour and invites the blow. Even if thou conquer for the moment, it is the worse for thee, for the blow shall come afterwards and cast thee down in the midst of thy triumph. But being pure cast aside all fear; for the hour is often terrible, a fire and a whirlwind and a tempest, a treading of the winepress of the wrath of God; but he who can stand up in it on the truth of his purpose is he who shall stand; even though he fall, he shall rise again, even though he seem to pass on the wings of the wind, he shall return. Nor let worldly prudence whisper too closely in thy ear; for it is the hour of the unexpected, the incalculable, the immeasurable. Mete not the power of the Breath by thy petty instruments, but trust and go forward.

But most keep thy soul clear, even if for a while, of the clamour of the ego. Then shall a fire march before thee in the night and the storm be thy helper and thy flag shall wave on the highest height of the greatness that was to be conquered.

Beyond Good and Evil

God is beyond good and evil; man moving Godwards must become of one nature with him. He must transcend good and evil.

God is beyond good and evil, not below them, not existing and limited by them, not even above them, but in a more absolute sense excedent and transcendent of the ideas of good and evil. He exceeds them in his universality; they exist in him, but the values of good and evil which we give to things is not their divine or universal value, they are only their practical value created by us in our psychological and dynamic dealings with life. God recognises them and seems to deal with us on the basis of this valuation of life, but only to such an extent as may serve his purpose in Nature. In his universal action he is not limited by them. But into his transcendent being of which his highest universal is the image, they do not at all enter; there in the highest universal which is to us transcendent is only the absolute good of which both our good and evil have in them certain differentiated elements. Neither our good nor our evil are or can of themselves give the absolute good; both have to be transformed, evil into good, good into pure and self-existent good, before they can be taken up into it.

This explains the nature of the universe which would otherwise be inexplicable, inconsistent with the being of God, a forcefully inconscient and violently active enigma. God must be beyond limitation by our ideas of good, otherwise the universe such as it is could not exist whether as the partly manifested being of a divine Existence or a thing created or permitted by a divine Will. He cannot, either, be evil, otherwise in man, his highest terrestrial creature or his highest terrestrial manifestation, there could not be this dominant idea of good and this stream of tendency towards righteousness. He cannot be a mixture of good and evil, whether a self-perplexed and struggling or a mysteriously ordered double principle, Ormuzd and Ahriman, or at least he cannot be limited by this duality, for there is much in the universe which is neither good nor evil. Perhaps the greatest part of the totality is either supramoral or inframoral or simply amoral. Good and evil come in with the development of mental consciousness; they exist in their rudimentary elements in the animal and primitive human mind, they develop with the human development. Good and evil are things which arrive in the process of the evolution; there is then the possibility that they will disappear in the process of the evolution. If indeed they are essential to its highest possible point of culmination, then they will remain; or if one of them be essential and the other non-essential, then that one will remain and its opposite will disappear.

The Divine Superman

This is thy work and the aim of thy being and that for which thou art here, to become the divine superman and a perfect vessel of the Godhead. All else that thou hast to do, is only a making thyself ready or a joy by the way or a fall from thy purpose. But the goal is this and the purpose is this and not in power of the way and the joy by the way but in the joy of the goal is the greatness and the delight of thy being. The joy of the way is because that which is drawing thee is also with thee on thy path and the power to climb was given thee that thou mightest mount to thy own summits.

If thou hast a duty, this is thy duty; if thou ask what shall be thy aim, let this be thy aim; if thou demand pleasure, there is no greater joy, for all other joy is broken or limited, the joy of a dream or the joy of a sleep or the joy of self-forgetting. But this is the joy of thy whole being. For if thou say what is my being, this is thy being, the Divine, and all else is only its broken or its perverse appearance. If thou seek the Truth, this is the Truth. Place it before thee and in all things be faithful to it.

It has been well said by one who saw but through a veil and mistook the veil for the face, that thy aim is to become thyself; and he said well again that the nature of man is to transcend himself. This is indeed his nature and that is indeed the divine aim of his self-transcending.

What then is the self that thou hast to transcend and what is the self that thou hast to become? For it is here that thou shouldst make no error; for this error, not to know thyself, is the fountain of all thy grief and the cause of all thy stumbling.

That which thou hast to transcend is the self that thou appearest to be, and that is man as thou knowest him, the apparent Purusha. And what is this man? He is a mental being enslaved to life and matter; and where he is not enslaved to life and matter, he is the slave of his mind. But this is a great and heavy servitude; for to be the slave of mind is to be the slave of the false, the limited and the apparent. The self that thou hast to become, is the self that thou art within behind the veil of mind and life and matter. It is to be the spiritual, the divine, the superman, the real Purusha. For that which is above the mental being, is the superman. It is to be the master of thy mind, thy life and thy body; it is to be a king over Nature of whom thou art now the tool, lifted above her who now has thee under her feet. It is to be free and not a slave, to be one and not divided, to be immortal and not obscured by death, to be full of light and not darkened, to be full of bliss and not the sport of grief and suffering, to be uplifted into power and not cast down into weakness. It is to live in the Infinite and possess the finite. It is to live in God and be one with him in his being. To become thyself is to be this and all that flows from it.

Be free in thyself, and therefore free in thy mind, free in thy life and thy body. For the Spirit is freedom.

Be one with God and all beings; live in thyself and not in thy little ego. For the Spirit is unity.

Be thyself, immortal, and put not thy faith in death; for death is not of thyself, but of thy body. For the Spirit is immortality.

To be immortal is to be infinite in being and consciousness and bliss; for the Spirit is infinite and that which is finite lives only by his infinity.

These things thou art, therefore thou canst become all this; but if thou wert not these things, then thou couldst never become them. What is within thee, that alone can be revealed in thy being. Thou appearest indeed to be other than this, but wherefore shouldst thou enslave thyself to appearances?

Rather arise, transcend thyself, become thyself. Thou art man and the whole nature of man is to become more than himself. He was the man-animal, he has become more than the animal man. He is the thinker, the craftsman, the seeker after beauty. He shall be more than the thinker, he shall be the seer of knowledge; he shall be more than the craftsman, he shall be the creator and master of his creation; he shall be more than the seeker of beauty, for he shall enjoy all beauty and all delight. Physical, he seeks for his immortal substance; vital he seeks after immortal life and the infinite power of his being; mental and partial in knowledge, he seeks after the whole light and the utter vision.

To possess these is to become the superman; for [it] is to rise out of mind into the supermind. Call it the divine mind or Knowledge or the supermind; it is the power and light of the divine will and the divine consciousness. By the supermind the Spirit saw and created himself in the worlds, by that he lives in them and governs them. By that he is Swarat Samrat, self-ruler and all-ruler.

Supermind is superman; therefore to rise beyond mind is the condition.

To be the superman is to live the divine life, to be a god; for the gods are the powers of God. Be a power of God in humanity.

To live in the divine Being and let the consciousness and bliss, the will and knowledge of the Spirit possess thee and play with thee and through thee, this is the meaning.

This is the transfiguration of thyself on the mountain. It is to discover God in thyself and reveal him to thyself in all things. Live in his being, shine with his light, act with his power, rejoice with his bliss. Be that Fire and that Sun and that Ocean. Be that joy and that greatness and that beauty.

When thou hast done this even in part, thou hast attained to the first steps of supermanhood.

Section Five

1927 and after

The Law of the Way

First be sure of the call and of thy soul's answer. For if the call is not true, not the touch of God's powers or the voice of his messengers, but the lure of thy ego, the end of thy endeavour will be a poor spiritual fiasco or else a deep disaster.

And if not the soul's fervour, but only the mind's assent or interest replies to the divine summons or only the lower life's desire clutches at some side attraction of the fruits of Yoga-power or Yoga-pleasure or only a transient emotion leaps like an unsteady flame moved by the intensity of the Voice or its sweetness or grandeur, then too there can be little surety for thee in the difficult path of Yoga.

The outer instruments of mortal man have no force to carry him through the severe ardours of this spiritual journey and Titanic inner battle or to meet its terrible or obstinate ordeals or nerve him to face and overcome its subtle and formidable dangers. Only his spirit's august and steadfast will and the quenchless fire of his soul's invincible ardour are sufficient for this difficult transformation and this high improbable endeavour.

Imagine not the way is easy; the way is long, arduous, dangerous, difficult. At every step is an ambush, at every turn a pitfall. A thousand seen or unseen enemies will start up against thee, terrible in subtlety against thy ignorance, formidable in power against thy weakness. And when with pain thou hast destroyed them, other thousands will surge up to take their place. Hell will vomit its hordes to oppose thee and enring and wound and menace; Heaven will meet thee with its pitiless tests and its cold luminous denials. Thou shalt find thyself alone in thy anguish, the demons furious in thy path, the Gods unwilling above thee. Ancient and powerful, cruel, unvanquished and close and innumerable are the dark and dreadful Powers that profit by the reign of Night and Ignorance and would have no change and are hostile. Aloof, slow to arrive, far-off and few and brief in their visits are the Bright Ones who are willing or permitted to succour. Each step forward is a battle. There are precipitous descents, there are unending ascensions and ever higher peaks upon peaks to conquer. Each plateau climbed is but a stage on the way and reveals endless heights beyond it. Each victory thou thinkest the last triumphant struggle proves to be but the prelude to a hundred fierce and perilous battles... But thou sayest God's hand will be with me and the Divine Mother near with her gracious smile of succour? And thou knowest not then that God's grace is more difficult to have or to keep than the nectar of the Immortals or Kuvera's priceless treasures? Ask of His chosen and they will tell thee how often the Eternal has covered his face from them, how often he has withdrawn from them behind his mysterious veil and they have found themselves alone in the grip of Hell, solitary in the horror of the darkness, naked and defenceless in the anguish of the battle. And if his presence is felt behind the veil, yet is it like the winter sun behind clouds and saves not from the rain and snow and the calamitous storm and the harsh wind and the bitter cold and the grey of a sorrowful atmosphere and the dun weary dullness. Doubtless the help is there even when it seems to be withdrawn, but still is there the appearance of total night with no sun to come and no star of hope to pierce the blackness. Beautiful is the face of the Divine Mother, but she too can be hard and terrible. Nay, then, is immortality a plaything to be given lightly to a child or the divine life a prize without effort or the crown for a weakling? Strive rightly and thou shalt have; trust and thy trust shall in the end be justified; but the dread Law of the Way is there and none can abrogate it.

Man and the Supermind

Man is a transitional being, he is not final; for in him and high beyond him ascend the radiant degrees which climb to a divine supermanhood.

The step from man towards superman is the next approaching achievement in the earth's evolution. There lies our destiny and the liberating key to our aspiring, but troubled and limited human existence — inevitable because it is at once the intention of the inner Spirit and the logic of Nature's process.

The appearance of a human possibility in a material and animal world was the first glint of a coming divine Light, — the first far-off intimation of a godhead to be born out of Matter. The appearance of the superman in the human world will be the fulfilment of that distant shining promise.

The difference between man and superman will be the difference between mind and a consciousness as far beyond it as thinking mind is beyond the consciousness of plant and animal; the differentiating essence of man is mind, the differentiating essence of superman will be supermind or a divine gnosis.

Man is a mind imprisoned, obscured and circumscribed in a precarious and imperfect living but imperfectly conscious body. The superman will be a supramental spirit which will envelop and freely use a conscious body, plastic to spiritual forces. His physical frame will be a firm support and an adequate radiant instrument for the spirit's divine play and work in Matter.

Mind, even free and in its own unmixed and unhampered element, is not the highest possibility of consciousness; for mind is not in possession of Truth, but only a minor vessel or an instrument and here an ignorant seeker plucking eagerly at a mass of falsehoods and half-truths for the unsatisfying pabulum of its hunger. Beyond mind is a supramental or gnostic power of consciousness that is in eternal possession of Truth; all its motion and feeling and sense and outcome are instinct and luminous with the inmost reality of things and express nothing else.

Supermind or gnosis is in its original nature at once and in the same movement an infinite wisdom and an infinite will. At its source it is the dynamic consciousness of the divine Knower and Creator.

When in the process of unfolding of an always greater force of the one Existence, some delegation of this power shall descend into our limited human nature, then and then only can man exceed himself and know divinely and divinely act and create; he will have become at last a conscious portion of the Eternal. The superman will be born, not a magnified mental being, but a supramental power descended here into a new life of the transformed terrestrial body. A gnostic supermanhood is the next distinct and triumphant victory to be won by the spirit descended into earthly nature.

The disk of a secret sun of Power and Joy and Knowledge is emerging out of the material consciousness in which our mind works as a chained slave or a baffled and impotent demiurge; supermind will be the formed body of that radiant effulgence.

Superman is not man climbed to his own natural zenith, not a superior degree of human greatness, knowledge, power, intelligence, will, character, genius, dynamic force, saintliness, love, purity or perfection. Supermind is something beyond mental man and his limits, a greater consciousness than the highest consciousness proper to human nature.

Man is a being from the mental worlds whose mentality works here involved, obscure and degraded in a physical brain, shut off from its own divinest powers and impotent to change life beyond certain narrow and precarious limits. Even in the highest of his kind it is baulked of its luminous possibilities of supreme force and freedom by this dependence. Most often and in most men it is only a servitor, a purveyor of amusements, a caterer of needs and interests to the life and the body. But the superman will be a gnostic king of Nature; supermind in him even in its evolutionary beginnings will appear as a ray of the eternal omniscience and omnipotence. Sovereign and irresistible it will lay hands on the mental and physical instruments, and, standing above and yet penetrating and possessing our lower already manifested parts, it will transform mind, life and body into its own divine and luminous nature.

Man in himself is hardly better than an ambitious nothing. He is a narrowness that reaches towards ungrasped widenesses, a littleness straining towards grandeurs which are beyond him, a dwarf enamoured of the heights. His mind is a darkened ray in the splendours of the universal Mind. His life is a striving exulting and suffering wave, an eager passion-tossed and sorrow-stricken or a blindly and dully toiling petty moment of the universal Life. His body is a labouring perishable speck in the material universe. An immortal soul is somewhere hidden within him and gives out from time to time some sparks of its presence, and an eternal spirit is above and overshadows with its wings and upholds with its power this soul continuity in his nature. But that greater spirit is obstructed from descent by the hard lid of his constructed personality and this inner radiant soul is wrapped, stifled and oppressed in dense outer coatings. In all but a few it is seldom active, in many hardly perceptible. The soul and spirit in man seem rather to exist above and behind his formed nature than to be a part of its visible reality; subliminal in his inner being or superconscient above in some unreached status, they are in his outer consciousness possibilities rather than things realised and present. The spirit is in course of birth rather than born in Matter.

This imperfect being with his hampered, confused, ill-ordered and mostly ineffective consciousness cannot be the end and highest height of the mysterious upward surge of Nature. There is something more that has yet to be brought down from above and is now seen only by broken glimpses through sudden rifts in the giant wall of our limitations. Or else there is something yet to be evolved from below, sleeping under the veil of man's mental consciousness or half visible by flashes, as life once slept in the stone and metal, mind in the plant and reason in the cave of animal memory underlying its imperfect apparatus of emotion and sense-device and instinct. Something there is in us yet unexpressed that has to be delivered by an enveloping illumination from above. A godhead is imprisoned in our depths, one in its being with a greater godhead ready to descend from superhuman summits. In that descent and awakened joining is the secret of our future.

Man's greatness is not in what he is but in what he makes possible. His glory is that he is the closed place and secret workshop of a living labour in which supermanhood is made ready by a divine Craftsman.

But he is admitted to a yet greater greatness and it is this that, unlike the lower creation, he is allowed to be partly the conscious artisan of his divine change. His free assent, his consecrated will and participation are needed that into his body may descend the glory that will replace him. His aspiration is earth's call to the supramental Creator.

If earth calls and the Supreme answers, the hour can be even now for that immense and glorious transformation.

The Involved and Evolving Godhead

The involution of a superconscient Spirit in inconscient Matter is the secret cause of this visible and apparent world. The key-word of the earth's riddle is the gradual evolution of a hidden illimitable consciousness and power out of the seemingly inert yet furiously driven force of insensible Nature. Earth-life is one self-chosen habitation of a great Divinity and his aeonic will is to change it from a blind prison into his splendid mansion and high heaven-reaching temple.

The nature of the Divinity in the world is an enigma to the mind, but to our enlarging consciousness it will appear as a presence simple and inevitable. Freed we shall enter into the immutable stability of an eternal existence that puts on this revealing multitude of significant mutable forms. Illumined we shall become aware of the indivisible light of an infinite consciousness that breaks out here into multiform grouping and detail of knowledge. Sublimated in might, we shall share the illimitable movement of an omnipotent force that works out its marvels in self-imposed limits. Fixed in griefless bliss we shall possess the calm and ecstasy of an immeasurable Delight that creates for ever the multitudinous waves and rhythms and the ever increasing outward-going and inward-drawing intensities of its own creative and communicative world-possessing and self-possessing bliss. This, since we are inwardly souls of that Spirit, will be the nature of our fourfold experience when the evolving Godhead will work here in its own unveiled movement.

If that full manifestation had been from the beginning, there would be no terrestrial problem, no anguish of growth, no baffled seeking out of mind and will and life and body towards knowledge and force and joy and an immortal persistence. But this Godhead, whether within us or outside in things and forces and creatures, started from an involution in inconscience of

Nature and began by the manifestation of its apparent opposites. Out of a vast cosmic inconscience and inertia and insensibility, an initial disguise that is almost non-existence, the Spirit in Matter has chosen to evolve and slowly shape, as if in a grudging and gradually yielding material, its might and light and infinity and beatitude.

The significance of the terrestrial evolution lies in this slow and progressive liberation of some latent indwelling Spirit. The heart of its mystery is the difficult appearance, the tardy becoming of a divine Something or Someone already involved in physical Nature. The Spirit is there with all its potential forces in a first formal basis of its own supporting, yet resistant substance. Its greater subsequent and deliberately emerging movements, life and mind and intuition and soul and supermind and the light of the Godhead are already there, locked up and obscurely compressed into the initial power and first expressive values of Matter.

Before there could be any evolution, there must needs be this involution of the Divine All that is to emerge. Otherwise there would have been not an ordered and significant evolution, but a successive creation of things unforeseeable, not contained in their antecedents, not their inevitable consequences or right followers in sequence.

This world is not an apparent order fortuitously managed by an inexplicable Chance. Neither is it a marvellous mechanism miraculously contrived by a stumblingly fortunate unconscious Force or mechanical Necessity. It is not even a structure built according to his fancy or will by an external and therefore necessarily a limited Creator. Mentally conceivable, each of these solutions can explain one side or appearance of things; but it is a greater truth that can alone successfully join all the aspects and illumine all the facts of the enigma.

If all were indeed a result of cosmic Chance, there would be no necessity of a new advance; nothing beyond mind need appear in the material world, — as indeed there was then no necessity for even mind to arise at all out of the meaningless blind material whirl. Consciousness itself would be only a fortuitous apparition, a strange hallucinating reflection or ghost of Matter.

Or if all were the work of a mechanical Force, then too mind need not have appeared at all as part of the huge grinding engine; there was no indispensable call for this subtler and yet less competent groping mechanic contrivance. No frail thinking brain should have been there to labour over the quite sufficient cogs and springs and pistons of the first unerring machine. A supermind added on this brilliant and painful complication would be still more a superfluity and a luminous insolence; it could be nothing more than a false pretension of transitory consciousness to govern and possess the greater inconscient Force that is its creator.

Or if an experimenting, external and therefore limited Creator were the inventor of the animal's suffering life and man's fumbling mind and this huge mainly unused and useless universe, there was no reason why he should not have stopped short with the construction of a mental intelligence in his creatures, content with the difficult ingenuity of his labour. Even if he were all-powerful and all-wise, he might well pause there, — for if he went farther, the creature would be in danger of rising too near to the level of his Maker.

But if this is the truth of things that an infinite Spirit, an eternal Divine Presence and Consciousness and Force and Bliss is involved and hidden here and slowly emerges, then is it inevitable that its powers or the ascending degrees of its one power should emerge too one after the other till the whole glory is manifested, a mighty divine Fact embodied and dynamic and visible.

All mental ideas of the nature of things, are inconclusive considerations of our insufficient logical reason when it attempts in its limited light and ignorant self-sufficiency to weigh the logical probabilities of a universal order which after all its speculation and discovery must remain obscure to it still and an enigma. The true witness and discoverer is our growing consciousness; for that consciousness is itself the sign and power of the evolving Divine, and its growth out of the apparent inconscience of the material universe is the fundamental, the one abiding, progressive index event of the long earth-story.

Only when this evolving consciousness can grow into its own full divine power will we directly know ourselves and the world instead of catching at tags and tail ends of an insufficient figure of knowledge. This full power of the consciousness is supermind or gnosis, — supermind because to reach it we have to pass beyond and turn upon mind as the mind itself has passed and turned upon life and inconscient matter and gnosis because it is eternally self-possessed of Truth and in its very stuff and nature it is dynamic substance of knowledge.

The true knowledge of things is denied to our reason, because that is not our spirit's greatest essential power but only an expedient, a transitional instrument meant to deal with the appearance of things and their phenomenal process. True knowledge commences only when our consciousness can pass beyond its present normal limit in man: for then it becomes directly aware of its self and of the Power in the world and begins to have at least an initial knowledge by identity which is the sole true knowledge. Henceforward it knows and sees, no longer by the reason groping among external data, but by an ever increasing and always more luminous self-illumining and all illuminating experience. In the end it will become a conscious part of the Divine revealing itself in the world; its life will be a power for the conscious evolution of that which is still unmanifested in the material universe.

The Evolution of Consciousness

All life here is a stage or a circumstance in an unfolding progressive evolution of a Spirit that has involved itself in Matter and is labouring to manifest itself in that reluctant substance. This is the whole secret of earthly existence.

But the key of that secret is not to be found in life itself or in the body; its hieroglyph is not in embryo or organism, — for these are only a physical means or base: the one significant mystery of this universe is the appearance and growth of consciousness in the vast mute unintelligence of Matter. The escape of Consciousness out of an apparent initial Inconscience, — but it was there all the time masked and latent, for the inconscience of Matter is itself only a hooded consciousness — its struggle to find itself, its reaching out to its own inherent completeness, perfection, joy, light, strength, mastery, harmony, freedom, this is the prolonged miracle and yet the natural and all-explaining phenomenon of which we are at once the observers and a part, instrument and vehicle.

A Consciousness, a Being, a Power, a Joy was here from the beginning darkly imprisoned in this apparent denial of itself, this original night, this obscurity and nescience of material Nature. That which is and was for ever, free, perfect, eternal and infinite, That which all is, That which we call God, Brahman, Spirit, has here shut itself up in its own self-created opposite. The Omniscient has plunged itself into Nescience, the All-Conscious into Inconscience, the All-Wise into perpetual Ignorance. The Omnipotent has formulated itself in a vast cosmic self-driven Inertia that by disintegration creates; the Infinite is self-expressed here in a boundless fragmentation; the All-Blissful has put on a huge insensibility out of which it struggles by pain and hunger and desire and sorrow. Elsewhere the Divine is; here in physical life, in this obscure material world, it would seem almost as if the Divine is not but is only becoming, θεος ουκ ἐστιν αλλα γιγνεται. This gradual becoming of the Divine out of its own phenomenal opposites is the meaning and purpose of the terrestrial evolution.

Evolution in its essence is not the development of a more and more organised body or a more and more efficient life — these are only its machinery and outward circumstance. Evolution is the strife of a Consciousness somnambulised in Matter to wake and be free and find and possess itself and all its possibilities to the very utmost and widest, to the very last and highest. Evolution is the emancipation of a self-revealing Soul secret in Form and Force, the slow becoming of a Godhead, the growth of a Spirit.

In this evolution mental man is not the goal and end, the completing value, the highest last significance; he is too small and imperfect to be the crown of all this travail of Nature. Man is not final, but a middle term only, a transitional being, an instrumental intermediate creature.

This character of evolution and this mediary position of man are not at first apparent; for to the outward eye it would seem as if evolution, the physical evolution at least were finished long ago leaving man behind as its poor best result and no new beings or superior creations were to be expected any longer. But this appears to us only so long as we look at forms and outsides only and not at the inner significances of the whole process. Matter, body, life even are the first terms necessary for the work that had to be done. New living forms may no longer be appearing freely, but this is because it is not, or at least it is not primarily, new living forms that the Force of evolution is now busied with evolving, but new powers of consciousness. When Nature, the Divine Power, had formed a body erect and empowered to think, to devise, to inquire into itself and things and work consciously both on things and self, she had what she wanted for her secret aim; relegating all else to the sphere of secondary movements, she turned toward that long-hidden aim her main highest forces. For all till then was a long strenuously slow preparation; but throughout it the development of consciousness in which the appearance of man was the crucial turning point had been kept wrapped within her as her ultimate business and true purpose.

This slow preparation of Nature covered immense aeons of time and infinities of space in which they appeared to be her only business; the real business strikes on our view at least when we look with the outward eye of reason as if it came only as a fortuitous accident, in or near the end, for a span of time and in a speck and hardly noticeable corner of one of the smallest provinces of a possibly minor universe among these many boundless finites, these countless universes. If it were so, we could still reply that time and space matter not to the Infinite and Eternal; it is not a waste of labour for That — as it would be for our brief death-driven existences — to work for trillions of years in order to flower only for a moment. But that paradox too is only an appearance — for the history of this single earth is not all the story of evolution — other earths there are even now elsewhere, and even here many earth-cycles came before us, and many are those that will come hereafter.

Nature laboured for innumerable millions of years to create a material universe of flaming suns and systems; for a lesser but still interminable series of millions she stooped to make this earth a habitable planet. For all that incalculable time she was or seemed busy only with the evolution of Matter; life and mind were kept secret in an apparent non-existence. But the time came when life could manifest, a vibration in the metal, a growing and seeking, a drawing in and a feeling outward in the plant, an instinctive force and sense, a nexus of joy and pain and hunger and emotion and fear and struggle in the animal, — a first organised consciousness, the beginning of the long-planned miracle. Thenceforward she was busy no more exclusively with matter for its own sake, but most with palpitant plasmic matter useful for the expression of life; the evolution of life was now her one intent purpose. And slowly too mind manifested in life, an intensely feeling, a crude thinking and planning vital mind in the animal, but in man the full organisation and apparatus, the developing if yet imperfect mental being, the Manu, the thinking, devising, aspiring, already self-conscient creature. And from that time onward the growth of mind rather than any radical change of life became her shining preoccupation, her wonderful wager. Body appeared to evolve no more; life itself evolved little or only so much in its cycles as would serve to express Mind heightening and widening itself in the living body; an unseen internal evolution was now Nature's great passion and purpose.

And if Mind were all that consciousness could achieve, if Mind were the secret Godhead, if there were nothing higher, larger, [no] more miraculous ranges, man could be left to fulfil mind and complete his own being and there would or need be nothing here beyond him, carrying consciousness to its summits, extending it to its unwalled vastnesses, plunging with it into depths unfathomable; he would by perfecting himself consummate Nature. Evolution would end in a Man-God, crown of the earthly cycles.

But Mind is not all; for beyond mind is a greater consciousness; there is a supermind and spirit. As Nature laboured in the animal, the vital being, till she could manifest out of him man, the Manu, the thinker, so she is labouring in man, the mental being till she can manifest out of him a spiritual and supramental godhead, the truth conscious Seer, the knower by identity, the embodied Transcendental and Universal in the individual nature.

From the clod and metal to the plant, from the plant to the animal, from the animal to man, so much has she completed of her journey; a huge stretch or a stupendous leap still remains before her. As from matter to life, from life to mind, so now she must pass from mind to supermind, from man to superman; this is the gulf that she has to bridge, the supreme miracle that she has to perform before she can rest from her struggle and discontent and stand in the radiance of that supreme consciousness, glorified, transmuted, satisfied with her labour.

The subhuman was once here supreme in her, the human replacing it walks now in the front of Time, but still, aim and goal of the future there waits the supramental, the superman, an unborn glory yet unachieved before her.

The Path

The supramental Yoga is at once an ascent towards God and a descent of Godhead into the embodied nature.

The ascent can only be achieved by a one-centred all-gathering upward aspiration of the soul and mind and life and body; the descent can only come by a call of the whole being towards the infinite and eternal Divine. If this call and this aspiration are there, or if by any means they can be born and grow constantly and seize all the nature, then and then only a supramental uplifting and transformation becomes possible.

The call and the aspiration are only first conditions; there must be along with them and brought by their effective intensity an opening of all the being to the Divine and a total surrender.

This opening is a throwing wide of all the nature on all its levels and in all its parts to receive into itself without limits the greater divine Consciousness which is there already above and behind and englobing this mortal half-conscious existence. In the receiving there must be no inability to contain, no breaking down of anything in the system, mind or life or nerve or body under the transmuting stress. There must be an endless receptivity, an always increasing capacity to bear an ever stronger and more and more insistent action of the divine Force. Otherwise nothing great and permanent can be done; the Yoga will end in a break-down or an inert stoppage or a stultifying or a disastrous arrest in a process which must be absolute and integral if it is not [to] be a failure.

But since no human system has this endless receptivity and unfailing capacity, the supramental Yoga can succeed only if the Divine Force as it descends increases the personal power and equates the strength that receives with the Force that enters from above to work in the nature. This is only possible if there is on our part a progressive surrender of the being into the hands of the Divine; there must be a complete and never failing assent, a courageous willingness to let the Divine Power do with us whatever is needed for the work that has to be done.

Man cannot by his own effort make himself more than man; the mental being cannot by his own unaided force change himself into a supramental spirit. A descent of the Divine Nature can alone divinise the human receptacle.

For the powers of our mind, life and body are bound to their own limitations and, however high they may rise or however widely expand, they cannot rise above their natural ultimate limits or expand beyond them. But, still, mental man can open to what is beyond him and call down a supramental Light, Truth and Power to work in him and do what the mind cannot do. If mind cannot by effort become what is beyond mind, supermind can descend and transform mind into its own substance.

If the supramental Power is allowed by man's discerning assent and vigilant surrender to act according to its own profound and subtle insight and flexible potency, it will bring about slowly or swiftly a divine transformation of our present semiperfect nature.

This descent, this working is not without its possibility of calamitous fall and danger. If the human mind or the vital desire seizes hold on the descending force and tries to use it according to its own limited and erring ideas or flawed and egoistic impulses, — and this is inevitable in some degree until this lower mortal has learned something of the way of that greater immortal nature, — stumblings and deviations, hard and seemingly insuperable obstacles and wounds and suffering cannot be escaped and even death or utter downfall are not impossible. Only when the conscious integral surrender to the Divine has been learned by mind and life and body, can the way of the Yoga become easy, straight, swift and safe.

And it must be a surrender and an opening to the Divine alone and to no other. For it is possible for an obscure mind or an impure life force in us to surrender to undivine and hostile forces and even to mistake them for the Divine. There can be no more calamitous error. Therefore our surrender must be no blind and inert passivity to all influences or any influence, but sincere, conscious, vigilant, pointed to the One and the Highest alone.

Self-surrender to the divine and infinite Mother, however difficult, remains our only effective means and our sole abiding refuge. Self-surrender to her means that our nature must be an instrument in her hands, the soul a child in the arms of the Mother.

Part Two

From Man to Superman

Notes and Fragments on Philosophy,

Psychology and Yoga

1912–1947

The notes, drafts and fragments collected in this part were not written by Sri Aurobindo in the present sequence nor intended by him to form a single work. They have been arranged by the editors by topic in three sections — Philosophy: God, Nature and Man; Psychology: The Science of Consciousness; Yoga: Change of Consciousness and Transformation of Nature.

Section One

Philosophy

God, Nature and Man

God
The One Reality

The Divine Eternal and Infinite

1

There are three Powers with whom we have to reckon, three and no others; for no others are in the universe or out of the universe: God, the Soul and Nature. And these three are, as it were, different fronts of One Being.

2

All existence, whatever its appearance or its process of being, is and draws its substance, origin, energy, truth from a Spirit which is the beginning, middle and end of all — itself being eternal, infinite, self-existent beyond end or beginning, beyond Space and Time, beyond Form and Quality and Circumstance as well as in Space and Time, in Form and Quality and Circumstance. This is the fundamental Reality which is hidden from our knowledge, the one Truth on which all other truths depend, those that affirm it as well as those that seem to contradict it. To be conscious of this Reality and its right relations with the other truths or appearances of existence, to live in it and govern by its Truth all our being, consciousness, nature, will, action would then be the law of a perfect life. If human life is imperfect, it is because its consciousness moves seeking, groping, experimenting in a fundamental ignorance of the real truth of its own being and is therefore unable to know or to effectuate the true law of its life. It is only if man can overcome this ignorance and inability that he can hope to perfect his life and nature. If there is no means of doing that, then he can never hope to escape from his imperfection — and the suffering which is its consequence. He can only either die in his ignorance escaping from an incurable imperfection and suffering by a physical extinction or escape out of it by a spiritual extinction gained through an awakening of the soul to the illusoriness of birth and world and Nature or [. . .] & hope to get [out] of it into some other supraterrestrial state of existence. Human life on earth can then never grow into anything fundamentally other, better or more perfect than it is now. The hope that by using our reason and observing or utilising the laws of Nature we can arrive at a perfect life here is futile, for our nature here being itself ignorant and imperfect cannot arrive at anything better than a mitigated imperfection and ignorance. But if there is a means by which we can arrive at a true knowledge of the reality behind things and enter into its Truth and Light and Power then there is no reason why our life here should not become divine and perfect. It is through Yoga that this means can be found and this emergence become possible.

3

A greater existence and consciousness than what we are now or are in our surface being, to which yet we can by certain means raise ourself and become or enter into that, — this is the postulate of all Yoga.

What is this greater consciousness and existence? It is something or someone eternal and infinite, absolute or perfect, in which all is, from which all comes, to which all returns and which is the secret self of all things. All is by its existence, all is conscious by its consciousness, continues to be by its Ananda of being, thinks by its Mind, lives by its life, is a form of its Energy in the Cosmos. But still the existence we live, the consciousness we use, the highest joy of being which we experience, our mind, life, body, force are but a fragmentary phenomenon of or in It. That Eternal is the All, the whole, our greater Self, our completeness, our universe, yet is it more than any universe. If no universe were, it still would be.

This Eternal and Infinite is not only an Eternal of endless Time and Space. For its eternity can be realised not only in the endless progression of the years and aeons but in a single moment of Time, its infinity not only in the boundless extension of space to which we can assign no end or border, but in the most infinitesimal atom of an atom. But beyond the moment and the endless aeons the eternity of the Eternal is timeless and beyond the spatial Infinite and Infinitesimal the infinity of the Infinite is spaceless.

4

All begins from the Divine, from the Eternal, from the Infinite, all abides in it alone and by it alone, all ends or culminates in the divine Eternal and Infinite. This is the first postulate indispensable for our spiritual seeking — for on no other base can we found the highest knowledge and the highest life.

All time moves in the Eternal; all space is spread in the Infinite; all creatures and creations live by that in them which is Divine. This is patently true of an inner spiritual but also proves in the end to be true of this outer space and time. It is known to our inmost being that it lives because it is part of the Divine, but it is true also of the external and phenomenal creature compounded of ignorant Mind, blind life and subconscious Matter.

A secret Self is the Alpha and Omega of this manifested existence; it is also the constant term, the omnipresent x into which all things resolve separately or together and which is their sum, their constituting material and their essence. All here is secretly the Divine, all is the Eternal, all is the Infinite.

But this secret truth of things is contradicted by the world's external appearances, it is denied by all the facts placed before us by our mind and senses, inconsistent with the sorrow and suffering of the world, incompatible with the imperfection of living beings and the unchangeable inconscience of things. What then pushes the mind to affirm it? what compels us to admit a seeing of things which is in conflict with our outer seeing and experience?

For on the surface of our consciousness and all around us there is only the temporal and transient, only [the] confined and finite. What seems largest to us finds its limit, what we dreamed to be enduring comes to an end; even this vast universe with its masses of worlds upon worlds which seemed to stretch into infinity is convicted in the end of being only a boundless finite. Man claiming to be a divine soul and an all-discovering intellect is brought up short by Nature's rude proof of his ignorance and incompetence and exhibits constantly in his thoughts the proneness to self-confident error and in his feelings and acts the petty faultiness, meanness, and darkness or suddenly the abysses of falsehood or foulness or cruelty of his nature. In the management of his world the much that is undivine prevails easily over the little that is divine or they are inextricably mixed together. The ideal fails in practice, religion degenerates quickly into a settled sectarian fanaticism or formality, the triumphant good turns into an organised evil. The Christian doctrine of the fall, the Indian idea of the wandering of the Soul in a cosmic illusion or the sceptic affirmation of an inconscient material Nature producing the freak of consciousness seems often to be the kernel of the whole matter.

And yet if we go deep enough into ourselves, we strike against something valid that proves to be a veiled divine element which affirms its immortality, Soul. If we go beyond our embodied mind and senses we break suddenly into something permanent that feels itself to be eternal and infinite, that cannot see itself as anything else and we also cannot conceive of it as anything else, an infinite Self, an eternal Spirit. Moreover in our most secret essence we are convinced of perfection or of perfectibility — perfection in our deepest spiritual being, perfectibility in our nature; we have the instinct and intuition of the Divine.

Even to Time and Space our mind cannot fix or conceive a beginning or an end; it cannot conceive a first bound or a last, a primary or ultimate moment without at once looking beyond it. If we see the imperfection of things, the very idea implies a potentiality of a perfection by comparison with which they are imperfect, and this potentiality points to a beyond Mind and beyond Sense which is the integrally and permanently perfect. Every relative supposes an absolute.

For a long time we have been asked not to believe in these

things, to put our trust only in the measuring rods of science and its calculations and crucibles, to accept only what is materially ascertainable and measurable. But these measurements are those of something that is limited — how can we ascertain by it whether there is or is not the Illimitable? The instruments by which we question Nature in order to find out what is ascertainable have been proved to give only the results which are already contained in the question or in the questioner. Science gives us the measures and process of things within the physical limit, but it has failed [to] tell us what things are, their final origin or their reason of existence.

In all this questing by one end or the other we cannot get beyond ourselves and it is better then to look into the inner side of ourselves, — why should we limit ourselves only to our responses to an outer evidence? Let us explore ourselves and not only our sense or perception of what is around us. And in ourselves let us look not only at our surfaces but at the inner and the inmost of our being and nature.

This self-knowledge pursued far enough shows us a deeper than the surface mind and a deeper than the physical sense, a profounder than the outward life. It shows us also a Beyond-Mind and Beyond-Sense, a Beyond-Life; the limited passes into [the] illimitable. If there were not this capacity of research, we would have to be content with an unsatisfied agnosticism; but the means is there by which we can know ourselves and this Alpha and X and Omega of things or if not absolutely It at any rate its status and its dynamis, the law of its being and the law of its nature quite as deeply and more deeply than Science can show us the law and process of the physical universe.

For the moment let us affirm only this result that this spiritual search and knowledge leads us beyond the phenomenon which apparently contradicts it to that which beyond the phenomenon brings us to the Divine Eternal and Infinite.

5

The rooted and fundamental conception of Vedanta is that there exists somewhere, could we but find it, available to experience or self-revelation, if denied to intellectual research, a single truth comprehensive & universal in the light of which the whole of existence would stand revealed and explained both in its nature and its end. This universal existence, for all its multitude of objects and its diversity of faces, is one in substance and origin; and there is an unknown quantity, X or Brahman to which it can be reduced, for from that it started and in & by that it still exists.

6

Brahman is that which was before the beginning and will be after the end of things. In the beginning, says the Upanishad, Self was, Being was or Non-Being was; that saw world-creation in itself or from that Non-Being or eternal Being temporal existence was born. What prevents the timeless Eternal from conceiving Time in himself and ceasing from the conception? But the very idea supposes time[.]

7

One says "In the beginning was the Self, the Spirit, God, the Eternal." But there was never a beginning, for the Eternal and its works are always and for ever.

"In the beginning" is a phrase that has no meaning unless we speak of sections of existence, sections of it in Time, sections of it in Space, sections of it in substance; for these have a beginning and an end. Existence in itself has no end even as it never had a beginning.

It is not of pure existence only that this [can be said], existence in its essence without any expressive motion or feature, but of existence with all it contains and reveals in its depths as on its surface. For pure existence is only a state of being and not being in its whole truth and integral significance.

And even this state, although it appears to the quiescent mind featureless, motionless, concentrated in bare uniqueness, is still not empty or without feature, — it contains enveloped in itself all truth of feature, all power of motion, all that ever was, is or shall be manifested in this or any universe.

But the supreme divine Being is beyond any distinction of pure existence and phenomenal existence, feature or no feature, form or no form, being or non-being, manifestation and the unmanifest — for these are distinctions, separate states, opposite ideas to the mind, separate experiences to the Soul on the mental level, *manomaya purusha*. But the Supreme is beyond Mind and has no need for these divisions and contradictions of its nature.

Ekamevadvitiyam: One Without a Second

8

All existence is existence of the one Eternal and Infinite. Ekamevadvitiyam, — there is one without a second and there can be nothing else at any time or anywhere.

Even existence in Time is that, even the finite is that; for the finite is only a circumstance of the Infinite and Time is only a phase of Eternity. What we call undivine is that, for it is only a disguise of the omnipresent Divinity.

9

All existence is the existence of the one Divine Eternal and Infinite, there is and can be nothing else; not only the infinite is that but the finite, not only the timeless but Time and all that is in Time, not only the Impersonal but the Person, quality and number and that which [is] beyond quality and number; the Formless and form, the individual no less than the cosmic and supracosmic, matter and life and mind as well as the spirit, the relative and the absolute. All is that: *ekam evadvitiyam*.

All that is is reality of the Real; there is no need to invent an eternal illusive principle of Maya to account for world existence. The idea that the Supreme Reality is incapable of self-manifestation and that its only power is a power of self-delusion is a last desperate refuge of the human Mind and Reason trying to escape from a difficulty which is of its own creation, its own self-imposed illusion or Maya and does not exist for the true and perfect supramental consciousness of the luminous Spirit.

There is no incompatibility between the Eternal and existence in Time. Time and the Timeless are the same Eternity in a self-contained status and a self-developing movement. The Timeless is eternal and knows itself in an everlasting present; Time too is eternal and is known in an indivisible movement of past, present and future. It is our consciousness poising itself in the mobile moment that gives us the impression of a divided Time, of consciousness moving from moment to moment, losing its past, gaining its future, connecting the three only by an act of memory which binds the is to the was and the to be. In the eternal Consciousness the past still exists and extends through the present into the future. To suppose that the Timeless is debarred by its timelessness from throwing itself out in a movement of Time and that Time therefore and all in time is an illusion or to suppose that Time alone exists and we are its temporal creations is to impose the ignorance and limitation of our little surface consciousness on the Divine Eternal. In reality we ourselves below our surface are the timeless developing in movement our existence in eternal Time.

10

One sole Reality constitutes all the infinite, the One, the Divine, the Eternal and Infinite — there is That alone and no other existence. Ekamevadvitiyam.

Infinite, but the finite existence is also that one being, that infinite Being; it has no separate reality: Eternal, but the temporal is nothing more than a movement of that Eternity, Time has no independent self-sustenance: Divine, but all that seems undivine is a disguise of the Divinity, it is no creation out of some unaccountable Opposite.

The Divine Reality is unconfined by form or quality; but form and quality also are his, infinite quality, innumerable figure, vessel of that earth, coin of that gold, colour inherent in that transcendent whiteness. All is the divine Eternal and Infinite.

Impersonal and Personal are not contrary appearances or

even dual aspects nor is the Person our convenient imagination of an ever impersonal Entity, but rather both are for ever the One.

All is the Divine, even that which is undivine. There is no not self; all this is the eternal Self; all this universe and every other universe is the Time existence of the timeless Spirit.

11

There is one sole reality and there can be no other, the One, the Divine, the Eternal and Infinite. *Ekam evadvitiyam brahma.*

The One is at the same time the All, for it exists in all, all exists by it, it *is* all. Whatever be [the] plane of being, whatever be the cosmos, whatever be the individual, the truth of its existence is the same; that it or he is the One; for there is and can be no other. The Transcendent is the Divine, the universal is the Divine, the individual is the Divine; all are the one Reality.

Not only what we see as the Infinite, but the finite also is that One Existence; it has no separate and independent reality. Not only the Eternal [is] that, but the temporal also, for the temporal is only a circumstance of the Eternal apart from which Time has no self-existence. Not only what we see as Divine is that, but the undivine is no more than a disguise of the one Divinity, it is no creation out of an unaccountable Opposite.

12

All existence is one; it is existence of the One Being, divine, infinite, eternal, absolute.

What we see as the Many, is the multiplicity of the One. All these apparently separate persons and objects are also the one existence; they are beings of the One Being. For That is their one self; in their spiritual essence they are That, even in the play and form of their being they are That; they are personalities of the one Person, they are manifestations of the one Existence, they are so many realities of the only Real. In no way are they separate and independent from It, but in every way live by It, are of It, can be nothing else. All forces are powers of the one Force, the sole Power of the One Being; there is no other force than his. All objects are formations of the one Existence; there is nothing that exists in itself and apart from That, nothing that is of an individual essence other than the one Essence of the universe.

What we see as finite is not other than the Infinite. All is in the Infinite, all exists by the Infinite, all is of the stuff of the Infinite. No object or person could come into being or remain in being by its own finite and individual power; none exists by its own limited substance and essence other than the substance and essence of all others; all are at bottom indissolubly one. There is effective determination, definition, demarcation, diverse formation in the universe but no essential separation or division. A tree is separate as an object or phenomenon, but it is not a separate existence divided from all around it; there is a one-existence and a one-energy that has taken form of tree, constitutes every atom, molecule, fibre of it, pervades and is its whole structure of being and this existence, this energy not only abides in all of it and flows through all of it but extends everywhere around and is, constitutes, energises all other objects in the cosmos. Each finite is in fact the Infinite; all apparently separate or divided existence is only a front of the Indivisible.

All that we see as temporal is not other than the Eternal. The form of that which is in Time is or appears to be evanescent, but the self, the substance, the being that takes shape in that form is eternal and is one self, one substance, one being with all that is, all that was, all that shall be. But even the form is in itself eternal and not temporal, but it exists for ever in possibility, in power, in consciousness in the Eternal. Form is manifested and withdrawn from manifestation; it may be manifested by immediate apparition or it may be manifested by construction and withdrawn from manifestation by destruction or disaggregation, but in either case it exists beforehand in the consciousness and being of the Eternal. If it did not so preexist in power and possibility, it could not be created in actuality. For the actual proceeds from the possible and the possible is always a possibility of the truth of the Eternal.

13

All existence of whatever nature is existence of the One Divine, the Eternal and Infinite.

For not only the Infinite is that existence, but the finite also; not only the existence of the One, but the existence of the Many, not only the existence of the Unmanifest, but the existence of the manifested universe and of all actual or possible universes, not only the Impersonal, but the Personal, not only the Pure Existence, Consciousness, Bliss of Sachchidananda but all forms of existence or consciousness blissful or unblissful, not only the existence of the Absolute but the existence of all that is relative. There is nothing that is not the existence of the One Divine, the Eternal and Infinite. *Ekam evadvitiyam.*

14

There is one Being, infinite, eternal and divine, the sole Reality. All is the [   ], there is nothing else in the universe or outside the universe. *Ekam evadvitiyam.*

This eternity is not of Time; the eternity of Time is an extension in movement of the Timeless.

This infinity is not of Space; the infinity of Space is an extension in self of this spaceless Infinite.

15

All existence is the existence of the Eternal, the Infinite, the Divine, the Ineffable — existence in Time no less than existence in Eternity, existence in the finite no less than existence in the Infinite, of the Many no less than of the One, of the Personal no less than of the Impersonal, of the individual and the cosmos no less than of the supercosmic, of the relative no less than of the Absolute. *Ekam evadvitiyam Brahma.*

The Eternal is in his very truth of being Existence, Consciousness and Bliss of existence. These three are a trinity and inseparable — they are not three but one; it is only in a certain play of the Manifestation that they can be distinguished and separated from each other or turned phenomenally into their opposites. What appears to us as Nonexistence (Asat, Nihil or Sunya) is only an existence other than the existence of which we are aware. What appears to us as Inconscience is only a veiled or involved consciousness or else a consciousness to which our mind or sense has no access. What affects us as pain or suffering is only Ananda turned against itself, a distorted and tortured Bliss of existence. These contradictions are real in the Ignorance and because of the Ignorance, but to the true consciousness they are only phenomenal and superficial, not true truths of being.

Non-Being, Being and the Absolute

16

Nothing can arise from Nothing. Asat, nothingness, is a creation of our mind; where it cannot see or conceive, where its object is something beyond its grasp, too much beyond to give even the sense of a vague intangible, then it cries out "Here there is nothing." Out of its own incapacity it has created the conception of a Zero. But what in truth is this zero? It is an incalculable Infinite.

Our sense by its incapacity has invented darkness. In truth there is nothing but Light, only it is a power of light either above or below our poor human vision's limited range.

For do not imagine that light is created by the Suns. The Suns are only physical concentrations of Light, but the splendour they concentrate for us is self-born and everywhere.

God is everywhere and wherever God is, there is Light. Jnanam chaitanyam jyotir Brahma.

*

Of all that we know we know only the outside; even when we imagine that we have intimately seized the innermost thing, we have touched only an inner external. It is still a sheath of the covering, only it is a second or third or even a seventh sheath, not the most outward and visible.

It is the same when we think we know God or have possession of our highest inmost Self or have entered intimately into the inmost and supreme Spirit. What we know and possess is power or some powers of God, an aspect or appearance or formulation of the Self; what we have entered into is only one wideness or one depth of the Spirit.

This is because we know and possess by the mind or even what is below the mind, and when we find ourselves most spiritual, it is the mind spiritualised that conceives of itself as spirit. Imagining that we have left mind behind us, we take it with us into its own spiritual realms and cover with it the Supramental Mystery. The result is something to us wonderful and intense; but compared with That Intensity and Wonder, it is something thin and inadequate.

17

All existence, — as the mind and sense know existence, — is manifestation of an Eternal and Infinite which is to the mind and sense unknowable but not unknowable to its own self-awareness.

Whatever the manifestation spiritual or material or other may be, it has behind it something that is beyond itself, and even if we reached the highest possible heights of manifested existence there would be still beyond that even an Unmanifested from which it came.

The Unmanifested Supreme is beyond all definition and description by mind or speech; no definition the mind can make, affirmative or negative, can be at all expressive of it or adequate.

To the Mind this Unmanifest can present itself as a Self, a supreme Nihil (Tao or Sunya), a featureless Absolute, an Indeterminate, a blissful Nirvana of manifested existence, a Non-Being out of which Being came or a Being of Silence out of which a world-illusion came. But all these are mental formulas expressing the mind's approach to it, not That itself; impressions which fall from That upon the receiving consciousness, not the true essence or nature (swarupa) of the Eternal and Infinite. Even the words Eternal and Infinite are only symbolic expressions through which the mind feels without grasping some vague impression of this Supreme.

If we say of it neti neti, this can mean nothing except that nothing in the world or beyond it of which the mind can take cognisance is the Supreme in Its entirety or Its essence. If we say of it iti iti, this can mean at the most that what we see of it in the world or beyond is some indication of something that is there beyond and by travelling through all these indications to their absolutes we may get a step or two nearer to the Absolute of all absolutes, the Supreme. Both formulas have a truth in them, but neither touches the secret truth of the Supreme.

18

The Origin and eternal Supporter of all existence, as of all that seems to ignorant Mind to be non-existence, is a supreme infinite and absolute. This Infinite is an essential, not, except in manifestation, a mobile temporal or extended spatial infinite; this Absolute is an expressibly positive, not a merely negating absolute — not excluding, but containing all relatives; for in it they find their own eternal and stable truth behind their present temporary and fluctuating appearance.

The Supreme is knowable to itself but unknowable to mind, inexpressible by words, because mind can grasp and words coined by the mind can express only limited, relative and divided things. Mind gets only misleading inadequate indefinite impressions or too definite reflective ideas of things too much beyond itself. Even here in its own field it grasps not things in themselves, but processes and phenomena, significant aspects, constructions and figures. But the Supreme is to its own absolute consciousness for ever self-known and self-aware, as also to supramental gnosis it is intimately known and knowable.

This Infinite and Eternal is the supreme Self of all, the supreme Source, Spirit and Person of all, the supreme Lord of all; there is nothing beyond it, nothing outside it. A million universes for ever persist or for ever recur because they are substantial expressions and manifestations of the supreme Infinite and Eternal.

19

All is existence. Non-existence is a fiction of the mind; for we describe as non-existent all that has never been within the range of our limited consciousness or is not in that range at the moment or was there once but has gone beyond it.

20

Being is not Parabrahman nor is Non-Being Parabrahman; these are only affirmative & negative terms in which Consciousness envisages its self-existence.

Parabrahman is beyond Knowledge because Knowledge cannot comprehend that which comprehends it & is anterior to itself.

The beginning of Wisdom is to renounce the attempt to know the Unknowable.

Nevertheless vast shadows of the Unknowable are reflected in Knowledge & to these infinities we give names, the Absolute, the Relative, Being, Non-Being, Consciousness, Force, Bliss, God, Self, the Personal, the Impersonal, Krishna, Shiva, Brahman.

Each thing in the universe is All in the Universe and also That which is beyond the universe, — what Knowledge sees of it is only the face that the All presents in some play of Its infinite consciousness. We are our own Knowledge & all that is unknown to our Knowledge.

What matters in the universe is the play of the All in Itself & its ultimate self-fulfilment in Knowledge, Bliss & Being.

There is an individual self-fulfilment, a collective, a cosmic & an extra-cosmic. We may move towards any of these ultimate affirmations, but he who accepts them all & harmonises them, is the highest human expression of Parabrahman. He is the Avatar or the divine Unit.

21

All being is the Eternal, the Infinite, the Divine; there is nothing beyond the Eternal and Infinite, neither is there anything else anywhere whether in existence or in non-existence.

All being ranges between the Manifestation and the Non-Manifestation. These are the two poles of the Infinite.

The Non-Manifestation is not a Non-Existence. Non-Existence is a term created by the mind and has no absolute significance; there is no such thing as an absolute Nihil or Zero. It is agreed even by the philosophies of the Nihil, Tao or Zero (Sunya) that the Non-Existence of which they speak is a Nought in which all is and from which all comes. Tao, Nihil or Zero is not different from the Absolute or the Supreme Brahman of Vedanta; it is only another way of describing or naming it. The Supreme is an Existence beyond what we know of our existence and therefore only it can seem to our mind as a Zero, a Nihil, a Non-Existence. There is nothing there of what we know as existence, for though all is in Tao, yet all is there in a way of which our mind can have no conception or experience, therefore to the mind it has no reality and brings no concept of existence.

The manifestation in the Ignorance, that in which we live, has also been described as Asat, a non-existence, because it is not real, eternal, infinite, divine; it must therefore be an illusion, since only That exists and nothing else. But even Illusionism agrees that the manifested world is not without reality, — it is practically real, but not eternal. Moreover manifestation even if illusory in this sense, has no end or beginning in itself, but only to the soul that withdraws from it. It goes on existing eternally to other souls, it goes on existing to the Eternal. It is in the eternal consciousness that it exists, though apart from that consciousness it has no existence. Moreover the stuff of which it is made is not nothingness or void, but the Eternal itself which manifests it from itself and out of its own substance cast into form and force. It is therefore not a real Nihil, but a limited and constantly renewed, recurrent or mutable existence.

It is therefore permissible to say that all being ranges between Manifestation and Non-Manifestation, for both are degrees of existence, the one rising towards the Absolute, the other in appearance, but in appearance only, determined and relative.

Nature
The World-Manifestation

The Divine and the Manifestation

22

All existence is Brahman, Atman & Iswara, three names for one unnameable reality which alone exists. We shall give to this sole real existence the general name of God, because we find it ultimately to be not an abstract state of Existence not conscious of itself, but a supreme & self-aware One who exists — absolutely in Himself, infinitely in the world & with an appearance of the finite in His various manifestations in the world.

God in Himself apart from all world manifestation or realisable relation to world manifestation is called the Paratpara Brahman, & is not knowable either to the knowledge that analyses or the knowledge that synthetically conceives. We can neither say of Him that He is personal or impersonal, existence or non-existence, pure or impure, Atman or unAtman. We can only say to every attempt to define Him positively or negatively, neti neti, Not this, not this. We can pass into the Paratpara Brahman, but we cannot know the Paratpara Brahman.

God in the world is Brahman-Iswara-Atman, Prakriti or Shakti and Jiva. These are the three terms of His world-manifestation.

23

The One and the Many are both of them eternal aspects of the Absolute Parabrahman which is Itself neither one nor many in an exclusive sense. It is beyond unity and multiplicity in its essential truth as it is beyond all other oppositions, but neither unity nor multiplicity, neither the One nor the Many are illusions, they are both of them truths of the Absolute, otherwise they could have no existence nor could they come into existence. The world is a manifestation, and in it the absolute Parabrahman manifests as the Ishwara, the one Eternal, but also It manifests the multiplicity of the One in the Jiva. This creates in the manifestation the double aspect of Being and Becoming. But becoming does not mean that Being becomes what it never was before or that it ceases to be its eternal self; it manifests something that is already in its existence, a truth, a power, an aspect of itself; only the forms are temporal and can be deformed by the Ignorance. The Power of itself which thus manifests what is in its being is its Shakti, Maya or Prakriti, three names for the same thing. It is called Prakriti when it is seen in its executive aspect as working out the manifestation for the Purusha or Ishwara.

Whether we regard the soul that manifests in a body as a portion of the Divine, eternal therefore like the Divine, as is held by the Gita, or the Divine himself in his aspect of multiplicity, or a separate being dependent on the Divine, as is held by the dualists, or an illusory self-perception of the soul subject to Maya, the reality being the Divine himself, indivisible and ever unmanifested — one thing is certain that what appears as the Jiva is something unborn and eternal.

24

The self which we have to perfect, is neither pure atman which is ever perfect nor the ego which is the cause of imperfection, but the divine self manifested in the shifting stream of Nature.

Existence is composed of Prakriti & Purusha, the consciousness that sees and the consciousness that executes & formalises what we see. The one we call Soul, the other Nature. These are the first double term from which our Yoga has to start. When we come to look in at ourselves instead of out at the world and begin to analyse our subjective experience, we find that there are two parts of our being which can be, to all appearance, entirely separated from each other, one a consciousness which is still & passive and supports, and the other a consciousness which is busy, active & creative, and is supported. The passive & fundamental consciousness is the Soul, the Purusha, Witness or Sakshi; the active & superstructural consciousness is Nature, Prakriti, processive or creative energy of the Sakshi. But the two seem at first to stand apart & distinct, as if they had no share in each other.

The Purusha, still & silent witness of whatever Prakriti chooses to create, not interfering with her works, but reflecting only whatever forms, names & movements she casts on the pure mirror of his eternal existence and the Prakriti restlessly creating, acting, forming & effecting things for the delight of the Purusha, compose the double system of the Sankhyas. But as we continue analysing their relations and accumulate more and more experience of our subjective life, we find that this seeing of the Purusha is in effect a command. Whatever Prakriti perceives it to be the pleasure of the Purusha to see, she tends to preserve in his subjective experience or to establish; whatever she perceives it to be his pleasure to cease to see, she tends to renounce & abolish. Whatever he consents to in her, she forces on him & is glad of her mastery & his submission, but whenever he insists, she is bound eventually to obey. Easily found to be true in our subjective experience, this ultimate principle of things is eventually discovered by the Yogin to determine even objective phenomena. The Purusha & Prakriti are therefore not only the Witness & the Activity witnessed, but the Lord & his executive energy. The Purusha is Ishwara, the Prakriti is His shakti. Their play with each other is both the motive & the executive force of all existence in the universe.

25

The Divine is the eternal Self and Spirit; but Nature too is everlasting power of the Self, eternal conscious-Force of the Spirit.

Mind, life and Matter are powers of that Power, energies of that Force, substance of that Spirit, Spirit and Matter are not separate and contrary creations, but Matter itself is a self-creation of the Spirit.

Being and Becoming are the single One. The One does not become the Many, but the One is for ever the Many even as the Many are for ever the One.

This by a self-existent self-knowledge thou shalt know, through a supramental knowledge by identity — the problem, the opposition, the shifts of philosophy, the rifts of Science, the fragmentary upliftings of Religion are the devices of a still ignorant consciousness, a [. . .] seeking knowledge.

26

All existence is one in the Reality; manifold in its manifestation of the Reality. The Reality is the Absolute, the Spirit, the Self, the Being, the One-Existence, which is all and everywhere, but which is also more than all and nowhere. This One can be all because it is no one in particular, it can be all-pervading and eternal in its essence because it is not bound by Space or by Time. It is One but it is also multitudinous, its multitudes are the self-expression, not the denial, the abundance, not the division or fragmentation of its oneness. Each being of its multitudes seems to be a portion of the One, a finite of the Infinite, a time-face and time-form of the Eternal; but in and behind this appearance is the Reality, and there each is itself the One displaying something of itself, each is the Infinite in a finite phenomenon of itself, each is the Eternal playing in Time. But Time too is eternal, Time is eternity in extension and movement, therefore each is in its reality an eternal being of the Eternal, an infinite of the Infinite, a spirit of the One spirit, a self of the One Self. For the Reality is beyond our oppositions of one and many; its oneness and its multitude are for ever inherent in each other; yet it is bound neither by its unity nor its multiplicity, though both are true, because it is that of which both are intimate aspects, — it is the Absolute.

27

God is not a Being who creates & governs the universe, but the universe itself & all besides that is Timeless & Spaceless.

God is also a Being who creates the universe in Himself & governs it; for the universe is only one term of His existence. If one could conceive a centre that contains its own circle, we might have a just definition of God in the universe.

What is the Impersonality of God? It is the fact of the Is Not, the Is & the Becoming. And what is the personality of God? It is the fact that all this, the Is like the Becoming, the Is not like the Is, is aware of itself in Time & Space & beyond them.

The Impersonality of Love is a self-existent Delight which embraces, possesses & makes one in being all that manifests in Brahman. The Personality of Love is One who is aware of self-Delight & extends His Love in all creatures.

Personality & Impersonality are the same reality differently conceived by Knowledge. Ego is the consciousness of the One Infinite Personality reflected in a limiting form of consciousness & distorted by the limitation. The form itself is a face of the All which has forgotten in the succession of Time moments, in the coherence of Space-units all that is behind itself & involved in itself. Ego is a bridge by which it awakes to self-Ignorance & returns towards self-Knowledge.

If we stand on the bridge facing the world of Forms we tend towards the Relative; if we face away from them we tend towards the Absolute. It is only when we have crossed the bridge that we can easily & perfectly embrace the Relative in the Absolute.

Spirit & Matter, Pure Being & Being formally extended in Space are the two poles of the universe. In Spirit there is no ego; in substance of Matter there is no ego. In each pole ego loses itself, but in Spirit through synthesis, in Matter through dissolution.

Substance of matter, life & mind are the material which Ego uses to develop its conscious existence; there are higher infinite affirmations in which it fulfils its conscious existence.

There is a unity of essence & a unity of sum. The latter is only a synthetic formula & affirmation of multiplicity. The unity of essence is the true unity.

Unity & multiplicity are necessary to each other & one reality. Multiplicity is unity extended in its possibility; unity is multiplicity self-gathered into its essence[.]

28

The infinite Being in rest aware of its own eternal oneness. There is the everlasting silence of the Absolute.

The infinite Conscious Power in movement aware of its own eternal many-ness — the everlasting movement and creation of the Supreme.

As in the immobile ether arises, first sign of the creative impulse of Nature, vibration, Shabda, and this vibration is a line of etheric movement, is ether contacting ether in its own field of mobile self-force and that primal stir is sufficient to initiate all forms and forces, even such is the original movement of the Infinite.

But this vibration is not the stir of any material force or substance and this contact is not material contact. This is a vibration of consciousness in spiritual essence; this is the contact of consciousness with itself in spiritual substance.

This original movement, not original or first in Time, for it was from ever and continues for ever, but original in that action of consciousness which is an eternal repetition of all things in an eternal present. Or, if you will, an eternal past-present-future, the three simultaneous times of that ever packed Time of the Infinite that translates [to] our blind finite conception as the void timelessness of the Absolute.

29

All existence and all force proceeds from the One Supreme and all works of whatever being or whatever force are movements of the Universal and take place in the Eternal and Infinite.

The Supreme is not manifest to our minds encased in matter; numberless superphysical planes separate our terrestrial consciousness from all direct touch of our Source, and there can be no question of an unveiled immediate intimate presence and guidance of that Ineffable. And yet the Divine Consciousness and Force, the everlasting Chitshakti, the original Power, the transcendent and eternal Mother, because she holds the Supreme concealed in her, can put us into some kind of touch with that inexpressible Glory and communicate to us a highest Will and its consequence. This cannot be done through the mind; for the thinking mind can only form some inadequate and quite abstract conception of an Absolute or a supreme Person or an impersonal Principle or Presence. And even the higher mind that experiences returns only a pale reflection of Sachchidananda which it takes for that Ineffable or a vague sense of the Eternal or the Infinite. It cannot lay hold upon That and it cannot enter, for if it tries, either that vanishes from it or itself it disappears in a featureless trance, extinction, annihilation, void or dissolution, nirvikalpa samadhi, nirvana, vinasha, shunya, laya. But what the mind cannot do, the soul and a great secret Overmind [can.]

To the earth-mind God does not exist or is only a mental idea, an emotional [   ] or the Life-mind's projection and self-image[.]

30

Chitshakti not mind has created the world. Chitshakti is the thing which the Scientists call in its various aspects Force & Energy, but it is no material Force or Energy, it is the divine power of self-conscious Being forming itself not materially, not in substance of matter but in the substance of that self-consciousness into these images of form and force which make up the world. What we call world, is a harmony of things seen not by the individual mind or even by universal mind, but rather seen through universal mind, as through a reflecting medium, by the Eye of divine Being. The eye that sees is immaterial, the things seen are immaterial; for matter itself is only a form, image & appearance of eternal Spirit.

31

How, it is asked, do we make a permanent and changeless world out of a world of changing and transient objects? But this is to create a problem where there is none. We do nothing of the kind; what we do is to perceive by the senses a world of stability in constant motion, of sameness in spite of change. It is the world that is like that; we do not make it so; our senses receive, they do not create; if there is an error in their perceptions or images it is a passive imperfection of sensing that causes the wrong or altered image, it is not a willed and dynamic change like the liberties the artist takes with Nature.

Men are always changing, but man has a permanent character which does not alter. Tigers differ from each other and from themselves in the process of time, but the tiger is always the same animal and always as such recognisable. It is the details that vary and change, the type, the fundamental pattern is constant. So far our senses and our mind standing upon their data do not betray or deceive us. If they see a world that is stable and the same in spite of constant mobility and mutation, it is because the world is like that and it is therefore that we have to see it so and cannot see it otherwise. If there is a problem it is not what we make of it, not a problem of our psychology but why it is so, what is behind the mobility of the world and its stability, what is the cause or the significance or reality of it. There is no doubt the problem of what are mind and sense and their nature, their reality, their relation to the world and its cause or significance; but that too is a problem of metaphysics.

Are there then two worlds, the one changing and existing in time, the other changeless and eternal? Or are there rather two ways of knowing one and the same world? These questions, as they are put, are meaningless; for it is obvious that it is one world we are seeing and not two and that objects here belong to the same universe and not to two different universes at the same time. It cannot be the truth that man belongs to one world and men in their mutability to another or that in seeing the changes and variations of the species tiger we are seeing the world in one way and when we see the persistence of type of the species we are knowing it in a different way. These artificial problems are the result of looking at words and concepts instead of things; we concentrate on the words and concepts "sameness" and "change", see that they represent as abstractions ideas that stand opposed to each other, imagine that they are as opposed in fact as in our minds, are incompatible and therefore cannot coexist in the same world or cannot be true at the same time or in the same world-perception. As a matter of fact there is no such incompatibility; something that is permanently the same may be in constant change of its details of existence without losing its constant fundamental sameness. There is no reason why something should not be transient (not therefore unreal) in many of its phenomena, yet permanent in itself, in its being, whether that permanence be only a duration in time or eternal. No doubt, two worlds may meet, world of mind or spirit enter into world of Matter, but then their elements combine into one world, a world let us say of mind-informed or spirit-governed Matter; it is not two separate worlds that we are seeing at the same time and confusing together by the erroneous action of our mind and senses. Our souls, our minds may belong by origination to the mind world or spirit world, but here they are in the same world as the changing life and body and in so seeing it, we make no error.

32

A philosophy of change?[1] But what is change? In ordinary parlance change means passage from one condition to another and that would seem to imply passage from one status to another status. The shoot changes into a tree, passes from the status of

---

[1] *These notes were written apropos of Bergson's "philosophy of change"; "you" below would refer to a proponent of this philosophy.*

shoot to the status of tree and there it stops; man passes from the status of young man to the status of old man and the only farther change possible to him is death or dissolution of his status. So it would seem that change is not something isolated which is the sole original and eternal reality, but it is something dependent on status, and if status were non-existent, change also could not exist. For we have to ask, when you speak of change as alone real, change of what, from what, to what? Without this "what" change could not be.

Change is evidently the change of some form or state of existence from one condition to another condition. Otherwise, what is it? Is it itself fundamental and absolute, not explicable or definable by any other term than itself, perceivable and intelligible as the sole reality by a naked intuition which feels and cries out "Change = reality" and then falls dumb and can say no more?

An object changes, a person changes, a condition of things changes. But can it be said that the object is no real object but only a continuity of change, or that a person is not a person but a continuity of change, a condition of things is not a condition and there are no things but there is only a continuity of change? This seems to be an illustration of the besetting sin of metaphysics — to exalt a word into a reality or an idea into a reality — without fathoming what is the reality which it tries to indicate. For to label with a word or name is not to fathom and to define, to erect a concept is not to fathom. Fathom for us then what is change before you ask us to accept it as the only reality. You may say I have fathomed it, I have seen it to be the one constant real, but do not ask me to define what it is; "listen rather in silence to the silence of Nature and you too will fathom". But what if, so listening, I fathom other realities than change — let us say, immutable being as well as mutable force, status as well as change? To prevent that you plunge into speech and not silence, into dialectics of the intellect instead of the undebatable certitudes of intuition, and so abandon your own methodology. If intuition alone is to be used, then you must give a place to my intuition as well as yours and all, however contradictory in appearance must stand until a greater intuition comes in to put all in their place, reconcile, include in a consistent whole.

In the world of our experience contradictories [are] often complements and necessary to each other's existence. Change is possible only if there is a status from which to change; but status again exists only as a step that pauses, a step in the continuous passage of change or a step on which change pauses before it passes on to another step in its creative passage. And behind this relation is a duality of eternal status and eternal motion and behind this duality is something that is neither status nor change but contains both as its aspects — and That is likely to be the true Reality.

Existence, Consciousness-Force, Bliss

33

The nature of the Eternal is infinite Being, the nature of Being is Self-Awareness and all-Awareness or Consciousness, the nature of conscious Being is conscious Force aware of its self and its action, the nature of conscious self-awareness is infinite Bliss[.]

34

Identity is the first truth of existence; division is the second truth; all division is a division in oneness. There is one Existence which looks at itself from many self-divided unities observing other similar and dissimilar self-divided unities by the device of division.

Being is one; division is a device or a secondary condition of consciousness; but the primary truth of consciousness also is a truth of oneness and identity. One consciousness organised in many self-divided unities of consciousness is the subjective nature of existence.

The objective side of consciousness is force, because consciousness is a power of being. The eternal primary action of this force is to make for its own consciousness forms or figures of its being.

All force is inherently conscious force. Inhabiting and supporting every individual or universal form of being there is and must be some conscious power of being. But conscious force has the faculty of absorbing itself in its works and forms; there is in consciousness the power of self-oblivion. This self-oblivion is the primary phenomenon of material existence. But as [in] the sleeping or unconscious or self-oblivious man there is a subliminal self which neither sleeps nor forgets itself nor is unconscious, so in what appears to [be] inconscient form worked by an inconscient force or power of being there is, discoverable by extending knowledge, such a conscious power and that must be part of the conscious force of being of the one existence.

The nature of being aware of itself, in possession of all its consciousness and force is the inherent delight of its own existence. For experience shows that all complete possession of self is delight, only imperfection of possession creates imperfection or apparent absence of delight. But the one existence takes an equal delight in all the universal forms and figures of its own being, and this delight is the cause and support of universal and individual existence. For this reason all creation also and all action of force has secretly or overtly delight or a seeking for delight or [?some] attraction as its first motive cause, although the apparent object or aim of the action may seem to be of a different character.

These truths do not appear entirely to us because we start from division but they become self-evident when we get to a larger consciousness open to the conscious unity underlying things or one with the one conscious existence.

The One Existence whether we call it or him God, Brahman, Purusha or by some other name is in its or his nature infinite existence aware of itself and its own eternal bliss of existence. Or speaking less in terms of division and analysis it is one existence, consciousness, bliss in an inalienable unity.

35

The object and condition of Life is Ananda; the means of Ananda is Tapas; the nature of Tapas is Chit; the continent and basis of Chit is Sat. It is therefore by a process of Sat developing its own Ananda through Tapas which is Chit that the Absolute appears as the extended, the eternal as the evolutionary, Brahman as the world. He who would live perfectly must know Life, he who would know Life, must know Sacchidananda.

Pleasure is not Ananda; it is a half-successful attempt to grasp at Ananda by means which ensure a relapse into pain. Therefore it is that pleasure can never be an enduring possession. It is in its nature transient and fugitive. Pain itself is obviously not Ananda; neither is it in itself anything positive, real and necessary. It has only a negative reality. It is a recoil caused by the inability to command pleasure from certain contacts which becomes habitual in our consciousness and, long ingrained in it, deludes us with the appearance of a law. We can rise above transitory pleasure; we can get rid of the possibility of pain.

Pleasure, therefore, cannot be the end & aim of life; for the true object and condition of Life is Ananda and Ananda is something in its nature one, unconditioned and infinite. If we make pleasure the object of life, then we also make pain the condition of life. The two go together and are inseparable companions. You cannot have one for your bed-fellow without making a life-companion of the other. They are husband and wife and, though perpetually quarrelling, will not hear of divorce.

But neither is pain the necessary condition of life, as the Buddhists say, nor is extinction of sensation the condition of bliss.

36

The world lives in and by Ananda. From Ananda, says the Veda, we were born, by Ananda we live, to Ananda we return, and it adds that no man could even have the strength to draw in his breath and throw it out again if there were not this heaven of Bliss embracing our existence as ether embraces our bodies, nourishing us with its eternal substance and strength and supporting the life and the activity. A world which is essentially a world of bliss — this was the ancient Vedantic vision, the drishti of the Vedic drashta, which differentiates Hinduism in its early virility from the cosmic sorrow of Buddhism and the cosmic disillusionment of Mayavada. But it is possible to fall from this Bliss, not to realise it with the lower nature, in the Apara Prakriti, not to be able to grasp and possess it. Two things are necessary for the fullness of man's bliss, — the fullness of his being and the fullness of his knowledge creating by their union the fullness of his strength in all its manifestations, viryam, balam, bhrajas, tejas, ojas. For Ananda, Sat & Chit make one reality, and Chit is in its outward working pure force to which our Rishis gave the name of Tapas. To attain even here upon earth this fullness of bliss dependent upon fullness of existence, illumination and force, must always be humanity's drift, man's collective endeavour. To attain it within himself here and beyond, iha ca amutra ca, must always be the drift of the human unit, the individual's endeavour. Wherever the knowledge in him thinks it can grasp this bliss, it will fix its heaven. This is Swarga, Vaikuntha, Goloka; this is Nirvana.

37

The bliss of the Brahman can be described as the eternity of an uninterrupted supreme ecstasy. There is no opposition or incompatibility between these two states in the nature of the Brahman. Bliss there is the keen height and core of peace; peace there is the intimate core and essence of bliss. There is no turbidity or turbulence in the being of the Brahman; its ineffable poignancy is eternal in its self-poise.

The essential mark of the descent of the consciousness from its highest grade in the supreme spirit is the constant diminution of the power of Sachchidananda, the intensity of its force, force of being, force of consciousness, force of bliss. The intensity of all these three in the supreme status is ineffable;

in the Supermind the intensity of consciousness is ever luminous and undiminished; in overmind it is already diminished and diffuse; the highest intensity of mind is a poor thing in comparison with the splendour of overmind, and so it goes diminishing till it reaches an apparent zero which we call inconscience.

The degree and amount of pain which mind, life and body can bear is by our human standards considerable; but their capacity for pleasure is very limited and pale in its intensity, low in its degree. What we call ecstasy would seem to a god to be ridiculously thin and vapid and edgeless. Its capacity of duration also is pitifully brief and measurable by the moments.

38

In experience even on the spiritual plane so long as we do not transcend the spirit in mind, there is a difference between peace and Ananda. Peace is the Divine static, Ananda the Divine dynamic. Peace is a negative-positive; it is positive of itself, of status, of eternity, of the essential, of the abstract-concrete, of force in rest. It is or tends to be negative of all that is less than itself, contradictory to itself or more than itself, of the dynamic, of action, of creation, of time and happening, of the substantial concrete, of force in motion. Or when it allows these things or even feels or supports them, it is with a certain disinterested separateness. It has essentially the character of the Witness Spirit or at the most of the disinterested Witness-Creator. Ananda is in its every fibre a positive of positives. It affirms and rejoices in all that is native to peace, but it affirms too and rejoices in all that peace negates or regards with a sovereign separateness. Ananda is an all embracing and creative force. There can be in the world's tangle of conflicting forces an Ananda of pain and suffering and in the full manifestation pain and suffering no longer remain themselves but are transformed into Ananda. But these opposing differences prove in the end to be part of the separative mental creation, the disjunctive Maya in which we live. In supermind experience peace is always full of Ananda and by its Ananda can act and create; Ananda is for ever full of the divine peace and its most vehement ecstatic intensity contains no possibility of disturbance. At the height of the supramental Infinite peace and Ananda are one. For there status and dynamis are inseparable, rest and action affirm each other, essence and expression are one indivisible whole.

39

One that is Two that are Many, — this is the formula of the eternal and timeless manifestation in the worlds of Sachchidananda.

One who is Two and becomes the Two who become Many, — this is the formula of the perpetual manifestation in time in the three worlds of Mind, Life and Matter.

One who is in himself for ever the Two and for ever innumerably All and Eternal and Infinite, this is the indication of the Supreme who is beyond Time and Timelessness in the highest Absolute.

*

The One is Four for ever in his supramental quaternary of Being, Consciousness, Force and Ananda.

Brahma, Vishnu, Shiva, Krishna, these are the eternal Four, the quadruple Infinite.

Brahma is the Eternal's Personality of Existence; from him all is created, by his presence, by his power, by his impulse.

Vishnu is the Eternal's Personality of Consciousness; in him all is supported, in his wideness, in his stability, in his substance.

Shiva is the Eternal's Personality of Force; through him all is created, through his passion, through his rhythm, through his concentration.

Krishna is the Eternal's Personality of Ananda; because [of] him all creation is possible, because of his play, because of his delight, because of his sweetness.

Brahma is Immortality, Vishnu is Eternity, Shiva is Infinity; Krishna is the Supreme's eternal, infinite, immortal self-possession, self-issuing, self-manifestation, self-finding.

Manifestation, Not Illusion

40

As earth when it becomes pot, floor or oven, never ceases to be earth, so the Being even though it becomes all things and persons, is ever and immutably the same.

Becoming does not cancel Being; after millions of events in a million universes have passed in the Infinite, its infinity remains the same for ever.

The Mayavadins fix their definition, their rigid iti to the Parabrahman, the Absolute, and say that since it is that, it can never be anything else and therefore the world must be an illusion. But the Absolute is beyond all definitions, descriptions, qualifications, he is [not] bound by them, neither by features nor featurelessness, by unity nor multiplicity[.]

41

It is said by certain Adwaitists with an unusual largeness of philosophic toleration that the views of all other philosophies are true on the way or at least useful and mark stages in the realisation of the Truth, but the highest realisation is the truth of Monistic Adwaita — there is only the One and nothing else. This concession comes to nothing; for it means that other spiritual experiences are only temporarily helpful delusions or helpful half truths and the only true truth is Adwaita. The dispute remains; for all the other schools also will claim theirs as the highest truth. The mind cannot arrive at a perfect toleration, because the mind needs a cut and defined truth opposed or superior to all others. In the supermind, the aspect of the One is true like all other aspects; all are equally true but none solely true.

42

The position taken up by the Illusionists must first be firmly stated; for often there is a great nebulousness in the minds both of its supporters and antagonists which leaves room for much confused thinking and the real issue, the vital point gets obscured. We must first give this admission to the defence for whatever it is worth, that Illusionism does not affirm the absolute non-existence of the universe but only that it is an existence which is in its beginning and its end a non-existence and in its middle it is an existence which amounts to non-existence. It is real while it lasts to the mind that creates it; but it is not really real, — it is only phenomenally existent, like a dream, like a hallucination, like the imaginations of a person in delirium. Three questions arise from this proposition. Is this hallucinatory creation of the universe a truth or is the theory itself a hallucination of the logical mind or of the experiencing consciousness? Secondly, if true, how does the illusion come about and how is it possible? Thirdly, who is the victim of the hallucination?

The whole theory arises from and turns on one original proposition of which it is the logical consequence. It is this that Brahman the one real, original and eternal existence is, firstly, self-existent, secondly, featureless and relationless, thirdly, unmodifiable, immutable, incapable therefore of developing feature and relation, fourthly, solely existent, for there is and can be nothing else but that in existence. None of these original positions about the Brahman imposes itself irrefutably upon the intellect; there are philosophies which deny them one and all and with quite as good a show of logic as any the logical apparatus of the Mayavada can furnish us. In fact, what we first see as the one experience of our consciousness is not this at all, but just the opposite. We see that every thing reduces itself not to an existence at all, but to a continuity of the action of Force, Karma as the Buddhists call it. We see that this action of Force exists only by an infinite flux of feature and relation, the stream of the Buddhist figure. Apart from that it is nothing, it is the Buddhist sunya or Nihil, and the reduction of the universe to

Nature: The World-Manifestation

its original starting point, the escape out of it is not a return to the self-existent, but a return to Nihil, a Nirvana or extinction. Far, then, from being immutable and incapable of modification, it is in its very nature a constant modification and mutation. Eliminate the stream of becoming and the result is not Being, but a zero. This is the difficulty which the Mayavada has to surmount, the logic which it has to refute.

For it cannot be denied that the universe, the thing from which all our conscious experience starts, is such a constant stream of becoming, a round of mutations and modifications, a mass of features and relations. The question is how is it maintained? what is [it] that gives an appearance of permanence to the impermanent, of stability to the unstable, of a sum of eternal sameness in which all the elements of the sum are in constant instability and all capable of mutation? The Buddhist admits that it is done by an action of consciousness, by idea and association, vijnana, sanskara; but ideas and associations are themselves Karma, action of Force, themselves impermanent, only they create an appearance of permanence, by always acting in the same round, creating the same combination of forms and elements, as the flame and stream appear always the same, though that which constitutes them is always impermanent. The modern Materialist says that it is material Force or an eternal Energy which takes the form of Matter and follows always the same inherent law of action. The Mayavadin says on the contrary that it is Consciousness, but a consciousness which is in its reality immutable and unmodifiable self-existence, only it produces a phenomenon of constant modification and mutation. How is this possible? There lies the riddle, for it is a direct self-contradiction. To escape from it, he alleges that the phenomenon has no reality at all, but is an illusion.

To deal with this theory at all, we have first to admit that consciousness is the cause and continent of the universe and that it exists only in consciousness and not at all in itself. How does he [*the Mayavadin*] propose to prove it? It is by an appeal to reason and experience. Our reason tells us that we have no knowledge of the existence of the universe except by our conscious mentality, no possibility of knowing it; the universe can only be allowed to exist by a consciousness admitting its existence, supporting it by its assent. If by any chance, law or process our consciousness can cease finally to be aware of the universe, then so far as we are concerned, the universe no longer exists; it is annulled to us, it was an illusion from which we are released, as when a dream or hallucination ceases. Any such final upshot proves that originally also the universe was non-existent, for otherwise, if it had existed for us eternally without beginning, it would also continue for us eternally without end. But even if it ceases for us, it still continues in existence, is capable of being observed and lived in by others. How is that? We must suppose, that since it exists cosmically, its existence must be admitted and supported by the assent of a universal consciousness by which and for which it is or rather seems to be. Well, if by any chance, law or process this universal consciousness ceases finally to be aware of the universe, then the universe no longer exists for anybody or anything at all; it is proved to be an utter illusion, existent phenomenally only so long as the universal consciousness admitted it, but capable of coming to an end and therefore shown to be non-existent in its beginning and in its end non-existent. Now our ultimate experience is that there is a last and highest state of consciousness in which the universe does thus cease for the individual to be. What is that state? It is samadhi, a trance of consciousness in which the sole experience is thus expressed, "I am in bliss" and the sole memory brought back is "I was in bliss." In this state the universe has for the individual no existence; he is released from it. Therefore this highest state of experience is one of which only three things can be affirmed, existence, consciousness of existence, bliss of the consciousness of existence; but it is a pure existence without other feature or any relation. But how is this proved to be the ultimate state of our conscious being? Well, it is the knowledge of the sages who have entered into it that it is the ultimate state, it is the knowledge left behind them that they have finally passed away into it not to return to consciousness of the phenomenal world, and it is confirmed by the authority of the Veda. Reason tells us that such a condition must be the ultimate condition, since it is one infinitely beyond the phenomenal and to which the phenomenal arrives by self-elimination, and being the ultimate it must be also the original: the phenomenal which disappears from it, must originally have been imposed on it. There is no rational escaping from that conclusion.

Well, the individual soul can escape from consciousness of the universe, but what of the universal consciousness? For so long as the universe goes on existing — and who shall say that it is not for all eternity? — this escape may only prove that the individual soul goes into a state of unconsciousness or absorbed self-consciousness, like a man going to sleep or falling into a trance, while the world goes on around him just as before essentially unaffected and not at all annulled by his unconsciousness of it. But in the first place this highest power of the individual consciousness cannot be peculiar to it, for it must be a power of the general and universal; the individual reflects the universal, for it is only the law of the universal that can be repeated with individual modifications in the law of the individual. Secondly, the universal soul is the same in all; for that is the experience of the highest knowledge and consciousness, that there [is] one self in all, featureless, immutable, unmodifiable, the same amidst all the changes of phenomena. As this self can draw back that which supports the individual into it, so it is and must be capable of drawing back that which supports the universal. In one case the stream of phenomena centred around its individual reflection ceases, in the other the stream of phenomena centred around its universal reflection. A theory only? But it is justified by reason acting on our total experience which sees the lower or phenomenal and the higher or eternal and sees how the phenomenal disappears, vanishes away from the face of the eternal.

We have then as a fact a supreme state of existence which is self-existent, the original I am, which is featureless bliss and consciousness of being, immutable, eternal and this seems to be common to all beings, secret in all, the real self of all. But what then of the world? It is a mass of constant modifications of consciousness and being, itself in its nature modification of consciousness or of being or of both. It cannot be a modification of nothing, it must be a modification of something. If consciousness and being are the first fact, real, eternal, is it not a modification of conscious being, of this real, this eternal something, and itself therefore real? Is it not itself eternal, an eternal continuity of modification, uninterrupted continual or else interrupted and recurringly continual? Must we not then suppose two states of the Brahman, a primary state of eternal unmodified being, a secondary state of eternal continuity of modifications of being, becomings of the Brahman? Does not the Vedantic statement that all comes from the Brahman, exists by it, returns to it, imply that all is eternally contained in it and all are modifications of it? In that case, we cannot say that the Eternal Being is absolutely unmodifiable. No, says the Illusionist, the supreme eternal self is not only unmodified, but unmodifiable and nothing else but the eternal unmodifiable self exists really: all else is seeming. How then do all these modifications come about? What is the clue to this mystery, the cause of this magic of illusion?

Maya, answers the Illusionist. And what is Maya? It is a power of the eternal consciousness of Brahman by which there comes about an apparent modification of consciousness of which all these modifications we call the universe are the outcome. The modification is apparent, not real, yet a fact, unreally, non-existently existent. Maya exists, yet does not exist; and its results too are apparent, not real, yet while Maya lasts, they are a fact we have to deal with, unreally, non-existently existent. We have to escape from them, by escaping from Maya. We do not understand. How can the unmodifiable consciousness undergo at all even an apparent modification, to say nothing of such portentous results of the modification? To that there is no explanation, there can be no explanation. It takes place beyond the intellect, before the intellect can at all exist and cannot be understood by the intellect; it must be accepted as a fact; it is a fact that Maya is, it is a fact that Maya can be escaped from, and therefore not being eternal, is transient, is unreal, is not. To see this and escape is our only business. Only while it lasts, are we concerned with the modifications. But what is meant by saying while it lasts and who is it that is subject to it and escapes from it? Is it Brahman who is subject to Maya? No, Brahman the eternally unmodifiable consciousness aware only of the bliss of its self-existence cannot be subject to Maya, does not behold this phenomenal illusion. For if he did, we returning into that, should also behold it and could not by the returning escape from it. It is the individual soul only that is subject to Maya and escapes from it. But who is this individual soul? Is it the self in the individual, the Jivatman, and is the self in the individual different from the eternal Self? No, the individual self is the eternal Brahman, for there is only one self and not many. But then the Jivatman also cannot be subject to Maya or escape from it. There is then nobody subject to it, nobody who escapes. And really that is so, says the illusionist, but what seems to us now to be the individual self, is a reflection of the eternal Self in the mind, and it is that which is subject to Maya and suffers by it. But what then is Mind? It is a result of Maya, it is an illusory movement of consciousness, it is that for which and by which the universe exists. Get rid of its action, its movement, and the illusion will cease; you will be free. But then again who is this you? If I am really the eternal, then I, the individual do not exist; my real self, to use a desperately foolish language, — since that means an individual in possession of a self which cannot be, as my individuality is an illusion, — my real self is in eternal bliss and not being affected cannot care whether this false, nonexistently existent I is bound or escapes, suffers or is in bliss. To whom then does it matter? Only to Maya and mind. Well, then, it is an affair between Maya and mind, and they can settle it between themselves. Precisely, the Illusionist will reply; to you, the mental being, it does matter because you are in Maya, you suffer, however phenomenally, however unreally, and the only way to get rid of it is to abolish Maya by abolishing yourself, your mental individuality, her result by which alone she exists; then you will not exist, Maya and the world will exist for other mental beings; but you will undergo extinction in the Brahman, for you Brahman only will exist. How for me, since I can only be either in Maya or out of it, either individually aware of Maya and not of my real self or else non-existent individually? How can 'I' be aware of my real self only and of nothing else? It is possible; for as the mind falsely reflects Brahman by Maya as the individual, so free from Maya, it can truly reflect Brahman and it ceases to be individual mind, although in an individual body it still seems to be individually released. Really, it is Brahman expelling Maya from the consciousness, then the mind is taken up into Samadhi, extinguished in Samadhi, and this is the [?prefatory] sign. Fix your mind upon that, look at things practically, and do not ask inconsistent questions, as to how there can be individual salvation when there is no individual self to be saved. These questions do not arise once the release is made, they arise in Maya which is a practical fact and can receive only a practical solution.

Well that is a kind of answer. But how am I to know that it is not an evasion of the difficulty? What if I say that really the unmodifiable Brahman is not the highest truth? that the Brahman is aware at once of his unmodified eternal self and of his eternally modified cosmic existence, Akshara and Kshara, but he is himself beyond both, and that my real way of escape is to be the same, to be aware of my eternal self and of all the universe as modifications of my self; that with this transcendence and universality comes perfect bliss, and that the fact that I, still existing in Maya, can be blissfully aware of one Self everywhere and of all things in the universe is a proof of my assertion? This seems to me at least as good a theory as your theory of Maya; and if you say, how is that possible, I can either allege reasons or answer like you, it is a supraintellectual fact and we have to take it as a fact and find the practical way of realising it. If you want me to reject it in favour of your theory, give me at least some help. Make me realise how the world can be nonexistently existent, how the unmodifiable can be apparently modified, how I can exist only beyond the world and yet exist in it so palpably that I must struggle to get out of it, how Brahman exists only beyond Maya and yet by me exists in Maya, how mind is the result of Maya, an instrument to see world and is yet capable of getting rid of Maya and seeing only the Brahman, how being by my individuality subject to Maya, and only able to escape by getting rid of my individuality, I am yet to become individually aware of Brahman and get an individual salvation, while all the rest of the world by which alone I am individual in my experience is still subject to it, how an unreal individual can realise Brahman.

The Mayavadin answers that as it is the Maya power of the Self which creates the ignorance in each individual, so it is the Self in each individual which enables him to have the knowledge by removing from him the Maya power. How this can be, can only be explained by analogies. As a man mistakes a rope for a snake, and then discovers it is a rope and there is no snake, so the mind thinks there is a world where there is only Brahman and discovers in the end that there is only Brahman; — or as a man mistakes mother of pearl for real pearl and runs after it and is then disillusioned and leaves it to go after the reality. As a pot is only a name and form of earth and earth is the only reality, so the world and the individual are only a name and form; break the pot, it will go back to its original earth; break the name and form in the consciousness, get rid of the individual, and there will be only Brahman in the consciousness. There are many golden ornaments, but the reality of them all is the gold; it is that alone which has value. So Brahman only is worth having; the rest is name and form and mere vanity. Or if these analogies seem to be only physical images not valid for a supraphysical fact, observe how you dream. The dream has no reality, yet is real to your consciousness while it lasts. The you in the dream is an unreal you; you awake to your real self. So the world is a dream; falling asleep to the world, the dream ceases; awake to the Brahman, the dream is convinced of unreality. That is the only possible and a quite sufficient answer.

Is it a sufficient answer? Does it prove the main point that the world consciousness is an apparent and unreal modification of the ever unmodifiable Brahman and therefore to be dispelled as quickly as possible, so that I may cease to exist, except insofar as I already eternally exist, not at all as I, but as the Brahman?

Above all, does it show that my one practical business is to get rid of a world consciousness which is of no value and has no purpose except self-bewilderment, and become again what I ought never to have ceased to be in my unreal consciousness, as indeed I am still that in my real consciousness, the featureless and immutable Spirit? Is the world really a valueless dream, a purposeless delirium of ignorance? Have we no other true spiritual business here except to get out of it? These are the real questions that the soul of man asks of the illusionist thinker, and we have to judge his answer.

43

Existence is not a fluke, a random creation by nobody, a thing that unaccountably happened to be. It carries in itself the Word of God, it is full of a hidden Divine Presence.

Existence is not a blind machine that somehow came and started a set ignoble motion without object or sense or purpose. Existence is a Truth of things unfolding by a gradual process of manifestation, an evolution of its own involved Reality.

Existence is not an illusion, a Maya that had no reason, no business to exist, could not exist, does not exist but only seems to be. A mighty Reality manifests in itself this marvellous universe.

44

All that is is the manifestation of a Divine Infinite. The universe has no other reason for existence.

There is an eternal manifestation and there is a temporal manifestation; both are without end or beginning even as That which manifests is without end or beginning. Time and its creations are for ever.

The temporal manifestation is cast partly in a gradation of enduring types; partly it moves through a long unrolling series of vicissitudes of change and new formation and is evolutionary in its process.

The typal worlds do not change. In his own world a god is always a god, the Asura always an Asura, the demon always a demon. To change they must either migrate into an evolutionary body or else die entirely to themselves that they may be new born into other Nature.

45

All that is is the manifestation, even as all that is not is the self-reservation, of a Supreme, an Infinite who veils himself in the play of impersonal forces, in the recesses of a mysterious Inconscience and will at last rediscover here his most intimate presence, his most integral power, light, beauty, Ananda and all vast and ineffable being through a growing illumination of the still ignorant consciousness now evolving in Matter, a consciousness of which Man is only one stage, at once the summit of an ascent that is finished and the starting point of a far greater ascension that is still only preparing its commencement.

All manifestation that is not evolution is a play and self-formulation of the One Infinite in one term or another of his existence, consciousness-force, Ananda, his self-knowledge, self-power, self-delight, for the glory, joy and beauty of the play and for no other reason.

All evolution is the progressive self-revelation of the One to himself in the terms of the Many out of the Inconscience through the Ignorance towards self-conscient perfection.

The evolution has a purpose, but it is a purpose in a circle. It is not a straight line or other figure of progression from the not to the is, from the less to the more.

There is no beginning or end of the Universe in space or time; for the universe is the manifestation of the Eternal and Infinite.

Manifestation is not an episode of the Eternal. It is his face and body of glory that is imperishable, it is the movement of his joy and power that needs not to sleep or rest as do finite things from their labour.

In the beginning, it is said, was the Eternal, the Infinite, the

One. In the middle, it is said, is the finite, the transient, the many. In the end, it is said, shall be the One, the Infinite, the Eternal.

For when was the beginning? At no moment in Time, for the beginning is at every moment; the beginning always was, always is and always shall be. The divine beginning is before Time and in Time and beyond Time for ever. The Eternal Infinite and One is an endless beginning.

And where is the middle? There is no middle; for the middle is only the junction of the perpetual end and the eternal beginning; it is the sign of a creation which is new at every moment. The creation was for ever, is for ever, shall be for ever. The eternal Infinite and One is the magical middle term of his own existence; it is he that is this beginningless and endless creation.

And when is the end? There is no end. At no conceivable moment can there be a cessation. For all end of things is the beginning of new things which are still the same One in an ever developing and ever recurring figure. Nothing can be destroyed for all is He who is for ever. The Eternal Infinite and One is the unimaginable end that is the never closing gate upon new interminable vistas of his glory.

Man and Superman

Man and the Evolutionary Process

46

Man is a transitional being, he is not final. He is a middle term of the evolution, not its end, crown or consummating masterpiece.

47

Man is not final, he is a transitional being. Beyond him awaits formation the diviner race, the superman.

48

God is the beginning, middle and end of all things; but in the beginning He is concealed, in the middle partly and progressively manifest, in the end revealed.

The universe is such a manifestation of God under certain conditions and in the terms of a gradually unfolding harmony. These conditions and the movements which govern the rhythms of the harmony are the universal laws.

In this manifestation the two terms are involution and evolution. The material universe starts from an involution of God in the movement of inconscient Force and the forms of inert Matter and it is impelled by the divine impulse within it to the evolution of God through the increasing manifestation of consciousness and conscious power which must culminate in a perfect and infinite self-knowledge, self-mastery and self-delight. By the involution we mean a self-concealing of the Divine in a descent of which the last rung is Matter, by the evolution a self-revealing of the Divine in an ascent of which the last rung is Spirit.

Since evolution or a gradual self-unfolding is the essential movement of the universe, the impulse of all life in the universe must be to self-fulfilment and the realisation of its utmost potentialities. Behind each form of life there is a divine idea which determines its form and its limits and the form circumscribes the potentialities of the life. Therefore the self-fulfilment of the life is contained within certain limits fixed by the nature of the life and the law of its being and action which that nature determines.

The idea which thus determines is the cause and the form which thus limits the sign of the Finite in the universe. The universe is an infinity creating innumerable finite expressions of itself in idea and form within its own infinite being. The one and infinite is the soul and reality of each finite; the multiple finite is the rhythm, movement and harmony of the infinite.

Therefore in and behind all finite life in the universe there is an infinite reality seeking to arrive at itself which must in its self-unfolding create finite forms of life which are yet able in their consciousness and movement to manifest and realise the infinite. Man is such a finite-infinite and the sole type of such a form of life that yet exists upon the earth.

49

All life and mind on earth is the story of a Being, a Consciousness, a Power, a Joy that is darkly imprisoned in the apparent inconscience of Matter and is struggling for liberation. Blinded, cabined, drugged, immured, it is yet ever striving to come out of the black cell of this obscurity into its own light, wideness, conscious sight and force, self-aware action, bliss, freedom, harmony, perfection. It starts with small beginnings, as a vibration in the metal, as a feeling out and drawing in and a groping and [?infusing] in the plant, as a crude or minute power of sensory life-urge rising to an instinctive reason and mind and purposeful force in the insect, as a more organised and conscious and emotional, even a roughly and narrowly thinking and planning vital being in the animal, and has persevered till it has broken into some half opening on itself in the thinking, reasoning, willing and aspiring nature of man, the Manu, the mental creature. Here at present it stands not by any means satisfied, but it would seem, feeling out for something more entirely itself, some supreme manhood or supermanhood, some beginning of godhead that would be at last its true self-finding and triumphant manifestation out of matter, even here in this limited and limiting earthly Nature.

This striving and slow outburst of Something that was hidden all along in Matter, in the Inconscient, is the whole sense of Evolution — not the mere development of a more and more organised living body out of protoplasm, as the scientists with their eyes fixed only or mainly on physical things would have it, but the struggle of Consciousness somnambulised in Matter to wake and free, find and possess itself more and more completely, the emancipation and slow self-revealing of a Soul secret at first in Force and Form, the growth of a Spirit.

This evolution, it is sometimes pretended, ends in man, man is the term and end; but this is because we miss the real values of the process. At first indeed we see this Spirit spending numberless millions of years to evolve a material system of worlds empty in the beginning of life, a lesser but vast enough series of millions to develop an earth on which life can inhabit, a lesser series of millions to make possible and train, raise life itself with but a feeble and restricted apparatus of mind; but once it has found a body, a brain, a living apparatus not perfect, but still sufficient it is no longer concerned mainly with evolving a body or [. . .] an embodied life but can at last grapple with its own proper business. Evolution henceforth means the evolution of the consciousness, of mind and, if any such thing there be, of what is beyond mind, — and in that case as its last stride has been the evolution of the mental being, man, out of the vital being, the animal, so its next stride will be to evolve out of mental man a greater spiritual and supramental creature.

50

All mind and life on earth are the progressive manifestation of a Spirit or Being that has involved itself in Matter and is slowly evolving in Matter, against the inconscient resistance of a first rigid material self-formation and under its conditions, its own secret powers and nature. In the Inconscience in which it has involved itself, these powers, this nature seem not only to be hidden but contradicted; cast into their own opposites they emerge with difficulty and labour at first in flickers and faint glimpses, then growing into a better but still much diminished figure. But the evolution cannot be considered at an end until these diminished figures growing more and more free, developed, powerful arrive at their own complete fulfilment, revelation of their truth, native perfection, beauty and greatness. This is the aim of terrestrial existence — to reveal in Matter, in Time-Space, in figure and body what was once self-held only in an eternal unembodied self and spirit.

In order that this evolution might be, an implacable plunge of supreme Consciousness and Being into an apparent void of insentience, inconscience, non-existence was inevitable; for without that plunge, immergence, seeming yet effective annihilation [in] its opposite the creation of that phenomenon of cosmic Energy which we call Matter would have been impossible. Yet however effective this appearance is only an appearance. In the void of that Non-Existence all the powers of being are held involved and latent; in the impenetrable darkness of that Inconscience all the possibilities of consciousness lie ready to be evolved; in that insentience is a drowned Delight of Existence which emerging in the contradictory figures of pleasure and pain can struggle upwards towards cosmic expression of its own truth of the Bliss that supports all things.

To ask why this plunge was taken at all, why such an evolution slow, gratuitous, painful should ever have been undertaken is natural for man struggling painfully with his own transience, ignorance and suffering — inevitable consequences of that plunge or fall — but from the cosmic point of view irrelevant and otiose. A possibility was there in the Infinite and outlined itself for manifestation, the lines of an evolutionary world amidst the numberless possibility or numbered reality of various universes, and it was undertaken because the Spirit in things is afraid of no possibility of itself but is rather ready to sanction all by its will towards manifest existence. To the Cosmic Spirit which sees things as a whole, the working out of this universe or any universe is self-justified, the obscure labour of the emergence no less than the glory of its completion and final perfection in a yet unattained light, bliss and greatness.

At any rate into this world of evolution something of the eternal spirit has thrown itself, with all in it that consented to the descent and to fulfil the world, not to escape from it, is the deepest meaning of the Spirit and Godhead within us and the universe.

This then must be our will in terrestrial existence — being mind in matter to grow into the Spirit, being man-animal to emerge into the Godhead, to expand out of our limited sense of existence into freedom and infinite wideness, out of the half figure of consciousness we have realised to be illumined into true consciousness, out of weakness to realise divine Mastery, out of the dual experience of pain and pleasure to emerge into possession of the cosmic Bliss of existence, out of the dull chrysalis of our limited selves to flower into oneness with the Divine Self that we are. For this is not an egoistic will in us but the meaning of the Divine Inhabitant for which he has undertaken bodily life and terrestrial existence.

51

Before there could be any evolution, there must needs be an involution of the Divine All that is to emerge. Otherwise there would be not an evolution, but a successive creation of things new, not contained in their antecedents, not their inevitable consequences or followers in a sequence but arbitrarily willed or miraculously conceived by an inexplicable

Chance, a stumblingly fortunate Force or an external Creator.

The long process of terrestrial formation and creation, the ambiguous miracle of life, the struggle of mind to appear and grow in an apparent vast Ignorance and to reign there as interpreter and creator and master, the intimations of a greater something that passes beyond the finite marvel of mind to the infinite marvels of the Spirit, are not a meaningless and fortuitous passing result of some cosmic Chance with its huge combination of coincidences; they are not the lucky play of some blind material Force. These things are and can be only because of something eternal and divine that concealed itself in energy and form of Matter.

The secret of the terrestrial evolution is the slow and progressive liberation of this latent indwelling spirit, the difficult appearance, the tardy becoming [of a] divine Something or Someone already involved with all its potential forces in a first formal basis of supporting substance, its greater slowly emerging movements locked up in one initial expressive power of Matter.

Man the thinker and seeker would not be here if he were not an embodied portion of an all-conscious Infinite that is superconscient above him but lies also hidden in the inconscience of the material universe.

The development of forms is not the most important or the most significant part of the evolutionary process; it is one sign of the thing that is being done, but it is not its essence. Material form is only a support and means for the progressive manifestation of the Spirit.

If all were chance or play of inconscient or inconsequent Force, there would be no reason why man with all his imperfections should not be the last word of this feat of unconscious intelligence or this haphazard miracle. It is because the Divine Spirit is there and his manifestation the meaning of the movement that a new power must emerge in the series that started from Matter.

The material universe would be a waste if wonderful desert

if Life had not appeared as the first index to some marvellous utility and an ultimate profound and moving significance. But life too by itself would be a movement without sequence to its purposeful initiation or any light to its own mystery if in Life there were not concealed an interpretative or at least a seeking power of consciousness that could turn upon its powers and try to grasp and direct them towards their own realised issue.

52

Our life is neither an accident nor a mechanism; it is not a freak of some wide-spread self-organising Chance, nor is it the result of a blind unaccountable material Necessity.

What we call Chance is a play of the possibilities of the Infinite; what we call Necessity is a truth of things working itself out in a Time-sequence of the Infinite.

It [*our life*] seems indeed to be born from a cosmic Inconscience which, pushed somehow towards world-building, does what it can or does what it must but in either case knows nothing of itself or of its own action. Yet is there a meaning in these workings, a conscious intention; our life is led by the will of some secret Being, secret perhaps within its own phenomenon, towards the solution of this packed cosmic Mystery, the unrolling of a willed and mighty Enigma.

What we see in and around us is a play of God, a "Lila". It is a scene arranged, a drama played by the One Person with his own multitudinous personalities in his own impersonal existence, — a game, a plan worked out in the vast and plastic substance of his own world-being. He plays with the powers and forces of his Nature a game of emergence from the inconscient Self out of which all here began, through the mixed and imperfect consciousness which is all we have now reached, towards a supreme consciousness, a divine nature.

This we cannot now know; our eyes are fixed on a partial outer manifestation which we see and call the universe — though even now we see and know very little of it or about it, know perhaps a few of its processes but nothing fundamental, nothing of its reality, — and an inner partial manifestation which we do not see but experience and feel and call ourselves. Our mind is shut up in a cleft between these two fragments and tends to regard it as the whole of things and the only tangible and real existence.

It is so that the frog regards himself and his well. But we have to grow out of this frog consciousness and exceed the limits of this well. In the end we come to perceive that we have a truer and divine being of which our petty personality is only a surface and corrupted output, a truer and divine Consciousness in which we must become self-aware and world-aware discarding our present fragmentary and bounded mental vision of self and things.[1]

The term of our destiny is already known to us; we have to grow from what we are into a more luminous existence, from pleasure and pain into a purer and vaster and deeper bliss, from our struggling knowledge and ignorance into a spontaneous and boundless light of consciousness, from our fumbling strength and weakness into a sure and all-understanding Power, from division and ego into universality and unity. There is an evolution and we have to complete it: a human animality or an animal humanity is not enough. We must pass from the inadequate figure of humanity into a figure of the Godhead, from mind to supermind, from the consciousness of the finite to the consciousness of the Infinite, from Nature into Supernature.

*

This is no vaulting imagination, but the inevitable outcome of our still unfulfilled being and incomplete nature, a necessity of the evolutionary world-urge: because things are what they are,

---

[1] *The following sentence from an earlier draft was not incorporated in the final version of this piece:*

  Our life is a journey towards the bliss of a vaster and happier existence, — not merely elsewhere in a far-off Paradise, but already here upon earth, *ihaiva*, in the terrestrial life and in an earthly [body.]

this too must be. For things are what they are, but not what they were; they cannot remain for ever what they are, but must grow into what they can be and shall be. And what they shall be can be nothing less than the exceeding of their present imperfection, the fullness of what they have only half become; but it may and must be something more than that, they must grow into their own concealed reality, their nature must reveal what is now concealed, their real self.

The perfection of species or of types is not what is aimed at; the type is often perfect [within its] limits, for it is the limits that make the type; the species too can be perfect in itself, perfect in its own variation of the genus and the genus perfect by the number and beauty or curiosity of its variations. But what we see in Nature is that it strives ever to exceed itself, to go beyond what it has yet done. For having achieved in the animal the whole of which animality was capable, it did not in achieving man endeavour to produce the perfect synthetic animal, it began at once working out something more than the animal. Man is to a certain extent a synthesis of several animals; he might even be said to synthetise all, from the worm and the skink, to the elephant and the lion; but as an animal he is terribly imperfect. His greatness lies in his being more than an animal and by this new nature he has exceeded the animal and made up for all his deficiencies even in the region of the struggle for life. Comparatively defenceless at first, he has become the master of the earth; he is not merely *primus inter pares*; he is a sovereign and the others are not any longer, even if they were ever his equals.

53

The world we live in is not a meaningless accident that has unaccountably taken place in the void of Space; it is the scene of an evolution in which an eternal Truth has been embodied, hidden in a form of things, and is secretly in process of unfoldment through the ages. There is a meaning in our existence, a purpose in our birth and death and travail, a consummation of all our labour. All are parts of a single plan; nothing has been idly made in the universe; nothing is vain in our life.

The evolution is arranged or arranges itself according to this plan. It begins here with a system of worlds which seem to be dead, yet in perpetual motion; it proceeds towards birth and life and consciousness, justifying Matter; it finds the justification of birth in thinking man; [?   ] to divinity. A slow [?   ] of godhead in Matter, this is the sense of the material universe.

Man is a transitional being, he is not final. He is too imperfect for that, too imperfect in capacity for knowledge, too imperfect in will and action, too imperfect in his turn towards joy and beauty, too imperfect in his will for freedom and his instinct for order. Even if he could perfect himself in his own type, his type is too low and small to satisfy the need of the universe. Something larger, higher, more capable of a rich all embracing universality is needed, a greater being, a greater consciousness summing up in itself all that the world set out to be. He has, as was pointed out by a half blind seer, to exceed himself; man must evolve out of himself the divine superman: he was born for transcendence. Humanity is not enough, it is only a strong stepping stone; the need of the world is a superhuman perfection of what the world can be, the goal of consciousness is divinity. The inmost need of man is not to perfect his humanity, but to be greater than himself, to be more than man, to be divine, even to be the Divine.

To rest in humanity is to rest in imperfection; the perfect man would be a self-contented finality of incompleteness. His nature is transitional and there is therefore in it an innate tendency to strive towards something more.

— Unless indeed he turned aside from his destiny, became a two-legged termite content with a perfectly arranged or sufficiently comfortable material order. He would [. . .   . . .] exist, deteriorate or become stable like the ant or the dung-beetle or after attaining complete efficiency, disappear like the sloth, the mammoth, the pterodactyl or the dinosaur. His innate reason for existence would have ceased and with it his necessity for being.

But this cannot be; there is something in him that forbids it.

But this most — that humanity cannot realise itself except by passing into supermanhood.

The saint, the sage, the seer, the inspired man of action, the creator, — these are his summits of being. Beyond him is the supramental being, the spiritual superman.

54

Our existence in the cosmic order is not an accident, the purposeless freak of a Chance which happened to organise itself into a world or the product of a blind Force which has somehow managed to exist in what we call a void Space and executes there [?soulless] inexplicable revolutions, as if compelled by its own causeless necessity; nor is man the result of a chemical combination of gases by an Energy which has somehow, being radically inconscient, succeeded without intending it to produce consciousness and started writing poems, painting pictures, producing civilisations, conceiving an inexistent God and invisible Creator. There is surely more in it than that; there was [an] Idea somewhere [and if it] has emerged it is because it was [. . .] and had to emerge.

If there is an intelligence which has appeared in Matter and is constantly developing its height and its range, this can only be because there was already an intelligence there, asleep, involved, latent or in some way a possibility of Matter, which has come forth from latency when things and conditions were ready. Or else it [is] because behind or in the world immanent in it there is an Intelligence which has created or is manifesting this world and at the right time has sent this power of itself [. . .   . .]

The nature of evolution according to physical Science is a development of forms more and more suitable to an increasingly complex and subtle development of Life and incidentally only to a more and more complex and subtle consciousness serving the ends of Life. This consciousness is a temporary phenomenon beginning in each form with birth and ending with death of the body. Consciousness then is a circumstance of body and incapable of survival of the body. There is no such thing per se as consciousness. A consciousness not dependent on the body, expressing itself in it as its instrument, a soul or spirit, is therefore a myth, an imagination; if it existed, it would be an unwarrantable intrusion into the nature of things as seen in this material universe; or, since everything in this universe is dependent on Matter, arose from Matter, is a circumstance or result of Matter and returns to Matter, soul too would be a circumstance or result of Matter, would act by it and in it only, would return finally to Matter. Consciousness itself is a phenomenon of Matter, is nothing but Matter in action, a combination of phenomenal action of chemical or other physical entities and operations and can be nothing else. It is unproven and unprovable, — though it may be that it is also not disproved and not disprovable. Either it must be left in a barren light or no light of agnosticism or is at most a matter of faith and not of knowledge.

But all this only means that Science has not any adequate means to deal precisely with the supraphysical nor can it collect and handle all the necessary data; it can deal only with the physical and with the physical side of the supraphysical; and that is not enough. Faith and knowledge are themselves supraphysical things with which Science cannot deal; for psychology at present is not a science; it is only a dispute between different bundles of inferences and guesses.

*

Man is not final, he is a transitional being.

This imperfect thinker embarrassed by the limitations of his brain and senses, this ignorant mind seeking after the truth of himself and things and never arriving at a certain knowledge, this stumbling reasoner capable only of speculation and stiff logical conclusions but not of indubitable conclusions or of a complete or direct knowledge, this imperfect liver divided between his reasoning will and his half-governed impulsions and instinctive desires, this thing of bundles of ideas and sensations and lusts and longings, this hunter after forms and formulas, this suffering and sorrowing mixture of wisdom and imbecility we call man is not the final essay of Nature, her last word, the crown of her evolution, the summit of consciousness, her master creation.

*

The central fact, the essential and cardinal significance of the evolution is not development and perfection of the outer and instrumental form, but the development [and] increasing perfection of consciousness. If human consciousness had been something complete, consummate, a ne plus ultra, then we could confidently say that here was the summit, here the crown and end of things and beings, here the perfected creation and the supreme terrestrial creator. Or if his consciousness though imperfect showed signs that it could arrive [at] the very top of possibility, rule earth and discover heaven, then we might believe that man was the last instrument by which Nature was passing from the terrestrial to the highest stage developing out of her initial inconscience a supreme conscient being.

But man seems to be by his very mould of nature a being with an animal living out of which he grew and a mental boundary beyond which he cannot pass.

For mind is the man, mind cramped into a body and entangled in the intricate machinery of a laborious and precarious physical organism which helps it less than it hampers. Mind's only data for knowledge are the motions of terrestrial life, the motions and processes of the physical world and its own processes and motions. Its notions about other things are merely speculations, guesses, imaginations; it thinks about them by means of abstractions, it cannot grasp anything concrete. It can observe life and know it by observation and inferences from observation or it can know by theory; it can find out its constituent parts and its processes. Its knowledge of itself is of the same variety; it traces out the processes of thinking, demarcates the observed constituents of personality; it evaluates men from what they say and do, not from what they are, for that it cannot see. It discovers by analysis or makes a synthesis by fitting together the fragments of things. Eventually it discovers the phenomenon, but misses the reality; it knows things as objects but knows nothing about things in themselves. Reality is beyond its grasp, it is only sure about the appearance. This is much for one who emerged out of nescient Matter and started as the ignorant animal, but it is not enough to make of man the crown of creation and the last apex of the evolution.

If man's knowledge and his way of knowledge are imperfect, still more imperfect are his living and his doing. [His] works sometimes attain perfection. Some men have done well in poetry and the arts and crafts, more have done badly, most are conventional copyists or botchers. In science and works with a scientific basis, men have certainly done well and their works were often efficient or masterly, for there all is method and rule and there the human mind seeks to master and execute what he has to do and that he can always do. Few have insight in works, fewer have any originality. Journeyman's work he can do, for man is essentially a journeyman. He is skilful in putting things [up], buildings, a job, a swindle. In pulling down he is perfect, a destroyer ne plus ultra. The world is full of his constructions, but more pervasive is his destruction; but that leaves few traces. But still the great doers are few in number, the good doers are many, the poor doers are legion, the evil doers hardly less. All this shows that he is a transitional and evolving animal, the highly evolved are rare, the poorly evolved numerous, the ill-evolved a multitude.

Living is more difficult than doing; though it is universal, and ought to have become easy by practice, it is commonly ill done, almost universally botched or half worked out. Human society is a ramshackle affair; it is top-heavy, over-elaborate and opulent at the top, below a multitudinous level. When he tries to reform his world, he sets out to level everything down towards or even to the worst. He can force all things down to the level of a universal proletariat, but he cannot make of the proletariat a universal aristocracy.

55

There are two states of being, two levels or limits between which all existence stands or moves, a highest limit of supreme consciousness, an omniscient Superconscience, a nethermost limit of supreme unconsciousness, an omnipotent Inconscience. The secret of consciousness reveals itself only when we perceive these two limits and the movement between them which we call the universe.

There can be no consciousness without existence, for the consciousness of a Void or a Nihil is a vain imagination, a thing impossible. For Nothing cannot be conscious of anything — cannot be conscious of itself; if it were conscious of itself, it would at once be an existence aware of itself, it would cease to be a Nihil; it would at once be evident that it was all the time an Existence appearing to be Nihil, that it was Being or a Being unconscious, but now grown conscious of its own existence. A void conscious of itself is conceivable, but it would then be a void existence and not Nihil. There might be an eternal Non-Being, but that too could not be Nihil; eventually it could only be a supreme superconscient existence exceeding our notion of Being. A true Nihil would necessarily be as incapable of consciousness as of existence; out of it nothing could come as in it nothing could be, neither spirit nor soul nor mind nor Matter.

We have then at one end of things a supreme superconscient existence and [at the other] a supreme inconscient existence and between them we have consciousness in the universe; but both are two states of one Being; what is between also is movement of that one Being between its two ends, its two highest and lowest levels of self-manifestation. *Ekam evadvitiyam.*

56

All existence upon earth is an evolution of what has come down from a superconscious Eternity to be involved here in a subconscious Infinite.[2]

That Eternity and this Infinite are the same Essence in opposite powers, but the one appears as a dark shadow of the other. The Superconscient is hidden from us because it is wrapped in its own being of illimitable light; the Inconscient escapes our search because it is plunged in its own veil of impenetrable darkness.

All that manifested from the Eternal has already been arranged in worlds or planes of its own nature, planes of subtle Matter, planes of Life, planes of Mind, planes of Supermind, planes of the triune luminous Infinite. But these worlds or planes are not evolutionary but typal.

A typal world is one in which some ruling principle manifests itself in its free and full capacity and energy and form are plastic and subservient to its purpose. Its expressions are therefore automatic and satisfying and do not need to evolve; they stand so long as need be and do not need to be born, develop, decline and disintegrate.

For evolution to be necessary there must be an opposing medium or recalcitrant instruments or an involution of the thing in its opposite. This is what has happened in the terrestrial world. Spirit has to evolve out of matter, consciousness out

---

[2] *Three drafts of this piece exist; the first paragraph of each of them is identical, or almost so. From the third paragraph, the second and third drafts were developed on different lines by Sri Aurobindo. These two drafts have been printed as pieces 56 and 57. The first draft, much shorter, contains a few phrases not taken up in either of the other drafts. It is printed in its entirety below:*

All existence upon earth is an evolution, in an ascending series of figures, of what came down from a superconscious Eternity to be involved here in a subconscient Infinite.

What was involved evolves slowly; each manifested term of the evolution is a step in the series and presupposes another step beyond it. There can be no finality until a perfect potential is reached which can express all the possibilities of the involved Godhead.

The evolution is from the Inconscient; therefore at first ignorant, feeling its way rather than consciously finding it. But its significant element is a growing consciousness which must at last emerge out of ignorance into Knowledge. When that happens the evolution will become conscious, aware of its way, no longer a stumbling search or precarious growth but a luminous outblossoming of the Divine.

of the Inconscient, life out of inanimation, mind out of a life that is void of thought; out of mind and its fragmentation and difficult piecing together of things the automatic completeness of the supramental knowledge.

There is a secret self-compulsion in the Inconscient to manifest what is involved — gaoled, suppressed and inactive within it, but also there is a stupendous Inertia, as of some fathomless cosmic sleep, that resists the will to manifest and retards the evolution. There is thus an upward levitation towards the luminous eternity of the Spirit strongly countered by a downward gravitation back towards the Inconscience.

This Inertia was needed in order that the evolution might be gradual by aeonic process and not an explosion of the concealed elements either into a rapid self-ordered typal series or into their original superconscience.

As a consequence of this retarding force what is involved evolves with difficulty and slowly. Evolution is a struggle between an insistent call to manifestation and an iron retardatory reluctant Inertia. Evolutionary existence is precarious because the downward gravitation back to its source contradicts powerfully both the stress from within towards permanence and the pull from above towards self-transcendence. Matter in our world can easily dissolve into its elements, life sink back into death, mind relapse into unconsciousness. A type evolved, animal or man, struggles slowly and with much difficulty into manifestation, it is less difficult for it to disappear, as disappeared the mastodon and the dinosaurus. Hence the law of a precarious impermanence laid on the forms of Matter which is corrected only for a time by the lavish will to reproduction in Nature.

As the evolution is from the Inconscient, it is not only a precarious but also an ignorant movement feeling its way rather than consciously finding it. But still its most significant term is a growing consciousness which must at last emerge out of ignorance into knowledge. When that happens, the evolution will become a willed and conscious movement, aware of its process and its way, no longer a stumbling search or a precarious growth but a luminous outflowering of the Divine.[3]

The call to manifestation is composed of a double current of Force moving between two poles. There is a will or at least an urge in the Inconscient itself, slow, dumb, obscure but imperative and inevitable towards the revelation of its involved contents. But there is also a pressure from above from the already established Powers for their manifestation in Space-Time here and for their evolutionary possibilities in the world of Matter. A world of subtle Matter presses on the shapeless Inconscient for the manifestation of forms; a world of essential Life presses on form of Matter for the manifestation of an embodied life; a world of essential Mind presses on animate life for the manifestation of mind in the living body. This compulsion is so great as to contradict and counteract finally the refusing and retarding Inertia.

Above on the summits of existence is all that is beyond Mind and all that is the complete splendour of the Spirit. These too wait for their hour of manifestation, their turn for revelation in Time and Space and the evolving series of the powers of the Eternal.

57

All existence upon earth is an evolution of what has come down from a superconscious Eternity to be involved here in a subconscious Infinite.

The superconscious Eternity to which we tend and the subconscious Infinite from which we rise — for we are a part of both and we stand between them as their developing link — are opposite powers of the same Being, are indeed, in their essence, one and the same Being; but one appears to our experience as a dark and void shadow of the other. The Superconscient is hidden

---

[3] *The incomplete passage that follows apparently was intended for insertion here:*
 A third consequence of the origin of the evolution is its character of struggle and suffering. For all is involved here in its opposite. Being descends into the phenomenon of Non-Being and has to emerge from it. Consciousness descends into the worldwide Inconscience and is involved in its night. Force descends into

from us because it is wrapped in its own being of illimitable light; the Inconscient escapes our search because it is plunged in its own veil of impenetrable darkness.

What comes down from the Superconscient is self, spirit, the wide and all-containing Essence of the eternal existence. It plunges, carrying its powers in it, into an infinite ocean of inconscience, *apraketam salilam*, and hides itself there. It hides itself and its powers from itself — it appears in us as its own opposite.

The Self is an immortal and unseizable essence and substance of all things, it is a pure omnipresent omniscient omnipotent existence. It appears to our experience when we emerge from the subconscient as a mysterious Void or Nihil, indeterminable yet from it all things and forms are, inconscient yet flowering into consciousness, inert yet manifesting enormous energies, lifeless yet the parent of life, insensible yet a fountain of pain and pleasure. This impossibility, this universal contradiction is unreal and born of our ignorance; yet that ignorance is not ours, but a result of the inconscience which was imposed on itself as a veil by the involved Self and Spirit. For if that Inconscience were not there, the evolutionary emergence of the Self which is the law and object of this universe would not have been possible; all would have flowered into a manifestation too immediate, too irresistibly powerful in its process, too absolute.

The Self, the Spirit is a pure existence, a spiritual substance that is self-aware and therefore all-aware. It is in its nature an absolute and omniscient consciousness, eternally comprehending all itself, all in itself and would naturally manifest as an absolute, unwalled, indivisible knowledge. It becomes an inconscience out of which consciousness struggles brokenly into light, seeking and groping for itself, groping after signs and intimations of its substance, but finding at first only fragmentary signs and separated forms and objects which seem not itself. The consciousness in the individualised form becomes aware of itself by the shock of things outside that are or seem to be not itself. It becomes aware of itself as a separated form and only when it grows more and more deeply self-conscious slowly becomes aware of all outside it as part of its own continuous indivisible existence.

The nature of the Spirit's consciousness is a self-existent Force which in action becomes a spontaneously self-manifesting or, as it seems to us, self-creating and self-determining energy. It is omnisciently omnipotent and creates out of itself what it wills under whatever conditions it wills — for its will is that of an infinite and infinitely variable self-aware oneness whose steps, no matter what they are, are by necessity the movement of a perfect Truth and Knowledge. But it is by an equal necessity the very opposite when the manifestation of the Substance of things becomes the working of a void Inconscience. For even if that Inconscience be only apparent because an all-knowledge and its force are hidden there, yet this error, this phenomenon of Inconscience is and was intended to be dynamic and operative. In other words, all had to look and appear as the gropings of an Inconscience whose results in their upshot were yet those of an ordered and imperative Intelligence. An inert Soul guiding with a strange and blind sureness the steps of a somnambulist Nature would be no inadequate image of the apparent Spirit of this material universe.

This material world sprung from the subconscious Infinite appears to us as if [it] were the sole actual universe and even perhaps the only creation possible. But that is because we are limited by our senses which we now know to be restricted in their field and even there fallible. The material senses by their very nature can perceive only material things and from that our still infantile external reason infers that only material things exist and there is nothing else. All forms that are immaterial or of another substance than ours are and cannot but be illusions, hallucinations, unreal images. But a being otherwise constituted in consciousness or sense could well see this world in other figures than present themselves to ours. Another would see perhaps other worlds made of another, a subtler material or an essentially mental or vital or spiritual substance. A world is only an arrangement of things as experienced by consciousness of the Spirit and this consciousness can see all kinds of things in all kinds of ways according to whatever plane of itself, whatever medium and whatever instruments it has produced for its cosmic purpose. We shall understand nothing of existence if we confine our vision to the particular view of things our primary consciousness and its instruments which are physical impose upon us; for this consciousness is only a surface phenomenon of ourselves and our total being is far deeper, higher and vaster than that, our possibilities extend infinitely beyond their present limit, and the world also is far more complex than the first crude inexplicable mystery of Matter would lead us to imagine.

The immense material world in which we live is not the sole reality but only one of innumerable potential and existent universes; all of them need not have either Matter as we know it or the Inconscient for their base. Indeed this world of matter is itself dependent on many planes of consciousness and existence which are not material; for these have not this gross substance as their foundation or as the medium of their instrumentation of energy and consciousness or their primary condition of existence.

All the powers that are involved here in the inconscient Infinite and that we see rising out of it, — mind, life and what is beyond mind no less than matter itself — have their previous existence and are not merely evolutionary results of Nature in this universe. They have not only a preexistence but also their separate planes of manifestation in which each in turn is, as matter is here, the foundation, the medium of instrumentation, the primary condition of existence.

58

All terrestrial existence is the slow surge of a hidden Consciousness mounting up out of an apparent Inconscience towards its own perfect and luminous manifestation. This is the secret of evolution and its significance.[4]

There is a spirit secret even in things immobile, — there is an All-Consciousness disguised in the Inconscient. In Matter life

---

[4] *Sri Aurobindo left out the sentence that follows when he revised the first draft of this piece:*
   All else is only veils and means and forms, conditions and stages, action and counter-action of this great half-veiled becoming which is the heart of the earth's enigma.

is embedded, in Life is an enveloped mind, in Mind is concealed a greater supramental and spiritual being not yet manifested. These are the significant and illumining terms of the riddle.

Evolution is the labour of Nature, or let us say at once of the Energy of the secret Spirit, working in the semblance and under the limiting conditions of an inconscient Power to release these latencies each in its turn out of their involution in the original Inconscience.

It is an All-consciousness that is working, the force of a self-aware cosmic Spirit, and the emergence of its secret powers is implied in the very nature of existence; therefore the result is inevitable.

Science has discovered a physical evolution hidden in the past history of the earth of which the living record remains in the embryo; but the physical evolution is only an outward sign, means and material condition of a still more secret evolution. A spiritual evolution, an evolution of consciousness is the inner fact which alone illumines the problem of earth existence and opens to it its true solution; apart from it our life here has no intelligible significance.

Ancient Indian thought discovered an evolution from birth to birth, from the life of tree and plant to the life of insect and animal, from the life of the animal to the life of man, attained with difficulty through the ages. This slowly attained human life it took to be the key of release from the baffling circle of the enigma. After some eighty and more lakhs of births, says the Tantra, a soul reaches the human form and consciousness and sooner or later finds the secret of escape from birth in time into the birthless and deathless Eternity from which it came.

These two discoveries seem at first sight quite unconnected and disparate. In one it is a physical Life in the cosmos that evolves and the individual is only an ephemeral member of the species, the species a means of this cosmic evolution. Mind is indeed the term and the mental human being the crown of this inexplicable emergence; when human progress is over, when the race decays and perishes, the cosmic evolution will be at an end, for it has nothing more then it can do. In man it has shot its bolt; nothing more is possible. Consciousness emerging out of the Inconscient has achieved this shoddy and splendid, this winging and limping miracle of the ever-seeking creative Mind of Man and sinks back into the Inconscient; its emergence had no discoverable significance, its brief play and cessation make no difference to the meaningless rounds of an inconscient universe.

In the Indian view it is the individual that evolves from birth to birth and the hierarchy of the vegetal, animal, human kinds [is] a fixed unchanging ladder for its ascent. A successive creation of higher and higher species is envisaged in the Upanishads as well as the Puranas and heredity affirmed as a means of conscious continuity of the human embodiment of the Spirit, but still the evolution is individual and not cosmic, spiritual not physical. Yet here too this persistent phenomenon of spiritual embodiment appearing from the bodiless Spirit and evolving back into the bodiless Spirit seems to be devoid of significance.

If stripped of their limitations the two discoveries can be regarded as complementary rather than disparate. There is evidently an evolution; Matter first manifests out of the Formless — inanimate in appearance; in Matter life manifests unconscious in appearance; in life mind manifests in the animal but instinctive and irrational in appearance; in life-mind thinking mind appears rational but yet self-ignorant in appearance, — for it seeks to know but yet does not know the secret and significance of its own existence. It is not yet undisputed but it is affirmed that in thinking man spirit is moving towards manifestation, spirit aware of itself and of its own secret and significance. Thus far at least an evolution is indisputable and we may affirm without hesitation that there is a cosmic Existence here which first achieves a material manifestation of itself or a manifestation in itself, a material formula, then on that basis a life formulation, a vital formula, on that again a mental formulation, a mind formula. It is possible that on that again it is preparing a spiritual formulation of self-affirmation and self-knowledge which will complete the emergence.

There is also very evidently an evolution of forms, generic

and individual in the genus and species, which enables the formulation to be effective, each in its own kind, organised so as to express more and more definite and superior possibilities of matter, more and more definite and superior possibilities of life, more and more definite and superior possibilities of mind, — more than this cannot yet be positively asserted, but this much is asseverable. If we can add that in the mental formula, in the mentalised life and body of man, a spiritual emergence is in process which has not yet reached its full possibility and that possibility is the emergence of the spiritual man or supramental being, then the object of the physical evolution and its significance becomes clear. The evolution of bodies is only a means for the evolution of consciousness and the spiritual formulation will be that in which the cosmic Existence will find its own full affirmation, manifest through the original veil of Matter its self-awareness, self-knowledge, self-realisation. The Cosmic Spirit hidden in the Inconscience is then the Alpha, its manifestation in the consciousness of spiritualised man the Omega.

The Stages of Evolution
Matter, Life, Mind, Supermind

59

The evolution of the earth nature is not finished because it has manifested only three powers out of the seven-fold scale of consciousness that is involved in manifested Nature. It has brought out from its apparent inconscience only the three powers of Mind and Life and Matter.

60

Matter, one might say from a certain viewpoint, is purely a matter of mathematics. That cannot be said of Mind or of Life.

Then again, Matter is a matter of formulas. Everything purely material is created according to a formula.

Again, Matter is a matter of magic. It is a thing of magical and irrational or suprarational formulas.

Lastly, all Matter is *matra*, a thing of degrees, measures, quantities.

*

We find that water is produced by a combination in a fixed quantity of the two first elements, hydrogen and oxygen. We do not know or do not yet know why this should be so. All we can say is that [it] is a fixed law of Nature that when this formula is scrupulously followed without deviation something called water appears, — becomes a phenomenon of material Nature. There seems to be no reason in this miracle. We could partly understand if oxygen and hydrogen by their very nature tended to produce in any combination water or something like water, but only in the fixed amounts could bring out the perfect article.

But this is not the case; only by the fixed relative combination can it be done. This formula then is of the nature of a magic formula. Only by pronouncing a fixed combination of words or syllables or sounds can the [. . .] magic result follow and not otherwise. Any variation voids the effect and leaves the incantation barren.

Hydrogen itself is produced by a combination of a fixed number of electrons or electric particles of energy in a fixed relative position in their movement. Oxygen is produced by another such combination. The elements are alike in kind, it is a positional quantitative [*remainder of piece missing*]

61

Ether and material space are different names for the same thing. Space, in its origin at least if not in its universal character, is an extension of the substance of consciousness in which motion of energy can take place for the relations of being with being or force with force and for the building up of symbolic forms on which this interchange can be supported. Ether is space supporting the works of material energy and the symbolic forms it creates; it is, speaking paradoxically but to the point, immaterial or essential matter[.]

62

Matter is but a form of consciousness; nevertheless solve not the object entirely into its subjectivity. Reject not the body of God, O God lover, but keep it for thy joy; for His body too is delightful even as His spirit.

Perishable and transitory delight is always the symbol of the eternal Ananda, revealed and rapidly concealed, which seeks by increasing recurrence to attach itself to some typal form of experience in material consciousness. When the particular form has been perfected to express God in the type, its delight will no longer be perishable but an eternally recurrent possession of mental beings in matter manifest in their periods & often in their moments of felicity.

63

Evolution is the one eternal dynamic law and hidden process of the earth-nature.

An evolution of the instruments of the spirit in a medium of matter is the whole fundamental significance of the values of the earth-existence. All its other laws are its values of operation and process; the spiritual evolution is its one pervading secret sense.

*

The history of the earth is first an evolution of organised forms by the working of material forces.

There follows on this initial stage an evolution of life in the form and an organisation of a hierarchy of living forms by the working of liberated life-forces. The next step is an evolution of mind in living bodies and an organisation of more and more conscious lives by the process of developing mind forces. But even this is not the end; for there are higher powers of consciousness beyond mind which await their turn and must have their act in the great play, their part of the creative Lila.

*

Matter, the medium of all this evolution, is seemingly inconscient and inanimate; but it so appears to us only because we are unable to sense consciousness outside a certain limited range, a fixed scale or gamut to which we have access. Below us there are lower ranges to which we are insensible and these we call subconscience or inconscience. Above us are higher ranges which are to our inferior nature an unseizable superconscience.

The difficulty of Matter is not an absolute inconscience but an obscured consciousness limited by its own movement, vaguely, dumbly, blindly self-aware, only mechanically responsive to anything outside its own form and force. At its worst it can be called not so much inconscience as nescience. The awakening of a greater and yet greater consciousness in this Nescience is the miracle of the universe of Matter.

This nescience of Matter is a veiled, an involved or a somnambulist consciousness which contains all the latent powers of the Spirit. In every particle, atom, molecule, cell of Matter there lives hidden and works unknown all the omniscience of the Eternal and all the omnipotence of the Infinite.

The evolution of forms and powers by which Matter will become more and more conscious until passing beyond form and life and mind it becomes aware with the supernal awareness of the eternal and infinite Spirit in his own highest ranges, this is the meaning of earth existence. The slow self-manifesting birth of God in Matter is the purpose of the terrestrial Lila.

* * *

Matter is at once a force and a substance. Matter is original being, Brahman made concrete in atomic division; Matter is original substance-force, Brahman-Shakti made active in an obscure involution of the spirit's powers, in a self-forgetful nescience.

Matter-force casts matter-substance, material Shakti casts Matter-Brahman into form expressive of its own most characteristic powers. When that has been done, the physical world is ready for the splendid intrusion of conscious Life into the force-driven inertia of material substance.

Matter is not the only force, nor the only substance. For Life and Mind too and what is beyond Mind are also forces that are substances but of another kind and degree.

Spirit is the original force-substance; all these others are kinds and derivations of force of spirit, degrees and modifications [of] substance of spirit. Matter too is nothing but a power and degree of the spirit; Matter too is substance of the Eternal.

But the Matter that we see and sense is only an outermost sheath and coating; behind it are other subtler degrees of physical substance which are less dense with the atomic nescience and it is easier for Life and Mind to enter into them and operate. If finer invisible physical layers or couches did not exist supporting this gross visible physical world, that world could not abide; for then the fine operations of transmission between Spirit and Matter [could not] be executed at all and it is these that render the grosser visible operations possible. The evolution would be impossible; life and mind and beyond-mind would be unable to manifest in the material universe.

There is not only this material plane of being that we see, there is a physical life plane proper to the vital physical operation of Nature. There is a physical mind plane proper to a mental physical operation of Nature. There is a physical supermind plane proper to the supramental physical operation of Nature. There is too a plane of physical spirit power or infinite physical Being-Consciousness-Force-Bliss proper to the spiritual physical operations of Nature. It is only when we have discovered and separated these planes of Nature and of our physical being and analysed the synthesis of their contributions to the whole play that we shall discover how the evolution of vital, mental and spiritual consciousness became possible in inconscient Matter.

But there is more; for beyond these many couches of the physical existence are other supraphysical degrees, a many layered plane of Life, a many layered plane of Mind, planes of Supermind, of Bliss, of Consciousness Force and of infinite Being on which the physical existence depends for its origination and its continuance. It is higher planes that flood the constantly unfolding unseen energies which have raised its evolution from the obscurity in which it began to the splendour of a light of consciousness to which the highest human mind shall only be the feeble glimmer of a glowworm fire before the sun in its flaming glories.

There is a stupendous hierarchy of grades of consciousness between darkest Matter and most luminous spirit. Consciousness in Matter has to go on climbing to the very top of the series and return with all it has to give us before the evolution can utterly fulfil its purpose.

* *

Matter, Life, Mind, Supermind or Gnosis, and beyond these the quadruple power of a supreme Being-Consciousness-Force-Bliss — these are the grades of the evolutionary ascent from inconscience to the Superconscience.

Life does not wholly come into the earth from outside it; its principle is there always in material things. But, imprisoned in the apparent inanimate inertia or blind force movement of Matter, it is bound by its movements and unable to manifest its own independent or dominant existence.

Life is there in the earth, rock, metal, gas, atom, electron and the other more subtle yet undiscovered forces and particles that constitute material energy and form. It is in everything, but at first a hardly detectable presence organised only to support secretly material energies, processes, formations and transformations; it is there as an involved power for the building and expression of Form of Matter, not for the expression of Life. It is not in possession of itself, not self-conscious in the form, not pushed towards self-manifestation; a helpless tool and instrument, not a free agent, it is a servant of Matter and a slave of the Form, not the master of the house.

But above the material world there is a plane of dominant Life that presses down upon this material universe and seeks to pour into it whatever it can of its own types, powers, forces, impulsions, manifesting creative godheads. When in the material world form is ready, the Gods and Life-Daemons of this higher plane are attracted to put their creative touch upon Matter. Then there comes a rapid and sudden efflorescence of Life; the plant, the animalcule, the insect, the animal appear. A Life-Soul and a Life-Force with its many and always more complex movements are manifested in what seemed once to be inert and inanimate substance. Life souls, life minds, animal existences are born and evolve; a new world appears that is born and contained in this world of Matter and yet surpasses it in its own dynamic nature.

64

At each capital step of Nature's ascent there is a reversal of consciousness in the evolving spirit. As when a climber turns on a summit to which he has laboured and looks down with an exalted and wider power of vision on all that was once above or on a level with him but is now below his feet, the evolutionary being not only transcends his past self, his former now exceeded status, but commands from a higher grade of self-experience and vision, with a new apprehending feeling or a new comprehending sight and effectuating power, in a greater system of values, all that was once his own consciousness but is now below his tops and belongs to an inferior creation. This reversal is the sign of a decisive victory and the seal of a radical progress in Nature.

The new consciousness attained in the spiritual evolution is always higher in grade and power, always larger, more comprehensive, wider in sight and feeling, richer and finer in faculties, more complex, organic, dominating than the consciousness that was once our own but is now left behind us. There are greater breadths and spaces, heights before impossible, unexpected depths and intimacies. There is a luminous expansion that is the very sign manual of the Supreme upon his work.[5]

Mark too that each of the great radical steps forward already taken by Nature has been infinitely greater in its change, incalculably vaster in its consequences than its puny predecessor. There is a miraculous opening to an always richer and wider expression, there is a new illuminating of the creation and a dynamic heightening of its significances. There is in this world we live in no equality of all on a flat level, but a hierarchy of ever-increasing precipitous superiorities pushing their mountain-shoulders upwards towards the Supreme.

Plant-life is a most significant progress upon the mineral, but the difference is as nothing compared with the gulf that divides the dumb vitality of the plant from the conscious experience of the animal. The hiatus between the animal and the human is so great in consciousness, however physically small, that the scientists' alleged cousinship of monkey and man looks psychologically almost incredible. And yet the difference between vital animal and mental man is as nothing to that which will be between man's mind and the superman's vaster consciousness and richer powers. That past step will be to this new one as the snail's slow march in the grass to a Titan's sudden thousand league stride from continent to continent.

Evolution on the terrestrial plane, even in the dullest brute matter is only in outward appearance a progression of physical function and form; in its essential fact, in its inner meaning, in its significant power, it is a progression of consciousness, a spiritual or psychological change.

At each step the spirit heightens its stature, perfects its instruments, organises better its self-expression; a new consciousness comes in, takes up the old and gives it an extended movement and another significance, adds greater, richer, more

---

[5] *The following passage from the first draft of this piece was not incorporated by Sri Aurobindo in the present draft:*

Illuminating his creation here and pointing out to it its own significance it suggests the culmination of ever-ascending superiorities in the Supreme and the opening of released ever-increasing widenesses in the Infinite.

complex movements of which the first formulation was incapable.

In the sub-vegetal world all movements, all stimulus, all reaction are of a material and if dynamic, of a mechanically dynamic character. Even the life movements that exist there, as in the mineral, are of the most rigidly automatic, unindividualised and mechanical and external nature, birth, formation, fatigue, sleep, death. Mental or psychic powers and significances there are, as an occult knowledge discovers, but of these the form seems not aware; it is something behind the life of the mineral, a consciousness supporting rather than inhabiting it, using but not used by it, that is their possessor.

In the plant world for the first time a true vital consciousness appears in earth Nature.

65

All the trend and purpose of Nature in terrestrial existence is to manifest the yet unmanifested. Her continual aim is to develop out of what has been evolved that which has not been evolved but is waiting to [be] liberated out of latency. This continual evolution is the whole meaning of terrestrial existence.

What has already been evolved is form of matter with life and mind housed in it, what has yet to be evolved is supermind liberating from their narrow limits and transforming mind and life and matter.

Here on earth and in the material universe matter has been the first term, the basis of things, the condition of all that must evolve here. Life can evolve here only so far as it can persuade or compel matter to give it a form and an instrumentation. Mind too has to accommodate itself to the means given it by an organised living body. There is no reason to suppose however that life in itself is limited in its possibilities to the small range realised by the living animal or human body; or the potentialities [of] mind limited to the field of powers accorded to it by the brain, nerves and physical senses, its ingenious but still very poor and unreliable instruments here.

In a world where life and not matter was the first term, condition and basis, in a vital world life would be free to organise itself in its own way with a free energy in plastic and pliable forms and its ranges of possibilities would be immense and circumscribed by no rigid limits.

66

But what shall be the gain won for the earth-consciousness we embody by this unprecedented ascent out of mind to whatever may be beyond it and what the significance of the supramental change? To what end shall man leave his safe human limits for this godlike but hazardous adventure?

First consider what was gained when earthly Nature passed from the brute inconscience and inertia of the first organised forms in what seems to us inanimate Matter to the vibrant sensibility of the plant range. Life was gained; the gain was the beginning of the mute groping and involved consciousness that reaches out to growth, to sense-vibration, to waking and sleep, to hunger and thirst, to physical pain and pleasure, to a preparation for vital yearnings and a living joy and beauty. That was begun which still is unfinished — the first step towards a conscious consciousness and what shall yet be the divine Ananda.[6]

In the plant earth-nature achieved a first figure of life, but the creature she made could not possess it, because this first organised life-consciousness had feeling and seeking, woke and slept, hungered and was satisfied, thirsted and drank and grew and flourished, had pleasure of some contacts and suffered from others, but was still externally blind, dumb, deaf, chained to the soil from which it was born, involved in its own nerve and tissue. It could not get out of this primitive formula, could not get behind its nerve-self as does the vital mind of the animal, still less could turn down from above it to know and realise its own motions as does the thinking and observing mind of man and to

---

[6] Not joy or pleasure, but the bliss of existence and its movements from which the world arose.

control them. This was a decisive but an imprisoned gain; for there was still a gross oppression of the original Inconscience which had covered up with the brute phenomenon of Matter and energy of Matter all signs of the Spirit. Nature could nowise stop here, because she held so much in her that was still occult, potential, unexpressed, unorganised, suppressed, latent; the evolution had perforce to go farther. The animal had to replace the plant at the head and top of Nature.

And what then was gained when Nature passed from the obscurity of the plant kingdom to the awakened sense and desire and emotion and the free mobility of animal life? The gain was liberated sense and feeling and desire and courage and cunning and the contrivance of the objects of desire, passion and action and hunger and battle and conquest and the sex-call and play and pleasure, and all the joy and pain of the conscious living creature. Not only the life of the body which the animal has in common with the plant but a life-mind that appeared for the first time in the earth-story and grew and grew from form to more organised form till it reached in the best the limit of its own formula.

The animal achieved a first form of mind, but could not possess it, because this first organised mind consciousness was enslaved in a narrow scope, tied to the first functionings of the physical body and brain and nerve, tied to serve the physical life and its desires and needs and passions, limited to the insistent uses of the vital urge, to natural longing and feeling and action, bound by its own inferior instrumentation, its spontaneous combinings of association and memory and instinct. It could not get away from them, could not get behind them as man's intelligence gets behind them to observe them; still less could it turn down on them from above as do human reason and will to control, enlarge, reorder, exceed, sublimate.

67

Mind emerges out of life in matter; it is incapable of manifesting directly in the material form. It is there, but it acts mechanically in the somnambulism of an original force of inconscience and inertia. This and no more is what we mean by the inconscience of Matter; for although consciousness is there, it is involved, inorganic, mechanical in its action; it supports the works of Force by its inherent presence, but not by its light of active intelligence. This is why material Nature does the works of a supreme and miraculous intelligence and yet there seems to be no intervention of any indwelling Seer or Thinker.

68

Because man is a mental being, he naturally imagines that mind is the one great leader and actor and creator or the indispensable agent in the universe. But this is an error; even for knowledge mind is not the only or the greatest possible instrument, the one aspirant and discoverer. Mind is a clumsy interlude between Nature's vast and precise subconscient action and the vaster infallible superconscient action of the Godhead.

There is nothing mind can do that cannot be better done in the mind's immobility and thought-free stillness.

When mind is still, then Truth gets her chance to be heard in the purity of the silence.

Truth cannot be attained by the mind's thought but only by identity and silent vision. Truth lives in the calm wordless Light of the eternal spaces; she does not intervene in the noise and cackle of logical debate.

Thought in the mind can at most be Truth's brilliant and transparent garment; it is not even her body. Look through the robe, not at it, and you may see some hint of her form. There can be a thought-body of Truth, but that is the spontaneous supramental Thought and Word that leap fully formed out of the Light, not any difficult mental counterfeit and patchwork. The supramental Thought is not a means of arriving at Truth, for Truth in the supermind is self-found or self-existent, but a way of expressing her. It is an arrow from the Light, not a bridge to reach it.

Cease inwardly from thought and word, be motionless within you, look upward into the light and outward into the vast cosmic consciousness that is around you. Be more and more one with the brightness and the vastness. Then will Truth dawn on you from above and flow in on you from all around you.

But only if the mind is no less intense in its purity than its silence. For in an impure mind the silence will soon fill with misleading lights and false voices, the echo or sublimation of its own vain conceits and opinions or the response to its secret pride, vanity, ambition, lust, greed or desire. The Titans and the Demons will speak to it more readily than the divine Voices.

Silence is indispensable, but also there is needed wideness. If the mind is not silent, it cannot receive the lights and voices of the supernal Truth or receiving mixes with them its own flickering tongues and blind pretentious babble. Active, arrogant, noisy, it distorts and disfigures what it receives. If it is not wide, it cannot house the effective power and creative force of the Truth. Some light may play there but it becomes narrow, confined and sterile. Or the force that is descending is cabined and thwarted and withdraws again from this rebellious foreign plane to its vast native heights. Or even if something comes down and remains, it is a pearl in the mire; for no change takes place in the nature or else there is formed only a thin intensity that points narrowly upward to the summits but can hold little and diffuse less upon the world around it.

69

Reason is a clarified, ordered and organised Ignorance. It is a half-enlightened Ignorance seeking for truth, but a truth which it insists on founding upon the data and postulates of the Ignorance. Reason is not in possession of the Truth, it is a seeker. It is [unable to] discover the Truth or embody it; it leaves Truth covered but rendered into mental representations, a verbal and ideative scheme, an abstract algebra of concepts, a theory of the Ignorance. Sense-evidence is its starting point and it never really gets away from that insecure beginning. Its concepts start from sense-data and though like a kite it can fly high into an air of abstractions, it is held to the earth of sense by a string of great strength; if that string is broken it drifts lazily [in] the clouds and always it falls back by natural gravitation to its original earth basis — only so can it receive strength to go farther. Its field is the air and sky of the finite, it cannot ascend into the stratosphere of the spiritual vision, still less can it move at ease in the Infinite.

70

Mind can never be a perfect instrument of knowledge. For even if it could be free from all positive error, even if it could be all intuitive and infallibly intuitive, it could still present and organise only half truths or separated truths and these too not in their own body but in luminous representative figures put together to make an accumulated total or a massed structure[.]

71

The office of intellect is not to fathom reality, but to fabricate and preside over action; intellect cannot comprehend life and reality. Intellect (logic) goes round the object, intuition enters into the object; one stops at the [?   ], the other enters into the absolute[.]

72

Intuition, — but what do we mean when we speak of intuition? What is its origin, nature, working, and how is it connected with intelligence and sense and instinct, our other ways of knowing, or what is the difference? Is intuition the one means of true and complete knowledge or does it need intelligence, sense, instinct to complete it? Is there a greater power of direct and absolute and complete knowledge of which intuition is only a special or part action, — some first and last potency, the Alpha and Omega of an all-knowledge, the all-knowledge that we attribute to God or to the Spirit of the universe?

These are the queries it is proposed to answer here; but the answer can come only from intuition itself, from a direct seeing and experience, for if intuition exists, it and its way of working must obviously be something beyond the reasoning intelligence and therefore not entirely seizable by the reasoning intelligence.

I know myself because I am myself, I know the movements of my mind, joy, anger, love, thought, will, because they are myself or parts of myself; I have a direct knowledge of myself, a knowledge by identity. Observation, reasoning there can be as a subsidiary process; but it is not by observation or reasoning that I know them; I feel and know my anger or love as part of myself and have no need to observe or to reason in order to know that I am angry or that I love.

Intuition is a direct knowledge self-existent and independent of means and devices; it is naturally self-existent and founded upon a knowledge by identity; or when it is gained, it is either by identification or by a knowledge arising from some intimate contact made possible by an underlying or occult identity.

73

Nothing has the value of truth for the supramental if it is only thought or understood with the intelligence. That is a shadow or reflection and shadows can always distort, at best only adumbrate; reflections can always misform or mistranslate and at best have not the truth-substance. It is only when the object is entered into, seen with an inner and surrounding vision, possessed in experience, taken into our living universal & identifying individual consciousness, made one with us in the Truth that is, holds, comprehends, actuates all things, — only then is there the characteristic process of the supermind, the way of directness, the sincerity and power, the magnificence and general wholeness of the gnosis[.]

74

But what is supermind and where is it in this world of half lights, in which consciousness is a constructor of ideas, images and sensations that at once inform and mislead, representations that are half truths, half misrepresentations, symbols of things, not things in themselves, relative impressions but nothing absolute. Our senses give us the forms of things as they seem to our senses, not as they are; for they would appear quite different to other senses than ours; our mind builds the great mass of its idea of the world and things on this insecure basis, or if it corrects the evidence of the senses, it is in the light of a reason whose conceptions of Time, Space and Substance are equally imperfect, equally relative, empirically valid up to a certain point, but fundamentally dubious and insecure. Is not this the only consciousness possible, or at least the highest of which we are capable and have we any evidence of a higher power of awareness and knowledge or any ground to suppose that there are beings greater than man who possess it? Is not this world and must it not be always a world of Ignorance, knowledge partial at the best, all knowledge here relative, pragmatic, indirect and no knowledge either here or anywhere that can be called supreme, direct or absolute? If absolute knowledge there is it must be the sheer consciousness of the Featureless Infinite, the One Self, the void or formless Spirit, and there can be no other.

75

I mean by the supermind a power, a level, an organisation of consciousness which is not only above the human mind, but above all that can be called mind, — another higher and wider essence and energy of consciousness altogether. Mind is that which seeks after truth of any kind or of all kinds within its range, labours to know it, attempts to direct and utilise it. But by supermind I mean a divine awareness which inherently possesses truth, knows it by its own intrinsic identity with it and puts it into action or effect spontaneously by its own sovereign power without any need of endeavour or labour. Mind even though it seeks after knowledge and can sometimes grasp its figure or touch its shadow, is a product of the cosmic Inconscient or of a Half-Conscience-Ignorance; supermind is an eternal Truth-consciousness, a divine Knowledge self-maintained for ever and luminous in its own right beyond all Ignorance.

The Emergence of the Superman

76

A god has veiled himself in the earth & mire and beauty and perfection lie unevolved in masses of ordure. This is the play of God with His substance in Matter.

In the atom there is hidden all the will & intelligence & joy that created the universe. In Man they have emerged, but blinking & dazzled by the gleam of their own sunlight, bewildered at themselves & each other. They stumble up against each other, strive & wrestle blindly; for they cannot even [in] the highest man accomplish altogether their own unity & harmony.

An ignorance in which is packed up all knowledge, a mighty inertia in which all cosmic force strives helplessly, an insensibility which conceals the pain and strain of all ecstasy present, but held back, this is the outer face of material Nature and our starting point.

The Spirit awakening out of this veil gradually and with difficulty but inevitably is the secret sense of life. The power to accomplish the perfect awakening against accumulated difficulties, is God's offer to man throughout his cycles.

The perfection & the unity of the divine knowledge, will, delight in the mould of his universalised individuality is the destiny of man, his ascent to Godhead and the unfolding in him of Superman.

Mind evolved is man; supermind unevolved conceals in him the superman.

77

This is the meaning of our existence here, its futuristic value and inherent trend of power, to rise above ourselves, to grow into gods, to reveal God in a world of material forms and forces.

Earth and conscious life upon earth are not a freak of cosmic Chance, a meaningless accident in the vacant history of nebula and electron and gas and plasm; they are the field of a game of the Gods with the destiny of our souls as the stake of their wager.

To evolve Godhead out of the mud of matter, some divinest consciousness out of a primal inconscience and a struggling ignorance, immortality out of death, undying bliss out of pain and sorrow, the everlasting Truth out of the falsehoods and denials of this relative world is their great and daring gamble.

All life upon earth is the evolution of a divine Spirit that is concealed as by a self-formed mask and robe in the appearance of Matter. Out of that involution it evolves, manifests by a series of ascendent steps its suppressed powers and, once this process has begun, will not cease till the Godhead is manifest in Matter.

Man is a struggling transitional term, an intermediate being who has gathered up into himself the consciousness of the mineral and the vegetable, of the insect and the animal, and is fashioning and refining in the confused twilight and chaos of a half knowledge founded on Ignorance the materials of the god that is to be born.

The instrument of man is mind and thinking and willing mind-force — just as the instrument of the animal is life instinct and feeling and remembering life force and the instrument of the plant and tree existence is the vital push and the dynamism of material energy turning into force of life. As these lower states developed up to a point at which Mind-intelligence could descend into the organised living body and take up the earth-past to mentalise and transform it, so Mind in man has to develop up to a point at which a consciousness greater than Mind can descend into the mind and living body and take up the human material to supramentalise and transform it into godhead. This is man's rise to the Infinite.

An air from a consciousness greater than mind has already been felt by many of those who have climbed to the human summits and to the glow that has come from above they have given many names, *bodhi*, intuition, gnosis. But these things are only the faint edge of that greater light thrust into the pallid twilight that we call mind. Only when the lid between mind and supermind has been utterly rent apart and the full power of the sun of a divine Gnosis can pour down — not trickling through mind as in diminished and deflected beams — and transform the whole mind and life and body of the human creature, can man's labour finish. Then only shall begin the divine play and the free outpouring of the liberated self-creating Spirit.

To rise into this greater consciousness above our mental level of humanity as man has risen above the level of the life-mind of the beast, to grow from mind into supermind, from twilight into light, from the mind's half-consciousness into what is now to us superconscient, from a narrow imprisoned ego into the transcendent and universalised individual, from a struggling half effective into a throned and master power, from little transient joys and sorrows into an unalloyed divine delight, this is the goal of our journey, the secret of our struggle.

This is our way of emergence from the now dark riddle of the earth and unsolved problem of human life. If there were not this secret sense in all we are and do, there would be no significance in the material world and no justification for our earth-existence.

A gnostic superman is the future master of the earth and rescuer of the divine meaning out of the ambiguous terms of this great world-enigma.

78

All that baffles us in existence can find its solution, if we can read it in the light of intention that comes from its source. The original Light points us from our preoccupation with our roundabout and puzzling course to the revealing significance of its aim; for the world's source and origin and its aim are one.

The Cause and Fount of all things is the Divine and the end and aim of all things is the Divine. The finite in Time reveals its own deep and abiding sense when it opens to the Eternal and throws itself into the Infinite.

The only true knowledge — for all the rest is either false or only true in a limited field, half-true and therefore, from the vision of the whole, false — is that which reads everything in the sense and light of the Divine. If man would open himself to the Divine Light, he would begin at last to know; but he prefers always to read everything in the light of man's consciousness, man's sense, man's aims and hopes in his little half lit circle.

But man was not the beginning of the manifested universe or even of the earth-cycle, so also he is not its end and fulfilment. There was much before he appeared; there will be much after he has gone — or fallen into a subordinate place.

Human consciousness is a half term in earth nature's climb from the electron and atom, gas and metal through the vegetable and animal and human formulas to the god and Titan and through the god to the Divine. It is not in the light of the realised alone that we should read the earth-riddle; it is in the light of the unrealised that we shall understand the realised and know why all was and to what all was moving in Nature.

At present what we know best is man and mind and what mind and its several senses see or infer about the universe. But mind is not the highest possible instrument and mental man is not the last creation possible to the capacities of creative evolution in the material universe.

There is indeed the real man as well as this that is apparent. The apparent is this imperfect and struggling humanity, the real is the Purusha, the conscious being within us. The Conscious Being within us, one with the Being in whom we live and move, is indeed the cause and beginning and the end and aim of existence. But our humanity is only a transitory phase of the Conscious Being within us.

Man is not final.

79

The transition from manhood to supermanhood is, in one sense, a self-exceeding, a ceasing to be what we now are in order to become something else or more. In another sense it is a self-becoming, a flowering out of something concealed by our present state, a latent godhead that already is and always was our true being.

Supermanhood is for us a self-exceeding because man, pragmatically and to his own surface awareness, is a small, confused, limited, still ignorant formation of evolutionary Nature, — if supermanhood is intended, then either he has himself to become superman or, if he cannot or will not achieve it, he must make way for some creature greater than he who will have both the will and the power.

But again supermanhood is at bottom a self-becoming because what we now call ourselves is only the surface man, a thinking and living body; but this [is] only the top of a wave, not the whole sea that secretly we are. All that makes supermanhood is there at least in material in our secret depths and on our still more occult height; what in outward fact, in appearance, in present self-awareness man is not but must become, is already there within him; he has only to find himself in order to become that greater self and nature.

80

Man [is a] transitional being, not the final end of the evolution and the crown of terrestrial existence.

This ignorant, imperfect and divided being, with his labouring uncertain thought and half-successful will, this toiling and fluctuating experiment, this field of the attempt at emergence of a thousand things that are striving to be, is no consummation of the struggle of cosmic Force; he is only a laboratory in which Nature seeks for its own concealed secret, makes tentative efforts at what she has been missioned to achieve.

As man arose out of the animal, so out of man superman shall come.

81

Man is a transitional being; he is not final. As it did not begin with him, neither does it end with him. He is not its evident crown, not its highest issue, not the last clear sum of Nature. Nature has not brought out in man her highest possibilities; she has not reached in him the supreme heights of consciousness and being; as there was before him the infrahuman, the insect and animal, so there shall be after him the superhuman, the superman.

Man may himself become the superman, he may become all that he is not now; but for that he must exceed himself. It is not by clinging to his present imperfect consciousness that he can take the next step in the evolution. He must discover and release the spiritual godhead within him, realise his divine possibilities, be himself the giant potential something, the divine someone who has been struggling into emergence out of the original plasm that imprisoned it since began the mystery of terrestrial Nature.

82

Man cannot be final, he is a transitional being. This is very clear from the incompleteness and imperfection of all his powers of consciousness; he can only arrive at some limited form of temporary and unstable perfection by much labour and struggle; and yet the search for perfection is ingrained in his nature. There is something that he is not yet which he has to be; he is reaching always towards the something yet unrealised; his whole life and nature is a preparation, an endeavour of Nature towards what is beyond him.

The human consciousness is limited in every direction; it does not know itself, it does not know the world around it, it does not know the origin and meaning and use of its existence.

But it strives always to know, to find the truth of its being, the right use of its life, the end towards which Nature in him is tending; this it does with a seeking and blundering movement; man's consciousness is an ignorance struggling towards knowledge; it is a weakness training itself for power; it is a thing of pleasure and suffering that tries to lay hands on the true delight of existence.

All that we see in us and around us in this material world is a mystery-play of the Eternal and Infinite; it is the large total and the curiously variable detail of steps and circumstances in a self-discovery or self-unfolding of a Divinity who has hidden his real from his manifested self in the vast black disguise of the inconscience of Nature.

This is the constant miracle that is the key to the meaning of existence, — the miracle of the birth and growth of life and consciousness in the inanimation and inconscience of the material universe.

The birth and growth of consciousness is the whole sense of evolution. For evolution is not in its inner and essential character a development of more and more organised forms of Matter. This development is only an outer instrumentation for the evolution of life and of consciousness in life. That again in its deepest inmost sense is a growth embodying the slow self-discovery and self-revelation of a soul or spirit in a form of living matter.

The evolution has been an ascension starting from forms that seem to be inanimate and inconscient objects, for in them the spirit in things is asleep, through a leisurely waking in plant and animal till it reached with difficulty a beginning of self-awareness in man the mental being, the first and only speaking, thinking, reasoning creature. But there is no ground for the idea cherished by this imperfect human being that he is the summit and last word of the evolution. Humanity is one step in the destiny of the evolving spirit, the last before it assumes something of its own divinity delivered and apparent; his imperfect life and consciousness must develop itself into the type of the fully conscious being, after man or out of him must be born the superman.

This consummation can only take place by an evolution of the consciousness of the individual and humanity beyond its present stage of development; it can take place only if man is ready to take the turn towards which Nature has been slowly leading him, to discover himself, to know himself as soul and spirit, to see and lay firm hold on the Reality behind world and life and things after which he has been seeking through the ages. Nature's first evolution has been an evolution of Matter, of physical objects, of the stage, scenery, external conditions and instruments of the drama of an evolving conscious Life in Matter. In life itself she has been content at first to organise a physicality, an externality of life; the evolution of the body has been the sign, the instrument, the apparent cause of the evolution of consciousness. Even when she has arrived at the evolution of Mind, the mind of a humanity which is capable not only of knowing outwardly the external world but of going within itself, of knowing itself, of knowing the secret things, powers, forces which are behind itself and behind the works of a surface external Nature, still she has been most careful to organise a surface Mind dealing with surface and external things and an organisation of personality which is superficial and not the whole of ourselves, a wave only of the ocean of our hidden being, our secret reality. To build an ego which will deal with material life and nature as its user but also as its subject, a life that is bound by matter, a mind that is bound by both matter and life has been her main preoccupation. But still the evolution of consciousness is the real and central fact which gives a significance otherwise altogether lacking to the mechanical structure of the universe. Man is here not merely to utilise his world for the service of his individual and collective ego; he is here as a medium in which the Spirit within, the secret growing Consciousness can evolve farther its self-manifestation, arrive from a partial to a complete consciousness and, since life itself is there only as a means of this evolution and an image of it, at a complete and perfect individual and social life. If the psychological truth of our being is the real and central truth, more central and important than the physical, this must be its true nature, a conscious being growing towards its own completeness of consciousness and growing too towards its expression and formation in a complete individual and social life.

Section Two

Psychology

The Science of Consciousness

The Problem of Consciousness

The Triple Enigma

83

Existence, consciousness and the significance of our conscious being, — a triple enigma confronts us when we look at them to discover their origin, foundations, nature, their innermost secret. We begin with a riddle, we end with a mystery.

Existence itself is the first riddle. What it is we do not know, we are ignorant how it came to be at all, we cannot say whether it is an eternal fact or a temporary phenomenon. It may be only an appearance or it may be real, not in itself but as a manifestation of some hidden Reality; but then of what is it the manifestation and how came it into being or why had it to be?

Consciousness of existence is a second insoluble miracle. It seems not to have been and now is and it may be that some day it will not be; yet it is a premier fact and without it being would not know of its own existence. Things might exist, but only as a useless encumbrance of a meaningless space, — consciousness makes being self-aware, gives it a significance. But what then is consciousness? Is it something in the very grain of being or an unstable result or fortuitous accident? To whom does it belong? to the world as a whole? or is it peculiar to individual being? Or has it come from elsewhere into this inanimate and inconscient universe? To what end this entry?

The significance of our conscious being in an inconscient material world is the last and worst enigma. What is the sense and justification of the individual, his consciousness, his feeling of self, his personality? Is our individuality real or apparent, temporary or permanent, a minor circumstance or a central secret of the whole? Has it a meaning in the universe or in something beyond the universe? or is it only a chance outburst of Nature with no sense in it or any but a mechanical purpose?

*

All these problems arise in our consciousness and in our consciousness alone can be found their solution — or to it or through it perhaps from a greater consciousness the solution must come. On the nature and validity of our consciousness depends the nature and validity of the discovery we shall make or the conclusions to which we can come. On the power of our consciousness depends the possibility or impossibility of putting into the terms of life the solutions our knowledge discovers. But most of all the appearance and development of consciousness in the inconscient world is the decisive factor, the one thing that gives its existence a light of meaning, a possibility of purpose, a hope of fulfilment and the soul's self-finding. To know, then, the nature of consciousness, its process, its birth, growth and destiny is for us a study of supreme importance.

84

All the problem of existence turns around three things, the nature of being, the nature of consciousness and the secret of the dynamics, the energy of existence by which being and consciousness find each other and manifest what is within them. If we can discover these three things, all is known which we fundamentally need to know; the rest is application and process and consequence.

The problem of consciousness is the central problem; for it links the other two together and creates their riddle. It is consciousness that raises the problem it has to solve; without it there would be no riddle and no solution. Being and its energy would then fulfil themselves in form and motion and in cessation of form and motion without any self-awareness and without any enjoyment or fruition of their form and motion.

Existence would be a fact without significance, the universe an inanimate machine turning for ever — or for a time, — without any reason or issue in its turning. For it to have any significance there must be either a Mind or some other kind of Awareness that observes it, originates it perhaps, has joy in its turning, works out something by the turning of the machine for its own satisfaction or dissatisfaction; or there must be a consciousness that emerges by the turning and reveals being and energy to themselves and leads them to some kind of fulfilment. Even if it is only a temporary consciousness that emerges, yet that must be the one significant fact of being, the one thing that lights up its movements, makes it aware of itself, raises it to something that is more than a mere dead or blank self-existence, a One or a Many that is yet worth no more than a zero.

Even if what fundamentally is in being, is not consciousness but a superconscience, yet that must be one supreme kind of self-awareness, if not also all-awareness; for otherwise there would be no difference between superconscience and inconscience; the two would be only top-side and bottom-side of the same blank, yet mysteriously but vainly fruitful reality.

In the ancient tradition eternal and infinite Being and Consciousness carry in them as the result of their oneness or coexistence an eternal significance of Bliss, Ananda. If we suppose Being-Consciousness to carry in them an eternal and infinite energy that creates, as we say, expresses, as the Sanskrit term better puts it, the universe, then the bliss of eternal conscious being would contain in itself a bliss of eternal energy of consciousness and being finding itself in the joy of self-expression, self-manifestation, self-creation. That would be a sufficient explanation of the appearance of a phenomenal universe, there is in fact no other that is satisfactory. These then are there the three or the four terms underlying all the secret of existence, — Being, Consciousness-Energy, Bliss of being, Ananda.

It would not materially affect the fundamental satisfactoriness of this explanation that the world we live in is not a world of bliss, not a world of consciousness, — though it is in its evident appearance, a world of being and of energy of being, that it is in its phenomenal basis inconscient and works itself out through process and labour and, when consciousness appears, through joy of being but also through pain of being. If the eternal creative Energy takes joy in that, has the Ananda of it (and without consciousness there can be no joy or Ananda), as a poet in the creation of his tragedy or comedy, then that would be a sufficient explanation of the existence of this universe, though we would still have to seek for its significance, the reason of this choice of pain and labour.

Consciousness then is the centre of the riddle. If we know what is Consciousness, where its action begins and ends — if it has a beginning and an ending, what is its process and the significance of its temporal appearance and action, we shall then be able to look deeply into being and its energy and understand and solve all their enigma.

*

But here in our world of Matter the original and fundamental phenomenon we meet everywhere is a universal Inconscience, Consciousness appears to come in as only an incident, a development, a strange consequence of some ill-understood operations of Energy in inconscient Matter. It arises out of an original Inconscience, it dissolves or sinks back into the Inconscience. Once it has appeared it persists indeed but as a general phenomenon precariously manifested in individual living beings. It has the seeming either of an uncertain freak of inconscient Nature, — a disease some would conjecture, a phosphorescence playing upon the stagnant waters of inconscient being, active at certain points of animation, or a guest in a world in which it is alien, a foreign resident with difficulty able to maintain itself in a hardly amicable environment and atmosphere.

According to the materialist hypothesis consciousness must be a result of energy in Matter; it is Matter's reaction or reflex to itself in itself, a response of organised inconscient chemical substance to touches upon it, a record of which that inconscient substance through some sensitiveness of cell and nerve becomes inexplicably aware. But such an explanation may account, — if we admit this impossible magic of the conscious response of an inconscient to the inconscient, — for sense and reflex action [yet] becomes absurd if we try to explain by it thought and will, the imagination of the poet, the attention of the scientist, the reasoning of the philosopher. Call it mechanical cerebration, if you will, but no mere mechanism of grey stuff of brain can explain these things; a gland cannot write Hamlet or pulp of brain work out a system of metaphysics. There is no parity, kinship or visible equation between the alleged cause or agent on the one side and on the other the effect and its observable process. There is a gulf here that cannot be bridged by any stress of forcible affirmation or crossed by any stride of inference or violent leap of argumentative reason. Consciousness and an inconscient substance may be connected, may interpenetrate, may act on each other, but they are and remain things opposite, incommensurate with each other, fundamentally diverse. An observing and active consciousness emerging as a character of an eternal Inconscience is a self-contradictory affirmation, an unintelligible phenomenon, and the contradiction must be healed or explained before this affirmation can be accepted. But it cannot be healed unless either the Inconscient has a latent power for consciousness — and then its inconscience is phenomenal only, not fundamental, — or else is the veil of a Consciousness which emerges out of a state of involution which appears to us as an inconscience.

There is no doubt a connection and interdependence between consciousness and the inconscient substance in which it resides and through which it seems to operate. Consciousness depends upon the body and its functionings, on the brain, nerves, gland-action, right physiological working, for its own firm state and action. It uses them as its instruments and, if they are injured or unable to act, the action of the consciousness may also be in part or whole impaired, impeded or suspended. But this does not prove that the action of consciousness is an action of the body and nothing else. There is an instrumentation and if the instrument is impaired, the user of the instrument can no longer manifest himself rightly through it; if it is destroyed, he cannot operate any longer unless or until he can get another instrument. This then has to be seen whether the phenomena of consciousness are such that they make it necessary to suppose such a use or instrumentation of the body.

If so then either there must be a conscious being in us that is other than the body or else a conscious Energy that thinks, senses, observes, acts intelligently through the physical instrument. This is what we actually observe in our experience of ourselves that there is such a being or else such an energy at work in us and this self-experience is surely as valid, as binding as the accompanying experience of an inconscient substance or building of inconscient Matter which is its field and habitat. Both sides of the phenomenon must be given their value; to reject Matter as an illusion of Consciousness or Consciousness as a freak or disease of Matter are equally one-eyed views which miss the true problem and are not likely to lead to a satisfying solution.

It is certainly possible, prima facie, that Consciousness may be a subordinate phenomenon dependent on Matter or, more accurately, on the Energy that formulates Matter. Our need then is to discover its exact nature, origin, function in a material world and the utmost limit of its possibilities for the human being; for to man matter is only a basis of his life, a material of his works, an opportunity; what is really important to him is consciousness, for it is his consciousness and use of consciousness that gives him his significance and importance to himself and the world; without it he would be nothing and mean nothing.

At any rate this is the fact that faces us, that there is an apparent Energy that seems to have built up this world which first in the animal and then more amply in man has become and works as a conscious Energy and that this transformation is the crucial and capital fact of our universe. It may well be that in it lies the secret of the significance of that universe. It may turn out on deeper enquiry that a Conscious Energy has created as its field an inconscient substance and is veiled in its creation and emerges in it, a Power, a Godhead releasing itself slowly and with difficulty out of its self-made chrysalis of material Inconscience.

It is not sufficient to examine the material, the physiological processes accompanying the functioning of consciousness and attempt to explain the functioning by its physical processes. This leaves consciousness itself unexplained; if it accounts to some extent, but imperfectly, for sense phenomena or mechanical thinking, it does not account in the least for the most important powers of our conscious energy; it does not account for reason, understanding, will, creative thought, conscious selection, the conscious intellectual and spiritual action and self-development of the human being. Yet these are of capital importance, for it is here that consciousness begins to unfold itself out of its chrysalis or matrix of inconscience and a half conscious first working and reveal its true nature. Here consciousness acts in its own right, in its own field and not as a product of the body. To see how the body uses consciousness may be within limits a fruitful science, but it is more important to see how consciousness uses the body and still more important to see how it evolves and uses its own powers. The physiological study of the phenomenon of consciousness is only a side-issue; the psychological study of it independent of all reference to the body except as an instrument is the fruitful line of inquiry. A body using consciousness is the first outward physical fact of our existence, the first step of our evolution; a consciousness using a body is its inner spiritual reality, it is what we have become by our evolution and more and more completely are[.]

What Is Consciousness?

85

Consciousness — but what is consciousness? A word only conveniently ticketing a class of natural phenomena or a fundamental reality of existence?

Apparently a phenomenon which has only a small range intervening in an immense mass of things inconscient and without significance, consciousness alone gives a value to the universe. It seems to have taken no part in the creation of the universe; it was not there in the beginning or even during the greater part of the history of the earth; it may not be there at its end. In the middle it plays a great role in the life of animal and man, but its action is crude and ill-developed in the animal, imperfect in the human creature. Its evolution wears the character of an episode in the long history of an inconscient world, a chapter that began some time ago, but one knows not why it intervened at all or how it will end or whether its appearance has any meaning, whether its developing importance has an accidental and meaningless or a purposeful and revelatory character. It may be a freak of creative Chance or it may be or may carry in itself the whole meaning of the world-drama.

In an inconscient universe, in a Nature or the working of an Energy which is fundamentally material, the emergence [of] Consciousness has at first the air of a surprising, a contradictory, an impossible event. For in such a world, in the working of such a Nature or Energy, how could it ever come into existence? Either there is no real consciousness, only an action of Matter or unconscious Energy which takes this inexplicable and deceptive form, or Nature or Energy is not fundamentally inconscient. Consciousness was always a possibility which at a certain stage chanced or was bound to take place, or it was a latent power that has become manifest. Or even it may be all Nature is really conscious and it is we who foist inconscience upon her because we are limited to a certain range and character of consciousness and cannot communicate with her other ranges or even detect their existence.

It has been held by a certain opinion that consciousness in itself does not exist, there are only phenomena of reactions of Matter to Matter or of Energy in Matter to Energy in Matter to which by generalisation we give the name. There is no person who is conscious, thinks, speaks, perceives, wills, acts; it is an organised body in which certain chemical, molecular, cellular, glandular and nerve activities take place and certain material results and reactions of these activities take place in the brain which take the form of these phenomena. It is the body that thinks, perceives, wills, speaks, acts; it is Matter that goes through these operations and becomes aware of them; it may be said that brain-matter makes a record or notation of these actions and this notation is consciousness and this record is memory. There is nothing in the world except Matter and the operations of Matter.

This theory arose when physical Science concentrated on the operations of Matter, saw only Matter and energy of Matter everywhere; it persists even after that seeing of things has been severely shaken. For now we are driven to see and say that there is no such thing as Matter in itself; what we call Matter is only a mass of phenomena of Energy, events of energy, which our senses regard as objects and our minds classify under the general name of Matter. But we can still hold that all phenomena are phenomena of Energy acting in the forms or sensible events which we call Matter and the phenomena of consciousness are of that character. There is nothing else to it, nothing but the mobile and executive Energy, Nature, Prakriti; there is no soul, no Purusha. Consciousness would still be a general name for a brain-record and notation of these events of material Energy and this will still be the true character of thought, perception, will, speech, act. All these events are separate phenomena which may act and react on each other or group themselves together, but they are not the result or manifestations of any one general force or power of being that we can call Consciousness.

86

Consciousness, — but what is consciousness?

And first of all we have to face the possibility that there is no such thing. For many hold that the word is an unreal generalisation invented to cover a class of material phenomena having their origin in Matter and material in their nature and essence, an operation of Matter on Matter and in Matter. Thoughts are only vibrations of the grey matter of the brain; they are not something other [than] that or capable of existing beyond the material plane; they cannot exist independently of the brain; brain is not their instrument of expression or manifestation; they are [its] instrument made of its substance, dependent on [its] substance, inexistent without it. Mind is an action of Matter, not a separate power or force; there is nothing in it superior to the physicality of the body; it exists by the body and as a part of its activity, lasts along with it, dies with it. Mind is a product of gases, some operation of Nature's chemistry, glandular influences, nervous stimuluses; it is matter and records the operations of Matter.

But why then this appearance of mentality, of consciousness, of a conscious being? That too is only a trick of Matter. They are reflexes and reactions to the contacts of things outside, to other material objects, bodies, movements, forces. Sense and sensation are the reply of the nerves to stimulus of external and material things or to internal stimuli that are still material. To the experience of the body the result of these, recoils, reflexes, reactions, may seem mental, but that cannot alter the fact that they are material products of the workings of Matter.

Well, be it so; but still this mentality creates an awareness of self and things and the movements of self and things, even if both be only a body and so many other bodies, and it is difficult to describe awareness as an inconscient movement or condition or as the inconscient seeming to be conscious. Evidently we are in face of a general sophism invented by specialists of a limited field of data, the data of inconscient Matter, who are determined to force everything into its characteristic formulas and refuse to admit everything else. We must at least recover the right to see this awareness and its movements as they are or as they present themselves to us and see how far it leads us and whether indeed, even if it occurs in matter and the body, it does not lead us to something other than the body and other than Matter. The materialist contention that consciousness is not a separate power or force or manifestation of energy like electricity or magnetism or steam, but only a name for a particular bundle of brain phenomena, cannot hide the startling fact that inconscient and insentient Matter has become sentient and conscious even if it be only at points, in jets, in small masses.

This awareness has created at least the appearance of a

sentient and conscient being who not only becomes relatively aware of self and things, but can study them, discover their nature and process, determine and develop the possibilities of his own consciousness and the possibilities of the world's forces and processes, can will and can create, can ponder and philosophise, can write poetry and create works of art, can use [?] to modify and alter the world around him and make for himself a different life-environment, can look beyond Matter, can tend towards the heights of consciousness not yet developed, can envisage the Superconscient. If the consciousness that can do all this is not a force, a power in itself, it at least looks strangely like it. And we have the right, at least hypothetically, to study it as such a power or force and find out how far that leads us.

It may even lead us to the discovery of a Reality greater than the world of Matter or of Energy building up shapes of Matter and movements in Matter. It may take us beyond phenomena and appearances to the truth of things and to something that is the origin of all that seems to be[.]

*

At the other extreme of human mentality we meet a similar and more devastating denial. Consciousness has no real existence; or, so far as it exists at all, it is as a dynamic Power, a creator of illusions. There is nothing sound or real in what it builds; there is nothing true in what it sees; the world it shows us is [an] impossible chimera, a mass of figments and falsehoods. The sole consciousness that is true is the self-awareness of some absolute Silence, a spaceless immobile Infinite, a timeless featureless Eternity. Or, as the materialist sees only a bundle of phenomena material and dependent on Matter or a fortuitous result of material operations, so the Nihilistic Buddhist sees only a bundle of associations, *sanskaras*, which stuck together produce the false appearance of a continuity of concrete phenomena or a stream of momentary perceptions giving the impression of a false self and coherent world, a coherent personality, but if the bundle is dissolved, if the stream ceases to flow, all dissolves and collapses and shows the empty Nothingness which is the only eternal truth and the sole eternal reality. This superconscient Nothingness has no need of consciousness [for] the greatness of its emptiness or its everlasting peace of unconscious bliss. To return to Nothingness is the only use or meaning of existence.

Here too we seem to be in front of [the] sophism of a specialist seizing the sole salient and striking side, the one prominent aspect of Truth in which he is versed putting aside all the rest as inconsistent or invalid. After all the world exists and is too persistent and effective and solid a phenomenon to be put aside or merely whistled off the field with an airy "It is not"; — a mirage is ineffectual and recedes or fades if it is touched, an illusion dissolves if revealed but this is stupendously effective, overwhelmingly persistent and we have to sound all its possibilities before dismissing it as something vain and trifling. World-consciousness may be only one aspect of our being, but it is a big and momentous aspect and it too should be given its full chance of justifying itself before it is ruled out of court. The eternal reality of a pure immobile existence and its self-awareness is also a truth of our being. But it is not impossible that these are two aspects of one Reality and not so incompatible as the metaphysical logician imagines. This is what we propose to do integrally and with a full and exhaustive inquiry before we decide either way. The chances are that so enormous a thing as this world is something more than an astonishing chimera. The chances are that when two such great aspects of existence confront each other, there is a connection somewhere, a reconciliation of their contraries. It is possible that both are aspects, static and dynamic, of some absolute Reality from which both have drawn their own reality and in which they have their true and inevitable place.

*

In any case consciousness is the one thing by which we can consider or decide the question at all. It is the one thing by which we know at all that world exists or can inquire into its truth and its meaning. If consciousness has no reality and no value, then there is nothing by which we can know the truth, — one explanation of things has then as little value as the other, neither can be claimed as the truth. The consciousness by which we affirm the featureless sole Reality can be as fallacious as that by which we affirm our individual self and the universe.

If consciousness is the self-awareness of the eternal Existence, it can only be this self-awareness seeing its own power and the works of its power as a real world. If consciousness is a creation of the evolution, it is also the one thing by which it receives some value, the one thing by which its values can be reckoned, its [. . .], its one central and essential value. It is not by the development of forms that evolution reaches its height, but by the evolution of consciousness. The degree of consciousness is the degree of evolution; the extent to which consciousness has developed its powers, range, height, its fulness of vision and self-vision, is the measure of the evolution's development of its work and aim, its progress towards its goal, if goal indeed it has and is not the incoherent working out of an accidental Chance. Indeed, if we look at the way in which the Inconscient has devised the world and the sequences by which it has arrived at intelligence, we have some reason [to think] that it is a secret Consciousness which has made this world and under the mask of inconscience has emerged as a slow process of an Ignorance developing Knowledge.

If so, it may well be that it is the self-awareness of the [eternal Existence] that is working out in the formula of inconscient Matter and ignorant Life and half-awakened Mind its own self-manifestation in the material universe.

87

But what is consciousness and what its relation to existence? How and why did it come into being in an inconscient universe, a universe which even if it originated by an inexplicable chance, has assumed the proportions of a huge and complex inexorable mechanism repeating the same processes through the aeons without respite or cessation? By what spiritual or mechanical necessity? by what mechanical chance or accidental process of Energy? To what end or purpose, if any purpose there can be in an inconscient mechanism of brute Necessity or inexplicably organised Chance or any end in a movement which never had any reason for beginning? Does consciousness exist or is it a fortuitous illusion? Who or what is it that becomes conscious in the animal and in the body of the human being?

Three possible solutions. Consciousness has not come into being but was and is always there, a fundamental power of existence, latent or involved or concealed from our mind and sense even in what we call inanimate and unconscious things. It has not come into existence but has emerged from existence; involved it has evolved in the general evolutionary process. Or consciousness is only a phenomenon, a surprising result of certain inconscient processes of Nature, unintentional but actual, unnecessary and accidental or else somehow inevitable as an output of chemical and other physical energies which could not help imposing itself at a certain point of their activity in the natural course of things. It did not exist before that point was reached; when another point has been reached it may go out of existence. Or again the world is a creation of an extra-cosmic or immanent conscious Being personal or impersonal who has either put his consciousness or a consciousness resembling his into his mechanical creation to be an element there or else has infused it from within into the mechanical self-expression in which he has chosen to dwell as its upholder, inspirer, inhabitant.

What is meant by consciousness? what is this phenomenon which seems to have so small a part in the vast inconscient mass of things and is yet the sole element here that can give any value to the universe?

And to come to the heart of the difficulty — is it indeed only a phenomenon, an appearance that has emerged in the course of the workings of an Energy which was, is and will always remain inconscient? Or is it something fundamental, an inherent reality or a latent character or power of that Energy and bound to emerge at some time once it had begun its workings?

88

It is to a mass of ill-connected and ill-understood phenomena that we give this name of consciousness; when these are at work we say that a man or animal is conscious, when they are suspended we say that he or it is unconscious; where they are absent, as in a tree, we suppose the object, even if it has life, to be inconscient by its very nature, incapable of sensation no less than empty of thought and will. Where life is not, inconscience seems to us a still more self-evident character of the thing or being. Man alone is fully conscious, for he alone is aware of himself, reflective on things, in full possession of mental capacities and their aware and observant use. Mind and consciousness are almost synonymous to our ordinary notions; where consciousness is not mentalised, we find it difficult to recognise its presence, hardly possible to follow its movements; even in the animal we are apt to regard it as reflex movement not aware of itself, undeveloped, primitive.

89

All that exists or can exist in this or any other universe can be rendered into terms of consciousness; there is nothing that cannot be known. This knowing need not be always a mental knowledge. For the greater part of existence is either above or below mind, and mind can know only indirectly what is above or what is below it. But the one true and complete way of knowing is by direct knowledge.

All can be rendered into terms of consciousness because all is either a creation of consciousness or else one of its forms. All exists in an infinite conscious existence and is a part or a form of it. In proportion as one can share directly or indirectly, completely or incompletely in the eternal awareness of this Infinite, or momentarily contact or enter into it, or formulate some superior or inferior power of its consciousness or knowledge, one can know what it knows, in part or whole, by a direct knowing or an indirect coming to knowledge. A conscious, half conscious or subconscious participation in the awareness of the Infinite is the basis of all knowledge.

All things are inhabited by this consciousness, even the things that seem to us inconscient and the consciousness in one form can communicate with or contact the consciousness in another or else penetrate or contain or identify with it. This in one form or another is the true process of all knowledge; the rest is ignorant appearance.

All things are one self; it is the one Knower who knows himself everywhere, from one centre or another in the multiplicity of his play. Otherwise no knowledge would be possible.

The Secret below the Surface

90

All life, all existence is an enigma to the human mind, because the mind is a light which sees only the surfaces of things or at most a little below the surface and is moreover limited by its own circumscribed area of vision. It cannot see what is beyond those limits and yet there are an infinity of things beyond its circle. It cannot see what is above, it cannot see what is within, it cannot see what is below. But what is on the surface is never the truth of things; the surface presents us only with facts not with truths, with phenomena not with realities, with imperfect indications, not with the realisation of things in themselves. The secret, the truth, the reality of things is above, within, below, it is not on their surface.

91

There is a meaning in the universe, an intention in cosmic existence; there is a significance of the individual, his life is a sign and has a purpose.

The true truth of things is not apparent on the surface, it is something hidden. Truth is not obvious, it comes always as a discovery, Life is the working out of a secret, the process and progress of a mystery; we too are not what we seem to be, we have to find and become ourself.

What we seem to be is a thinking human animal. What we are and have to become is God; the secret purpose of our existence here is to find the occult Reality of ourselves and the world, to become Divine.

92

Our existence in the world has a reality which is other than that which strikes our mind and senses on the surface. It contains a secret, a mystery which we have to discover, for through that discovery we must move both to the realisation of our self and spirit and the perfection and fulfilment of our life in Nature.

Our life is not an illusion nor a delirium nor is Nature a Maya, a fabricator of dreams or a dealer in vanities as certain religions would have it nor is one the outcome of a blind Force or the trick [of] a blind self-regulating Chance, the other an unconscious Power as it must be if the materialists' dogma were true. Our life is neither a freak of God nor a freak of Nature; it has a conscious plan although a secret plan, a significance although an occult and mystic significance.

The plan, the significance are secret and mysterious to us because we live on the surface of ourselves and things and are not in touch with either their core or their height or depths. Science on one side, Religion and Philosophy on the other try to arrive at the hidden Truth, but each touches and only just touches one end of it and refuses to go farther and discover the other end or the link and reconciling relation between these two poles of existence.

It is said in the Veda of Agni, the flame of the creative Will and Force, that he hides his two extremities; only his middle is patent and visible. The head of Agni is occult in some superconscient height, his feet are plunged in the abyss of the material Inconscience. Consciousness emerging in the universe of life and mind is the bridge and link between the two poles. But our human consciousness is a term in the chain which is aware only of itself and sees all the rest in its own terms; it cannot identify itself with the other links and misses their significance and their purpose. It stands on the middle of the bridge looking all around it, but the bridgeheads are to its sight invisible. It cannot see what is there, but only speculate, infer or conjecture.

Science questing with its measuring rod of empirical experiment begins to have a dark glimpse of the Inconscient; it knows the universe as an organised freak that has emerged from the material Inconscience and will go back to its source. Religion and Philosophy rise on the wings of spiritual experience or in a balloon of metaphysical logic into some stratosphere of superconscient Reality, they seem to discover a God or Self or Spirit or Absolute and try to map it with the intellect or to turn it into a dynamic spiritual formula. But they are unable to reconcile these three terms of being; their physical experiments or their spiritual experiences are valid, but each has hold of only one end of the enigma.

Science has discovered Evolution; Religion and Philosophy have discovered something of that which is involved and evolves in this cosmic Existence. But the two discoveries have refused to shed light upon each other; each has shut itself up in its own formulas. This is because each is a creation and activity of Mind, Science of the concretising experimental mind, Philosophy of the abstracting intellectual mind, Religion of the dynamic spiritual mind. But Mind is bound always by its partial formulations of the Truth; Mind grasps formulas or images but is itself grasped by its own creations, it cannot get free from them or go beyond them. But the mind's concepts and formulas are only fragmentary representations of Truth or pointers or abstract schemas and images, not her very self and reality. Either a deeper inner soul-vision or a higher overmental or supramental consciousness is needed to discover Truth in her very face and body.

Then only can both ends of the riddle be firmly seized and connected together, the whole of existence seen in one gaze and life compelled to unmask its fathomless significance[.]

*

A mysterious something involved in Matter, concealed by it, evolving from it but in a material house or figure, striving to reveal itself in life and mind, but concealed by its forms of life, concealed by its forms of mind, shooting out from them glimpses of itself, glimpses that hint but do not elucidate, — this is what we can see, and we see no more; the rest is speculation and conjecture. Is this something native to Matter, born in it and destined to die in it? Or is it an alien, a temporary visitor? Is Matter itself only a mask of it, a phenomenon of Energy, as it now more and more seems to be? Energy itself is a movement, a force of concealed Consciousness, Consciousness the sign of a hidden spiritual Being. But if so, what possible significance or purpose can there be in this involution, this material self-concealment and self-imprisonment, this slow tormented emergence of the Spirit?

Two lines of enquiry seem to give, though imperfectly and in opposition, a positive base for a reply to the question and the riddle, — the experiments of the scientist and the experience of the mystic.

Consciousness and the Inconscient

Inconscience

93

World and life can be looked at from one of two opposite vision-bases — observed in the light of the knowledge that looks below and sees as the foundation of things the Inconscient from which our physical birth took its rise or experienced in the light of the knowledge that looks above and draws the radiations it throws upon all around it from the Superconscient which is our soul's source. These two conflicting light-streams — which yet at their extreme points seem almost to meet or at least touch the same mystery — yet shed at first opposite values on the phenomenon of conscious life in matter and illumine in contrary senses the destiny of man and his place in world-existence; for in the light from above it assumes a supreme significance, in the light from below a supreme insignificance.

For if we look from one side, consciousness appears as a circumstance, a thing secondary or even accidental, a little flickering temporary uncertain light in a vast darkness of inconscient world-systems; if we look from the other it is the slowly delivered but not yet perfectly released blaze of that which supported all along this seemingly inconscient creation, subtly concealed in its very cells, molecules, atoms, electrons or whatever still more infinitesimal whorls of motional force-substance have been made its base. Either then consciousness is a perishable jet of flame shooting up out of the slime of this obscure teeming morass we call Matter, a strange inexplicable temporary freak sprung from gas and plasm, chromosome and gene, gland and hormone — we know not well how even when we have found the process, and know not at all why and can never know and hardly need to know, since the whole thing is a meaningless and eventually purposeless miracle of incalculable Chance or blind Necessity, — or if it is not this, then it is the very Flame which, dynamic and hidden, has shaped all these things and now, overt and revealed, can work openly on them and on itself to use, to uplift, to subtilise, to refine, to liberate, to transfigure.

If the first view is right, the view so long pressed on us by physical Science, then this very universe itself is but a queer paradoxical movement of mindless eyeless Force or of a brute substance emanating purposeless energy, which yet works as if it had a purpose; for it produces by some inconscient compulsion on itself a steady succession of evolutionary forms that carry themselves as if they had an aim and a meaning, although in the nature of things they can really have none. The whole is a mechanism which automatically turns out what it must with a certain inevitability but has no comprehending Intelligence, no intuitive Power behind it to determine its use. Universal Nature is a Chance that works as if it were a Necessity or else perhaps a Necessity that works like a self-regulating Chance. What seems to be consciousness has come out of this machine just like everything else in this singular freak-universe, constituted somehow, miraculously, impossibly, as the plant and the flower came out of the seed, somehow constituted, or as different chemical atoms are mysteriously constituted out of variant numbers of identical electrons, or as water leaps inexplicably into birth by a combination in exact measure of two gases. We have discovered that by just this process it came, — consciousness, the flower, the atom, water, — but how it could come into being by such a process is an unsolved riddle and how it took this form out of such a mother or could be the result of such ingredients and what each of these things in itself is remains unknowable. It is or has so become (or perhaps is not, but only so seems to our senses) — but that is all, for more than this science limited by its methods cannot tell and speculative philosophy itself with all its range and licence can hardly conjecture. And it does not much matter; for after all this consciousness which emerged obscurely in Time will in a later

Time disappear with its living vessels and be as if it had never been leaving behind the Inconscient still busy with its perpetual and empty labour. And perhaps indeed this consciousness is not really consciousness at all but only a sort of strange vibrant typewriting of conventional signs by which the Inconscient records to itself its own mechanical values; for things are not what they seem, colour is not colour but only a fictitious sign, all things perhaps are mere signs of bundled vibrations and consciousness itself nothing else. However we look at it, it would seem very much as if this universal Energy which creates these strange, inexplicable, impossible things or semblances that yet in a way are, were only a sort of Maya, like that of the Illusionists, *aghatana-ghatana-patiyasi*, very skilful to make happen things that cannot happen, a huge senseless well organised paradox, a sequently arranged mass of inevitable inconsequences, a defiance to reason of which reason is the last brilliant but bewildered outcome. And of all these phenomenal appearances, the uprising of consciousness is perhaps the most paradoxical, the least inevitable, — Nature's most accidental, most startling inconsequence.

And again in this reading of the universe, more baffling than any unbelievable belief — *credo quia incredibile*, — with which ever dogmatic theology or mystic philosophy has challenged us, man loses all his cosmic value. An infinitesimal little creature on a tiny speck of matter lost amidst a whirling multitude of stupendous universes most or all of them perhaps vacant of life and thought and made for no other end but simply to whirl, he is (justifying Scripture) even as the worm is — only an edition de luxe, with copious developments and commentaries, of the same laborious but useless text, the same minute, careful, well-arranged, painstaking but insignificant script that we see already in the ant and the termite. Individual man lasts for a few years which are in the aimless vastness of the universe of no more matter than the few days or weeks or months of the insect. The race indeed has endured for millions of years and may endure for some centuries, some thousands, myriads or millions of years longer; but what are these millions in the incalculable aeons of the cosmos? The termite perhaps was before man and may be there when he has disappeared, perhaps massacring his kind out of existence or destroyed by his own science; it has like man done against adverse conditions extraordinary miracles of intelligence (having yet, it seems, no intelligence with which to do them), built immense fortified cities, cultivated earth, organised remarkable societies, adapted means to end and overcome a stepmotherly Nature. Each has an equal value for itself which arrives after all only to the passion Nature has put in each species for survival, for exploitation of its life; for each other their only significance is to come annoyingly and destructively in each other's way; for the universe — at least the universe as Science has described it — both have an equal non-value, for to it neither can matter, since they will disappear and the world go on interminably as it did without them. Vanity of vanities, Science teaches us even as did the world's Scriptures; out of nothingness we came and into nothingness we shall sink hereafter. All that we are and think and create [and] do, however wonderful to our own eyes, or even if really wonderful in the mind's values, is but a bubble, a vibration, a plasmic pullulation on the surface of Matter.

This is one side of the picture; but there is another.

94

If there is a consciousness in Matter, however secret and involved, there must be a consciousness secret and involved in the Inconscient.

But the question then arises whether such a thing can be any more than there can be a square circle [or] cold fire. "Not even a hundred declarations of the Veda," says Shankara, "could prove the coldness of fire." There are psychologists who deny that there is or can be any such thing as the subconscious, for it is a flat self-contradiction to speak of a consciousness which is below the level of consciousness. To be conscious is to be aware of self and things or at least of things, with whatever limitation, as a man's or an animal's waking mind is aware.

To a certain thought it might seem that only the surface of things is knowable, the rest either does not or cannot exist or must be left in the shadow of an inevitable agnosticism. There are no depths [or they] are, as Bertrand Russell would have us believe, an uninhabited emptiness; there is no inner sky except the sky of thought or an abstract void crossed by the wandering wings of the Idea; if there is a sky behind the sky, it is such a Void, a void of unattainable superconscience. But this too is an imagination, a nonexistence. There can be no consciousness in the Inconscient, no Conscious in unconscious things, no superconscience.

If that were so, it would be impossible to have any true or whole knowledge. For our mind is an Ignorance searching for knowledge and arriving at representations or figures of it, it can never be except by a miraculous transformation something that knows, still less knows truly and knows all. But knowledge exists somewhere, knowledge is possible and a seeking ignorance is not our first and last fate. Our boundaries are lost [. . .], the depths teem [or] are no longer vacant, the sky above mind is peopled with winged realities. The subconscient is disburdened of its strange contents, the superconscient becomes the top [of] consciousness, the peak of knowledge, there is a Conscient in unconscious things. Let us look then with the eye of the Ignorance first but also with the eye of this greater knowledge at the subconscient, at Inconscience, at the superconscient top of things. An immediate change will take place in our conception of self and our outlook on the universe.

95

The subconscious is a fact of our mentality. It is not the fact that our whole being, even our whole mentality, is on the surface. There are concealed heights, there are hidden gulfs, there are crowded spaces behind the front wall, below the threshold, in the unseen mental environment. There is a vast inconscient below us, an infinite superconscience above us. All these are part of a secret consciousness in the world, but also part of our own hidden being of which we are not aware or only intermittently and ignorantly or only, in our ultimate evolution, eventually aware.

Even in our ordinary experience there are moments in which one or other of these things becomes apparent, acts in our daily actions or peers out above the surface and replaces our absent and inattentive mind. We start writing and finish the writing without knowing what we have written. We are walking with our mind aware and guiding our course, — the [?outer] mind, — but we continue to walk and find ourselves after a time farther on the intended way or beyond the intended goal or turn and have to retrace our steps. In an unconscious or half conscious moment words pour from our lips which we would never have spoken if we had used our fully awake mind and will. What is it that thus takes up the writing, the walk, the speech and completes our intention or betrays us? It must be either something of the mind behind or below its active surface movement or something of a driving life-force or action of the body.

But in the first explanation there must be a part of the mind, not our conscious thought and will that is capable of continuing automatically a course once habitual or previously fixed or pursuing of itself the direction accustomed or repetitive. It is capable not only of execution but of a radical direction, even a misdirection. This means a consciousness at conscious work, however vague or latently automatic, and can only be described as a subconscious or at least partly subconscious or subjacent, an underlying something else akin to consciousness. This is the first sign of a subconscious mind or of a secret consciousness which may even underlie not only our own surface being, but the whole cosmic operation and its apparently inconscient functioning and driven interactions, its purposeless purpose.

If it is a life-force that goes on with the works of the life when the mind is not attending to them, then only this must be a subconscious action and where it continues an action initiated by the conscious mind, then some sort of mechanical consciousness must be attributed to it. If it is the body that takes up the action, it must equally be credited with a subconscience that can do under certain circumstances the work of consciousness.

I have written a letter and proceed to put the name and address on the envelope, but my mind gets absorbed in something else and I find that I have written another habitual name and address, not the one I intended. Memory evidently has done this uncalled for work, but not a conscious memory with the mind aware of what it was doing. A subconscious layer of memory must have come to the surface mistaking the call, or there must have been a double action of memory one deliberate, the other automatic, the temporary suspension of the first giving room to an inadvertent action of the subliminal working.

On the other hand I may complete a sentence with a phrase I had not intended or thought of; where did it come from if not from the subconscious mind? It may even be a phrase having no connection with the conscious thought or in itself incoherent or have the form of words but be unintelligible. What is it that has dictated these things?

96

As consciousness descends from the supreme and the higher to the lower levels, it loses progressively its force and intensity till it reaches the nadir of inconscience.

97

The figure of Inconscience is the mask of an all-conscious Creator; the Inconscient creates with an unerring art, adaptation of means to end, ingenious originality, spontaneity and [. . .] of device. The conscious creator man cannot even come near the inconscient Creator, God. But [the] Inconscient is only a mask on a mobile face; its blank rigidity hides from us the expression of the face of the Omnipresent.

The Inconscient Energy

98

At one end of existence, the nether material end, we observe the reign of a complete phenomenal Inconscience. No creative consciousness or will can be detected there; we start from something that is but is not aware that it is, things that are but are unconscious that they are or that anything is. Yet it is this vast impalpable Inconscient that seems to have created Matter and the whole material universe.

There is, obvious and undeniable, an Energy that creates and there is a creation; these are the only two affirmations we can make which are beyond doubt. Even if we take the creation to be illusory, still the illusory creation is there and there is a Force or Energy or Power that has created it, whether it be mere unconscious Energy, Prakriti, or an energy of deceptive consciousness, Maya.

What we actually experience here is an energy inconscient or seemingly inconscient which is in constant motion and in that motion takes on forms or produces forms and in these forms it enters into many kinds of activity and engenders a multitude of active relations. Energy and action and the results of action, Prakriti and Karma, this is the whole formula of the material universe. Objects innumerable there are, lives too and things living, a Mind or minds, a Consciousness or consciousnesses or else perhaps mere phenomena in the Inconscient to which we give these names; but all these appear to us as if they were temporary results, events ephemeral or long persistent of the movement of Energy and action, its Karma.

What is this Energy? is it something uncreated and unborn, eternal, absolute though all it produces is created, temporal, relative? If it is born, then whence came it? in or on what does it work? what set it going and towards what? We do not know and seem to have no means of knowing; at least our intellect does not know and has not yet found out any sure way to know; it can only speculate, speculate endlessly in an inconclusive circle.

It is not an unborn eternal Matter from which it is born or of which it is the eternal force or in and on which it works, as was once supposed and as some still suppose. For that is now only a construction of the speculative mind, an idea, a hypothesis, an arbitrary postulate for which there is no discoverable correspondent reality. Matter, as we now know it, is something that we can almost see coming into existence or at least can determine its process of creation; waves of energy materialising into particles and again becoming waves, but finally the waves coalesce and become atoms of what we must needs call Matter. This cannot be the inert inconscient Godhead, original and eternal, out of which all came, in and on which Energy works and produces by automatic necessity or a fortunately self-organising Chance the material world and all the lives, minds, souls — if souls there are — which in it live and move.

It can be said that this is only a conclusion of Science and Science is unfinished and everchanging; it may refute tomorrow what it affirms today; it may discover that electricity and light, the electron and proton and the photon are not the last word or the first fact; there may be a subtler Matter which is not that but something else — a Matter not formed but motional, vibratory, aetheric. But, still, what can that be but a subtler motion of Energy, a vibration of Energy in Space? And of Space too we do not know what it is, — whether a mere conception of our mind and its sense or an extension of something that exceeds the grasp of our mind and sense, — perhaps an unseizable Infinite.

The Sankhya philosopher affirmed an original indiscriminate Matter which evolves from Prakriti, from the eternal Energy, — is, we might say, its first state of manifestation. But as it is indiscriminate, it is not likely to be in any way determinable by our senses. And, after all, this too is only a creation of Energy, an evolution out of itself or a state which it assumes; we do not get away from the original formula, Energy and its actions and results, Prakriti and Karma.

99

An energy of some Inconscient Existence has created Matter and the material universe. All this material universe is indeed nothing but an inconscient Energy taking form or producing form and in and through its forms entering into all kinds of activity. Energy (Prakriti) and motion and action of Energy, Karma, and results of its action — this is the formula of our universe.

But whence then comes consciousness? How can things in their very nature inconscient and unaware become conscious or develop some kind of awareness? There is here a contradiction which is inexplicable and the more we look at it, becomes more and more inexplicable.

This is possible because inconscience is a phenomenon not a fundamental reality. A phenomenon is something that appears to us, but does not show to us the whole reality of existence or of its own existence; it is a front, a face, a circumstance of something more than itself that does not appear but is — the Reality. Inconscience is a phenomenal state; it is consciousness that is the Reality; consciousness is an inherent and eternal state of being, inconscience is its temporal, temporary and apparent condition when it forms itself by its own energy into Matter and material objects. Its consciousness involves itself in inanimate Matter and seems there an inconscience; its energy too acts as if it were an inconscient energy, doing things without knowing what it is doing, creating a universe but unaware of the universe it creates, contriving millions of devices, but without any intelligence. So it seems, but so it cannot be; there is something hidden from us which we have to discover. It is the consciousness behind the Energy, the conscious Being behind the action that we have to discover.

Consciousness, being, force, energy (shakti), these are the three first terms of the fundamental truth of existence. What we have to know is how they work out together in ourselves and the universe.

*

Chance, some say, does all; the phenomena of consciousness — for there is no such thing as consciousness in itself, only reactive phenomena of sense and mind provoked by outward impacts — are, like everything else, the products of Chance.

But what is Chance, after all? It is only a word, a notion formed by our consciousness to account for things of which we have no true knowledge — and it does not account for them.

When we do not know how or why a thing came to pass, we escape by saying, it was chance. We do not truly know how or why the universe happened or things in the universe, so we say "Chance made it; Chance did it." An intellectual escape, nothing more. If we said "A selection, mysterious to us, out of infinite possibility," then there would be some truth and some profundity in our thinking.

But the emergence of consciousness out of the Inconscient was more probably a necessity in the very being of being, in the innate movement of being, than merely a possibility. Necessity, then? an inevitable determination in Nature? or a self-determination in the conscious Spirit?

Consciousness and Immortality

100

Our existence is not a freak of some inconscient mechanical Force stumbling into consciousness nor an inexplicable activity on the surface of a blank Nothingness or an impassive inactive Infinite. There is a significance in our life, it moves towards a spiritual end, it fulfils the drive of an eternal reality.

Immortality is the nature of our being, birth and death are a movement and incident of our immortality. Birth is an assumption of a body by the spirit, death is the casting off [of] the body; there is nothing original in this birth, nothing final in this death. Before birth we were; after death we shall be. Nor are our birth and death a single episode without continuous meaning or sequel; it is one episode out of many, scenes of our drama of existence with its denouement far away in time.

101

All depends upon consciousness. For all world-existence is a form created by consciousness, upheld by consciousness, determined by consciousness. All that is is a consciousness veiled or unveiled, manifesting or concealing its own substance. All is energy of consciousness masked by movement of mind and life and matter and taking forms which are merely motions of the energy stabilised to appearance, yet always in movement; for the consciousness that constitutes these forms is always in dynamic movement; the visible rhythm and self-result of this self-repeating or self-continuing vibration and never resting motion and dynamis is what we call form. Disperse the energy that constitutes it and the form dissolves. Withdraw the consciousness that expresses itself in the energy and the energy can keep up no longer its sustaining rhythm; therefore it disperses, therefore the form dissolves. If we could so intensify the power of the consciousness put out in us that we could keep the energy always repeating, continuing, enlarging, progressing in its rhythm, then, the form might change but need not dissolve and even physically we should be immortal[.]

The Science of Consciousness

Vedantic Psychology

102

Body, brain, nervous system are instruments of consciousness, they are not its causes.

Consciousness is its own cause, a producer of objects and images and not their product. We are blinded to this truth because when we think of consciousness, it is of the individual we think.

We look at the world in the way and speak of it in the terms of individual consciousness; but it is of the universal consciousness that the world is a creation.

The individual participates subconsciently and superconsciently in the universal consciousness. But the embodied individual in his physical or waking mind does not so much participate as arrive at participation. He is not directly part of it, but reproduces it by a partial indirect action, and in reproducing selects and varies, combines, discombines, new combines and develops his selections.

In the body his waking mind receives its impressions from the outside world and reacts upon them. Body and nerves are his instrument for the impressions and the reaction; therefore all their apparent instrumentation is nervous, physical, atomically combined, a physiological apparatus for a battery of nervous energy.

Physical, nervous and sensory impressions are the means by which this individual is induced to put himself into waking relations with the physical universe. Physical, nervous and sensory reactions are his means for entering into that relation.

*

He, — but who is he? The mental being in his mentality.

Who is it that feels himself to be separate from the world or things in the universe to be outside his being? Not the Spirit, for the Spirit contains the universe, creates and combines all relations. All personalities act in the one spirit, as our own multiple personalities act in one being. Spiritual being is their continent, they are not its constituents, but its outer results and the diverse representative selves of its consciousness and action.

Not, either, the supramental being. For the supramental being is one with the spirit in its original or basic consciousness, in its idea-consciousness it is ideally comprehensive of cosmic things or, if we must speak in terms of space, commensurate with the universe. The supramental being with one action of his Idea-self can regard universal being as his object of will and knowledge. That attitude is the seed of mind. It can regard it as contained in itself and itself contained in it, and in that way know and govern it. But it can too, like Spirit in its real action know all things by identity and govern all things by identity. Externality of being does not enter into supramental experience.

Supermind can see mind externalising objects; it can itself take a particular viewpoint fronting objects but it is in itself that it fronts them, as we front our subjective operations in mind. It does not regard them as something outside its own being, as we regard physically objects.

Mind is a delegation from supermind, which primarily regards existence as an object fronting its vision. Mental being also need not regard the universe as quite separate from or outside its own being. Subliminal mentality is capable by extension of a comprehensive relation with cosmic things and of entering into unity with the universe. Mind's starting-point is not a containing universal vision or a knowledge by identity, but an individualised viewpoint from which it sees the universe. Still mind can arrive at a sort of containing vision, a mentalised cosmic consciousness.

What then compels embodied mind to see objects externally and by separation? It is compelled by the fact of physical embodiment. Body is a self-limitation of conscious being by which mind is rigidly bound down to its own tendency of separative individuation.

Body, including all physical formations from the atom upwards, is a device of Nature for the extreme of conscious individuation. Empirically it is immaterial whether it is an image created by consciousness or a real substance of being. For practical purposes we may take it as a substantial formation. In fact body is a knot of conscious being built up by its own energy, instinct with nervous or subnervous life, — because the energy is in dynamic actuality a living energy — cognizing and cognized by subconscious or superficially conscious sense, because the energy is in a certain inherent reality a conscious energy. It is a knot indivisible in reality from universal Consciousness and Force and Substance but in a certain empirical utility of selective action separative rather than separate. Body, not really separate, is limited by subconscious instinct of separation and energetic tendency of separation, but not capable of effecting real separation. All its movements are a practical result of selective experience and selective action which is based on a phenomenon of separate physical being.

Body is separated from other bodies by intervention of universal matter, but both of the separate bodies are one with the indivisible intervening matter, therefore not separate in reality, but indivisibly connected in energy, and one matter in fundamental reality.

Put otherwise, two bodies are images or formations of one indivisible ethereal space, which is in reality one indivisible movement of material energy, life-energy, mind energy.

This inseparable connection and fundamental unity of bodies become of immense importance when we examine the relation of the appearances of consciousness to its reality.

Mind in body has to begin from the separation proper to body. Embodied mind is bound down in its root-action to a separative view of the universe. This is its waking view; subliminally, whether in subconscious mentality or where it approaches or touches the superconscient being, it is capable of bridging the artificial separation.

Taking this separative basis of waking consciousness for itself and for a reality, the house of imprisoned awareness from which it looks at the world, it is bound to see objects as external to this awareness and this conscious vision. Embodied mind is as if a walled house were to have a thinking soul and spirit (air and ether) and look at things not in itself as things outside through windows (the senses), receive the touches of the outside air (nervous life-impacts) as if other than the air in itself; even its own ether as other than the rest of ether (my soul and other souls). This is the self and not-self of our mentality.

Mind subliminal is able, though not normally habituated, to bridge the gulf between self and not-self; where it approaches the superconscient, this gulf lessens and conscience of oneness grows upon the being.

Body is only the instrument and basis of this extreme separative individuation, not its first cause. Mind itself is a prior cause; but mentality in itself need not be rigidly separative: especially, subliminal mind has a large integrating power. Mind in itself is only the basis of a relatively separative plurality; mind in body increases this relation into a phenomenon of absolutely separative plurality.

From this basis of externalising individuation and separative plurality waking mental consciousness in the physical universe commences its operations.

103

Psychology is the knowledge of consciousness and its operations.

A complete psychology must be a complex of the science of mind, its operations and its relations to life and body with intuitive and experimental knowledge of the nature of mind and its relations to supermind and spirit.

A complete psychology cannot be a pure natural science, but must be a compound of science and metaphysical knowledge.

This necessity arises from the difference between natural or physical sciences and psychology.

A physical science is a knowledge of physical processes

which leads inevitably to action and use of physical processes. The scientist may only regard scientific truth and not utility; but he can find only truth of the process of things, not truth of the nature of things. His discoveries bring about inevitably an utility for action; for all truth of process is an utility for action. Even when not the aim of science, process and utility are the soul and body of physical science. Matter itself is only an utility of Spirit or Being or Nature for physical process and action. Material energy is an instrumental dynamis for that utility or else an original dynamis which has no other sense of its operations. We get beyond to a higher sense only when [we] get beyond material to mental, psychical and spiritual energy, to mind, soul and spirit.

Debateable it is whether if we knew the real essence of Matter and the basic, not only the apparent, relations of mind, soul and spirit to matter and material operations, we could not arrive at an infinitely more potent use of physical process and operations. But in any case these things cannot be discovered by physical science; it has its limits and cannot exceed its limits.

Psychology may begin as a natural science, but it deals already with superphysical and must end in a metaphysical enquiry. If one side of the process it studies and its method of enquiry is physical, the other and more important is non-physical; it is a direct observation of mental operations by mind without any regard to their physiological meaning, support, substratum or instrumentation.

If this is in the first place a study of process and involves an utility for psychological action, yet what it leads to inevitably is not that action but an enquiry into the nature of mental consciousness.

This necessity arises from the immediate perception by mind of something beyond and behind its operations, some energy of hidden consciousness greater than our apparent mentality. To know what that is, we have to resort to a metaphysical enquiry.

Consciousness is itself found to be not essentially a process, — although in mind it appears as a process, but the very nature of self-existent being. Being or the Self of things can only be known by metaphysical — not necessarily intellectual — knowledge.

This self-knowledge has two inseparable aspects, a psychological knowledge of the process of Being, a metaphysical knowledge of its principles and essentiality.

We find that one of these principles of being is energy. Energy is an eternal and inherent power of conscious being. Since all energy is convertible to action, this knowledge also contains a side of psychological and spiritual utility, — eventually perhaps even, since life and body are results of the energy of being and supports of its action, of vital and physical utility.

Two great utilities open before psychology. We may acquire the possibility of a greater being, consciousness and energy. We may open up the possibility and discover the psychical means or process [of] becoming consciously one with our original self-existent Being, with God, the Absolute, the Transcendence. To lead up to these possibilities is the aim of Vedantic psychology.

104

All psychology must result in and every complete statement of psychological truth must have for its frame a double schema of existence into which the facts it deals with must fall, a descending scale and an ascending scale.

The simplest elementary psychology deals with three notes of a limited scale, — the body and physical field and its impacts, the life and body and biological and physiological processes, the mental being and its conscious experience and action. This is a scale of ascension.

*

The nature of the physical field is the first fact; it determines everything else; it gives the impacts which awaken the consciousness, the impressions, images, subjects which are its matter, the starting-point and basis of all its conceptions, the body which is its support, instrument, fulcrum of action, the physical occasion of the sense of self.

Everything appears to be in the body or by the body and either for the body or for the I-sense in the body.

The body seems to be the principal if not the only cause or determinant of individual consciousness.

What is not of the body is of the physical field outside the body.

Whatever in consciousness seems not to be of the physical field, yet appears to be derived from it, to be a resultant, development or deformation from physical experience.

*

The life in the body is the necessary modification of the first fact of material being, without whose intervention consciousness is unable to manifest in any material form. The atom is a form of matter, the stone is a material body, but life in these things is either nil or not developed to the point where manifestation of consciousness becomes possible. Consciousness in the atom and the stone is either latent, non-manifest to us, suppressed, potential or nil.

Life in any degree is not sufficient for the manifestation of mental consciousness. A certain high degree of it or else a certain indispensable kind of organisation is needed for this third tone of the scale. Plants are living, even in a degree intensely living, they have a nervous organisation, but consciousness is either nil or latent, non-manifest at least to us, suppressed or else of another kind than ours, a submental nervous consciousness and not mentality.

Life supplies certain biological conditions and certain physiological processes which physically underlie the operations of conscious mental being.

Life gives the intermediate dynamic link between mind and body.

Life has two operations which serve the purpose of mentality, a necessary life power in a nervous apparatus and a capacity of instrumental development and modification. Without the power of life in the nervous apparatus consciousness in the body is impossible; without the power of developing modifications it might exist as in the lower animals, but it could not expand as in man.

The nervous apparatus is the initial biological fact necessary to mentality. Life power consists not of the nervous system, which is a physical element, but of a new power or energy of which the system is the vehicle, — the power of nervous communication, nervous charge, nervous discharge. This power is not sufficient to create mentality, for the plant too possesses them, yet does not appear to be a mental being, but it is the first condition of embodied mentality.

A power of biological and physiological development is the secondary, continuative factor necessary to farther evolution of mentality. Once the nervous vital power appears in material body, it shows a biological power of developing a more complex physical instrumentation for a more complex nervous activity. Once it has attained a certain complexity of physical instrumentation, life seems able indefinitely to refine in some subtle way its action of nervous power so as to support a more and more fine and complex action of mentality.

How far this development of mentality can go and how far it is dependent on the physical apparatus and the nervous action is one of the capital questions of psychology.

*

Mental being, power and operation of mental consciousness is the third note of the scale of being.

Mind cannot certainly be said to be constituted of life and body, nervous action and reaction in a physical body. Nervous action does not appear to constitute of itself consciousness, any more than physical impact and consequent atomic disturbance appears of itself to constitute nervous action. As a correspondent or resultant nervous communication, charge and discharge is necessary to manifest life, so a resultant or correspondent conscious action, — sensation, perception, thought, conscious motiving impulsion, desire, intention, will, — are necessary to manifest mind.

Mind may or may not be an exact result, reflection or correspondence of life action in body, life thinking itself out in body, body living and thinking out its experience in mind, but it is not the same thing as life and body.

Life is a new or second power emerging from or in material energy. Mind is a new or third power emerging from or in the life-energy.

*

But this is only the ascending scale.

Mind is not only awakened by life-action in the body at a certain evolutionary pitch of its operations; mind reacts upon and in certain ways uses, for its own characteristic purpose, modifies by its will to act and increase the life action and the ways of the body.

Mind is not limited in its thoughts by the life and body. There is an action in it which is more than a creative stress of life, an attempt to image supraphysical realities, which we may dismiss as an illusion or a result of abnormal physiological states, but may also follow as first clues to a greater truth and possibly a higher tone or tones of the scale of being.

In that case, mind appears as a larger thing than life and material being. Though apparently an evolution from life and the body, it may have been in reality a prior power, life and body only its occasions and means for self-manifestation on the material plane of being.

At any rate, psychology has to regard the scale not only from the upward point of view of body creating life, life creating mind, but from the downward point of view of mind creating new life in body.

Evidently mind is a greater thing, higher than life and body. In that case, besides the ascending scale of the lower rising to a highest possibility, we must regard a possibility of the descending scale, the highest reality involving itself in the lower conditions of being.

But the question arises whether mind itself is the highest possibility or the highest reality[.]

*

Vedantic psychology explores the idea and intuition of a higher reality than mind.

The intuition can only be verified by psychological experience exceeding the normal action of mind. This experience may lead to constantly ascending intuitions verified by an ascent of experience to some summit of being.

Beyond mind psychological experience finds another power of energy, another note in the scale of being. This we will call the supermind. This supermind lives and acts natively in a domain of experience of which the mind becomes aware by a reflective experience and calls vaguely spirit or spiritual being.

Spirit is found to have three tones of its being. Triune, it makes each successively a power of its energy, a status of spiritual experience and form of its action. Triune, they are inseparable, but one or other can be so stressed as to appear a leading principle.

But we have to note three essential facts about spirit: —

Spirit is infinite consciousness, even when it dwells upon finite formulations of conscious being.

Awareness of spirit is infinite self-awareness.

All its three essential principles must have this character of infinity.

Infinite self-conscious bliss is the first; infinite self-conscious conscious energy is the second; infinite self-conscious existence the third principle of spirit. Existence, consciousness, bliss are the three tones of infinity, the three basic colours of the Absolute.

*

The ascending scale of being presents then seven notes, matter, life, mind, supermind, bliss self, self of conscious energy, self of primary conscious existence.

But the experience we get as we ascend in the scale leads us to the discovery that what in evolution appears subsequent is prior in reality. Life evolves in matter, but was preexistent to matter, latent, omnipresent, waiting for matter to be ready to be manifest — which it does when the movement of energy reaches a certain intensity.

Mind evolves in embodied life, but was preexistent to matter and life, latent, omnipresent, involved, a hidden cause of action waiting for life and matter to be ready for its manifestation which comes when the movement of energy has reached a greater intensity. So supermind is prior to mind, latent, omnipresent, involved even in matter and life, a hidden cause of action and waits for mind to be ready for its manifestation, and since supermind acts only in spirit spirit too must be there latent, omnipresent, involved, a hidden cause of action. But spirit is not dependent on the evolution of supermind for its manifestation; it can appear to our mentality, to our life-consciousness, even to our physical mind.

The true nature and rationale of this priority appear in the descending scale. There we see the true development of the universe.

Spirit of self-being develops self of conscious energy which supports its self of cosmic bliss, which acts on the finite by supermind, which offers its differentiations to mind, relates them in life, fixes them phenomenally in body of material substance. This is the descending scale by which universe is created or made sensible to embodied soul.

But in the material world, all is first involved in matter and has to find itself by a development from material being and with material being as its support and basis. The evolving process of this self-discovery of the universal existence produces the phenomenon of evolution of higher and greater from lower and lesser principles which we call the ascending scale of being.

This phenomenon baffling now to the reason becomes a self-evident proposition when we observe the descending scale and find involution to have preceded evolution. The phenomenon arises inevitably from the nature of our being.

*

Schema of being has to be formulated from these two points of view, the results, though data of experience, being at first taken as a working hypothesis, subject to verification. We follow actually the ascending scale, but the descending scale has first to be shown, as otherwise the possible explanations of psychological phenomenon which result from this line of experience, would be unintelligible and would have either to be excluded or the whole enquiry restated in altered detail in the end.

All questions of the reality or unreality of the world, its fundamental or ultimate purpose or want of purpose, the destiny of the soul, must be left over till the psychological data have been understood. To proceed otherwise would be to determine them by metaphysical reasoning; but the object before us is to arrive at them by the road of psychology.

The whole psychology of Vedanta depends upon this double scale and without it could have no complete scientific verification. Because it exists experience of consciousness can give a clue to the nature of world existence. Metaphysical reasoning by itself could only give us philosophical opinions, psychological verification makes Vedantic truth a firm guide in life. It gives us a tangible ladder of ascension by which we rise to our highest truth of being[.]

105

The knowledge at which psychology arrives in its largest generalisations, is that there is one absolute and indefinable Reality which we call for psychological purposes the Self one, indivisible and common to all existence which manifests itself with an infinite variety in the universe and that every soul is an individual personality — we will use the word for want of a better — of that Self manifesting itself with a variety not precisely infinite, but indefinite, but in accordance with its individual nature which provides the principle of harmony, regulates the variety, casts it into a certain mould of unity. All existence is one, but with a constantly active principle of variation and individuation. There is a universal nature of things, but man while abiding within the principles of that nature, has also a nature of his own which distinguishes him from the animal and from lower forms of life. There is therefore this general individuality of Man which the totality of mankind represents in its full play of oneness and variety. Within that general individuality there are typal, racial, national, class individualities and each man has his own individual nature, one indeed in its general basis and materials with general human nature and with his type, race, class, nation, but yet possessed of its own principle of particular individuation. It is this which reigns in his mentality, vital being, physical being and stamps itself upon them, but in itself it is neither mental, vital nor physical, but proceeds from a secret principle superior to all these; mind, life and body are only means and values of his self-expression. So is it with every community, nation or other natural grouping of men.

Towards a True Scientific Psychology

106

When the ancient thinkers of India set themselves to study the soul of man in themselves and others, they, unlike any other nation or school of early thought, proceeded at once to a process which resembles exactly enough the process adopted by modern science in its study of physical phenomena. For their object was to study, arrange and utilise the forms, forces and working movements of consciousness, just as the modern physical Sciences study, arrange and utilise the forms, forces and working movements of objective Matter. The material with which they had to deal was more subtle, flexible and versatile than the most impalpable forces of which the physical Sciences have become aware; its motions were more elusive, its processes harder to fix; but once grasped and ascertained, the movements of consciousness were found by Vedic psychologists to be in their process and activity as regular, manageable and utilisable as the movements of physical forces. The powers of the soul can be as perfectly handled and as safely, methodically and puissantly directed to practical life-purposes of joy, power and light as the modern power of electricity can be used for human comfort, industrial and locomotive power and physical illumination; but the results to which they give room and effect are more wonderful and momentous than the results of motorpower and electric luminosity. For there is no difference of essential law in the physical and the psychical, but only a difference and undoubtedly a great difference of energy, instrumentation and exact process. The Supreme Existence which expresses itself equally in soul and matter, moves upon one fundamental principle on all its sevenfold levels, and even by one set of medial processes, but It varies their minute arrangement and organic functioning to suit the material which it is using and the objective which it has set before Itself in Its divine movement.

Exact observation and untrammelled, yet scrupulous experiment are the method of every true Science. Not mere observation by itself — for without experiment, without analysis and new-combination observation leads to a limited and erroneous knowledge; often it generates an empirical classification which does not in the least deserve the name of science. The old European system of psychology was just such a pseudo-scientific system. Its observations were superficial, its terms and classification arbitrary, its aim and spirit abstract, empty and scholastic. In modern times a different system and method are being founded; but the vices of the old system persist. The observations made have been incoherent, partial or morbid and abnormal; the generalisations are far too wide for their meagre substratum of observed data; the abstract & scholastic use of psychological terms and the old metaphysical ideas of psychological processes still bandage the eyes of the infant knowledge, mar its truth and hamper its progress. These old errors are strangely entwined with a new fallacy which threatens to vitiate the whole enquiry, — the fallacy of the materialistic prepossession.

107

Psychology ought to be rather than is the science of consciousness and of the motions of consciousness as distinguished from the science of form and of the motions of form. We are dealing, therefore, in psychology with a more subtle, flexible and versatile material than in the physical sciences; its motions are more elusive, its processes harder to fix; but when once grasped and ascertained, its laws and activities are found to be quite as regular, manageable and utilisable as the processes of physical Nature. They give room to even more wonderful and momentous results. There is no difference of essential law in the physical & psychical, but a great difference of instrumentation and exact process. For the Supreme Existence moves on one fundamental principle or one set of principles in all its manifestations, but varies its organic arrangement and functioning of the principles to suit the material which It is using & the objective which It intends to reach. In both fields observation & experiment are the only sound foundation of knowledge. But observation without experiment leads only to a limited and erroneous science, often to an empirical system of surface rules which do not deserve the name of science at all. It is this defect which has so long kept European psychology in the status of a pseudo-science; and, even now when real observation has begun & experimentation of an elementary kind is being attempted, the vices of the perishing sciolism mar and hamper this infant knowledge. It has not rid itself of all its old scholastic swaddling clothes; therefore it still walks on all fours and cannot yet learn to stand up erect and walk.

108

Psychology is the science of consciousness and its status and operations in Nature and, if that can be glimpsed or experienced, its status and operations beyond what we know as Nature.

It is not enough to observe and know the movements of our surface nature and the superficial nature of other living creatures just as it [is] not enough for Science to observe and know as electricity only the movements of lightning in the clouds or for the astronomer to observe and know only those movements and properties of the stars that are visible to the unaided eye. Here as there a whole world of occult phenomena have to be laid bare and brought under control before the psychologist can hope to be master of his province.

Our observable consciousness, that which we call ourselves, is only the little visible part of our being. It is a small field below which are depths and farther depths and widths and ever wider widths which support and supply it but to which it has no visible access. All that is our self, our being, — what we see at the top is only our ego and its visible nature.

Even the movements of this little surface nature cannot be understood nor its true law discovered until we know all that is below or behind and supplies it — and know too all that is around it and above.

For below this conscient nature is the vast Inconscient out of which we come. The Inconscient is greater, deeper, more original, more potent to shape and govern what we are and do than our little derivative conscient nature. Inconscient to us, to our surface view, but not inconscient in itself or to itself it is a sovereign guide, worker, determinant, creator. Not to know it is not to know our nether origins and the origin of the most part of what we are and do.

And the Inconscient is not all. For behind our little frontal ego and nature is a whole subliminal kingdom of inner consciousness with many planes and provinces. There are in that kingdom many powers, movements, personalities which are part of ourselves and help to form our little surface personality and its powers and movements. This inner self, these inner persons we do not know, but they know us and observe and dictate our speech, our thoughts, feelings, doings even more directly than the Inconscient below us.

Around us too is a circumconscient Universal of which we are a portion. This Circumconscience is pouring its forces, suggestions, stimulus, compulsions into us at every moment of our existence.

Around us is a universal Mind of which our mind is a formation and our thoughts, feelings, will, impulses are continually little more than a personally modified reception and transcription of its thought-waves, its force-currents, its foam of emotion and sensation, its billows of impulse.

Around us is a permanent universal life of which our petty flow of life-formation that begins and ceases is only a small dynamic wave.

109

Psychology is the science of Consciousness; it is the knowledge of its nature, its processes and the aim or results of its processes, its law or laws of being, its habitat and instruments, its what, why, where, whence and whither.

But what is consciousness and can there be a science of consciousness? We are not in presence of a body of concrete, visible or sensible facts, verifiable by all, which form an indisputable starting-point, are subject to experiment and proof, where theories can be tested at every point and discarded if they do not accord with the facts, with all the facts. The data here are subjective, fluid, elusive. They do not subject themselves to exact instruments, can lend themselves to varying theories, do not afford proofs easily verifiable by all. Their presentation is difficult and can hardly be more than scanty and often infantile in their insufficiency. Theories are numerous, but few or none have any solidity or permanence.

To understand the psychology of others we depend upon our observation of them and our own interpretation of the movements we observe and our comparison with our own psychological actions and reactions. But our observation is limited by the fact that what we observe is not the psychological events we wish to study but signs of speech, action, facial or bodily expression which seem to us to indicate them; but it is still more limited by the possibility of error in our observation and still more in our interpretation. Errors of wrong attribution, exaggeration, diminution, false [?evidence], false valuation, crop up at every turn; indeed, the whole observation may be nothing but error, the interpretation purely personal and mistaken. Comparison with ourselves may be a fruitful fountain of mistakes; there is no doubt a general similarity in the mass of human reactions, but the differences and variations are also marked and striking; there is here no source of certitude.

A direct experiential and experimental psychology seems to be demanded if psychology is to be a science and not merely a mass of elementary and superficial generalisations with all the rest guesswork or uncertain conclusion or inference. We must see, feel, know directly what we observe; our interpretations must be capable of being sure and indubitable; we must be able to work surely on a ground of sure knowledge.

*

Modern psychologists have aimed at certitude in their knowledge, have found it or thought they found it by mixing up psychology and physiology; our physiological processes are supposed to be not only the instrumentation or an instrumentation of our consciousness, but the base or constituents of our psychological processes. But by this method we can only arrive at an extended physiological, not at a true psychological knowledge. We learn that there is a physical instrumentation by which physical things and their contacts work upon our consciousness, reach it through the nerves and the brain and awake certain reactions in it which may however vary with the brain and the consciousness contacted; we learn that the consciousness uses certain physiological processes as well as physical means to act upon outward things and conditions; we learn too that physical conditions have an action upon our state of consciousness and its functionings. But all this was to be expected, since we are a consciousness embodied and not disincarnate, acting through a body and with a body as a habitation and instrument and not a pure consciousness acting in its own right[.]

Yogic Psychology

110

The problem of consciousness can only be solved if we go back to a radical state of our existence in which things get back to their reality. For there they are no longer a mass of phenomena which have to be cleared up, classified, organised by the perceptions, conceptions and relative logic of the human intellect. These perceptions, these concepts, this logic belong to an imperfect instrument and the arrangements they make can only be provisional and, at that, onesided and only half-true or a good deal less than half-true — and even that truth is of an inferior kind, a constructed representation and not truth itself in its own nature. In fact the intellect sees only the phenomenon, it cannot go back behind it; when it tries, it only arrives at other and more occult phenomena. The truth of things can only be perceived when one gets to what may be called summarily the spiritual vision of things and even there completely only when there is not only vision but direct experience in the very substance of one's own being and all being.

111

Consciousness is not an unaccountable freak or a chance growth or a temporary accident in a material and inconscient universe.

It may so appear on the surface and physical science, since by its very terms it is limited to the examination of appearances and must start from the surface phenomenon, may choose or may have no alternative but to treat it on that basis. But surface appearances are not the reality of things, they may be a part of the truth but they are not the whole reality. One must look beyond the external appearances of things before one can know things in themselves: especially first appearances are apt to be deceptive. It is not by regarding a flash of lightning as a chance ebullition of fiery temper in a cloud that one can know the truth of electricity. We must go far and dig deep before we can get at the truth about the Force that manifested the lightning. Consciousness may similarly appear as a phenomenon, an outbreak of sentience in the obscurity of an originally nescient being; but we must go far beyond that specious appearance if we would know the true nature and origin and discover the entire possibilities of this apparently strange and anomalous force. For anomalous it is, since it occurs in a fundamentally inconscient universe of Matter and strange and curious it is in its reactions, aberrations, workings, destiny.

Physical science — and psychology in its present methods is only an extension of physical science — conducts its search into things from down upwards; it regards Matter as the foundation and the bottom of things and having searched into that foundation, got as it thinks to the very bottom, it believes, or once believed, it has by that very fact understood their depths, their centre, their height and top. But this is a naive error. The truth of things is in their depths or at their centre and even at their top. The truth of consciousness also is to be found at its top and in its depths or at its centre; but when we enter into the depths of consciousness or when we try to reach its centre, we go off into trance and likewise before we get to its top, we go off into trance.

Our searches into Matter also are vitiated by the fact that in Matter consciousness is in a trance and gives no apparent response to our probings. In living Matter, not yet mental, still subconscious, it does give sometimes a reply, but not one that we can understand, and, as for mind in the animal, it is only consciousness half awakened out of the original trance of inconscient Matter: even in the human being it starts from an original nescience, its expressions, its data, all that we can ordinarily observe of it, are the movements of Ignorance fumbling for knowledge. We cannot understand from these alone what consciousness really is nor discover its source or its supreme possibilities or its limits, if indeed it has any limits and is not like being itself infinite and illimitable. Only if we can get away from this imperfection and ignorance to some top of its possibilities or to its latent depths or some hidden centre, can we discover its true nature and through it the very self and reality of our being.

How do we know that there is a top to consciousness or an inner centre, since these are not apparent on the face of things? By its supernormal, not its normal manifestations and phenomena, for the top of things is always supernormal, it is only the bottom and what is near to the bottom that are normal, at any rate to our ordinary consciousness in the material universe. Especially we can know by the supernormal becoming normal to us — by Yoga.

112

I mean by Yogic psychology an examination of the nature and movements of consciousness as they are revealed to us by the processes and results of Yoga.

This definition at once takes us out of the field of ordinary psychology and extends the range of our observation to an immense mass of facts and experiments which exceed the common surface and limited range very much as the vastly extended range of observation of Science exceeds that of the common man looking at natural external phenomena only with the help [of] his unaided mind and senses. The field of Yoga is practically unlimited and its processes and instrumentation have a plasticity and adaptability and power of expansion to which it is difficult to see or set any limit.

It is true that modern psychology has probed the internal law of living matter and consciousness and arrived at results which are remarkable but limited and fundamentally inconclusive. We know from it that the movements of consciousness are affected and on a certain side determined by the functioning of the physical organs. But still the nature, origin and laws of consciousness remain unknown; all that has been proved is that the body provides for it an engine or instrumentation for its manifestation in living physical bodies and that certain lesions, alterations or deteriorations of the engine may lead to considerable or serious results in the functioning of the embodied consciousness. This was to be expected and can at once be conceded; but there is no proof that consciousness is a function of matter or that it was originated by the chemical or biological processes of the body or that it perishes with the dissolution of life in the body. The cessation of its functioning in the body at death proves nothing, for that was to be expected whatever the origin of consciousness or its fundamental nature. Its disappearance may be a departure, a disappearance from the body, but not a disappearance from existence.

It is true also that modern inquiry probing into psychological (as opposed to physiological) phenomena has discovered certain truths that are equally discovered by Yogic process, the role of the subconscient, the subliminal, double or multiple personality; but its observations in these fields are of an extremely groping and initial character and one does not see easily how it can arrive at the same largeness of results here as in physiology, physics, chemistry or other departments of physical Science.

It is only by Yoga process that one can arrive at an instrumentation which will drive large wide roads into the psychological Unknown and not only obscure and narrow tunnels. The field of psychology needs a direct inner psychological instrumentation by which we can arrive at sure data and sure results in ourselves verified [by] equally sure data [and] results in our observation of others and of the hidden psychological world and its play of unseen forces. The physical is the outwardly seen and sensed and needs physical instruments for its exploration; the psychological is the physically unseen and unsensed, to be discovered only by an organisation of the inward senses and other now undeveloped and occult means. It is through consciousness, by an instrumentation of consciousness only that the nature and laws and movements of consciousness can be discovered — and this is the method of Yoga.

Section Three

Yoga

Change of Consciousness and
Transformation of Nature

The Way of Yoga

Change of Consciousness: The Meaning of Yoga

113

Yoga is a means by which one arrives at union with the Truth behind things through an inner discipline which leads us from the consciousness of the outward and apparent to the consciousness of the inner and real. Yoga consciousness does not exclude the knowledge of the outer apparent world but it sees it with the eyes of an inner, not an outer seeing and experience, alters and sets right all its values in the light of an inner deeper greater truer consciousness and applies to it the Law of the reality, exchanging the law of the creature's Ignorance for the rule of a divine Will and Knowledge.

A change of consciousness is the whole meaning of the process of Yoga[.]

114

Yoga is the science, the process, the effort and action by which man attempts to pass out of the limits of his ordinary mental consciousness into a greater spiritual consciousness[.]

115

All yoga is in its essential [. . . . .] heightening or deepening of our consciousness so that it may become capable of something beyond our ordinary consciousness and our normal Nature. It is an entering into depths, an ascent towards heights, a widening beyond. Or it is contact with depths within, heights above, vastnesses beyond us, an opening to their greater influences, beings, movements or a reception of them into our surface consciousness and being so that the outer [is] altered, enveloped, governed by what is not our ordinary self. For the Reality which we are seeking does not lie on our surface or, if it is there, it is concealed and only a deeper, higher or wider consciousness than any to which we now have access can reach, touch or know and possess it. Even if we dive below our normal consciousness to find what is there it is some aspect of the Reality into which we enter.

116

By Yoga is meant — the word is not here used in the limited sense given to it in the disputations of Pandits — the use and [?   ] of certain processes of self-discipline [and] self-exercise or spontaneous and automatic self-intensification and self-extension of the mind and whatever in us is limited and that by which we enter into a larger deeper consciousness than is ordinarily ours.

This consciousness is aware of external things not only through the physical mind and senses but by other though often similar means of Mind, an inner sense or senses, an inner tact or feeling such as a projective or responsive awareness of things at a slight or great distance, a premonitory sense of things about to happen [or] preparing to happen, a feeling of things or persons not seen, an inner vision of physical objects and happenings not before the eye and hundreds of other phenomena not normal to the ordinary mind. These phenomena are ordinarily labelled occult or psychic or described as hallucinatory according to the point of view of the speaker, but such epithets explain nothing. This range of phenomena exists and for anyone who would know the nature and origin and possibilities of consciousness an examination of them is imperative.

This range of phenomena is however only an outer fringe of Yoga. It is more important that it admits to an inner field of experiences of the utmost import, to a growth of psyche and spirit, to deepest realities and [?finally] to the deepest of all; [... ...]

But what precisely do we mean by the word Yoga? It is used here in the most general sense possible as a convenient name including all processes or results of processes that lead to the unveiling of a greater and inner knowledge, consciousness, experience. Any psychic discipline by which we can pass partly or wholly into a spiritual state of the consciousness, any spontaneous or systematised approach to the inner Reality or the supreme Reality, any state of union or closeness to the Divine, any entry into a consciousness larger, deeper or higher than the normal consciousness common to humankind, fall automatically within the range of the word Yoga. Yoga takes us from the surface into the depths of our consciousness or it admits us into its very centre; it takes us up to the hidden topmost heights of our conscious being. It shows to us the secrets of the Self and the secret of the Divine. It gives us the knowledge, the vision, the presence of the Immanent and the Cosmic and the Transcendent Reality; that is its supreme purpose. On a lower grade it gives us the key to an inner and larger consciousness that is subliminal to us and brings out its experiences, its powers and possibilities and unless we know these things the secret of Consciousness and the knowledge of our whole being must escape us. It is through this door that we pass from a nescience of our true nature into a full light of self-knowledge.

But there are methods, schools, disciplines of Yoga that are turned towards one restricted aim, follow each a different path, win control of a separate province and by following that exclusive path we shall know that province of our being only or reach a single summit. It is by the integrality of Yoga that one can attain the integrality of consciousness. Our aim must be to embrace in this new knowledge all the planes of consciousness and all its summits. Then in the light of the knowledge brought to us and its widening and heightening of our consciousness, it is in the light of the top of things that we have to see and know all. It is then only that our ignorance or a very partial and surface awareness of ourselves can be flooded by a light of self-revelation and turn into self-knowledge.

117

Yoga is in its essence a passage from the ordinary consciousness in which we are aware only of appearances into a higher wider deeper consciousness in which we become aware of realities and of the one Reality. Not only do we become aware of it, but we can live in it and act from it and according to it instead of living in and according to the appearance of things. Yoga is a passage from ignorance to self-knowledge, from our apparent to our true being, from an outer phenomenal mental vital material life-existence to an inner spiritual existence and a spiritualised nature.

By Yoga we pass from the phenomenal to the real Man, from the consciousness of our own apparent outer nature to the consciousness of our real self, Atman, an inner and inmost man, Purusha, that which we truly and eternally are. This self or true being remains constant through all the changes of our phenomenal being, changes of the mind, life or body or changes of our apparent personality; it is permanent, perpetual and immortal, a portion or manifestation of the Eternal.

By Yoga we pass also from our consciousness of the phenomenal appearance or appearances of the cosmos or world around us to a consciousness of its truth and reality. We become aware of the world as a manifestation of or in universal being who is the true truth of all that we see, hear, experience. We become aware of a cosmic Consciousness which is the secret of the cosmic Energy, a cosmic Self or Spirit, the cosmic Divine, the universal Godhead.

But by Yoga we become aware also that our own Self or true being is one with the cosmic Self and Spirit, our nature a play of the cosmic Nature; the wall between ourselves and the universe begins to disappear and vanishes altogether. We realise the selfsame Pantheos in ourselves, in others and in all universal existence.

But also by Yoga we become aware of something that is more than our individual being and more than the cosmic being, a transcendent Being or Existence which is not dependent on ours or the existence of the universe. Our existence is a manifestation of and in that Being, the cosmos also is a manifestation of and in that one Supreme Existence.

This then is the Truth or Reality to which we arrive by Yoga, a one and supreme Being or Existence and Power of Being which manifests as a cosmic Self or Spirit and a cosmic Energy or Nature and in that again as our own self or spirit which becomes aware of itself as an individual being and nature.

Union: The Aim of Yoga

118

It is the aim of all Yoga to pass by a change of consciousness into the Reality that is behind things and live no longer in their appearance. To enter into some kind of union or communion or participation in that is the common object of all Yoga.

But the Reality presents itself to the consciousness of man the mental being under many aspects. We seek after union or closeness to the Divine, whatever the Divine may be. We see the Divine as a personal Godhead or as an impersonal Existence. A God of Love or compassion attracts us or a God of might and power. It is a divine Friend who meets us or a Divine Master or a World Father or World Mother or an almighty Lord of all or a Divine Lover. We are in the presence of a Cosmic Spirit in whose universal consciousness we lose our separate ego or a Supracosmic Absolute in whom we lose altogether our cosmic as well as our individual existence. We find our own highest Self or the Self of all or we pass into a sublime

Mystery without relation or feature where neither self nor all can exist any longer. Or it may be the inexpressible mystery of an original Nihil that abolishes for us all suffering along with all existence — or else that Nihil may be a mystic All that is far other than the false and illusory being created for us by mind and life experience.

119

Yoga is our union with some Being or some Reality, which is greater than ourselves or is our own greatest and real Self; it is That which by Yoga we join, enter into or become.

120

All Yoga strives towards union with the Highest, the Spirit, the Self, the Divine, or whatever other name or aspect we seize of the One Eternal and Infinite.

And by union we mean, first, contact constant and increasing with the consciousness of the Divine or Infinite, then to assimilate it or assimilate ourselves to it, then to become not only like to it and full of it, but to enter into it and dwell in it, to become that divine consciousness and being, essence of its essence and so abolish all division that separates us from the Divinity from whom we came.

121

To be one with the Eternal is the object of Yoga; there is no other object, because all other aims are included in this one divine perfection.

To be one with the Eternal is to be one with him in being, consciousness, power and delight. All that is is summed in these four terms of the infinite, for all else are but their workings.

To be one with the Eternal is also to live in the Eternal and in his presence and from his infinite nature, — sayujya, salokya, samipya, sadrishya. These four together are one way of being and one perfection.

To live in the Eternal is also to live with the Eternal within us. Whosoever consciously inhabits his being, his conscious presence inhabits. God lives and moves and acts in us when we live and move and act in him[.]

122

Yoga is the contact of the humanity in us with the deity in which it dwells, of the finite with the Infinite, of the as yet accomplished evolving & imperfect humanity with its yet unevolved attainable perfection, of the outwardly active waking consciousness which is controlled with the inwardly active controlling consciousness, of man with God, of the changing outward apparent ego with the secret real and immutable Self. By that contact the lower rises to the higher, the unevolved evolves, the unborn is created, humanity assumes some part of godhead, man moves upward to God. This upward and self-expanding movement is the utility of Yoga.

123

To be one in all ways of thy being with that which is the Highest, this is Yoga. To be one in all ways of thy being with that which is the All, this is Yoga. To be one in thy spirit and with thy understanding and thy heart and in all thy members with the God in humanity, this is Yoga. To be one with all Nature and all beings, this is Yoga. All this is to be one with God in his transcendence and his cosmos and all that he has created in his being. Because from him all is and all is in him and he is all and in all and because he is thy highest Self and thou art one with him in thy spirit and a portion of him in thy soul and at play with him in thy nature, and because this world is a scene in his being in which he is thy secret Master and lover and friend and the lord and sustainer and aim of all thou art, therefore is oneness with him the perfect way of thy being[.]

124

The human being on earth is God playing at humanity in a world of matter under the conditions of a hampered density with the ulterior intention of imposing law of spirit on matter & nature of deity upon human nature. Evolution is nothing but the progressive unfolding of Spirit out of the density of material consciousness and the gradual self-revelation of God out of this apparent animal being.

Yoga is the application, for this process of divine self-revelation, of the supreme force of tapas by which God created the world, supports it & will destroy it. It substitutes always some direct action of an infinite divine force for the limited workings of our fettered animal humanity. It uses divine means in order to rise to divinity.

All Yoga is tapasya and all siddhi of Yoga is accomplishment of godhead either by identity or by relation with the Divine Being in its principles or its personality or in both or simultaneously by identity and relation.

Identity is the principle of Adwaita, relation of Dwaita, relation in a qualified identity of Visishtadwaita. But entire perfection comes by identity with God in essential experience & relation of difference with Him in experience of manifestation.

125

In the end a union, a closeness, a constant companionship in the soul with the Divine, and a yet more wonderful oneness and inliving[.]

Yoga Partial and Complete

126

Yoga means union and the whole object of Yoga is the union of the human soul with the supreme Being and of the present nature of humanity with the eternal, supreme or divine Nature.

The greater the union, the greater the Yoga, the more complete the union, the more complete the Yoga.

There are different conceptions of the supreme Being and to each conception corresponds a school of Yoga with its separate idea and discipline. But these are partial and not complete systems; or rather they are complete in themselves, but do not cover the whole human being and nature. Most of them lead away from life and are useful only to the few who are moved to turn away from human existence and seek the bliss of some other state of being. To humanity at large this kind of Yoga has no real message. The complete Yoga will be one which accepts God in the world and oneness with all beings and solidarity with the human kind, fills life and existence with the God-consciousness and not only raises man the individual but leads man the race towards a total perfection.

127

The aim put before itself by Yoga is God; its method is tapasya.

God is the All and that which exceeds & transcends the All; there is nothing in existence which is not God but God is not anything in that existence, except symbolically, in image to His own consciousness. Humanity also is a symbol or eidolon of God, we are made in His image; and by that is meant, not a formal image, but in the image of His being and personality, the essence of divinity & its quality, the divine being & divine knowledge.

There are in every thing existing phenomenally or, as we shall say, symbolically, two parts, the thing in itself & the symbol, Self & Nature, res (thing that is) & factum (thing that is made), immutable being & mutable becoming, that which is supernatural in it & that [which] is natural.

Everything in existence has something in it which seeks to transcend itself; Matter moves towards becoming Life, Life moves towards becoming Mind, Mind moves towards becoming ideal Truth, ideal Truth rises to become divine & infinite Spirit.

The reason is that every symbol, being a partial expression of God, reaches out to & seeks to become its own entire reality; it aspires to become its real self by transcending its apparent self. Thing that is made is attracted towards Thing that is, becoming towards being, the natural to the supernatural, symbol towards Thing in itself, Nature towards God.

The upward movement is the means towards fulfilment of existence in the world; downward movement is destruction, Hell, perdition. Everything tends [to] move upward; once it is assured of its natural existence, it seeks the supernatural. Every nature is a step towards some supernature, something natural to itself but supernatural to what is below it. Life is supernatural to Matter, Mind supernatural to Life, ideal being supernatural to mental being, infinite being supernatural to ideal being. So too man is supernatural to the animal, God is supernatural to man. Man too as soon as he has assured his natural existence, must insist on his upward movement towards God. The upward movement is towards Heaven, the downward movement towards Hell.

The animal soul fulfils itself when it transcends animality & becomes human. Humanity also fulfils itself when it transcends humanity & becomes God.

By yielding to Nature, we fall away both from Nature & from God; by transcending Nature we at once fulfil all the possibilities of Nature & rise towards God. The human touches first the divine & then becomes divine.

There are those who seek to kill Nature in order to become the Self; but that is not God's intention in humanity. We have to transcend Nature, not to kill it.

Every movement of humanity which seeks to destroy Nature, however religious, lofty or austere, of whatever dazzling purity of ethereality, is doomed to failure, sick disappointment, disillusionment or perversion. It is in its nature transient, because it contradicts God's condition for us. He has set Nature there as a condition of His self-fulfilment in the world.

Every movement of humanity which bids us be satisfied

with Nature, dwell upon the earth & cease to look upwards, however rational, clearsighted, practical, effective, comfortable it may be is doomed to weariness, petrifaction & cessation. It is in its nature transient because it contradicts God's intention in us. He dwells secret in Nature & compels us towards Him by His irresistible attraction.

Materialistic movements are as unnatural & abnormal as ascetic & negatory religions & philosophies. Under the pretence of bringing us back to Nature, they take us away from her entirely; for they forget that Nature is only phenomenally Nature but in reality she is God. The divine element in her is that which she most really is; the rest is only condition, process & stage in her development of the secret divinity.

Not to be ensnared, emmeshed and bound by Nature, not to hate & destroy her, is the first thing we must learn if we would be complete Yogins & proceed towards our divine perfection.

Being still natural in the world to transcend Nature internally so that both internally & externally we may master & use her as free & lord, swarat samrat, is our fulfilment.

Being still the symbol to reach through it the thing that symbolises itself, to realise the symbol, is our fulfilment.

Being still a figure of humanity, man among men, a living body among living bodies, though housed in life & matter yet a mental being among mental beings, being & remaining all this that we are apparently, yet to exceed all this apparent manhood and become in the body what we are really, God, spirit, supreme & infinite, pure Bliss, pure Force, pure Light, this is our fulfilment.

Our whole apparent life is a becoming, but all becoming has for its goal & fulfilment being & God is the only being; to become divine in the nature of the world, in the symbol of humanity is our fulfilment.

Yoga in its practice may be either perfect or partial, either selective or comprehensive. Perfect and comprehensive Yoga avoids limitations by aspects and leads to entire divinity.

If we are to exceed our human stature and become divine,

we must first, in our Indian phrase, get God; for this human ego is the lower imperfect term of our being, God is its higher perfect term. God in us is the possessor of our super-nature and without Him there is no effectual rising. The finite cannot become infinite, unless it perceives & desires to touch its own secret infinity; nor can the symbol-being, unless it knows, loves and pursues its Self-Reality, overcome the present limits of its merely apparent nature. This necessity is the imperative justification of religion, — not of a church, creed or theology; for these things are all outward religiosity rather than the truth of religion, but of that personal and intimate religion, a thing of temper and spirit and life, not of views or ceremonies which draws each man to his own vision of the Supreme or his own idea of something higher than himself. Without the worship of the Supreme in the heart, the aspiration towards it in the will or the thirst for it in the temperamental cravings we shall not have the impulse or the strength for the difficult and supreme effort demanded of us. Therefore have the prophets spoken and the Avatars descended, so that mankind may be inspired to this great call upon its upward-straining energies. The aim of rationalism & Science is to make man content with his humanity and contradict Nature, baffling her evolution; the aim of religion, — but not unhappily of the creeds & Churches — is to farther the great aim of Nature by pushing man towards his evolution.

The attainment of God is the true object of all human effort for which all his other efforts political, social, literary, intellectual, are only a necessary condition & preparation of the race; but then there are both differences in the state of the attainment, differences in its range & effectivity. Three states of divine attainment may usefully be distinguished, touch with God, indwelling in Him & becoming He. The first is initial & elementary; unless passing the veil of our ordinary nature we touch the divine Being or He leaning down impose His touch [on] us, unless we come first into contact with Him either in our heart, our mind, our works or our being, we cannot go on to indwell in Him. If we are strong in spirit, the touch may indeed be rapid & summary & we may wake at once & stride forward to the state of divine indwelling, soul of man in the soul of God, the individual in the universal; but the touch must be there. To enforce this preliminary step, to bring man into some kind of contact with God, is the common and sometimes the sole preoccupation of human religions. It does not matter greatly to Nature for her purpose how it is done, — in however crude & elementary a way, through whatever intellectual errors & emotional blunders or ethical outrages, the touch must be established; this imperatively & above all things the religious spirit demands. Nature, as is always her way, presses on to her all-important, immediate steps and is willing to purchase a single great & general gain by any number of particular losses. Man, besides, is so various in the arrangement of his human qualities, the master spring as well as the peculiar temperament differs so greatly or so subtly in each individual that there can never be, for this purpose of Nature's, too many sects, disciplines or different religions. Swami Vivekananda has well seen the consummation of religion in a state when each human individual has his own religion dictated by his own spiritual needs & nature; for collective creeds, Churches & theologies, in spite of their temporary necessity & some undeniable permanent advantages, help to formalise the upward effort & deprive it of its adaptability, freedom & perfect individual sincerity. The priest & dogma will seldom leave God & the soul free to meet each other in that solitude & spontaneity which gives the union its highest force & delight. They are always pressing in to control & preside at the marriage & legitimise it with formulas, rites & official registration.

Moreover the intellect of natural man is narrow, his effort soon exhausted & easily satisfied with imperfection. If he is led to think that his way of contact with the Divine is the only way, his own freedom of higher development is fettered or entirely taken away from him & in his intellectual & religious egoism he militates against the freedom of others. Most religions tend easily to believe that the contact with God once established, no matter with what limitations or of what kind, all is done that needs to be done, all fulfilled that God demands of us.

Popular religions tend naturally to be dualistic and to preserve a trenchant distinction between man & God dividing the symbol being from That which expresses itself in him; while with one hand they raise man towards his super-nature, with the other they hold him down to his ordinary nature. The lower is suffused with the glow of the higher & touched with its power & rapture, but it does not itself rise into & dwell within it. At its lowest the dualistic soul cherishes the taint of its imperfections, at its highest, unless in rare self-transcending moments, keeps itself distinct in awe & reverence from the divine Lover, worships at His feet but cannot hide itself in His bosom.

Therefore Nature, still following her upward surge, has provided a mightier rank of human souls who are capable of going forward beyond this preliminary effort & having entered into the very being of God, of dwelling there in beatitude. Entering into the consciousness of the Infinite, feeling it all around them & in them, ever thrilling with its touch, aware of identity with It in nature, joy and inner awareness, they yet preserve a constant separateness of their special being in that identity. They do not plunge themselves wholly into the divine ocean or, if they go down into it, they keep hold on a fathomline which will preserve their touch with the surface. In their nature — whatever be their opinions — such men are Visishtadwaitins, souls not drawn towards entire oneness. But unless man plunges himself wholly into God caring not whether he reemerge, unless the human sacrifices himself wholly to the divinity, keeping back no particle of his being, not even the least particle of separateness of the individual ego, jivatman, the divine purpose in man cannot be utterly accomplished. Therefore Nature or the Will of God — for Nature is nothing but the Will of God in action — has provided that some, having indwelt in God, human soul in divine soul, shall be irresistibly called immediately, with brief respite or at long & last to the utter immersion. These go onward & throw away the last trace of Ego into God. Some of us, it has been said by a great teacher, are jivakotis, human beings leaning so preeminently to the symbol-nature that, if they have lost it utterly for a while in the Reality, they lose themselves; once immersed, they cannot return; they are lost in God to humanity; others are ishwarakotis, human beings whose centre has already been shifted upwards or, elevated in the superior planes of our conscious-existence from the beginning, was established in God rather than in Nature. Such men are already leaning down from God to Nature; they, therefore, even in losing themselves in Him yet keep themselves since in reaching God they do not depart from their centre but rather go towards it; arrived they are able to lean down again to humanity. Those who can thus emerge from this bath of God are the final helpers of humanity & are chosen by God & Nature to prepare the type of supernatural man to which our humanity is rising.

There are, then, these three divine conditions, states separately conceived of humanity's God attainment. Man being limited in energy & discriminative rather than catholic in intellect, fastens usually on this separate conception & limits himself to one or other of these conditions; Yogic method, also, being careful of the different natures of men, suits itself to their limitations, becomes selective and concentrates upon one of these conditions or another. Or even it becomes partial as well as selective; for in its contact with God, it relates itself to a part of divine quality rather than the perfect divinity, to a God of mercy, the God of Justice, the Divine Master, the Divine Friend, or else with some aspect of divine impersonal being, to Infinite Rapture, to Infinite Force or to Infinite Calm & Purity. In the indwelling there may be the same limitations, in the becoming also they may persist. There is no fault to be found with this selective process or with this partiality. They are necessary; human limitations demand this device; human perfectibility itself finds its account in these concessions. Nature knows her task & she proceeds to it with a wide, flexible & perfect wisdom which smiles at our impatient logical narrownesses & rigid, onesighted consistencies. She knows she has an infinitely complex & variable material to deal with & must be infinitely complex & variable in her methods. We only consider precise method & ultimate fulfilment; she has to reckon on her way with thousand-armed struggles & infinite possibilities.

Nevertheless, her ultimate aim & the perfect & comprehensive Yoga is that which embraces rather than selects. We are meant to be within the symbol of humanity what God is in Himself & universally. Now God is free, absolute from these limitations & all-comprehensive. He is always one in his being, yet both one with & separate from his symbols & in that differentiated oneness able to stand quite apart from them. So we too in our ultimate divine realisation when we have become one with our divine Self, may & should be able also to stand out as the self still one in all things and beings, yet differentiated in the symbol, so as to enjoy a blissful divided closeness such as that of the Lover & Beloved mingling yet separate in their rapture; & may & should even be able to stand away from God with a sort of entire separateness holding His hand still, unlike the pure dualist, but still standing away from Him so that we may enjoy that infinity of human relation with God which is the wonder & beauty & joy of dualistic religions. To accomplish this is the full, the purna Yoga, and the sadhak who can attain to it, is in his condition the complete Yogin.

Is such a triune condition of the soul possible? Logically, it would seem impossible; logically, all trinities are chimeras and a thing must be one thing at a time & cannot combine three such divergent states as oneness, differentiated oneness & effective duality. But in these matters an inch of experience runs farther than a yard of logic, & experience, you will find, affirms that the triune God-state is perfectly possible & simple once you have attained God's fullness. We must not apply to the soul a logic which is based on the peculiarities of matter. It is true of a clod that it cannot be at the same time a clod hanging up or pasted on some bough, a clod protruding from the earth and a shapeless mass trodden into the mother soil. But this is because the clod is divided from the earthly form. The soul is not divided from God by these barriers of material & dimension. What is true [of] matter is not true of Spirit, nor do the standards of form become facts applied to the formless. For matter is conscious being confined in form, the spirit is conscious being using form but unconfined in it; & it is the privilege of Spirit that though indivisible in its pure being, it is freely self-divisible in its conscious experience & can concentrate itself in many states at a time. It is by this tapas, by this varied concentration of self-knowledge that Divine Existence creates & supports the world & is at one & the same [time] God & Nature & World, Personal & Impersonal, Pure & Varied, Qualitied & without Qualities, Krishna & Kali, Shiva & Brahma & Vishnu, man & animal & vegetable & stone, all aspects of Himself & all symbols. We need not doubt therefore that we, recovering our divine reality, shall not be bound to a single condition or aspect but can command a triune or even a multiple soul-experience. We, becoming God, become that which is the All & exceeds & transcends the All. Sarvabhutani atmaivabhud vijanatah. The soul of the perfect knower becomes all existent things & That transcendental in which all things have their existence, ihaiva, without ceasing to possess his human centre of separate experience. For this is the entire divinity that is the result of the perfect & comprehensive Yoga.

Partial Systems of Yoga

Jnana Yoga: The Yoga of Knowledge

128

All existence is the existence of the One, the Eternal and Infinite, the beginning and middle and end, the source and substance and continent and support of all things. There is not and cannot be any other existence, anything that is other than or outside of or above or below or beyond or in any way separate from the existence of the one Eternal and Infinite. All that appears as finite, temporal, multiple and phenomenal is still in reality being of the being of the Infinite and the Eternal. *Ekam evadvitiyam.*

This is the first and abiding truth without which no other can be understood in the truth of things or put in its proper place in the integrality of the Whole. It is therefore the fundamental realisation at which the seeker of the Yoga must arrive.

129

God is, is the first seed of Yoga. It is Tat Sat of the Vedanta. I am, is the second seed. It is So'ham of the Upanishads. God is infinite self-existence, self-conscious force of existence, self-diffused or self-concentrated delight of existence; I too am that infinite self-existence, self-consciousness, self-force, self-delight; this is the double third seed. It is Sachchidananda of the worldwide transcendental conclusion of all human thinking.

130

Self-knowledge is the foundation of the complete Yoga. Affirm in yourselves self-knowledge.

Self-knowledge and knowledge of the Brahman is one; for I am He. Of this let there be no doubt in thy mind.

Self is twofold, essential and phenomenal, being & becoming[.]

131

First be aware of thy inner self and spirit. Next be aware of that self and spirit one with thine in others.

132

All Yoga starts from the perception that what we are now or rather what we perceive as ourselves and so call is only an ignorant partial and superficial formulation of our nature. It is not our whole self, it is not even our real self; it is a little representative personality put forward by the true and persistent being in us for the experience of this brief life; we not only have been in the past and can be in the future but we are much more than that in the present secret totality of our being and nature. Especially, there is a secret soul in us that is our true person; there is a secret self that is our true impersonal being and spirit. To unveil that soul and that self is one of the most important movements of Yoga[.]

133

The sense of a greater or even of an ultimate Self need not be limited to a negative and empty wideness whose one character is to be without limitation or feature. The first extreme push of our recoil from what we now are or think ourselves to be may and does often at first carry us over into this annihilating experience. A negation of our present error, a release from our petty irksome aching bonds may seem to be the only thing worth having, the only thing true. The rest is infinity, freedom, peace. We feel an Infinity that needs nothing but its own infinite to fill it. We rejoice in a freedom of which any form, name or description, any creative activity, any movement, any impulse would be a disturbing denial and the beginning of a relapse into the error of will and desire, the ignorance of the illusory finite. To accept nothing but the bare bliss of infinity is the condition of this peace. The mind escaping from itself denies all thought, all form-making, all motion or play of any kind; for that would be a grievous return to itself, a miserable imprisonment and renewed hard-labour. The life released from the toil of labouring and striving and living, demands only immobility and no more to be, a sleep of force, the surety and rest of an immutable status. The body accepts denial and dissolution, for to be dissolved is to cease to breathe and suffer. A bodiless, lifeless, mindless infinite breadth and supreme silence shows to us that we are in contact with the Absolute.

134

This method of extinction is imposed on our mind and our mental ego, because all that is eternal, infinite, absolute is superconscient to mind; mind and its ego cannot remain awake in that greater consciousness, they must disappear. But if we can change or evolve from mental into supramental beings, then the superconscient becomes our normal consciousness. We can then hope to wake in That and not fall asleep in it, to grow into it and not abolish ourselves in it, to last in identity and not lose ourselves in identity with the supreme Existence.

135

It is possible for the reason, the thinker in us to rest and cease satisfied in this sole spiritual experience and to discard all others on the ground that they are in the end illusory or of a minor phenomenal significance. The logical mind drives naturally towards a pursuit of the abstract, towards pure essences, an indefinable substratum of all experiences, a nameless X without contents, an ineffable and featureless Absolute. Itself a creator of definitions without which it cannot think but none of which can give it any abiding sense of an ultimate, it escapes from itself with a sense of relief into the Indefinable. But if the mind finds its account in cessation and release, the other parts of our being have in this solution to be cast away from us or put to silence. The heart remains atrophied and unfulfilled; the will is baulked of its last dynamic significances. These too tend towards an absolute, the heart towards an absolute of ineffable Love and Bliss, the will towards an absolute of ineffable Power. And there is nothing to prove that the knowledge at which the reason arrives is alone true. There is no reason to suppose that the heart and will and the deeper soul within us have not too their own sufficient doors opening upon the Supreme, their key to the mystery of the Eternal.

Bhakti Yoga: The Yoga of Devotion

136

The integral Yoga of Devotion proceeds through seven stages each of which opens out from the one that precedes it:

Aspiration and self-consecration; devotion; adoration and worship; love; possession of the whole being and life by the Divine; joy of the Divine Love and the beauty and sweetness of the Divine; the absolute Bliss of the Absolute.

Faith is our first need; for without faith in the Divine, in the existence and the all-importance of the Divine Being there can be no reason to aspire or to consecrate, there can be no power in the aspiration or force behind the consecration.

Doubts do not matter, if the faith central and fundamental is there. Doubts may come, but they cannot prevail against [the rock] of faith in the centre of the being. The rock may be covered awhile by surges of doubt and despondency, but the rock will emerge firm and indestructible. Faith is of the heart, the inner heart where lives the psychic being. The outer heart is the seat of the vital being, the life personality. That like the mind may believe and then lose its belief, doubt comes from the mind, the vital and the physical consciousness. [The greater the intensity] of the psychic fire, the less will be the power of doubt to soil and darken the mind, the life and the consciousness of the body.

137

Three are the words that sum up the first state of the Yoga of devotion, faith, worship, obedience.

Three are the words that sum up the second state of the Yoga of devotion, adoration, delight, self-giving.

Three are the words that sum up the supreme state of the Yoga of devotion, love, ecstasy, surrender.

*

These are the seven ecstasies of Love —

The ecstasy of the body in the clasp of the Lover.

The ecstasy of the life consecrated and self-given to the Lord.

The ecstasy of the Mind made one in idea and [will] with the divine Consort.

The ecstasy of the supermind united with mind and body and enjoying the bliss of difference.

The ecstasy [of the] soul in the pure bliss of the Beatific.

The ecstasy of the spirit united in consciousness and force with the Universal.

The ecstasy of the pure being absolute and one with the Transcendent.

Karma Yoga: The Yoga of Works

138

All spiritual paths lead to a higher consciousness and union with the Divine and among the many paths one of the greatest is the

Way of Works: it is as great as the Way of Bhakti or the Way of Knowledge.

Do not imagine that works are in their nature nothing but a bondage, they can be a powerful means towards liberation and divine perfection. All depends on the spirit in our works and their orientation towards the inner and the higher Light away from desire and ego.

Works are a bondage when they are done out of desire or for the sake of the ego, by a mind turned outwards, involved in the act and not detached and free, bound to the ignorance of this lower nature.

139

To create the union of his soul with the Divine Presence and Power through a perfect surrender of the will in all his activities, is the high aspiration of the seeker on the Way of Works.

To put off like a worn-out disguise the ignorant consciousness and stumbling will that are ours in our present mind and life-force and to put on the light and knowledge, the purity and power, the tranquillity and ecstasy of the divine Essence, the spiritual Nature that awaits us when we climb beyond mind, is the victory after which he reaches.

To make mind and heart and life and body conscious, changed and luminous moulds of this supramental Spirit, instruments of its light and power and works, vessels of its bliss and radiance, is the glory he assigns to his transfigured human members.

On one side a darkened mind and life, ignorant, suffering, spinning like a top whipped by Nature always in the same obscure and miserable rounds, on the other a soul touched by a ray from the hidden Truth, illumined, conscious, concentrated in a single unceasing effort towards its own and the world's Highest, — this is the difference between man's ordinary life and the way of the divine Yoga[.]

*

It is not a mental or moral ideal to which is turned the seeker of the Way, but a truth of the spirit, the experience of a hidden Reality living and concrete, a Light, a Power, a Joy that surpasses the mental understanding and is beyond any merely mental experience.

The ideals created by the mind are constructions in the air that have no sufficient foundation in our vital and physical nature; therefore they can change a side of our mind and colour a part of our actions, but they cannot transform our lives, cannot find here their physical body. Ideals touch and pass, mankind remains the same; after religions, ideals, moralities without end we keep always the same ignorant and imperfect human nature.

Moral rules and ideals are a harness for the ignorant soul, bridle and bit for the passions, reins that compel it to an assigned road, yoke and poles and traces that bind it to be faithful to the burden it carries. Morality checks and controls but does not purify or change the vital nature.

In ethics there is an artificial shaping of the mind's surfaces, but no spiritual freedom, no satisfying perfection of the whole dynamic nature.

The mind's ideals like the life's seekings are at once absolute each in its own demand and in conflict with one another; neither mind nor life knows the means either of their complete or their harmonised fulfilment. The mind labours through the centuries but human nature remains faithful to its imperfections and man's life amid its changes always the same.

Beyond mind on spiritual and supramental levels dwells the Presence, the Truth, the Power, the Bliss that can alone deliver us from these illusions, display the Light of which our ideals are tarnished disguises and impose the harmony that shall at once transfigure and reconcile all the parts of our nature.

*

The first secret of Yoga is to get back behind the mind to the spirit, behind the surface emotional movements to the soul, —

behind the life to the universal force that builds these outward shapes and movements, — behind matter to the eternal Existence that puts on the robe of the body.

The second secret of Yoga is to open these discovered powers to their own supreme Truth above matter, above life, above the mind. This Truth, secret in the Superconscient, has four gradations or movements of its power, infinite supermind or Gnosis, infinite Bliss, Ananda, infinite Consciousness and Power, Chit-Tapas, infinite Being — Sat-Chid-Ananda.

The third secret of Yoga is, once arisen beyond mind, to bring down the power [*sentence not completed*]

140

The progressive surrender of our ignorant personal will and its merger into a greater divine or on the highest summits greatest supreme Will is the whole secret of Karma Yoga. To bring about the conditions in which alone this vast and happy identity becomes possible and to work out the lines we must follow to their end if we are to reach it, is all the deeper purpose of this discipline. The first condition is the elimination of personal vital desire, for if desire intervenes, all harmony with the supreme Divine Will becomes impossible. Even if we receive it, we shall disfigure its working and distort its dynamic impulse. To give up all desire, all insistence upon fruit and reward and success must be renounced from our will and all vital attachment to the work itself excised from our nature; for attachment makes it our own and no longer the Godhead's. The elimination of egoism is the second condition, not only of the rajasic and tamasic egoisms that twine around desire, but of the sattwic egoism that takes refuge in the idea of the I as the worker.

The ordinary consciousness of man cannot accept this difficult renunciation or, if it accepts it, cannot achieve this tremendous change. The human mind is too ignorant, narrow and chained to its own limited movements, the human life-instincts too blind, selfish, obscure, shut up in their own earth-bound pursuits and satisfactions, the human body too clumsy and hampering a machine. There is here no freedom, no large and infinite room, no willing and happy plasticity for the greater play of the Divine in Nature. A certain half-seeing and imperfect subordination of the personal will to an ill-understood greater Will and Power, a stumbling and occasional intuition or at best a brilliant lightninglike intimation of its commands and impulsions, a confused, clouded and often grossly distorted execution of the little one seizes of a divine Mandate seems to be the uttermost that the human consciousness as it is at its best seems able to accomplish. Only by a growth into a greater superhuman and supramental consciousness whose very nature is to be attuned to the Divine can we achieve the true and supreme Karma Yoga.

This transformation is only possible after certain steps of a divine ascent have been mastered and to climb these steps is the object of the Yoga of Works as it is conceived by the Gita. The extirpation of desire, a wide and calm equality of the mind, the life soul and the spirit, annihilation of the ego, an inner quietude and expulsion or transcendence of ordinary Nature, the Nature of the three gunas and a total surrender to the Supreme are the successive steps of this preliminary change. Only after all this has been done, can we live securely in an infinite consciousness not bound like our mental human nature. And only then can we receive the Light, know perfectly the will of the Supreme, attune all our movements to the rhythm of its Truth and execute perfectly from moment to moment its imperative commandments. Till then there is no firm achievement, but only an endeavour, seeking and aspiration, all the stress and struggle of a great and uncertain spiritual adventure. Only when these things are accomplished is there for the dynamic parts of our nature the beginning of a divine security in its acts and a transcendent peace.

141

Desire is always sinning against the Truth; it thins it and prevents it from taking body. Desire does not eternalise descending Truth;

it disintegrates, makes temporal, minimises and soon or at last abandons from dissatisfaction (vairagya) its maimed creation.

142

To do works in a close union and deep communion with the Divine in us, the Universal around us and the Transcendent above us, not to be shut up any longer in the imprisoned and separative human mind, the slave of its ignorant dictates and narrow suggestions, this is Karmayoga.

To work in obedience to a divine command, an eternal Will, a transcendent and universal impulsion, not to run under the whips of ego and need and passion and desire, and not to be goaded by the pricks of mental and vital and physical preference, but to be moved by God only, by the highest Truth only, this is Karmayoga.

To live and act no longer in human ignorance, but in divine Knowledge, conscient of individual nature and universal forces and responsive to a transcendent governance, this is Karmayoga.

To live, be and act in a divine, illimitable and luminous universal consciousness open to that which is more than universal, no longer to grope and stumble in the old narrowness and darkness, this is Karmayoga.

Whosoever is weary of the littlenesses that are, whosoever is enamoured of the divine greatnesses that shall be, whosoever has any glimpse of the Supreme within him or above him or around him let him hear the call, let him follow the path. The way is difficult, the labour heavy and arduous and long, but its reward is habitation in an unimaginable glory, a fathomless felicity, a happy and endless vastness.

Find the Guide secret within you or housed in an earthly body, hearken to his voice and follow always the way that he points. At the end is the Light that fails not, the Truth that deceives not, the Power that neither strays nor stumbles, the wide freedom, the ineffable Beatitude.

The heavens beyond are great and wonderful, but greater

and more wonderful are the heavens within you. It is these Edens that await the divine worker.

143

A peace and bliss inconceivable to the pleasure-bound and pain-racked mind, and immeasurable by the limited capacities of our present bodily sense, is the reward of the seeker's insistent self-discipline, his painful struggle, his untiring endeavour.

*

At first a consecration, then a surrender and subordination of our human personal will, then its merger in a greater divine or greatest supreme Will is the central secret and core of intention of the Karmayoga. But this cannot be entirely done by our mental consciousness in its little human boundaries. Our Yoga must help us to leave it and enter into a greater consciousness enlightened by a truer radiance of knowledge, armed with a mightier unerring strength, open to that vaster delight in which are drowned for ever our petty human pain and pleasure. Still even what can be done within the limits of our human consciousness brings a great liberation.

But even to do that little is not easy to the physical mind of man, even when his higher mind and will consent and demand it. There is something in us wedded to ignorance, eternally in revolt against all surrender, attached to its own blind activity, its own freedom of will, a "freedom" that rattles its hundred chains at every step; — but to that element in us even that seems a divine music. And our human mind will invent a hundred good reasons against any such surrender to something not ourselves or even to our highest Self, — unless that be nothing more than a magnified reflection of our ego; for then it will be willing enough to surrender. And even our highest spiritual achievement on the mental plane is tainted and limited, when it is not distorted, by this ever unredeemed element in our nature.

Our only safety is to push on beyond the mind to a Truth-consciousness with a larger dynamic light in it that is ever free by its inherent knowledge and illumined power from these pettinesses and this egoistic darkness. For in this supramental consciousness is the Truth and there we meet it and its Master. The supermind is the primal creative and organic instrument of the Supreme Will, the Will that is free from error because eternal, one and infinite.

Integral Yoga

Integrality

144

Most Yoga has for its aim one or other of two great ends, either the abandonment of the world and departure into some reality of supracosmic existence or some form of limited perfection, knowledge, bliss or mastery in the world. But there is a third objective of Yoga in which there is a harmony between world existence & supracosmic freedom. God is possessed; the world is not renounced or rather renounced as an aim in itself, but possessed as the play of God. A selfless and transcendent perfection in the divine existence is the goal in this path of Yoga.

145

There are many Yogas, many spiritual disciplines, paths towards liberation and perfection, Godward ways of the spirit. Each has its separate aim, its peculiar approach to the One Reality, its separate method, its helpful philosophy and its practice. The integral Yoga takes up all of them in their essence and tries to arrive at a unification (in essence, not in detail) of all these aims, methods, approaches; it stands for an all-embracing philosophy and practice.

146

To enter into the entire consciousness of the Divine Reality with all our being and all parts and in every way of our being and to change all our now ignorant and limited nature into divine nature so that it shall become the instrument and expression of the

Divine Reality that in our self and essence we are, — this is the complete fulfilment of our existence and this is the integral Yoga.

To enter into the Divine either by the way of the thinking mind or by the way of the heart or by the way of the will in works or by a change of the psychological nature-stuff or a freeing of the vital force in the body is not enough; all this is not enough. Through all these together it must be done and by a change of our very sense and body consciousness even to the material inconscience which must become aware of the Divine and luminous with the Divine.

To be one with the Divine, to live in and with the Divine, to be of one nature with the Divine, this should be the aim of our Yoga.

147

The integral Yoga is so called because it aims at a harmonised totality of spiritual realisation and experience. Its aim is integral experience of the Divine Reality, what the Gita describes in the words *samagram mam*, "the whole Me" of the Divine Being. Its method is an integral opening of the whole consciousness, mind, heart, life, will, body to that Reality, to the Divine Existence, Consciousness, Beatitude, to its being and its integral transformation of the whole nature[.]

148

Our Yoga is the integral Yoga. Its object is the harmony of a total spiritual realisation and experience, a supreme consummation of the spirit and the nature.

149

This Yoga is called the integral Yoga, first because its object is integral covering the whole field of spiritual realisation and experience. It takes existence at its centre and in all its aspects and turns it into a harmony at once single and entire. It is the method of an integral God realisation, an integral self-realisation, an integral fulfilment of the being, an integral transformation and perfection of the nature[.]

150

What is the integral Yoga?

It is the way of a complete God-realisation, a complete Self-realisation, a complete fulfilment of our being and consciousness, a complete transformation of our nature — and this implies a complete perfection of life here and not only a return to an eternal perfection elsewhere.

This is the object, but in the method also there is the same integrality, for the entirety of the object cannot be accomplished without an entirety in the method, a complete turning, opening, self-giving of our being and nature in all its parts, ways, movements to that which we realise.

Our mind, will, heart, life, body, our outer and inner and inmost existence, our superconscious and subconscious as well as our conscious parts, must all be thus given, must all become a means, a field of this realisation and transformation and participate in the illumination and the change from a human into a divine consciousness and nature.

This is the character of the integral Yoga.

151

The integral Yoga is a single but many-sided way of the growth of our spirit and development of our nature. A total experience and a single and all embracing realisation of the integral Divine Reality is its consequence. There is too implied in it a radical change and transformation of the whole being and of every part of the nature. Our being is a nexus of the human mental-vital-physical nature of Ignorance, it is transmuted into a spiritual and supramental consciousness: it becomes a divine unity in a harmony of the infinite and universal and integrated will, love, bliss and knowledge.

The Infinite Reality presents itself to our limited consciousness in an infinity of aspects; different ways of Yoga try to realise one or other of these aspects. The integral Yoga takes all of them in its movement, but it limits itself to no aspect; its sole desire is to embrace the whole Divinity (samagram mam — Gita).

A highest aspect of the infinite Reality is the supracosmic Absolute, unthinkable, ineffable, without relation to the universe. There is a path of Yoga that [*sentence not completed*]

152

The heart of the integral Yoga is in a triple spiritual endeavour. It is a realisation of the Divine, of all the Divine by our whole being and through all the parts of our being. It includes a discovery and harmonisation, a unification of our total consciousness subliminal as well as supraliminal, the now superconscient and subconscient as well as the now conscient and its surrender to the Divine for a spiritual instrumentation here; it culminates in an evolution of this consciousness [*sentence not completed*]

The integral Yoga is integral by the totality or completeness of its aim, the completeness of its process and the completeness of the ground it covers in its process. This kind of integrality must by its nature be complex, manysided and intricate; only some main lines can be laid down in writing, for an excess of detail would confuse the picture.

The aim the Yoga puts before itself is in essence the same as the object of other Yogas — the realisation of the Divine. But it is not the Divine in one of its aspects, personal or impersonal, cosmic or transcendent, Self or Lord or [*sentence not completed*]

153

That Yoga is full or perfect which enables us to fulfil entirely God's purpose in us in this universe.

All Yoga which takes the soul entirely out of world-existence, is a high but narrow specialisation of divine tapasya.

God's purpose in us is that we should fulfil His divine being in world-consciousness under the conditions of the Lila.

With regard to the universe God manifests Himself triply, in the individual, in the universe, in that which transcends the universe.

In order to fulfil God in the individual, we must exceed the individual. The removal of limited ego and the possession of cosmic consciousness is the first aim of our sadhana.

In order to fulfil God in the cosmos, individually, we must transcend the universe. The ascension into transcendent consciousness is the second aim of our sadhana.

154

All Yoga aims at oneness or union or a close communion or contact with the Divine, infinite and eternal. To reach to this union or come by this contact it is necessary to enter or at least open into a greater consciousness than that of the human mental being who is shut up in the limitations of an individualised living body. To arrive wholly at the union or the constant communion one must enter the consciousness of the Divine, — whether into its infinite cosmic consciousness or that of its supracosmic eternity. Or else, uniting both these terms, one may add to them that of the individualised Divine in oneself and through this trinity arrive at a perfect union, one, satisfying and complete.

But the Divine Consciousness can manifest itself through any and every plane, on the mental, on the vital, on the physical, or on those which are higher than the mental[.]

155

All Yoga done through the mind alone or through the heart or the will or the vital force or the body ends in some one aspect of the infinite and eternal Existence and rests satisfied there, as the mind imagines for ever. Not through these alone shall thy Yoga move, but through all these at once and, supremely, through that which is beyond them. And the end of thy Yoga shall be the integrality of thy entrance not into one aspect, but into all the Infinite, all the Eternal, all the Divine in all its aspects indivisibly unified together.

Whatever is beyond mind and life and body is spirit. But spirit can be realised even on these lower levels, in the spiritualised mind, in the spiritualised life-force, even in the spiritualised physical consciousness and body. But if thou rise not up beyond the mind-level, then in these realisations the spirit must needs be modified by the medium through which thou attainest to it and its supreme truth can only be seized in a reflection, partial even in widest apparent universality, and the utmost essential integrality will escape thy seizure.

Rise rather into the supramental levels and then all the rest shall remain a part of thy experience, but wonderfully changed, transfigured by a supreme alchemy of consciousness into an element of the supramental glory. All that other Yogas can give thee, thou shalt have, but as an experience overpassed, put in its place in the divine Whole and delivered from the inadequacy of an exclusive state or experience.

The Supramental Yoga

156

All Yoga is in its very nature a means of passing out of our surface consciousness of limitation and ignorance into a larger and deeper Reality of ourselves and the world and some supreme or total Existence now veiled to us by this surface. There is a Reality which underlies everything, permeates perhaps everything, is perhaps everything but in quite another way than the world now seen by us; to It we are obscurely moving by our thought, life and actions; we attempt to understand and approach by our religion and philosophy, at last we touch directly in some partial or, it may be, some complete spiritual experience. It is that spiritual experience, it is the method, it is the attainment of this realisation that we call Yoga.

But the Reality is an Absolute or an Infinite; our consciousness, even our spiritualised consciousness is that of a finite being. It is inevitable therefore that our spiritual experience should be not that of a concrete integrality of this Absolute or Infinite, but of aspects of it; we are, so long at least as we are mental beings, the blind men of the story trying to tell what the Elephant Infinite is in its totality by our touch upon a part of it, some member of its spiritual body, tanum svam. One experiences it as Self or Spirit. It may be a Self of himself in which he finds his spiritual consummation, integrality, infinity, perfection. It may be a Self of the universe in which his individuality loses itself forever. It may be a Self transcendent in which the Ego disappears, but cosmos too is annulled forever in a formless Eternal and Infinite. Another may experience it as God; and God may be either the All of the Pantheist, a cosmic Spirit, an individual Deity, a supracosmic Creator; or all of these together. A Personal Godhead may be the spiritual Form in which He presents Himself to us or rather He may reject forms from his being [and] resolve Himself into an impersonal Existence. Moreover each of these aspects of the Reality can be variously experienced; for each suits itself to the grasp of our consciousness, even though it can be very apparent that it is the same Reality that these variations differently account for. But also there may [be] other realisations of the Reality such as the Zero of the Nihilistic Buddhists which is yet a mysterious All, a negation that is a positive Permanence. It is an error to take these variations as a proof that spiritual experience is unreliable. All religions, all philosophies are equally desperate in their attempts to give an account of the Real and Ultimate; science itself for all its matter of fact physical positivism draws back bewildered from the attempt to touch the Real and Ultimate. It is the nature of Mind to arrive at this result of uncertain certainty; our experience is true but it is not and cannot be the sole possible integral experience.

157

All human Yoga is done on the heights or levels of the mental nature; for man is a mental being in a living body. But mind if it is able to reflect some light of the divine Truth or even admit some emanations from her power, is incapable of embodying her.

There is an eternal dynamic Truth-consciousness beyond mind; this is what we call supermind or gnosis.

For mind is or can be a truth seeker, but not truth-conscious in its inherent nature; its original stuff is made not of knowledge, but of ignorance.

158

All Yoga has one supreme object; a permanent liberation from the ignorance and weakness of this limited and suffering human and earthly consciousness is its purpose and either an escape or a growth and swift flowering into a greater consciousness beyond mind, life and body, into a wider and diviner existence.

But this greater consciousness is differently conceived by different seekers, for in itself it is to the mind unseizably infinite. One, but multitudinously one, it presents itself in a million aspects. To some it appears as a great permanent Negative or a magnificent, a happy annihilation of all that we know as an existence. To others it is a featureless Absolute; the annihilation of personality and world-Nature is its key and silence and an ineffable peace its gate of our entrance. To others it is a Supreme, positive beyond all positives, an Existence, an absolute Consciousness, an illimitable Beatitude. To others it is the one Divine beyond all Divinities, an ineffable Person of whom all these three supreme things are the attributes. And so through an endless chapter. As is the power of our spirit and the cast of our nature, so we conceive of the one Eternal and Infinite.

This Eternal and Infinite, however we conceive it, is the one ultimate aim of Yoga. Other smaller aims there are that can be achieved by it and are pursued by many seekers; but these are crowns of the wayside or even flowers of the bye-paths and their pursuit for their own sake may lead us far aside or far away from our eternal home.

The object of supramental Yoga combines all the others, but uplifts and transforms the smaller aims into a part of the completeness of the one supreme object.

Not to lose oneself altogether in some ineffable featurelessness is its object, but to renounce ego for our true divine person one with the universal and infinite; not to abolish consciousness, but to exchange ignorance for a supreme and all-containing Knowledge, not to blot out joy but to renounce human pleasure for a divine griefless beatitude, not to give up but to transform all world-nature and world-existence into a power of the Truth of the Divine Existence. Asceticism is not the final condition or characteristic means of this Yoga, although it does not exclude, whenever that is needful ascetic self-mastery or ascetic endeavour.

To become one in our absolute being with the ineffable Divine and in the manifestation a free movement of his being, power, consciousness and self-realising joy, to grow into a divine Truth-consciousness beyond mind, into a Light beyond all human or earthly lights, into a Power to which the greatest strengths of men are a weakness, into the wisdom of an infallible gnosis and the mastery of an unerring and unfailing divinity of Will, into a Bliss beside which all human pleasure is as the broken reflection of a candle-flame to the all-pervading splendour of an imperishable sun, but all this not for our own sake [but] for the pleasure of the Divine Beloved, this is the goal and the crown of the supramental path of Yoga.

This change is a thing in Nature and not out of Nature; it is not only possible, but for the growing soul inevitable. It is the goal to which Nature in us walks through all this appearance of ignorance, error, suffering and weakness.

159

The supramental Yoga is at once an ascent of the soul towards God and a descent of the Godhead into the embodied nature.

The ascent demands a one-centred all-gathering aspiration

of soul and mind and life and body upward, the descent a call of the whole being towards the infinite and eternal Divine. If this call and this aspiration are there and if they grow constantly and seize all the nature, then and then only its supramental transformation becomes possible.

There must be an opening and surrender of the whole nature to receive and enter into a greater divine consciousness which is there already above, behind and englobing this mortal half-conscious existence. There must be too an increasing capacity to bear an ever stronger and more insistent action of the divine Force, till the soul has become a child in the hands of the infinite Mother. All other means known to other Yoga can be used and are from time to time used as subordinate processes in this Yoga too, but they are impotent without these greater conditions, and, once these are there, they are not indispensable.

In the end it will be found that this Yoga cannot be carried through to its end by any effort of mind, life and body, any human psychological or physical process but only by the action of the supreme Shakti. But her way is at once too mysteriously direct and outwardly intricate, too great, too complete and subtle to be comprehensively followed, much more to be cut out and defined into a formula by our human intelligence.

Man cannot by his own effort make himself more than man, but he can call down the divine Truth and its power to work in him. A descent of the Divine Nature can alone divinise the human receptacle. Self-surrender to a supreme transmuting Power is the key-word of the Yoga.

This divinisation of the nature of which we speak is a metamorphosis, not a mere growth into some kind of superhumanity, but a change from the falsehood of our ignorant nature into the truth of God-nature. The mental or vital demigod, the Asura, Rakshasa and Pishacha, — Titan, vital giant and demon, — are superhuman in the pitch and force and movement and in the make of their characteristic nature, but these are not divine and those not supremely divine, for they live in a greater mind power or life power only, but they do not live in the supreme Truth, and only the supreme Truth is divine. Only those who live in a supreme Truth consciousness and embody it are inwardly made or else remade in the Divine image.

The aim of supramental Yoga is to change into this supreme Truth-consciousness, but this truth is something beyond mind and this consciousness is far above the highest mind-consciousness. For truth of mind is always relative, uncertain and partial, but this greater Truth is peremptory and whole. Truth of mind is a representation, always an inadequate, most often a misleading representation, and even when most accurate, only a reflection, Truth's shadow and not its body. Mind does not live in the Truth or possess but only seeks after it and grasps at best some threads from its robe; the supermind lives in Truth and [is] its native substance, form and expression; it has not to seek after it, but possesses it always automatically and is what it possesses. This is the very heart of the difference.

The change that is effected by the transition from mind to supermind is not only a revolution in knowledge or in our power for knowledge. If it is [to] be complete and stable, it must be a divine transmutation of our will too, our emotions, our sensations, all our power of life and its forces, in the end even of the very substance and functioning of our body. Then only can it be said that the supermind is there upon earth, rooted in its very earth-substance and embodied in a new race of divinised creatures.

Supermind at its highest reach is the divine Gnosis, the Wisdom-Power-Light-Bliss of God by which the Divine knows and upholds and governs and enjoys the universe[.]

160

The supramental Yoga is a path of integral seeking of the Divine by which all that we are is in the end liberated out of the Ignorance and its undivine formations into a truth beyond the Mind, a truth not only of highest spiritual status but of a dynamic spiritual self-manifestation in the universe.

The object of this Yoga is not to liberate the soul from Nature, but to liberate both soul and nature by sublimation into the Divine Consciousness from whom they came.

The aim of the ordinary Yoga is to liberate the soul from Nature or, perhaps sometimes, to liberate the soul in Nature.

Our aim is to liberate both soul and nature into the Divine. Our aim is to pass from the Ignorance into the Divine Light, from death into Immortality, from Desire into self-existent Bliss, from limited human-animal consciousness into all-consciousness and God-consciousness, from the ignorant seeking of Mind into the self-existent knowledge of Supermind, from obscure half animal life into luminous God-force, from the material consciousness [*sentence not completed*]

161

It is at the high line where the surrender can become absolute that a divine gnostic consciousness commences and the first authentic and unconditioned workings of the supramental Nature.

162

The first word of the supramental Yoga is surrender; its last word also is surrender. It is by a will to give oneself to the eternal Divine, for lifting into the divine consciousness, for perfection, for transformation, that the Yoga begins; it is in the entire giving that it culminates; for it is only when the self-giving is complete that there comes the finality of the Yoga, the entire taking up into the supramental Divine, the perfection of the being, the transformation of the nature.

The Yoga of Transformation

163

This is a Yoga of transformation of the being, not solely a Yoga of the attainment of the inner Self or the Divine, though that attainment is its basis without which no transformation is possible. In this transformation there are four elements, the psychic opening, the transit through [the] occult, the spiritual release, the supramental perfection. If any of the four is unachieved, the Yoga remains incomplete.

I mean by the psychic the inmost soul-being and the soul nature. This is not the sense in which the word is used in ordinary parlance, or rather, if it is so used, it is with great vagueness and much misprision of the true nature of this soul and it is given a wide extension of meaning which carries it far beyond that province. All phenomena of an abnormal or supernormal psychological or an occult character are dubbed psychic; if a man has a double personality changing from one to another, if an apparition of a dying man, something of his mere vital sheath or else a thought-form of him, appears and stalks through the room of his wondering friend, if a poltergeist kicks up an unseemly row in a house, all that is classed under psychic phenomena and regarded as a fit object for psychic research, though these things have nothing whatever to do with the psyche. Again much in Yoga itself that is merely occult, phenomena of the unseen vital or mental or subtle physical planes, visions, symbols, all that mixed, often perturbed, often shadowy, often illusory range of experiences which belong to this intervening country between the soul and its superficial instruments or rather to its outermost fringes, all the chaos of the intermediate zone, is summed up as psychic and considered as an inferior and dubious province of spiritual discovery. Again there is a constant confusion between the mentalised desire-soul which is a creation of the vital urge in man, of his life-force seeking for its fulfilment and the true soul which is a spark of the Divine Fire, a portion of the Divine. Because the soul, the psychic being uses the mind and the vital as well as the body as instruments for growth and experience it is itself looked at as if it were some amalgam or some subtle substratum of mind and life. But in Yoga if we accept all this chaotic mass as soul-stuff or soul-movement we shall enter into a confusion without an issue. All that belongs only to the coverings of the soul; the soul itself is an inner divinity greater than mind or life or body. It is something that once it is released from obscuration by its instruments at once creates a direct contact with the Divine and with the self and spirit.

164

In the integral Yoga there is a progressive discovery of our spiritual status; this progression is accompanied by a dynamic new-creation of our nature. A triple transformation is its process and the revelation of its entire significance.

A first discovery is the unveiling of the soul out of its disguising mask, concealing curtain, blockading wall of mind, life and body — the psychic entity, the divine element in our nature which gives it its permanence and immortality, becomes the open ruler of our instruments and transmutes them into conscious spiritualised agents so that they are no longer a changing formulation of the nature of the Ignorance.

165

Yoga is not only a discovery of our concealed spiritual status but a dynamic spiritual self-creation; a triple transformation is the heart of its process and the revelation of its entire significance.

Its first step is the unveiling of the soul;[1] for there [is a] secret psychic being, a divine element in our depths that is concealed even more than garbed by the mind, body and life. To bring it

---

[1] *Reproduced below is another, incomplete version of this passage:*

Its first step is the unveiling of the soul, the psychic entity, now covered by the superficial activity of mind and life and body. The soul is the deep hidden natural divine element in us, a permanent portion of the Godhead which persists in a spiritual permanence and ensures our immortality of being; for without it there could be only a temporary mechanical formation and action of nature-energy and its phenomenon of substance. This unveiling is accompanied by a psychic transformation of the nature; mind, life and body become truly ensouled and ready for a spiritual change.

Its second step is the revelation of a self and spirit which supports our individual soul manifestation and soul development, but knows itself to be one being with cosmic Godhead and universal Nature and can stand back from that even as a transcendent spirit. By this discovery the being in us exceeds its separate individuality, enters into a cosmic consciousness, is released into a supracosmic transcendence.

out of its seclusion where it lives like a spiritual king without apparent power served and replaced by its ministers, so that it may take over the whole active government of the nature is the first great unfolding, the initial potent self-discovery of the Yoga. Mind the thinker is the prime minister in us who covers the king, but mind too is dominated and led by the vital powers, the strong and violent of the realm, who force it to serve their purpose and these too can only act with the means given them by the body and physical nature, the inert hardly conscious subject existence whose passive assent and docile instrumentation is yet indispensable to its rulers. This is our present constitution and it amounts to no more than a sort of organised confusion, a feudal order that is an ignorant half anarchy and cannot make the most of the possibilities and resources even of the limited tract of nature which we inhabit, much less reveal to us and exploit our spiritual empire. To reinstate the king-soul is the first step in a needed revolution — the soul directing the mind will exercise through it its sovereign power over the powers of life and subject to them in their turn an enlightened and psychically consenting body. But this is not all; for soul-discovery is not complete without a psychic new creation of the mental, vital and physical instrumentation of nature. The mind will be recast by the soul's intuition of Truth, the vital being by its perception of power and good, the body and whole nature by its command for light, harmony and beauty. Our nature will become that of a true psychic entity, not a brute creation unified by a precarious life and illumined by the candlelight of a struggling intelligence.

166

I mean by the integral Yoga a manysided way or means of self-liberation and self-perfection, a radical change of our entire being by which we grow out of its present mental, vital and physical human ignorance into a large and integral spiritual and divine Consciousness; — as a result of this liberation, this change or transformation there is a union in the spirit with our Divine Origin in its integral Reality, an ascent of all our being and nature into the Divine Existence, the Divine Consciousness, the Divine Bliss or Ananda, and a descent of the Divine infinite Wideness, Light, Knowledge, Force, Joy, Ananda into our entire nature.

167

Our Yoga is a Yoga of transformation, but a transformation of the whole consciousness and the whole nature from the top to the bottom, from its hidden inward parts to its most tangible external movements. It is neither an ethical change nor a religious conversion, neither sainthood nor ascetic control, neither a sublimation nor a suppression of the life and vital movements that we envisage, nor is it either a glorification or a coercive control or rejection of the physical existence. What is envisaged is a change from a lesser to a greater, from a lower to a higher, from a surface to a deeper consciousness — indeed to the largest, highest, deepest possible and a total change and revolution of the whole being in its stuff and mass and every detail into that yet unrealised diviner nature of existence. It means a bringing forward of what is now hidden and subliminal, a growing conscious in what is now superconscient to us, an illumination of the subconscient and subphysical. It implies a substitution of the control of the nature by the soul for its present control by the mind; a transference of the instrumentation of the nature from the outer to the now more than half-veiled inner mind, from the outer to the inner vital or life-self, from the outer to an inner subtler vaster physical consciousness and by this transference a direct and conscious instead of an indirect and unconscious or half conscious contact with the secret cosmic forces that move us; a breaking out from the narrow limited individual into a wide cosmic consciousness; an ascension from mental to spiritual nature; a still farther ascension from the spirit in mind or overspreading mind to the supramental spirit and a descent of that into the embodied being. All that has not only to be achieved but organised before the transformation is complete.

168

The ascent to supermanhood will be a radical change of consciousness, force and bliss-power, a potent building of all that is necessary to manifest the new godhead in mind, life and body. There will be at once an inner revelation and an outer transformation. Something will be born that was not here or was latent and hidden in its own invisible radiances and at the same time there will be a metamorphosis and reversal in our existing structure.

A creation by a consensus of superior and nether powers is the condition demanded by the Spirit for its decisive works; and this double action, this meeting, consensus, unification of the superconscient and subconscient gods in a growing consciousness is the key to the critical revolutions of Nature.

The creation of conscious supermind on the terrestrial plane will be done therefore not only from above by the Spirit but from below by the Earth-Power. The sun of supramental Truth will descend into the body, but also it will awake another secret sun of supramental Truth that was asleep in the foundations and very principle of Matter.

169

The boon that we have asked from the Supreme is the greatest that the earth can ask from the Highest, the change that is most difficult to realise, the most exacting in its conditions. It is nothing less than the descent of the supreme Truth and Power into Matter, the supramental established in the material plane and consciousness and the material world and an integral transformation down to the very principle of Matter. Only a supreme Grace can effect this miracle.

The supreme Power has descended into the most material consciousness but it has stood there behind the density of the physical veil demanding before manifestation, before its great open workings can begin, that the conditions of the supreme Grace shall be there, real and effective. And the first condition is that the Truth shall be accepted within you entirely and without reserve before it can be manifested in the material being and Nature.

A total surrender, an exclusive self-opening to the divine influence, a constant and integral choice of the Truth and rejection of the falsehood, these are the only conditions made. But these must be fulfilled entirely, without reserve, without any evasion or pretence, simply and sincerely down to the most physical consciousness and its workings[.]

170

Victory in this effort depends upon the sincerity within you, the purity of your aspiration, the burning core of your faith, the absoluteness of your will and surrender[.]

171

Two things are needed if thou wouldst follow the steep and difficult way of Yoga, the need and will within thee and the call of the Spirit.

The need is the need of the soul, awakened or awaking or striving to come to the surface. For all other may be transitory or false; but the soul's need is lasting and true.

Thy soul's need of divine light and the spirit's perfection can alone bear thee across the darkness of the many nights through which thou must pass, beyond the open or hidden pitfalls of the road, past the dangers of the precipice and the morass, through the battle with giant forces and the clutching of hands that mislead and the delusions of the night and the twilight, through false light and illusive glamour, triumphant over the blows and ordeals and nets and temptations of the gods and on and up to the immeasurable summits[.]

Part Three

Notes and Fragments on Various Subjects

The pieces collected in this part were written by Sri Aurobindo at different times and for various purposes. They have been arranged by the editors by subject in five sections.

Section One

The Human Being in Time

The Marbles of Time

Institutions, empires, civilisations are the marbles of Time. Time, sitting in his banqueting hall of the Ages, where prophets and kings are the spice of his banquet, drinking the red wine of life and death, while on the marble floor at his feet are strewn like flowers the images of the same stars that shone on the pride of Nahusha, the tapasya of Dhruv and the splendours of Yayati, that saw Tiglath-Pileser, Sennacherib and the Egyptian Pharaohs, Pompey's head hewn off on the sands of Egypt and Caesar bleeding at Pompey's sculptured feet, Napoleon's mighty legions thundering victorious at the bidding of that god of war on the field of Austerlitz and Napoleon's panic legions fleeing disordered with pursuit and butchery behind them from that last field of Waterloo, — Time, the Kala Purusha, drunk with the fumes of death and the tears and laughter of mortals, sits and plays there with his marbles. There are marbles there of all kinds, marbles of all colours, and some are dull and grey, some glorious with hearts of many colours, some white and pure as a dove's wings, — but he plays with them all equally and equally he thrusts them all away when he has done with them. Sometimes even, in his drunkenness, he hurls them out of his window or lifts his mace and deals blows here and there smashing into fragments the bright and brittle globes, and he laughs as they smash and crumble. So Time, the god, sits and plays for ever with his marbles.

A Theory of the Human Being

It is a superstition of modern thought that the march of knowledge has in all its parts progressed always in a line of forward progress deviating from it, no doubt, in certain periods of obscuration, but always returning and in the sum constituting everywhere an advance and nowhere a retrogression. Like all superstitions this belief is founded on bad and imperfect observation flowering into a logical fallacy. Our observation is necessarily imperfect because we have at our disposal the historical data and literary records of only a few millenniums and beyond only disjected and insufficient indices which leave gigantic room for the hardly-fettered activity of the mind's two chief helpers and misleaders, inference and conjecture. Our observation is bad because, prepossessed by the fixed idea of a brief & recent emergence from immemorial barbarism, imagining Plato to have blossomed in a few centuries out of a stock only a little more advanced than the South Sea islander, we refuse to seek in the records that still remain of a lost superior knowledge their natural and coherent significance; we twist them rather into the image of our own thoughts or confine them within the still narrow limits of what we ourselves know and understand. The logical fallacy we land in as the goal of our bad observation is the erroneous conception that because we are more advanced than certain ancient peoples in our own especial lines of success, as the physical sciences, therefore necessarily we are also more advanced in other lines where we are still infants and have only recently begun to observe and experiment, as the science of psychology and the knowledge of our subjective existence and of mental forces. Hence we have developed the exact contrary of the old superstition that the movement of man is always backward to retrogression. While our forefathers believed that the more ancient might on the whole be trusted as more authoritative, because nearer to the gods, and the less ancient less authoritative because nearer to man's ultimate degeneracy, we believe on the contrary that the more ancient is always on the whole more untrue because nearer to the unlettered and unenquiring savage, the more modern the more true because held as opinion by the lettered and instructed citizen of Paris or Berlin. Neither position can be accepted. Verification by experience & experiment is the only standard of truth, not antiquity, not modernity. Some of the ideas of the ancients or even of the savage now scouted by us may be lost truths or statements of valid experience from which we have turned or become oblivious; many of the notions of the modern schoolmen will certainly in the future be scouted as erroneous and superstitious.

Among the ancient documents held by the ancients to be deep mines of profound and fertile truth but to us forgetful and blind of their meaning the Veda & Upanishads rank among the very highest.

A Cyclical Theory of Evolution

[.....] Driven from all other fields by a perception of the slow and aeonic processes of Nature, the mushroom theory of existence took refuge in this ill-explored corner of scientific theory. Thence, although later discoveries have had an enlarging effect, it still hampers the growth of more thoughtful generalisations. The time-limit allowed for the growth of civilisation is still impossibly short and in consequence an air of unreality hangs over the application of the evolutionary idea to our human development. Nor is this essential objection cured by any evidence of the modernity of human civilisation. Its great antiquity is denied merely on the absence [of] affirmative data; there are no positive indications to support the denial; but where data are scanty, such a negative basis is in the last degree unsound and precarious. We can no longer argue that no ancient civilisations can have existed of which the traces have entirely perished and that prehistoric means, necessarily, savage and undeveloped. History on the contrary abounds with instances of great societies which were within an ace of disappearing without leaving any visible memorial behind them and recent excavations have shown that such disappearances in ancient times have been even not uncommon. We cannot have exhausted all that the earth contains. There should be the remains of other civilisations yet undiscovered & there may well have been yet others which because of the manner of their disappearance or for other causes have left no traces at all whether upon the surface of the earth or under it. Indeed with regard to no object or previous existence, no silent or imperfectly documented [?scene], is it safe to argue that because there are no traces or sufficient evidence of it, therefore it never existed. Yet in many fields of generalisation modern scholarship has used substantially this argument with a prodigal freedom. It is at least possible that mighty cities and noble civilisations filled with their rumour the now silent spaces of Time for countless millenniums before Egypt and Assyria rose into their historic greatness.

Brief lapse of time is not indeed the cardinal point of the savage theory and even if larger time-spaces are allowed, the theory itself need not fall. But I have urged the question of time as of primary moment not for the overthrow of the modern explanation but for the readmission of another and more ancient synthesis. For if once we allow the existence of prehistoric civilisations older, it would seem, than the Egyptian, — such as may be argued from the deep-buried cities of Asia, — and the presence in an unknown antiquity of great national cultures where now the savage or the semi-savage swarm uncreative and unreflecting, — such as may be argued from the ruins of Mashonaland or the state of mediaeval Barbary after the ravages of Moor and Vandal or even the fate which overtook for almost a millennium the magnificent structure of Graeco-Roman culture and threatened even to blot out its remnants and ruins, — the question then arises, what was the nature of these forgotten civilisations and how was the relapse to barbarism often of an extreme form, so completely effected. These gigantic spaces of time, this worldwide rise and fall of human society, this swaying to and fro from darkness to light and light to darkness leave the ground open for another explanation which is in some respects the reverse of the savage theory, — for the Hindu explanation.

For the Hindu mind has never admitted the principle in Nature of progress in a straight line. Progress in a straight line only appears to occur and so appears only because we concentrate our scrutiny on limited sections of the curve that Nature is following. But if we stand away from this too near and detailed scrutiny and look at the world in its large masses, we perceive that its journeying forward has no straightness in it of any kind but is rather effected in a series of cycles of which the net result is progress. The image of this apparent straight line is that of the ship which seems to its crew to be journeying on the even plain of the waters but is really describing the curve of the earth in a way perceptible only to a more distant and instructed vision. Moreover even the small section of the curve which we are examining & which to our limited vision seems to be a straight line is the result of a series of zigzags and is caused by the conflict of forces arriving by a continual struggle at a continual compromise or working out by their prolonged discord a temporary harmony. The image of the actual progress in cycles is the voyaging in Space of the planets which describe always the same curve round their flaming & luminous sun, image of the perfect strength, joy, beauty, beneficence and knowledge towards which our evolution yearns. The cycle is always the same ellipse, yet by the simultaneous movement of the whole system the completed round finds the planet at a more advanced station in Space than its preceding journey. It is in this way, by an ever-swaying battle, a prodigal destruction and construction, a labouring forward in ever-progressing curves and ellipses that Nature advances to her secret consummation.

These are the conceptions we find expressed in the Puranic symbols familiar to our imagination. There is the Kalpa of a thousand ages with its term of fourteen Manwantaras dividing a sub-cycle of a hundred chaturyugas; there is the dharma, the well-harmonised law of being, perfect in the golden period of the Satya, impaired progressively in bronze Treta and copper Dwapara, collapsing in the iron Kali only to open the way by its disintegration to the manifestation in the next Satya of the old law, truth or natural principle of existence arranged in a new harmony. There is throughout this zigzag, this rhythm of rise and fall and rise again brought about by the struggle of upward, downward and stationary forces. There are the alternate triumphs of deva and daitya, helping god and opposing or too violently forward-striving Titan; — the dharmasya glani and abhyutthanam adharmasya, when harmony is denied and discord or wrong harmony established, and then the Avatara and the dharmasya sansthapanam, eternal Light and Force descending, restoring, effecting a new temporary adjustment of the world's ways to the truth of things and of man.

Translated into more modern but not necessarily more accurate language these symbols point us to a world history not full of the continual, ideal, straightforward victory of good and truth, not progress conceived as the Europeans conceive it, a continual joyous gallop through new & ever new changes to an increasing perfection, but rather of the alternately triumphant forces of progress and regression, a toiling forward and a sliding backward, — the continual revolution of human nature upon itself which yet undoubtedly has but conceals & seems not to have its secret of definite aim and ultimate exultant victory. In certain respects the old Vedantic thinkers anticipate us; they agree with all that is essential in our modern ideas of evolution. From one side all forms of creatures are developed; some kind of physical evolution from the animal to the human body is admitted in the Aitareya. The Taittiriya suggests the psychological progress of man, and the psychological progress of race cannot be different in principle from the evolution of the individual — a proceeding from the material, the emotionally and mentally inert man upwards [?through] the mental to [?our] spiritual fulfilment. The Puranas admit the creation of animal forms before the appearance of man and in the symbol of the Ten Avatars trace the growth of our evolution from the fish through the animal, the man-animal and the developed human being to the different stages of our present incomplete evolution. But the ancient Hindu, it is clear, envisaged this progression as an enormous secular movement covering more ages than we can easily count. He believed that Nature has repeated it over & over again, as indeed it is probable that she has done, resuming briefly & in sum at each start what she had previously accomplished in detail, slowly & with labour. It is this great secular movement in cycles, perpetually self-repeating, yet perpetually progressing, which is imaged and set forth for us in the symbols of the Puranas. It is for this reason that he assigned to his civilisation those immense eras and those ancient and far backward beginnings which strike the modern as so incredible. He may have erred; recent discoveries & indications are increasingly tending to convince us that nineteenth century scholarship has erred equally in the opposite direction.

Translated again into modern language the Hindu idea of the chaturyuga, four Ages, with all the attendant Puranic circumstances persists as the tradition of a period just such as has been postulated, a period of natural and perfect poise in his knowledge, action and temper between man and his environment. The ideas, the knowledge, the temper, the spirit of this great epoch of civilisation, — but not its institutions or practices — is preserved for us in the Veda and Vedanta, and all existing human societies, civilised or barbarous, go back for the origins of their thought, character & effort to the general type of humanity that was then formed.

Section Two

The East and the West

A Misunderstanding of Continents

The peculiar and striking opposition of thought, temperament, culture and manners between Asia and Europe has been a commonplace of observation and criticism since the times when Herodotus noted in his history the objection of both men and women to be seen naked as a curious and amusing trait of Asiatic barbarism. Much water has flown under the bridges since Herodotus wrote and in this respect Asia seems not only to have infected Europe with this "barbaric" trait of manners, but to have been far outstripped by her pupil in the development of sartorial superfluities. Excessive wealth and gorgeous splendour was also quoted as a characteristic of Asiatic barbarism from the time of the classical poets. Europe has seen to it that this charge shall only apply now in a very minimum quantity to the eastern continent. Asia now stands, not only by choice of her ascetics, but by economic compulsion for the simple life, and the ostentation of wealth which was once depreciated as a sign of oriental barbarism now parades itself, much vulgarised, at least to our barbaric eastern notion of aesthetics as the splendid face of occidental civilisation. But if circumstances have changed, the essential opposition abides; East is still East in its soul and West is still West and the misunderstanding of continents still flourishes, not only in the minds of politicians and "statesmen", — where one would naturally expect to find it, since it is there that vulgar prejudices, half-truths, whole untruths and unintelligent commonplaces assume their most solemn and sententious form, coin themselves into glittering phrases or flow in rhetorical periods, — but in the minds too of critics, poets and leading intellectuals. Faced with this continued misunderstanding, one is obliged to ask whether it is really incurable, an antinomy on which Nature is resolved to insist until the end of this cycle.

Some of us, temerarious idealists, have thought that the

misconception, the want of understanding is not only curable, but that to cure it as soon as may be is essential to the future interests of humanity. For my part I hold that all antinomies and opposed powers in this world of contradictions would be much better for an attempt to understand each other's souls and find their meeting point, would find something helpful not only to tone down their own exaggerations, but to fill in and round themselves without losing what is essential to their own spirit. Recently there has been a distinct widening in many minds, a nearer approach to understanding, almost to fusion. A little while ago in the first lyrical enthusiasm of the war and its "sacred unions" one imagined that a decisive step had been taken and the peoples themselves would now be ready for sympathy and understanding. But it seems it is not quite so yet[.]

Towards Unification

The progress of distance-bridging inventions, our modern facility for the multiplication of books and their copies and the increase of human curiosity are rapidly converting humanity into a single intellectual unit with a common fund of knowledge and ideas and a unified culture. The process is far from complete, but the broad lines of the plan laid down by the great Artificer of things already begin to appear. For a time this unification was applied to Europe only. Asia had its own triune civilisation, predominatingly spiritual, complex and meditative in India, predominatingly vital, emotional, active and simplistic in the regions of the Hindu Kush and Mesopotamia, predominatingly intellectual, mechanical and organised in the Mongolian empires. East, West and South had their widely separate spirit and traditions, but one basis of spirituality, common tendencies and such commerce of art, ideas and information as the difficulties of communication allowed, preserved the fundamental unity of Asia. East & West only met at their portals, in war oftener than in peace and through that shock and contact influenced but did not mingle with each other. It was the discovery of Indian philosophy and poetry which broke down the barrier. For the first time Europe discovered something in the East which she could study not only with the curiosity which she gave to Semitic and Mongolian ideas and origins, but with sympathy and even with some feeling of identity. This metaphysics, these epics and dramas, this formulated jurisprudence and complex society had methods and a form which, in spite of their diversity from her own, yet presented strong points of contact; she could recognise them, to a certain extent she thought she could understand. The speculativeness of the German, the lucidity of the Gaul, the imagination and aesthetic emotionalism of the British Celt found something to interest them, something even to assist. In the teachings of Buddha, the speculation of Shankara, the poetry of Kalidasa their souls could find pasture and refreshment. The alien form and spirit of Japanese and Arabian poetry and of Chinese philosophy which prevented such an approximation with the rest of Asia, was not here to interfere with the comprehension of the human soul & substance. There was indeed a single exception which remarkably illustrates the difficulty of which I speak. The art of India contradicted European notions too vitally to be admitted into the European consciousness; its charm and power were concealed by the uncouthness to Western eyes of its form and the strangeness of its motives and it is only now, after the greatest of living art-critics in England had published sympathetic appreciations of Indian art and energetic propagandists like Mr. Havell had persevered in their labour, that the European vision is opening to the secret of Indian painting & sculpture. But the art of Japan presented certain outward characteristics on which the European could readily seize. Japanese painting had already begun to make its way into Europe even before the victories of Japan and its acceptance of much of the outward circumstances of European civilisation opened a broad door into Europe for all in Japan that Europe can receive without unease or the feeling of an incompatible strangeness. Japanese painting, Japanese dress, Japanese decoration are not only accepted as a part of Western life by the select few and the cultured classes but known and allowed, without being adopted, by the millions. Asiatic civilisation has entered into Europe as definitely though not so victoriously as European civilisation into Asia. It is only the beginning, but so was it only the beginning when a few scholars alone rejoiced in the clarity of Buddhistic Nihilism, Schopenhauer rested his soul on the Upanishads and Emerson steeped himself in the Gita. No one could have imagined then that a Hindu monk would make converts in London and Chicago or that a Vedantic temple would be built in San Francisco and Anglo-Saxon Islamites erect a Musulman mosque in Liverpool. It appears from a recent inquiry that the only reading, omitting works of fiction, which commands wide and general interest among public library readers is either scientific works or books replete with Asiatic mysticism. How significant is this fact when we remember that these are the two powers, Europe & Asia, the victorious intellect and the insurgent spirit, which are rising at this moment to do battle for the mastery of the unified world. Nevertheless it is not the public library reader, that man in the street of the literary world, but the increasing circle of men of culture and a various curiosity through whom the Orient & the Occident must first meet in a common humanity and the day dawn when some knowledge of the substance of [the] Upanishads will be as necessary to an universal culture as a knowledge of the substance of the Bible, Shankara's theories as familiar as the speculations of Teutonic thinkers and Kalidasa, Valmekie & Vyasa as near and common to the subject matter of the European critical intellect as Dante or Homer.

It is the difficulties of presentation that prevent a more rapid and complete commingling.

China, Japan and India

It is significant of the tendencies of the twentieth century that all its great and typical events should have occurred no longer as in the last few centuries in Europe, but in Asia. The Russo-Japanese war, the Chinese Revolution, the constitutional changes in Turkey & Persia and last but most momentous the revival however indeterminate as yet of the soul of India, are the really significant events of the young century. In Europe except in its one Asiatic corner there has been no event of corresponding magnitude & importance. The abortive orgy of revolutionary fury in Russia, the growth of enormous strikes, the failure of the peace movement, the increase of legislation stamped with the pressure of a materialistic Socialism, although they may hold in themselves germs of greater things, are so far mere indistinct material symptoms of disorganisation & a disease vainly doctored with palliatives, not events of a definite movement of new birth & regeneration. The importance of this new tendency lies in the fact that great events in Europe, even when they are outwardly spiritual, have usually an intellectual or social trend & significance, but great events in Asia have even when they are outwardly intellectual, social or political a spiritual significance. Therefore when Asia once more becomes the theatre of the world's chief events, it is a sure sign that some great spiritual revolution, perhaps a great age of spirituality is preparing for humanity.

Section Three

India

Renascent India

Everybody can feel, even without any need of a special sense for the hidden forces and tendencies concealed in the apparent march of things, for the signs are already apparent, that India is on the verge, in some directions already in the first movements of a great renascence, more momentous, more instinct with great changes and results, than anything that has gone before it. Every new awakening of the kind comes by some impact slight or great on the national consciousness which puts it in face of new ideas, new conditions, new needs, the necessity of readaptation to a changing environment. The spirit of the nation has to take account of its powers and possibilities and is stirred by a will to new formation and new creation. The change does not always amount to a renascence. But the impact in which we live at the present hour is nothing less than that of a new world. It is not merely the pressure of the whole Western civilisation upon the ancient spirit of the East or of modernism on a great traditional civilisation, but it is a great worldwide change, an approaching new birth of mankind itself of which the change in us is only a part. Therefore the result that we are face to face with, is a renascence, the birth of the Spirit into a new body, new forms in society and politics, new forms of literature, art, science, philosophy, action and creation of all kinds. And the question arises what in the great play of modification and interchange around us are we going to take from the world around us, how are we going to shape [it] in the stress of our own spirit and past traditions, and what are we going to bring out of ourselves and impress upon the world in exchange? In what new forms is the spirit of India going to embody itself and what relations will its new creations have with the future of the world?

Where We Stand in Literature

[Draft A]

Where we stand, not only in literature, but in all things, is at or near a great turning point in which the thoughts and forms of East and West, both in an immense ferment of change, are working upon each other to produce something great, unforeseeable and unprecedented. From the less worldwide viewpoint which most nearly concerns us in this country, we may say, that we find ourselves in a great hour of rebirth of the ancient soul of India. The momentous issues of this hour are producing their inevitable upheaval, change and effort at creation in the whole national life, politics, society, economical conditions, industry, commerce, as well as and more noisily than in literature. But it is perhaps in art, literature and science that the future will see what was most definitive in the creations of the present hour, the most significant thing in the Indian renascence; for these things reveal most freely the spirit which is coming to birth; they have found their field, discovered their motive; the rest is still only a primary effort to escape out of unnatural conditions; the field has there yet to be made clear, before the struggling spiritual motive can make itself dominant and create its appropriate forms. Especially, is the movement of literature most revelatory; for while music and art reveal perhaps more absolutely the soul of a nation, literature is the whole expression of its mind and psychology, — not only of what it is in action, or what it is in essence, but its thought, character and aspiration.

[Draft B]

In literature, as in all else, we stand in India at the opening of a new age, in an hour of national rebirth and in the midst of a number of tendencies, possibilities, movements of which only a few have as yet formed for themselves distinct shapes, plainly decipherable signs. It is an hour not yet of accomplishment, but of travail and inception. What will be born of this dim travail, these shapeless or half-shaped beginnings, is no doubt already decided in the secret spirit of the age and in the subconscient mind of the people. Behind the waverings and strivings of our twilit surface minds the soul of India knows no doubt what it intends and is moving us to great fulfilments. But it is well also for us to ponder and inquire what it is the national soul and the soul of humanity demand from us and on what paths we are most likely to give our energies and efforts the maximum power and serviceableness to the great age of mankind and of India on which we are entering. For at such a moment there are usually many false starts and many misdirected aims and by seeing our way and our goal more clearly we may better be able to avoid the waste of energy, talent and even genius to which they give rise.

Section Four

Genius, Poetry, Beauty

The Origin of Genius

When the human being puts forth a force in himself which is considerable but acts normally, we call it talent; when it is abnormal in its working we call it genius. It would seem, therefore, that genius is in reality some imperfect step in evolution by which mankind in its most vigorous and forward individuals is attempting to develop a faculty which the race as a whole is not strong enough as yet to command or to acclimatise. As always happens in such a movement, there is a considerable irregularity in the working of the new phenomenon. Sometimes Nature seems to prepare by heredity for these its new experiments & fine flowers of humanity[.]

Poetic Genius

The greatest poets are usually those who arise either out of a large simple and puissant environment or out of a movement of mind that is grandiose, forceful & elemental. When man becomes excessively refined in intellect, curious in aesthetic sensibility or minute & exact in intellectual reasoning, it becomes more & more difficult to write great and powerful poetry. Ages of accomplished intellectuality & scholarship or of strong scientific rationality are not favourable to the birth of great poets or, if they are born, not favourable to the free & untrammelled action of their gifts. They remain great, but their greatness bends under a load; there is a lack of triumphant spontaneity and they do not draw as freely or directly from the sources of human action & character. An untameable elemental force is needed to overcome more than partially the denials of the environment. For poetry, even though it appeals in passing to the intellect & aesthetic sense, does not proceed from them but is in its nature an elemental power proceeding from the secret & elemental Power within which sees directly & creates sovereignly, & it passes at once to our vital & elemental parts. Intellect and the aesthetic faculties are necessary to the perfection of our critical enjoyment; but they were only assistants, not the direct agents of this divine birth.

The Voices of the Poets

Out of the infinite silence of the past, peopled only to the eye of history or the ear of the Yogin, a few voices arise which speak for it, express it and are the very utterance and soul of those unknown generations, of that vanished and now silent humanity. These are the voices of the poets. We whose souls are drying up in this hard and parched age of utilitarian and scientific thought when men value little beyond what gives them exact and useful knowledge or leads them to some outward increase of power & pleasure, we who are beginning to neglect & ignore poetry and can no longer write it greatly & well, — just as we have forgotten how to sculpture like the Greeks, paint like the mediaeval Italians or build like the Buddhists, — are apt to forget this grand utility of the poets, one noble faculty among their many divine and unusual powers. The kavi or vates, poet & seer, is not the manishi; he is not [the] logical thinker, scientific analyser or metaphysical reasoner; his knowledge is one not with his thought, but with his being; he has not arrived at it but has it in himself by virtue of his power to become one with all that is around him. By some form of spiritual, vital and emotional oneness, he is what he sees; he is the hero thundering in the forefront of the battle, the mother weeping over her dead, the tree trembling violently in the storm, the flower warmly penetrated with the sunshine. And because he is these things, therefore he knows them; because he knows thus, spiritually & not rationally, he can write of them. He feels their delight & pain, he shares their virtue & sin, he enjoys their reward or bears their punishment. It is for this reason that poetry written out of the intellect is so inferior to poetry written out of the soul, is, — even as poetical thinking, — so inferior to the thought that comes formed by inscrutable means out of the soul. For this reason, too, poets of otherwise great faculty, have failed to give us living men and women or really to show to our inner vision even the things of which they write eloquently or sweetly, because they are content to write about them after having seen them with the mind only, and have not been able or have not taken care first to be the things of which they would write and then not so much write about them as let them pour themselves out in speech that is an image of the soul. They have been too easily attracted by the materials of poetry, artha & shabda; drawn by some power & charm in the substance of speech, captivated by some melody, harmony or colour in the form of speech, arrested by some strong personal emotion which clutches at expression or gropes for expression in these externals of poetry they have forgotten to bathe in the Muse's deepest springs.

Therefore among those ancient voices, even when the literature of the ages has been winnowed & chosen by Time, there are very few who recreate for us in poetic speech deeply & mightily the dead past, because they were that past, not so much themselves as the age & nation in which they lived and not so much even the age and nation as that universal humanity which in spite of all differences, under them and within them, even expressing its unity through them is the same in every nation and in every age. Others give us only fragments of thought or outbursts of feeling or reveal to us scattered incidents of sight, sound and outward happening. These are complete, vast, multitudinous, infinite in a way, impersonal & many-personed in their very personality, not divine workmen merely but true creators endowed by God with something of His divine power and offering therefore in their works some image of His creative activity.

Pensées

God has a personality but no character; He is as we say in our Eastern thought, Anantaguna, of an infinite variation of qualities without fixed limitation or rigid distinction and incompatibility. His superhuman cruelty melts into and harmonises with His ineffable pity; His fierce enmity is one mask of His intensest love. For, being alone existent, He is irresponsible and the harmonies He creates, are the figment of His own plastic will and governed by laws of aesthetics determined in His own unfettered but infallible fantasy. Out of His infinite personality He creates all these characters & their inevitable actions & destinies. So it is with every divine creator, — with Homer, Shakespeare, Valmiki, Kalidasa. It is perfectly true that each has his own style of language & creation, his own preferred system or harmony of the poetic Art, just as the creator of this universe has fashioned it in a particular style & rhythm & on certain preferred & fixed canons, differing from that of the other universes He may have built in His infinite Being. But within that style & harmony they are not bound by any fixed personality. It is rather the infinite they express though through their personality, than their personality through their works. The writers who are limited by their personality may be among the fine artists of literature; they cannot be among the greatest creators; for to the creator freedom & infinity are necessary attributes. It is the infinite alone that can create; the finite can only manufacture, reproduce or at the most bring out a fine art & craftsmanship. Among all the Elizabethan dramatists Shakespeare alone has produced living men; the rest are only admirable, trivial or monstrous sketches, caricatures or images of men. There is, however, one exception to this rule; every man can at his best moments cast out, create in some way or another — for in our Indian languages the word for creating is casting out, letting free out of one's own being — one living creature & character, — himself. Milton has produced several bold & beautiful or fine outlines or descriptions, but only one living being, the rebel Archangel Satan, and only so in the first four books of Paradise Lost does Satan really live. When Milton ceases to portray himself in his fallen state and thinks only of his plot & subject, Satan also ceases to live. But the great impersonal creators even in their slightest creations, cannot help creating life. Impersonal, I say, but I do not mean by impersonality the nirguna, devoid or pure of quality, but rather the unfixed & unlimited by quality, — an infinite & indefinable personality out of which is not manufactured or cunningly shaped but perfectly & inevitably arises under the compelling eye of an intuitive Will to be this created world of innumerable brilliantly-coloured variously outlined individual existences.

A Dream

This is the story of a dream that often came & always fled, a dream that continued by snatches and glimpses through a succession of nights, at intervals of weeks, the mind returning again and again to the unfinished vision, the imagination and intuition filling in the gaps & interstices of a half told tale. Visions of waters blue in an immortal sunlight or grey in the drifting of a magic welter of cloud & rain, rocks swept by the surf and whistling in their hollows with the wind, island meadows & glades many pictured above the sea, rivers and haze-purpled hills, a scene of unimaginable beauty where forms moved that had not lost the pristine beauty of man before the clutch stiffened on him of early decay & death, of grief and old age, where hearts beat that had not lost the pulsations of our ancient immortality and were not yet attuned to the broken rhythms of pain & grief. The impression of such an atmosphere & background remains which the linking of ineffective details & the effort of words which are laden with the thoughts of an afflicted and oppressed humanity, strive vainly to restore. For those colours we have lost. When we speak of brightness, it is a subdued brilliance that is the utmost our imaginations can conceive; we mean only a broken hint of rapture when we talk even most eagerly of enjoyment & bliss.

The Beauty of a Crow's Wings

It is not only that the sable blackness of the crow's wings has in it wonderful shades of green and violet and purple which show themselves under certain stresses of sunlight, but that the black itself, sable of wing or dingy of back & breast has itself a beauty which our prejudiced habits of mind obscure to us. Under its darkness, we see, too, a glint of dingy white.

Section Five

Science, Religion, Reason, Justice

Science

We live under the reign of Science, a reign which from the mouth of its hierophants claims to be a tyranny or at least an absolute monarchy. It makes this claim by right of the great things it has done, of the immense utilities with which it has served, helped, strengthened, liberated, mankind, right knowledge of the world, an increasing and already fabulous mastery of Nature, a clear and free intellectual vision of things and masterful dealing with them, liberation from the fetters of ignorance, from blind subjection to authority, from unquestioning political, social, religious and cultural tradition with all their hindrance and their evil.

Religion

In a word, the religious tendency, the religious spirit in man does not escape from the law of evolution that governs the other parts of his complex psychological nature. Even though its very reason of existence is the inner sense of a soul and spirit within and around us and the search for spiritual truth and experience, that must be in their very nature a suprarational truth and experience, it begins like the rest with an infrarational instinct, an infrarational formulation, falls under the influence of the reasoning mind and only at its [*sentence not completed*]

Reason and Society

A pragmatic mentalism would not be in its essential principle other than the attempt already made by the race to make the intellectual Reason the governor of life, but this has been done hitherto by a reason preoccupied with the external fact and subjected to it; mind has attempted to read the law of life and its possibilities and organise life anew within those limits by invention, device, regulation, mechanisms of many kinds, or it has attempted to govern life by mental ideals of an abstract order, such as democracy or socialism, and devise an appropriate machinery materialising that mental abstraction so as to make the dominance of the idea practical and viable. A subjectivist pragmatic mentalism would try to act more subtly and plastically on life; it would seek for "truth of being", some idea or ideal of its perfection or practice or efficiency, right way of being or living, and attempt to let that grow in the individual and govern his nature, grow in the collective life and govern its formations. Or it would place the development and organisation of the mental life of man as the primary consideration and life and society as a convenience for this true aim of human existence. A new civilisation no longer vitalistic or mainly political and economic, but intellectual, cultural, idealistic, taking up the ancient ideal of man, the perfected mental being in an ennobled life and sound body, a great expansion of human mind and intellect, a mankind more mentally alive, even a human race grown capable of culture and not only of a greater external civilisation, thus fulfilling on a large human and universal scale the tendencies which in the past appeared only in a few favoured countries and epochs and even then imperfectly and mostly in a cultured class, might be the consequence of this change. That prospect has its attractions, and for the humanist and the intellectual it is in one form or another their utopia of the future. But this would not really carry the human evolution farther; it would only give it for a time a larger, finer and freer movement in its widest attainable circle. If the mentality remained too pragmatic, too eager to rationalise or organise life according to the idea, the peril of mechanisation and standardisation would be there. If the mental ideas governing the individual and social life took a settled form, became a cultural system of the mind, this system would after a time exhaust its possibilities and human life would settle down into a groove, satisfied and non-evolutive, as happened in the Graeco-Roman world or in China or elsewhere where the mental intellect became the predominant power of life. If this arrest were avoided either by the multiplication of different cultures — different peoples acting upon each other but escaping the tendency to replication and standardisation which is the tendency of the human collective mind or by a free progressiveness of the human intelligence making constantly new ideas, new ideals, still the movement would eventually be in a circle or an ellipsis which could be a constant description of a new-old movement in the same field. In fact our external mind moving on the surface tends always to exhaust itself rapidly; if it expends itself slowly, conservatively, at a leisurely pace, it can create a civilisation and culture which will last for centuries or even for one or more thousands of years; but that too will exhaust itself in time; if it throws itself into a brilliant or rapid movement as in ancient Greece or in modern Europe a few centuries are likely to see the end of this flaming up as of a new star. Afterwards there must be stagnation, decline and a renewal of the mental circle.

This is because mind and thought are not the sovereign principle or highest term of our existence; mind and thought therefore can to a certain extent fulfil themselves, but they cannot fulfil life nor can they give to man his complete self. Mind is an instrument, not the self of man; nor the complete reality or highest reality of his being. It is a mediator between the being and life; it seeks to know truth of being and truth of life and bring them together. Truth of idea therefore is effective only so far as it can interpret truth of spirit and truth of life, it has itself no essential existence; when it erects itself as a mental abstraction, it has no reality and no effective power; it is only an index, a figure. It can become effective only by taking up life and catching hold of some vital force to effectuate it, but usually it ends by [. . .], exhausting or stereotyping and sterilising the force it uses; or it can become effective only when it canalises and brings out into action of mind and life an inner truth of being, a truth of spirit and it is then powerful only so long as it replenishes itself from its spiritual source and so keeps itself true and alive.

Justice

Justice, one says; but what is Justice? Plato's question applies to this as to every other sacred icon set up by men for their worship.

Justice for each man is what his own type of mind accepts as right and proper and equitable as between men and men. Or, it might be added, between the community and its constituents, the State and its citizens.

Part Four

Thoughts and Aphorisms

Sri Aurobindo wrote the main series of 540 aphorisms around 1913 in a single notebook under the headings "Jnana", "Karma" and "Bhakti". Seven additional aphorisms were not classified under these headings; the last five were written in a different notebook, probably somewhat later.

Part Four

Thoughts and Aphorisms

Jnana

Judas

Jnana

1.   There are two allied powers in man; knowledge & wisdom. Knowledge is so much of the truth seen in a distorted medium as the mind arrives at by groping, wisdom what the eye of divine vision sees in the spirit.

2.   Inspiration is a slender river of brightness leaping from a vast & eternal knowledge, it exceeds reason more perfectly than reason exceeds the knowledge of the senses.

3.   When I speak, the reason says, "This will I say"; but God takes the word out of my mouth and the lips say something else at which reason trembles.

4.   I am not a Jnani, for I have no knowledge except what God gives me for His work. How am I to know whether what I see be reason or folly? Nay, it is neither; for the thing seen is simply true & neither folly nor reason.

5.   If mankind could but see though in a glimpse of fleeting experience what infinite enjoyments, what perfect forces, what luminous reaches of spontaneous knowledge, what wide calms of our being lie waiting for us in the tracts which our animal evolution has not yet conquered, they would leave all & never rest till they had gained these treasures. But the way is narrow, the doors are hard to force, and fear, distrust & scepticism are there, sentinels of Nature, to forbid the turning away of our feet from her ordinary pastures.

6.   Late, I learned that when reason died, then Wisdom was born; before that liberation, I had only knowledge.

7. What men call knowledge, is the reasoned acceptance of false appearances. Wisdom looks behind the veil and sees.

8. Reason divides, fixes details & contrasts them; Wisdom unifies, marries contrasts in a single harmony.

9. Either do not give the name of knowledge to your beliefs only and of error, ignorance or charlatanism to the beliefs of others, or do not rail at the dogmas of the sects and their intolerance.

10. What the soul sees and has experienced, that it knows; the rest is appearance, prejudice and opinion.

11. My soul knows that it is immortal. But you take a dead body to pieces and cry triumphantly "Where is your soul and where is your immortality?"

12. Immortality is not the survival of the mental personality after death, though that also is true, but the waking possession of the unborn & deathless self of which body is only an instrument and a shadow.

13. They proved to me by convincing reasons that God did not exist, and I believed them. Afterwards I saw God, for He came and embraced me. And now which am I to believe, the reasonings of others or my own experience?

14. They told me, "These things are hallucinations." I inquired what was a hallucination and found that it meant a subjective or a psychical experience which corresponds to no objective or no physical reality. Then I sat and wondered at the miracles of the human reason.

15. Hallucination is the term of Science for those irregular glimpses we still have of truths shut out from us by our preoccupation with matter; coincidence for the curious touches of

artistry in the work of that supreme & universal Intelligence which in its conscious being as on a canvas has planned & executed the world.

16. That which men term a hallucination is the reflection in the mind & senses of that which is beyond our ordinary mental & sensory perceptions. Superstition arises from the mind's wrong understanding of these reflections. There is no other hallucination.

17. Do not, like so many modern disputants, smother thought under polysyllables or charm inquiry to sleep by the spell of formulas and cant words. Search always; find out the reason for things which seem to the hasty glance to be mere chance or illusion.

18. Someone was laying it down that God must be this or that or He would not be God. But it seemed to me that I can only know what God is and I do not see how I can tell Him what He ought to be. For what is the standard by which we can judge Him? These judgments are the follies of our egoism.

19. Chance is not in this universe; the idea of illusion is itself an illusion. There was never illusion yet in the human mind that was not the concealing [?shape] and disfigurement of a truth.

20. When I had the dividing reason, I shrank from many things; after I had lost it in sight, I hunted through the world for the ugly and the repellent, but I could no longer find them.

21. God had opened my eyes; for I saw the nobility of the vulgar, the attractiveness of the repellent, the perfection of the maimed and the beauty of the hideous.

22. Forgiveness is praised by the Christian and the Vaishnava, but for me, I ask, "What have I to forgive and whom?"

23. God struck me with a human hand; shall I say then, "I pardon Thee thy insolence, O God"?

24. God gave me good in a blow. Shall I say, "I forgive thee, O Almighty One, the harm and the cruelty, but do it not again"?

25. When I pine at misfortune and call it evil, or am jealous and disappointed, then I know that there is awake in me again the eternal fool.

26. When I see others suffer, I feel that I am unfortunate, but the wisdom that is not mine, sees the good that is coming and approves.

27. Sir Philip Sidney said of the criminal led out to be hanged, "There, but for the grace of God, goes Sir Philip Sidney." Wiser, had he said, "There, by the grace of God, goes Sir Philip Sidney."

28. God is a great & cruel Torturer because He loves. You do not understand this, because you have not seen & played with Krishna.

29. One called Napoleon a tyrant and imperial cut-throat; but I saw God armed striding through Europe.

30. I have forgotten what vice is and what virtue; I can only see God, His play in the world and His will in humanity.

31. I saw a child wallowing in the dirt and the same child cleaned by his mother and resplendent, but each time I trembled before his utter purity.

32. What I wished or thought to be the right thing, does not come about; therefore it is clear that there is no All Wise one who guides the world but only blind Chance or a brute Causality.

33. The Atheist is God playing at hide & seek with Himself;

but is the Theist any other? Well, perhaps; for he has seen the shadow of God and clutched at it.

34. O Thou that lovest, strike! If Thou strike me not now, I shall know that Thou lov'st me not.

35. O Misfortune, blessed be thou; for through thee I have seen the face of my Lover.

36. Men are still in love with grief; when they see one who is too high for grief or joy, they curse him & cry, "O thou insensible!" Therefore Christ still hangs on the cross in Jerusalem.

37. Men are in love with sin; when they see one who is too high for vice or virtue, they curse him & cry, "O thou breaker of bonds, thou wicked and immoral one!" Therefore Srikrishna does not live as yet in Brindavun.

38. Some say Krishna never lived, he is a myth. They mean on earth; for if Brindavun existed nowhere, the Bhagwat could not have been written.

39. Strange! the Germans have disproved the existence of Christ; yet his crucifixion remains still a greater historic fact than the death of Caesar.

40. Sometimes one is led to think that only those things really matter which have never happened; for beside them most historic achievements seem almost pale and ineffective.

41. There are four very great events in history, the siege of Troy, the life and crucifixion of Christ, the exile of Krishna in Brindavun and the colloquy with Arjuna on the field of Kurukshetra. The siege of Troy created Hellas, the exile in Brindavun created devotional religion, (for before there was only meditation and worship,) Christ from his cross humanised Europe, the colloquy at Kurukshetra will yet liberate humanity. Yet it is said that none of these four events ever happened.

42. They say that the Gospels are forgeries and Krishna a creation of the poets. Thank God then for the forgeries and bow down before the creators.

43. If God assigns to me my place in Hell, I do not know why I should aspire to Heaven. He knows best what is for my welfare.

44. If God draw me towards Heaven, then, even if His other hand strive to keep me in Hell, yet must I struggle upward.

45. Only those thoughts are true the opposite of which is also true in its own time and application; indisputable dogmas are the most dangerous kind of falsehoods.

46. Logic is the worst enemy of Truth, as self-righteousness is the worst enemy of virtue, — for the one cannot see its own errors nor the other its own imperfections.

47. When I was asleep in the Ignorance, I came to a place of meditation full of holy men and I found their company wearisome and the place a prison; when I awoke, God took me to a prison and turned it into a place of meditation and His trysting-ground.

48. When I read a wearisome book through and with pleasure, yet perceived all the perfection of its wearisomeness, then I knew that my mind was conquered.

49. I knew my mind to be conquered when it admired the beauty of the hideous, yet felt perfectly why other men shrank back or hated.

50. To feel & love the God of beauty and good in the ugly and the evil, and still yearn in utter love to heal it of its ugliness and its evil, this is real virtue and morality.

51. To hate the sinner is the worst sin, for it is hating God; yet he who commits it, glories in his superior virtue.

52.   When I hear of a righteous wrath, I wonder at man's capacity for self-deception.

53.   This is a miracle that men can love God, yet fail to love humanity. With whom are they in love then?

54.   The quarrels of religious sects are like the disputing of pots, which shall be alone allowed to hold the immortalising nectar. Let them dispute, but the thing for us is to get at the nectar in whatever pot and attain immortality.

55.   You say that the flavour of the pot alters the liquor. That is taste; but what can deprive it of its immortalising faculty?

56.   Be wide in me, O Varuna; be mighty in me, O Indra; O Sun, be very bright and luminous; O Moon, be full of charm and sweetness. Be fierce and terrible, O Rudra; be impetuous and swift, O Maruts; be strong and bold, O Aryama; be voluptuous and pleasurable, O Bhaga; be tender and kind and loving and passionate, O Mitra. Be bright and revealing, O Dawn; O Night, be solemn and pregnant. O Life, be full, ready & buoyant; O Death, lead my steps from mansion to mansion. Harmonise all these, O Brahmanaspati. Let me not be subject to these gods, O Kali.

57.   When, O eager disputant, thou hast prevailed in a debate, then art thou greatly to be pitied; for thou hast lost a chance of widening knowledge.

58.   Because the tiger acts according to his nature and knows not anything else, therefore he is divine and there is no evil in him. If he questioned himself, then he would be a criminal.

59.   The animal, before he is corrupted, has not yet eaten of the tree of the knowledge of good and evil; the god has abandoned it for the tree of eternal life; man stands between the upper heaven and the lower nature.

60.   One of the greatest comforts of religion is that you can get hold of God sometimes and give him a satisfactory beating. People mock at the folly of savages who beat their gods when their prayers are not answered; but it is the mockers who are the fools and the savages.

61.   There is no mortality. It is only the Immortal who can die; the mortal could neither be born nor perish. There is nothing finite. It is only the Infinite who can make for Himself limits; the finite can have no beginning nor end, for the very act of conceiving its beginning & end declares its infinity.

62.   I heard a fool discoursing utter folly and wondered what God meant by it; then I considered and saw a distorted mask of truth and wisdom.

63.   God is great, says the Mahomedan. Yes, He is so great that He can afford to be weak, whenever that too is necessary.

64.   God often fails in His workings; it is the sign of His illimitable godhead.

65.   Because God is invincibly great, He can afford to be weak; because He is immutably pure, He can indulge with impunity in sin; He knows eternally all delight, therefore He tastes also the delight of pain; He is inalienably wise, therefore He has not debarred Himself from folly.

66.   Sin is that which was once in its place, persisting now it is out of place; there is no other sinfulness.

67.   There is no sin in man, but a great deal of disease, ignorance and misapplication.

68.   The sense of sin was necessary in order that man might become disgusted with his own imperfections. It was God's corrective for egoism. But man's egoism meets God's device by being

very dully alive to its own sins and very keenly alive to the sins of others.

69. Sin & virtue are a game of resistance we play with God in His efforts to draw us towards perfection. The sense of virtue helps us to cherish our sins in secret.

70. Examine thyself without pity, then thou wilt be more charitable and pitiful to others.

71. A thought is an arrow shot at the truth; it can hit a point, but not cover the whole target. But the archer is too well satisfied with his success to ask anything farther.

72. The sign of dawning Knowledge is to feel that as yet I know little or nothing, & yet, if I could only know my knowledge, I already possess everything.

73. When Wisdom comes, her first lesson is, "There is no such thing as knowledge; there are only aperçus of the Infinite Deity."

74. Practical knowledge is a different thing; that is real and serviceable, but it is never complete. Therefore to systematise and codify it is necessary but fatal.

75. Systematise we must, but even in making & holding the system, we should always keep firm hold on this truth that all systems are in their nature transitory and incomplete.

76. Europe prides herself on her practical and scientific organisation and efficiency. I am waiting till her organisation is perfect; then a child shall destroy her.

77. Genius discovers a system; average talent stereotypes it till it is shattered by fresh genius. It is dangerous for an army to be led by veterans; for on the other side God may place Napoleon.

78.   When knowledge is fresh in us, then it is invincible; when it is old, it loses its virtue. This is because God moves always forward.

79.   God is infinite Possibility. Therefore Truth is never at rest; therefore, also, Error is justified of her children.

80.   To listen to some devout people, one would imagine that God never laughs; Heine was nearer the mark when he found in Him the divine Aristophanes.

81.   God's laughter is sometimes very coarse and unfit for polite ears; He is not satisfied with being Molière, He must needs also be Aristophanes and Rabelais.

82.   If men took life less seriously, they could very soon make it more perfect. God never takes His works seriously; therefore one looks out on this wonderful Universe.

83.   Shame has admirable results and both in aesthetics and in morality we could ill spare it; but for all that it is a badge of weakness and the proof of ignorance.

84.   The supernatural is that the nature of which we have not attained or do not yet know, or the means of which we have not yet conquered. The common taste for miracles is the sign that man's ascent is not yet finished.

85.   It is rationality and prudence to distrust the supernatural; but to believe in it, is also a sort of wisdom.

86.   Great saints have performed miracles; greater saints have railed at them; the greatest have both railed at them and performed them.

87.   Open thy eyes and see what the world really is and what God; have done with vain and pleasant imaginations.

88. This world was built by Death that he might live. Wilt thou abolish death? Then life too will perish. Thou canst not abolish death, but thou mayst transform it into a greater living.

89. This world was built by Cruelty that she might love. Wilt thou abolish cruelty? Then love too will perish. Thou canst not abolish cruelty, but thou mayst transfigure it into its opposite, into a fierce Love & Delightfulness.

90. This world was built by Ignorance & Error that they might know. Wilt thou abolish ignorance and error? Then knowledge too will perish. Thou canst not abolish ignorance & error, but thou mayst transmute them into the utter & effulgent exceeding of reason.

91. If Life alone were & not death, there could be no immortality; if love were alone & not cruelty, joy would be only a tepid & ephemeral rapture; if reason were alone & not ignorance, our highest attainment would not exceed a limited rationality & worldly wisdom.

92. Death transformed becomes Life that is Immortality; Cruelty transfigured becomes Love that is intolerable ecstasy; Ignorance transmuted becomes Light that leaps beyond wisdom and knowledge.

93. Pain is the touch of our Mother teaching us how to bear and grow in rapture. She has three stages of her schooling, endurance first, next equality of soul, last ecstasy.

94. All renunciation is for a greater joy yet ungrasped. Some renounce for the joy of duty done, some for the joy of peace, some for the joy of God and some for the joy of self-torture, but renounce rather as a passage to the freedom and untroubled rapture beyond.

95. Only by perfect renunciation of desire or by perfect satisfaction of desire can the utter embrace of God be experienced;

for in both ways the essential precondition is effected, — desire perishes.

96. Experience in thy soul the truth of the Scripture; afterwards, if thou wilt, reason & state thy experience intellectually & even then distrust thy statement; but distrust never thy experience.

97. When thou affirmest thy soul-experience & deniest the different soul-experience of another, know that God is making a fool of thee. Dost thou not hear His self-delighted laughter behind thy soul's curtains?

98. Revelation is the direct sight, the direct hearing or the inspired memory of Truth, drishti, sruti, smriti; it is the highest experience and always accessible to renewed experience. Not because God spoke it, but because the soul saw it, is the word of the Scriptures our supreme authority.

99. The word of Scripture is infallible; it is in the interpretation the heart and reason put upon the Scripture that error has her portion.

100. Shun all lowness, narrowness & shallowness in religious thought & experience. Be wider than the widest horizons, be loftier than the highest Kanchenjunga, be profounder than the deepest oceans.

101. In God's sight there is no near or distant, no present, past or future. These things are only a convenient perspective for His world-picture.

102. To the senses it is always true that the sun moves round the earth; this is false to the reason. To the reason it is always true that the earth moves round the sun; this is false to the supreme vision. Neither earth moves nor sun; there is only a change in the relation of sun-consciousness & earth-consciousness.

103. Vivekananda, exalting Sannyasa, has said that in all Indian history there is only one Janaka. Not so, for Janaka is not the name of a single individual, but a dynasty of self-ruling kings and the triumph-cry of an ideal.

104. In all the lakhs of ochre-clad Sannyasins, how many are perfect? It is the few attainments and the many approximations that justify an ideal.

105. There have been hundreds of perfect Sannyasins, because Sannyasa had been widely preached and numerously practised; let it be the same with the ideal freedom and we shall have hundreds of Janakas.

106. Sannyasa has a formal garb and outer tokens; therefore men think they can easily recognise it; but the freedom of a Janaka does not proclaim itself and it wears the garb of the world; to its presence even Narada was blinded.

107. Hard is it to be in the world, free, yet living the life of ordinary men; but because it is hard, therefore it must be attempted and accomplished.

108. When he watched the actions of Janaka, even Narada the divine sage thought him a luxurious worldling and libertine. Unless thou canst see the soul, how shalt thou say that a man is free or bound?

109. All things seem hard to man that are above his attained level, & they are hard to his unaided effort; but they become at once easy & simple when God in man takes up the contract.

110. To see the composition of the sun or the lines of Mars is doubtless a great achievement; but when thou hast the instrument that can show thee a man's soul as thou seest a picture, then thou wilt smile at the wonders of physical Science as the playthings of babies.

111. Knowledge is a child with its achievements; for when it has found out something, it runs about the streets whooping and shouting; Wisdom conceals hers for a long time in a thoughtful and mighty silence.

112. Science talks and behaves as if it had conquered all knowledge: Wisdom, as she walks, hears her solitary tread echoing on the margin of immeasurable Oceans.

113. Hatred is the sign of a secret attraction that is eager to flee from itself and furious to deny its own existence. That too is God's play in His creature.

114. Selfishness is the only sin, meanness the only vice, hatred the only criminality. All else can easily be turned into good, but these are obstinate resisters of deity.

115. The world is a long recurring decimal with Brahman for its integer. The period seems to begin and end, but the fraction is eternal; it will never have an end and never had any real beginning.

116. The beginning and end of things is a conventional term of our experience; in their true existence these terms have no reality, there is no end and no beginning.

117. "Neither is it that I was not before nor thou nor these kings nor that all we shall not be hereafter." Not only Brahman, but beings & things in Brahman are eternal; their creation and destruction is a play of hide and seek with our outward consciousness.

118. The love of solitude is a sign of the disposition towards knowledge; but knowledge itself is only achieved when we have a settled perception of solitude in the crowd, in the battle and in the mart.

119. If when thou art doing great actions and moving giant results, thou canst perceive that *thou* art doing nothing, then know that God has removed His seal from thy eyelids.

120. If when thou sittest alone, still & voiceless on the mountaintop, thou canst perceive the revolutions thou art conducting, then hast thou the divine vision and art freed from appearances.

121. The love of inaction is folly and the scorn of inaction is folly; there is no inaction. The stone lying inert upon the sands which is kicked away in an idle moment, has been producing its effect upon the hemispheres.

122. If thou wouldst not be the fool of Opinion, first see wherein thy thought is true, then study wherein its opposite and contradiction is true; last, discover the cause of these differences and the key of God's harmony.

123. An opinion is neither true nor false, but only serviceable for life or unserviceable; for it is a creation of Time and with time it loses its effect and value. Rise thou above opinion and seek wisdom everlasting.

124. Use opinion for life, but let her not bind thy soul in her fetters.

125. Every law, however embracing or tyrannous, meets somewhere a contrary law by which its operation can be checked, modified, annulled or eluded.

126. The most binding Law of Nature is only a fixed process which the Lord of Nature has framed and uses constantly; the Spirit made it and the Spirit can exceed it, but we must first open the doors of our prison-house and learn to live less in Nature than in the Spirit.

127. Law is a process or a formula; but the soul is the user of processes and exceeds formulas.

128. Live according to Nature, runs the maxim of the West; but according to what nature, the nature of the body or the nature which exceeds the body? This first we ought to determine.

129. O son of Immortality, live not thou according to Nature, but according to God; and compel her also to live according to the deity within thee.

130. Fate is God's foreknowledge outside Space & Time of all that in Space & Time shall yet happen; what He has foreseen, Power & Necessity work out by the conflict of forces.

131. Because God has willed and foreseen everything, thou shouldst not therefore sit inactive and wait upon His providence, for thy action is one of His chief effective forces. Up then and be doing, not with egoism, but as the circumstance, instrument and apparent cause of the event that He has predetermined.

132. When I knew nothing, then I abhorred the criminal, sinful and impure, being myself full of crime, sin and impurity; but when I was cleansed and my eyes unsealed, then I bowed down in my spirit before the thief and the murderer and adored the feet of the harlot; for I saw that these souls had accepted the terrible burden of evil and drained for all of us the greater portion of the churned poison of the world-ocean.

133. The Titans are stronger than the gods because they have agreed with God to front and bear the burden of His wrath and enmity; the gods were able to accept only the pleasant burden of His love and kindlier rapture.

134. When thou art able to see how necessary is suffering to final delight, failure to utter effectiveness and retardation to the last rapidity, then thou mayst begin to understand something, however faintly and dimly, of God's workings.

135. All disease is a means towards some new joy of health, all evil & pain a tuning of Nature for some more intense bliss &

good, all death an opening on widest immortality. Why and how this should be so, is God's secret which only the soul purified of egoism can penetrate.

136. Why is thy mind or thy body in pain? Because thy soul behind the veil wishes for the pain or takes delight in it; but if thou wilt — and perseverest in thy will — thou canst impose the spirit's law of unmixed delight on thy lower members.

137. There is no iron or ineffugable law that a given contact shall create pain or pleasure; it is the way the soul meets the rush or pressure of Brahman upon the members from outside them that determines either reaction.

138. The force of soul in thee meeting the same force from outside cannot harmonise the measures of the contact in values of mind-experience & body-experience, therefore thou hast pain, grief or uneasiness. If thou canst learn to adjust the replies of the force in thyself to the questions of world-force, thou shalt find pain becoming pleasurable or turning into pure delightfulness. Right relation is the condition of blissfulness, ritam the key of ananda.

139. Who is the superman? He who can rise above this matter-regarding broken mental human unit and possess himself universalised and deified in a divine force, a divine love & joy and a divine knowledge.

140. If thou keepest this limited human ego & thinkest thyself the superman, thou art but the fool of thy own pride, the plaything of thy own force and the instrument of thy own illusions.

141. Nietzsche saw the superman as the lion-soul passing out of camel-hood, but the true heraldic device & token of the superman is the lion seated upon the camel which stands upon the cow of plenty. If thou canst not be the slave of all mankind, thou

art not fit to be its master and if thou canst not make thy nature as Vasistha's cow of plenty with all mankind to draw its wish from her udders, what avails thy leonine supermanhood?

142. Be to the world as the lion in fearlessness and lordship, as the camel in patience and service, as the cow in quiet, forbearing & maternal beneficence. Raven on all the joys of God as a lion over its prey, but bring also all humanity into that infinite field of luxurious ecstasy to wallow there and to pasture.

143. If Art's service is but to imitate Nature, then burn all the picture galleries and let us have instead photographic studios. It is because Art reveals what Nature hides, that a small picture is worth more than all the jewels of the millionaires and the treasures of the princes.

144. If you only imitate visible Nature, you will perpetrate either a corpse, a dead sketch or a monstrosity; Truth lives in that which goes behind & beyond the visible & sensible.

145. O Poet, O Artist, if thou but holdest up the mirror to Nature, thinkest thou Nature will rejoice in thy work? Rather she will turn away her face. For what dost thou hold up to her there? Herself? No, but a lifeless outline & reflection, a shadowy mimicry. It is the secret soul of Nature thou hast to seize, thou hast to hunt eternally after the truth in the external symbol, and that no mirror will hold for thee, nor for her whom thou seekest.

146. I find in Shakespeare a far greater & more consistent universalist than the Greeks. All his creations are universal types from Lancelot Gobbo & his dog up to Lear & Hamlet.

147. The Greeks sought universality by omitting all finer individual touches; Shakespeare sought it more successfully by universalising the rarest individual details of character. That which Nature uses for concealing from us the Infinite, Shakespeare used for revealing the Ananta-guna in man to the eye of humanity.

148. Shakespeare, who invented the figure of holding up the mirror to Nature, was the one poet who never condescended to a copy, a photograph or a shadow. The reader who sees in Falstaff, Macbeth, Lear or Hamlet imitations of Nature, has either no inner eye of the soul or has been hypnotised by a formula.

149. Where in material Nature wilt thou find Falstaff, Macbeth or Lear? Shadows & hints of them she possesses but they themselves tower above her.

150. There are two for whom there is hope, the man who has felt God's touch & been drawn to it and the sceptical seeker & self-convinced atheist; but for the formularists of all the religions & the parrots of free thought, they are dead souls who follow a death that they call living.

151. A man came to a scientist and wished to be instructed; this instructor showed him the revelations of the microscope & telescope, but the man laughed and said, "These are obviously hallucinations inflicted on the eye by the glass which you use as a medium; I will not believe till you show these wonders to my naked seeing." Then the scientist proved to him by many collateral facts & experiments the reliability of his knowledge but the man laughed again & said, "What you term proofs, I term coincidences, the number of coincidences does not constitute proof; as for your experiments, they are obviously effected under abnormal conditions & constitute a sort of insanity of Nature." When confronted with the results of mathematics, he was angry & cried out, "This is obviously imposture, gibberish & superstition; will you try to make me believe that these absurd cabalistic figures have any real force & meaning?" Then the scientist drove him out as a hopeless imbecile; for he did not recognise his own system of denials and his own method of negative reasoning. If we wish to refuse an impartial & openminded enquiry, we can always find the most respectable polysyllables to cover our refusal or impose tests & conditions which stultify the enquiry.

152. When our minds are involved in matter, they think matter the only reality; when we draw back into immaterial consciousness, then we see matter a mask and feel existence in consciousness alone as having the touch of reality. Which then of these two is the truth? Nay, God knoweth; but he who has had both experiences, can easily tell which condition is the more fertile in knowledge, the mightier & more blissful.

153. I believe immaterial consciousness to be truer than material consciousness? Because I know in the first what in the second is hidden from me & also can command what the mind knows in matter.

154. Hell & Heaven exist only in the soul's consciousness. Ay, but so does the earth and its lands & seas & fields & deserts & mountains & rivers. All world is nothing but arrangement of the Soul's seeing.

155. There is only one soul & one existence; therefore we all see one objectivity only; but there are many knots of mind & ego in the one soul-existence, therefore we all see the one Object in different lights & shadows.

156. The idealist errs; it is not Mind which created the worlds, but that which created mind has created them. Mind only missees, because it sees partially & by details, what is created.

157. Thus said Ramakrishna and thus said Vivekananda. Yes, but let me know also the truths which the Avatar cast not forth into speech and the prophet has omitted from his teachings. There will always be more in God than the thought of man has ever conceived or the tongue of man has ever uttered.

158. What was Ramakrishna? God manifest in a human being; but behind there is God in His infinite impersonality and His universal Personality. And what was Vivekananda? A radiant glance from the eye of Shiva; but behind him is the divine gaze

from which he came and Shiva himself and Brahma and Vishnu and OM all-exceeding.

159. He who recognises not Krishna, the God in man, knows not God entirely; he who knows Krishna only, knows not even Krishna. Yet is the opposite truth also wholly true that if thou canst see all God in a little pale unsightly and scentless flower, then hast thou hold of His supreme reality.

160. Shun the barren snare of an empty metaphysics and the dry dust of an unfertile intellectuality. Only that knowledge is worth having which can be made use of for a living delight and put out into temperament, action, creation and being.

161. Become & live the knowledge thou hast; then is thy knowledge the living God within thee.

162. Evolution is not finished; reason is not the last word nor the reasoning animal the supreme figure of Nature. As man emerged out of the animal, so out of man the superman emerges.

163. The power to observe law rigidly is the basis of freedom; therefore in most disciplines the soul has to endure & fulfil the law in its lower members before it can rise to the perfect freedom of its divine being. Those disciplines which begin with freedom are only for the mighty ones who are naturally free or in former lives have founded their freedom.

164. Those who are deficient in the free, full and intelligent observation of a self-imposed law, must be placed in subjection to the will of others. This is one principal cause of the subjection of nations. After their disturbing egoism has been trampled under the feet of a master, they are given or, if they have force in them, attain a fresh chance of deserving liberty by liberty.

165. To observe the law we have imposed on ourselves rather

than the law of others is what is meant by liberty in our unregenerate condition. Only in God & by the supremacy of the spirit can we enjoy a perfect freedom.

166. The double law of sin & virtue is imposed on us because we have not that ideal life & knowledge within which guides the soul spontaneously & infallibly to its self-fulfilment. The law of sin & virtue ceases for us when the sun of God shines upon the soul in truth & love with its unveiled splendour. Moses is replaced by Christ, the Shastra by the Veda.

167. God within is leading us always aright even when we are in the bonds of the ignorance; but then, though the goal is sure, it is attained by circlings & deviations.

168. The Cross is in Yoga the symbol of the soul & nature in their strong & perfect union, but because of our fall into the impurities of ignorance it has become the symbol of suffering and purification.

169. Christ came into the world to purify, not to fulfil. He himself foreknew the failure of his mission and the necessity of his return with the sword of God into a world that had rejected him.

170. Mahomed's mission was necessary, else we might have ended by thinking, in the exaggeration of our efforts at self-purification, that earth was meant only for the monk and the city created as a vestibule for the desert.

171. When all is said, Love & Force together can save the world eventually, but not Love only or Force only. Therefore Christ had to look forward to a second advent and Mahomed's religion, where it is not stagnant, looks forward through the Imams to a Mahdi.

172. Law cannot save the world, therefore Moses' ordinances are dead for humanity & the Shastra of the Brahmins is corrupt

& dying. Law released into Freedom is the liberator. Not the Pandit, but the Yogin; not monasticism, but the inner renunciation of desire and ignorance & egoism.

173. Even Vivekananda once in the stress of emotion admitted the fallacy that a personal God would be too immoral to be suffered and it would be the duty of all good men to resist Him. But if an omnipotent supra-moral Will & Intelligence governs the world, it is surely impossible to resist Him; our resistance would only serve His ends & really be dictated by Him. Is it not better then, instead of condemning or denying, to study and understand Him?

174. If we would understand God, we must renounce our egoistic & ignorant human standards or else ennoble and universalise them.

175. Because a good man dies or fails & the evil live & triumph, is God therefore evil? I do not see the logic of the consequence. I must first be convinced that death & failure are evil; I sometimes think that when they come, they are our supreme momentary good. But we are the fools of our hearts & nerves & argue that what they do not like or desire, must of course be an evil!

176. When I look back on my past life, I see that if I had not failed & suffered, I would have lost my life's supreme blessings; yet at the time of the suffering & failure, I was vexed with the sense of calamity. Because we cannot see anything but the one fact under our noses, therefore we indulge in all these snifflings and clamours. Be silent, ye foolish hearts! slay the ego, learn to see & feel vastly & universally.

177. The perfect cosmic vision & cosmic sentiment is the cure of all error & suffering; but most men succeed only in enlarging the range of their ego.

178. Men say & think "For my country!" "For humanity!"

"For the world!" but they really mean "For myself seen in my country!" "For myself seen in humanity!" "For myself imaged to my fancy as the world!" That may be an enlargement, but it is not liberation. To be at large & to be in a large prison are not one condition of freedom.

179. Live for God in thy neighbour, God in thyself, God in thy country & the country of thy foeman, God in humanity, God in tree & stone & animal, God in the world & outside the world, then art thou on the straight path to liberation.

180. There are lesser & larger eternities, for eternity is a term of the soul & can exist in Time as well as exceeding it. When the Scriptures say "śaśwatih samah", they mean for a long space & permanence of time or a hardly measurable aeon; only God Absolute has the absolute eternity. Yet when one goes within, one sees that all things are secretly eternal; there is no end, neither was there ever a beginning.

181. When thou callest another a fool, as thou must, sometimes, yet do not forget that thou thyself hast been the supreme fool in humanity.

182. God loves to play the fool in season; man does it in season & out of season. It is the only difference.

183. In the Buddhists' view to have saved an ant from drowning is a greater work than to have founded an empire. There is a truth in the idea, but a truth that can easily be exaggerated.

184. To exalt one virtue, — compassion even, — unduly above all others is to cover up with one's hand the eyes of wisdom. God moves always towards a harmony.

185. Pity may be reserved, so long as thy soul makes distinctions, for the suffering animals; but humanity deserves from thee something nobler; it asks for love, for understanding, for comradeship, for the help of the equal & brother.

186. The contributions of evil to the good of the world & the harm sometimes done by the virtuous are distressing to the soul enamoured of good. Nevertheless be not distressed nor confounded, but study rather & calmly understand God's ways with humanity.

187. In God's providence there is no evil, but only good or its preparation.

188. Virtue & vice were made for thy soul's struggle & progress; but for results they belong to God, who fulfils himself beyond vice & virtue.

189. Live within; be not shaken by outward happenings.

190. Fling not thy alms abroad everywhere in an ostentation of charity; understand & love where thou helpest. Let thy soul grow within thee.

191. Help the poor while the poor are with thee; but study also & strive that there may be no poor for thy assistance.

192. The old Indian social ideal demanded of the priest voluntary simplicity of life, purity, learning and the gratuitous instruction of the community, of the prince, war, government, protection of the weak & the giving up of his life in the battlefield, of the merchant, trade, gain and the return of his gains to the community by free giving, of the serf, labour for the rest & material havings. In atonement for his serfhood, it spared him the tax of self-denial, the tax of blood & the tax of his riches.

193. The existence of poverty is the proof of an unjust & ill-organised society, and our public charities are but the first tardy awakening in the conscience of a robber.

194. Valmekie, our ancient epic poet, includes among the signs

of a just & enlightened state of society not only universal education, morality and spirituality but this also that there shall be "none who is compelled to eat coarse food, none uncrowned & unanointed or who is restricted to a mean and petty share of luxuries."

195. The acceptance of poverty is noble & beneficial in a class or an individual, but it becomes fatal and pauperises life of its richness & expansion if it is perverted into a general or national ideal. Athens, not Sparta, is the progressive type for mankind. Ancient India with its ideal of vast riches & vast spending was the greatest of nations; modern India with its trend towards national asceticism has finally become poor in life & sunk into weakness & degradation.

196. Poverty is no more a necessity of organised social life than disease of the natural body; false habits of life & an ignorance of our true organisation are in both cases the peccant causes of an avoidable disorder.

197. Do not dream that when thou hast got rid of material poverty, men will even so be happy or satisfied or society freed from ills, troubles & problems. This is only the first & lowest necessity. While the soul within remains defectively organised, there will always be outward unrest, disorder & revolution.

198. Disease will always return to the body if the soul is flawed; for the sins of the mind are the secret cause of the sins of the body. So too poverty & trouble will always return on man in society, so long as the mind of the race is subjected to egoism.

199. Religion & philosophy seek to rescue man from his ego; then the kingdom of heaven within will be spontaneously reflected in an external divine city.

200. Mediaeval Christianity said to the race, "Man, thou art in thy earthly life an evil thing & a worm before God; renounce

then egoism, live for a future state and submit thyself to God & His priest." The results were not over-good for humanity. Modern knowledge says to the race, "Man, thou art an ephemeral animal and no more to Nature than the ant & the earthworm, — a transitory speck only in the universe. Live then for the State & submit thyself antlike to the trained administrator & the scientific expert." Will this gospel succeed any better than the other?

201. Vedanta says rather, "Man, thou art of one nature & substance with God, one soul with thy fellow-men. Awake & progress then to thy utter divinity, live for God in thyself & in others." This gospel which was given only to the few, must now be offered to all mankind for its deliverance.

202. The human race always progresses most when most it asserts its importance to Nature, its freedom & its universality.

203. Animal man is the obscure starting-point, the present natural man the varied & tangled mid-road but supernatural man the luminous & transcendent goal of our human journey.

204. Life and action culminate and are eternally crowned for thee when thou hast attained the power of symbolising & manifesting in every thought & act, in wealth getting, wealth having or wealth spending, in home & government & society, in art, literature and life, the One Immortal in this lower mortal being.

Karma

Karma

205. God leads man while man is misleading himself, the higher nature watches over the stumblings of his lower mortality; this is the tangle & contradiction out of which we have to escape into the [?self-unity] to which alone is possible a clear knowledge & a faultless action.

206. That thou shouldst have pity on creatures, is well, but not well, if thou art a slave to thy pity. Be a slave to nothing except to God, not even to His most luminous angels.

207. Beatitude is God's aim for humanity; get this supreme good for thyself first that thou mayst distribute it entirely to thy fellow-beings.

208. He who acquires for himself alone, acquires ill though he may call it heaven and virtue.

209. In my ignorance I thought anger could be noble and vengeance grandiose; but now when I watch Achilles in his epic fury, I see a very fine baby in a very fine rage and I am pleased and amused.

210. Power is noble, when it overtops anger; destruction is grandiose, but it loses caste when it proceeds from vengeance. Leave these things, for they belong to a lower humanity.

211. Poets make much of death and external afflictions; but the only tragedies are the soul's failures and the only epic man's triumphant ascent towards godhead.

212. The tragedies of the heart & the body are the weeping of children over their little griefs & their broken toys. Smile within

thyself, but comfort the children; join also, if thou canst, in their play.

213. "There is always something abnormal and eccentric about men of genius." And why not? For genius itself is an abnormal birth and out of man's ordinary centre.

214. Genius is Nature's first attempt to liberate the imprisoned god out of her human mould; the mould has to suffer in the process. It is astonishing that the cracks are so few and unimportant.

215. Nature sometimes gets into a fury with her own resistance, then she damages the brain in order to free the inspiration; for in this effort the equilibrium of the average material brain is her chief opponent. Pass over the madness of such and profit by their inspiration.

216. Who can bear Kali rushing into the system in her fierce force and burning godhead? Only the man whom Krishna already possesses.

217. Hate not the oppressor, for, if he is strong, thy hate increases his force of resistance; if he is weak, thy hate was needless.

218. Hatred is a sword of power, but its edge is always double. It is like the Kritya of the ancient magicians which, if baulked of its prey, returned in fury to devour its sender.

219. Love God in thy opponent, even while thou strikest him; so shall neither have hell for his portion.

220. Men talk of enemies, but where are they? I only see wrestlers of one party or the other in the great arena of the universe.

221. The saint and the angel are not the only divinities; admire also the Titan and the giant.

222. The old writings call the Titans the elder gods. So they still are; nor is any god entirely divine unless there is hidden in him also a Titan.

223. If I cannot be Rama, then I would be Ravana; for he is the dark side of Vishnu.

224. Sacrifice, sacrifice, sacrifice always, but for the sake of God and humanity, not for the sake of sacrifice.

225. Selfishness kills the soul; destroy it. But take care that your altruism does not kill the souls of others.

226. Very usually, altruism is only the sublimest form of selfishness.

227. He who will not slay when God bids him, works in the world an incalculable havoc.

228. Respect human life as long as you can; but respect more the life of humanity.

229. Men slay out of uncontrollable anger, hatred or vengeance; they shall suffer the rebound now or hereafter; or they slay to serve a selfish end, coldly; God shall not pardon them. If thou slay, first let thy soul have known death for a reality & seen God in the smitten, the stroke & the striker.

230. Courage and love are the only indispensable virtues; even if all the others are eclipsed or fall asleep, these two will save the soul alive.

231. Meanness & selfishness are the only sins that I find it difficult to pardon; yet they alone are almost universal. Therefore these also must not be hated in others, but in ourselves annihilated.

232. Nobleness and generosity are the soul's ethereal firmament; without them, one looks at an insect in a dungeon.

233. Let not thy virtues be such as men praise or reward, but such as make for thy perfection and God in thy nature demands of thee.

234. Altruism, duty, family, country, humanity are the prisons of the soul when they are not its instruments.

235. Our country is God the Mother; speak not evil of her unless thou canst do it with love and tenderness.

236. Men are false to their country for their own profit; yet they go on thinking they have a right to turn in horror from the matricide.

237. Break the moulds of the past, but keep safe its gains and its spirit, or else thou hast no future.

238. Revolutions hew the past to pieces and cast it into a cauldron, but what has emerged is the old Aeson with a new visage.

239. The world has had only half a dozen successful revolutions and most even of these were very like failures; yet it is by great & noble failures that humanity advances.

240. Atheism is a necessary protest against the wickedness of the Churches and the narrowness of creeds. God uses it as a stone to smash these soiled card-houses.

241. How much hatred & stupidity men succeed in packing up decorously and labelling "Religion"!

242. God guides best when He tempts worst, loves entirely when He punishes cruelly, helps perfectly when violently He opposes.

243. If God did not take upon Himself the burden of tempting men, the world would very soon go to perdition.

244. Suffer yourself to be tempted within so that you may exhaust in the struggle your downward propensities.

245. If you leave it to God to purify, He will exhaust the evil in you subjectively; but if you insist on guiding yourself, you will fall into much outward sin and suffering.

246. Call not everything evil which men call evil, but only that reject which God has rejected; call not everything good which men call good, but accept only what God has accepted.

247. Men in the world have two lights, duty and principle; but he who has passed over to God, has done with both and replaced them by God's will. If men abuse thee for this, care not, O divine instrument, but go on thy way like the wind or the sun fostering and destroying.

248. Not to cull the praises of men has God made thee His own, but to do fearlessly His bidding.

249. Accept the world as God's theatre; be thou the mask of the Actor and let Him act through thee. If men praise or hiss thee, know that they too are masks & take God within for thy only critic and audience.

250. If Krishna be alone on one side and the armed & organised world with its hosts and its shrapnel and its Maxims on the other, yet prefer thy divine solitude. Care not if the world passes over thy body and its shrapnel tear thee to pieces and its cavalry trample thy limbs into shapeless mire by the wayside; for the mind was always a simulacrum and the body a carcass. The spirit liberated from its casings ranges and triumphs.

251. If thou think defeat is the end of thee, then go not forth to fight, even though thou be the stronger. For Fate is not purchased

by any man nor is Power bound over to her possessors. But defeat is not the end, it is only a gate or a beginning.

252. I have failed, thou sayest. Say rather that God is circling about towards His object.

253. Foiled by the world, thou turnest to seize upon God. If the world is stronger than thou, thinkest thou God is weaker? Turn to Him rather for His bidding and for strength to fulfil it.

254. So long as a cause has on its side one soul that is intangible in faith, it cannot perish.

255. Reason gives me no basis for this faith, thou murmurest. Fool! if it did, faith would not be needed or demanded of thee.

256. Faith in the heart is the obscure & often distorted reflection of a hidden knowledge. The believer is often more plagued by doubt than the most inveterate sceptic. He persists because there is something subconscient in him which knows. That tolerates both his blind faith & twilit doubts and drives towards the revelation of that which it knows.

257. The world thinks that it moves by the light of reason but it is really impelled by its faiths and instincts.

258. Reason adapts itself to the faith or argues out a justification of the instincts, but it receives the impulse subconsciously; therefore men think that they act rationally.

259. The only business of reason is to arrange and criticise the perceptions. It has neither in itself any means of positive conclusion nor any command to action. When it pretends to originate or impel, it is masking other agencies.

260. Until Wisdom comes to thee, use the reason for its God-given purposes and faith and instinct for theirs. Why shouldst thou set thy members to war upon each other?

261. Perceive always and act in the light of thy increasing perceptions, but not those of the reasoning brain only. God speaks to the heart when the brain cannot understand him.

262. If thy heart tell thee, Thus & by such means and at such a time it will happen, believe it not. But if it gives thee the purity and wideness of God's command, hearken to it.

263. When thou hast the command, care only to fulfil it. The rest is God's will and arrangement which men call chance and luck and fortune.

264. If thy aim be great and thy means small, still act; for by action alone these can increase to thee.

265. Care not for time and success. Act out thy part, whether it be to fail or to prosper.

266. There are three forms in which the command may come, the will and faith in thy nature, thy ideal on which heart and brain are agreed and the voice of Himself or His angels.

267. There are times when action is unwise or impossible; then go into tapasya in some physical solitude or in the retreats of thy soul and await whatever divine word or manifestation.

268. Leap not too quickly at all voices, for there are lying spirits ready to deceive thee; but let thy heart be pure and afterwards listen.

269. There are times when God seems to be sternly on the side of the past; then what has been and is, sits firm as on a throne and clothes itself with an irrevocable "I shall be". Then persevere, though thou seem to be fighting the Master of all; for this is His sharpest trial.

270. All is not settled when a cause is humanly lost and hopeless; all is settled, only when the soul renounces its effort.

271. He who would win high spiritual degrees, must pass endless tests and examinations. But most are anxious only to bribe the examiner.

272. Fight, while thy hands are free, with thy hands and thy voice and thy brain and all manner of weapons. Art thou chained in the enemy's dungeons and have his gags silenced thee? Fight with thy silent all-besieging soul and thy wide-ranging will-power and when thou art dead, fight still with the world-encompassing force that went out from God within thee.

273. Thou thinkest the ascetic in his cave or on his mountaintop a stone and a do-nothing? What dost thou know? He may be filling the world with the mighty currents of his will & changing it by the pressure of his soul-state.

274. That which the liberated sees in his soul on its mountaintops, heroes and prophets spring up in the material world to proclaim and accomplish.

275. The Theosophists are wrong in their circumstances but right in the essential. If the French Revolution took place, it was because a soul on the Indian snows dreamed of God as freedom, brotherhood and equality.

276. All speech and action comes prepared out of the eternal Silence.

277. There is no disturbance in the depths of the Ocean, but above there is the joyous thunder of its shouting and its racing shoreward; so is it with the liberated soul in the midst of violent action. The soul does not act; it only breathes out from itself overwhelming action.

278. O soldier and hero of God, where for thee is sorrow or shame or suffering? For thy life is a glory, thy deeds a consecration, victory thy apotheosis, defeat thy triumph.

279. Do thy lower members still suffer the shock of sin and sorrow? But above, seen of thee or unseen, thy soul sits royal, calm, free and triumphant. Believe that the Mother will ere the end have done her work and made the very earth of thy being a joy and a purity.

280. If thy heart is troubled within thee, if for long seasons thou makest no progress, if thy strength faint and repine, remember always the eternal word of our Lover and Master, "I will free thee from all sin and evil; do not grieve."

281. Purity is in thy soul; but for actions, where is their purity or impurity?

282. O Death, our masked friend and maker of opportunities, when thou wouldst open the gate, hesitate not to tell us beforehand; for we are not of those who are shaken by its iron jarring.

283. Death is sometimes a rude valet; but when he changes this robe of earth for that brighter raiment, his horseplay and impertinences can be pardoned.

284. Who shall slay thee, O soul immortal? Who shall torture thee, O God ever-joyous?

285. Think this when thy members would fain make love with depression and weakness, "I am Bacchus and Ares and Apollo; I am Agni pure and invincible; I am Surya ever burning mightily."

286. Shrink not from the Dionysian cry & rapture within thee, but see that thou be not a straw upon those billows.

287. Thou hast to learn to bear all the gods within thee and never stagger with their inrush or break under their burden.

288. Mankind have wearied of strength and joy and called sorrow and weakness virtue, wearied of knowledge and called

ignorance holiness, wearied of love and called heartlessness enlightenment and wisdom.

289. There are many kinds of forbearance. I saw a coward hold out his cheek to the smiter; I saw a physical weakling struck by a strong and self-approving bully look quietly & intently at the aggressor; I saw God incarnate smile lovingly on those who stoned him. The first was ridiculous, the second terrible, the third divine and holy.

290. It is noble to pardon thine own injurers, but not so noble to pardon wrongs done to others. Nevertheless pardon these too, but when needful, calmly avenge.

291. When Asiatics massacre, it is an atrocity; when Europeans, it is a military exigency. Appreciate the distinction and ponder over this world's virtues.

292. Watch the too indignantly righteous. Before long you will find them committing or condoning the very offence which they have so fiercely censured.

293. "There is very little real hypocrisy among men." True, but there is a great deal of diplomacy and still more of self-deceit. The last is of three varieties, conscious, subconscious and half-conscious; but the third is the most dangerous.

294. Be not deceived by men's shows of virtue, neither disgusted by their open or secret vices. These things are the necessary shufflings in a long transition-period of humanity.

295. Be not repelled by the world's crookednesses; the world is a wounded and venomous snake wriggling towards a destined off-sloughing and perfection. Wait; for it is a divine wager, and out of this baseness, God will emerge brilliant and triumphant.

296. Why dost thou recoil from a mask? Behind its odious, grotesque or terrible seemings Krishna laughs at thy foolish

anger, thy more foolish scorn or loathing and thy most foolish terror.

297. When thou findest thyself scorning another, look then at thy own heart and laugh at thy folly.

298. Avoid vain disputing; but exchange views freely. If dispute thou must, learn from thy adversary; for even from a fool, if thou listen not with the ear and the reasoning mind but the soul's light, thou canst gather much wisdom.

299. Turn all things to honey; this is the law of divine living.

300. Private dispute should always be avoided; but shrink not from the public battle; yet even there appreciate the strength of thy adversary.

301. When thou hearest an opinion that displeases thee, study and find out the truth in it.

302. The mediaeval ascetics hated women and thought they were created by God for the temptation of monks. One may be allowed to think more nobly both of God and of woman.

303. If a woman has tempted thee, is it her fault or thine? Be not a fool and a self-deceiver.

304. There are two ways of avoiding the snare of woman; one is to shun all women and the other to love all beings.

305. Asceticism is no doubt very healing, a cave very peaceful and the hill-tops wonderfully pleasant; nevertheless do thou act in the world as God intended thee.

306. Three times God laughed at Shankara, first, when he returned to burn the corpse of his mother, again when he commented on the Isha Upanishad and the third time when he stormed about India preaching inaction.

307. Men labour only after success and if they are fortunate enough to fail, it is because the wisdom and force of Nature overbear their intellectual cleverness. God alone knows when & how to blunder wisely and fail effectively.

308. Distrust the man who has never failed and suffered; follow not his fortunes, fight not under his banner.

309. There are two who are unfit for greatness and freedom, the man who has never been a slave to another and the nation that has never been under the yoke of foreigners.

310. Fix not the time and the way in which the ideal shall be fulfilled. Work and leave time and way to God all-knowing.

311. Work as if the ideal had to be fulfilled swiftly & in thy lifetime; persevere as if thou knewest it not to be unless purchased by a thousand years yet of labour. That which thou darest not expect till the fifth millennium, may bloom out with tomorrow's dawning and that which thou hopest and lustest after now, may have been fixed for thee in thy hundredth advent.

312. Each man of us has a million lives yet to fulfil upon earth. Why then this haste and clamour and impatience?

313. Stride swiftly for the goal is far; rest not unduly, for thy Master is waiting for thee at the end of thy journey.

314. I am weary of the childish impatience which cries & blasphemes and denies the ideal because the Golden Mountains cannot be reached in our little day or in a few momentary centuries.

315. Fix thy soul without desire upon the end and insist on it by the divine force within thee; then shall the end itself create its means, nay, it shall become its own means. For the end is Brahman and already accomplished; see it always as Brahman, see it always in thy soul as already accomplished.

316. Plan not with the intellect, but let thy divine sight arrange thy plans for thee. When a means comes to thee as thing to be done, make that thy aim; as for the end, it is, in world, accomplishing itself and, in thy soul, already accomplished.

317. Men see events as unaccomplished, to be striven for and effected. This is false seeing; events are not effected, they develop. The event is Brahman, already accomplished from of old, it is now manifesting.

318. As the light of a star reaches the earth hundreds of years after the star has ceased to exist, so the event already accomplished in Brahman at the beginning manifests itself now in our material experience.

319. Governments, societies, kings, police, judges, institutions, churches, laws, customs, armies are temporary necessities imposed on us for a few groups of centuries because God has concealed His face from us. When it appears to us again in its truth & beauty, then in that light they will vanish.

320. The anarchic is the true divine state of man in the end as in the beginning; but in between it would lead us straight to the devil and his kingdom.

321. The communistic principle of society is intrinsically as superior to the individualistic as is brotherhood to jealousy and mutual slaughter; but all the practical schemes of Socialism invented in Europe are a yoke, a tyranny and a prison.

322. If communism ever reestablishes itself successfully upon earth, it must be on a foundation of soul's brotherhood and the death of egoism. A forced association and a mechanical comradeship would end in a worldwide fiasco.

323. Vedanta realised is the only practicable basis for a communistic society. It is the kingdom of the saints dreamed of by Christianity, Islam and Puranic Hinduism.

324. "Freedom, equality, brotherhood," cried the French revolutionists, but in truth freedom only has been practised with a dose of equality; as for brotherhood, only a brotherhood of Cain was founded — and of Barabbas. Sometimes it calls itself a Trust or Combine and sometimes the Concert of Europe.

325. "Since liberty has failed," cries the advanced thought of Europe, "let us try liberty cum equality or, since the two are a little hard to pair, equality instead of liberty. For brotherhood, it is impossible; therefore we will replace it by industrial association." But this time also, I think, God will not be deceived.

326. India had three fortresses of a communal life, the village community, the larger joint family & the orders of the Sannyasins; all these are broken or breaking with the stride of egoistic conceptions of social life; but is not this after all only the breaking of these imperfect moulds on the way to a larger & diviner communism?

327. The individual cannot be perfect until he has surrendered all he now calls himself to the divine Being. So also, until mankind gives all it has to God, never shall there be a perfected society.

328. There is nothing small in God's eyes; let there be nothing small in thine. He bestows as much labour of divine energy on the formation of a shell as on the building of an empire. For thyself it is greater to be a good shoemaker than a luxurious and incompetent king.

329. Imperfect capacity & effect in the work that is meant for thee is better than an artificial competency & a borrowed perfection.

330. Not result is the purpose of action, but God's eternal delight in becoming, seeing and doing.

331. God's world advances step by step fulfilling the lesser unit before it seriously attempts the larger. Affirm free nationality first, if thou wouldst ever bring the world to be one nation.

332. A nation is not made by a common blood, a common tongue or a common religion; these are only important helps and powerful conveniences. But wherever communities of men not bound by family ties are united in one sentiment and aspiration to defend a common inheritance from their ancestors or assure a common future for their posterity, there a nation is already in existence.

333. Nationality is a stride of the progressive God passing beyond the stage of the family; therefore the attachment to clan and tribe must weaken or perish before a nation can be born.

334. Family, nationality, humanity are Vishnu's three strides from an isolated to a collective unity. The first has been fulfilled, we yet strive for the perfection of the second, towards the third we are reaching out our hands and the pioneer work is already attempted.

335. With the present morality of the human race a sound and durable human unity is not yet possible; but there is no reason why a temporary approximation to it should not be the reward of strenuous aspiration and untiring effort. By constant approximations and by partial realisations and temporary successes Nature advances.

336. Imitation is sometimes a good training-ship; but it will never fly the flag of the admiral.

337. Rather hang thyself than belong to the horde of successful imitators.

338. Tangled is the way of works in the world. When Rama the Avatar murdered Vali or Krishna, who was God himself,

assassinated, to liberate his nation, his tyrant uncle Kansa, who shall say whether they did good or did evil? But this we can feel, that they acted divinely.

339. Reaction perfects & hastens progress by increasing & purifying the force within it. This is what the multitude of the weak cannot see who despair of their port when the ship is fleeing helplessly before the storm wind, but it flees, hidden by the rain & the Ocean furrow, towards God's intended haven.

340. Democracy was the protest of the human soul against the allied despotisms of autocrat, priest and noble; Socialism is the protest of the human soul against the despotism of a plutocratic democracy; Anarchism is likely to be the protest of the human soul against the tyranny of a bureaucratic Socialism. A turbulent and eager march from illusion to illusion and from failure to failure is the image of European progress.

341. Democracy in Europe is the rule of the Cabinet minister, the corrupt deputy or the self-seeking capitalist masqued by the occasional sovereignty of a wavering populace; Socialism in Europe is likely to be the rule of the official and policeman masqued by the theoretic sovereignty of an abstract State. It is chimerical to enquire which is the better system; it would be difficult to decide which is the worse.

342. The gain of democracy is the security of the individual's life, liberty and goods from the caprices of the tyrant one or the selfish few; its evil is the decline of greatness in humanity.

343. This erring race of human beings dreams always of perfecting their environment by the machinery of government and society; but it is only by the perfection of the soul within that the outer environment can be perfected. What thou art within, that outside thee thou shalt enjoy; no machinery can rescue thee from the law of thy being.

344. Be always vigilant against thy human proneness to persecute or ignore the reality even while thou art worshipping its semblance or token. Not human wickedness but human fallibility is the opportunity of Evil.

345. Honour the garb of the ascetic, but look also at the wearer, lest hypocrisy occupy the holy places and inward saintliness become a legend.

346. The many strive after competence or riches, the few embrace poverty as a bride; but, for thyself, strive after and embrace God only. Let Him choose for thee a king's palace or the bowl of the beggar.

347. What is vice but an enslaving habit and virtue but a human opinion? See God and do His will; walk in whatever path He shall trace for thy goings.

348. In the world's conflicts espouse not the party of the rich for their riches, nor of the poor for their poverty, of the king for his power & majesty, nor of the people for their hope and fervour, but be on God's side always. Unless indeed He has commanded thee to war against Him! then do that with thy whole heart and strength and rapture.

349. How shall I know God's will with me? I have to put egoism out of me, hunting it from every lair & burrow, and bathe my purified and naked soul in His infinite workings; then He himself will reveal it to me.

350. Only the soul that is naked and unashamed, can be pure and innocent, even as Adam was in the primal garden of humanity.

351. Boast not thy riches, neither seek men's praise for thy poverty and self-denial; both these things are the coarse or the fine food of egoism.

352. Altruism is good for man, but less good when it is a form of supreme self-indulgence & lives by pampering the selfishness of others.

353. By altruism thou canst save thy soul, but see that thou save it not by indulging in his perdition thy brother.

354. Self-denial is a mighty instrument for purification; it is not an end in itself nor a final law of living. Not to mortify thyself but to satisfy God in the world must be thy object.

355. It is easy to distinguish the evil worked by sin & vice, but the trained eye sees also the evil done by self-righteous or self-regarding virtue.

356. The Brahmin first ruled by the book & the ritual, the Kshatriya next by the sword and the buckler; now the Vaishya governs us by machinery & the dollar, & the Sudra, the liberated serf, presses in with his doctrine of the kingdom of associated labour. But neither priest, king, merchant nor labourer is the true governor of humanity; the despotism of the tool and the mattock will fail like all the preceding despotisms. Only when egoism dies & God in man governs his own human universality, can this earth support a happy and contented race of beings.

357. Men run after pleasure and clasp feverishly that burning bride to their tormented bosoms; meanwhile a divine & faultless bliss stands behind them waiting to be seen and claimed and captured.

358. Men hunt after petty successes & trivial masteries from which they fall back into exhaustion & weakness; meanwhile all the infinite force of God in the universe waits vainly to place itself at their disposal.

359. Men burrow after little details of knowledge and group them into bounded & ephemeral thought systems; meanwhile

all infinite wisdom laughs above their heads & shakes wide the glory of her iridescent pinions.

360. Men seek laboriously to satisfy & complement the little bounded being made of the mental impressions they have grouped about a mean & grovelling ego; meanwhile the spaceless & timeless Soul is denied its joyous & splendid manifestation.

361. O soul of India, hide thyself no longer with the darkened Pandits of the Kaliyuga in the kitchen & the chapel, veil not thyself with the soulless rite, the obsolete law and the unblessed money of the dakshina; but seek in thy soul, ask of God and recover thy true Brahminhood & Kshatriyahood with the eternal Veda; restore the hidden truth of the Vedic sacrifice, return to the fulfilment of an older & mightier Vedanta.

362. Limit not sacrifice to the giving up of earthly goods or the denial of some desires & yearnings, but let every thought and every work & every enjoyment be an offering to God within thee. Let thy steps walk in thy Lord, let thy sleep and waking be a sacrifice to Krishna.

363. This is not according to my Shastra or my Science, say the men of rule, formalists. Fool! is God then only a book that there should be nothing true & good except what is written?

364. By which standard shall I walk, the word that God speaks to me, saying "This is My will, O my servant," or the rules that men who are dead, have written? Nay, if I have to fear & obey any, I will fear & obey God rather & not the pages of a book or the frown of a Pandit.

365. Thou mayst be deceived, wilt thou say, it may not be God's voice leading thee? Yet do I know that He abandons not those who have trusted Him even ignorantly, yet have I found that He

leads wisely & lovingly even when He seems to deceive utterly, yet would I rather fall into the snare of the living God than be saved by trust in a dead formulary.

366. Act according to the Shastra rather than thy self-will & desire; so shalt thou grow stronger to control the ravener in thee; but act according to God rather than the Shastra; so shalt thou reach to His highest which is far above rule & limit.

367. The Law is for the bound & those whose eyes are sealed; if they walk not by it, they will stumble; but thou who art free in Krishna or hast seen his living light, walk holding the hand of thy Friend & by the lamp of eternal Veda.

368. The Vedanta is God's lamp to lead thee out of this night of bondage & egoism; but when the light of Veda has dawned in thy soul, then even that divine lamp thou needest not, for now thou canst walk freely & surely in a high & eternal sunlight.

369. What is the use of only knowing? I say to thee, Act and be, for therefore God sent thee into this human body.

370. What is the use of only being? I say to thee, Become, for therefore wast thou established as a man in this world of matter.

371. The path of works is in a way the most difficult side of God's triune causeway; yet is it not also, in this material world at least, the easiest, widest & most delightful? For at every moment we clash against God the worker & grow into His being by a thousand divine touches.

372. This is the wonder of the way of works that even enmity to God can be made an agency of salvation. Sometimes God draws and attaches us most swiftly to Him by wrestling with us as our fierce, invincible & irreconcilable enemy.

373. Shall I accept death or shall I turn and wrestle with him

and conquer? That shall be as God in me chooses. For whether I live or die, I am always.

374. What is this thing thou callest death? Can God die? O thou who fearest death, it is Life that has come to thee sporting with a death-head and wearing a mask of terror.

375. There is a means to attain physical immortality and death is by our choice, not by Nature's compulsion. But who would care to wear one coat for a hundred years or be confined in one narrow & changeless lodging unto a long eternity?

376. Fear and anxiety are perverse forms of will. What thou fearest & ponderest over, striking that note repeatedly in thy mind, thou helpest to bring about; for, if thy will above the surface of waking repels it, it is yet what thy mind underneath is all along willing, & the subconscious mind is mightier, wider, better equipped to fulfil than thy waking force & intellect. But the spirit is stronger than both together; from fear and hope take refuge in the grandiose calm and careless mastery of the spirit.

377. God made the infinite world by Self-knowledge which in its works is Will-Force self-fulfilling. He used ignorance to limit His infinity; but fear, weariness, depression, self-distrust and assent to weakness are the instruments by which He destroys what He created. When these things are turned on what is evil or harmful & ill-regulated within thee, then it is well; but if they attack thy very sources of life & strength, then seize & expel them or thou diest.

378. Mankind has used two powerful weapons to destroy its own powers and enjoyment, wrong indulgence and wrong abstinence.

379. Our mistake has been and is always to flee from the ills

of Paganism to asceticism as a remedy and from the ills of asceticism back to Paganism. We swing for ever between two false opposites.

380. It is well not to be too loosely playful in one's games or too grimly serious in one's life and works. We seek in both a playful freedom and a serious order.

381. For nearly forty years I believed them when they said I was weakly in constitution, suffered constantly from the smaller & the greater ailments & mistook this curse for a burden that Nature had laid upon me. When I renounced the aid of medicines, then they began to depart from me like disappointed parasites. Then only I understood what a mighty force was the natural health within me & how much mightier yet the Will & Faith exceeding mind which God meant to be the divine support of our life in this body.

382. Machinery is necessary to modern humanity because of our incurable barbarism. If we must incase ourselves in a bewildering multitude of comforts and trappings, we must needs do without Art and its methods; for to dispense with simplicity & freedom is to dispense with beauty. The luxury of our ancestors was rich & even gorgeous, but never encumbered.

383. I cannot give to the barbarous comfort & encumbered ostentation of European life the name of civilisation. Men who are not free in their souls & nobly rhythmical in their appointments, are not civilised.

384. Art in modern times & under European influence has become an excrescence upon life or an unnecessary menial; it should have been its chief steward and indispensable arranger.

385. Disease is needlessly prolonged & ends in death oftener than is inevitable, because the mind of the patient supports & dwells upon the disease of his body.

386. Medical Science has been more a curse to mankind than a blessing. It has broken the force of epidemics and unveiled a marvellous surgery; but, also, it has weakened the natural health of man and multiplied individual diseases; it has implanted fear and dependence in the mind and body; it has taught our health to repose not on natural soundness but a rickety & distasteful crutch compact from the mineral and vegetable kingdoms.

387. The doctor aims a drug at a disease; sometimes it hits, sometimes misses. The misses are left out of account, the hits treasured up, reckoned and systematised into a science.

388. We laugh at the savage for his faith in the medicine man; but how are the civilised less superstitious who have faith in the doctors? The savage finds that when a certain incantation is repeated, he often recovers from a certain disease; he believes. The civilised patient finds that when he doses himself according to a certain prescription, he often recovers from a certain disease; he believes. Where is the difference?

389. The north-country Indian herdsman, attacked by fever, sits in the chill stream of a river for an hour or more & rises up free & healthy. If the educated man did the same, he would perish, not because the same remedy in its nature kills one & cures another, but because our bodies have been fatally indoctrinated by the mind into false habits.

390. It is not the medicine that cures so much as the patient's faith in the doctor and the medicine. Both are a clumsy substitute for the natural faith in one's own self-power which they have themselves destroyed.

391. The healthiest ages of mankind were those in which there were the fewest material remedies.

392. The most robust and healthy race left on earth were the African savages; but how long can they so remain after their

physical consciousness has been contaminated by the mental aberrations of the civilised?

393. We ought to use the divine health in us to cure and prevent diseases; but Galen and Hippocrates & their tribe have given us instead an armoury of drugs and a barbarous Latin hocuspocus as our physical gospel.

394. Medical Science is well-meaning and its practitioners often benevolent and not seldom self-sacrificing; but when did the well-meaning of the ignorant save them from harm-doing?

395. If all remedies were really and in themselves efficacious and all medical theories sound, how would that console us for our lost natural health and vitality? The upas-tree is sound in all its parts, but it is still an upas-tree.

396. The spirit within us is the only all-efficient doctor and submission of the body to it the one true panacea.

397. God within is infinite and self-fulfilling Will. Unappalled by the fear of death, canst thou leave to Him, not as an experiment, with a calm & entire faith thy ailments? Thou shalt find in the end that He exceeds the skill of a million doctors.

398. Health protected by twenty thousand precautions is the gospel of the doctor; but it is not God's evangel for the body, nor Nature's.

399. Man was once naturally healthy and could revert to that primal condition if he were suffered; but Medical Science pursues our body with an innumerable pack of drugs and assails the imagination with ravening hordes of microbes.

400. I would rather die and have done with it than spend life in defending myself against a phantasmal siege of microbes. If that is to be barbarous [and] unenlightened, I embrace gladly my Cimmerian darkness.

401. Surgeons save & cure by cutting and maiming. Why not rather seek to discover Nature's direct all-powerful remedies?

402. It should take long for self-cure to replace medicine, because of the fear, self-distrust and unnatural physical reliance on drugs which Medical Science has taught to our minds & bodies & made our second nature.

403. Medicine is necessary for our bodies in disease only because our bodies have learned the art of not getting well without medicines. Even so, one sees often that the moment Nature chooses for recovery is that in which the life is abandoned as hopeless by the doctors.

404. Distrust of the curative power within us was our physical fall from Paradise. Medical Science and a bad heredity are the two angels of God who stand at the gates to forbid our return and reentry.

405. Medical Science to the human body is like a great Power which enfeebles a smaller State by its protection or like a benevolent robber who knocks his victim flat and riddles him with wounds in order that he may devote his life to healing & serving the shattered body.

406. Drugs often cure the body when they do not merely trouble or poison it, but only if their physical attack on the disease is supported by the force of the spirit; if that force can be made to work freely, drugs are at once superfluous.

Bhakti

Bhakti

407. I am not a Bhakta, for I have not renounced the world for God. How can I renounce what He took from me by force and gave back to me against my will? These things are too hard for me.

408. I am not a Bhakta, I am not a Jnani, I am not a worker for the Lord. What am I then? A tool in the hands of my Master, a flute blown upon by the divine Herd-Boy, a leaf driven by the breath of the Lord.

409. Devotion is not utterly fulfilled till it becomes action and knowledge. If thou pursuest after God and canst overtake Him, let Him not go till thou hast His reality. If thou hast hold of His reality, insist on having also His totality. The first will give thee divine knowledge, the second will give thee divine works and a free and perfect joy in the universe.

410. Others boast of their love for God. My boast is that I did not love God; it was He who loved me and sought me out and forced me to belong to Him.

411. After I knew that God was a woman, I learned something from far-off about love; but it was only when I became a woman and served my Master and Paramour that I knew love utterly.

412. To commit adultery with God is the perfect experience for which the world was created.

413. To fear God really is to remove oneself to a distance from Him, but to fear Him in play gives an edge to utter delightfulness.

414. The Jew invented the God-fearing man; India the God-knower and God-lover.

415. The servant of God was born in Judaea, but he came to maturity among the Arabs. India's joy is in the servant-lover.

416. Perfect love casts out fear; but still keep thou some tender shadow and memory of the exile and it will make the perfection more perfect.

417. Thy soul has not tasted God's entire delight, if it has never had the joy of being His enemy, opposing His designs and engaging with Him in mortal combat.

418. If you cannot make God love you, make Him fight you. If He will not give you the embrace of the lover, compel Him to give you the embrace of the wrestler.

419. My soul is the captive of God, taken by Him in battle; it still remembers the war, though so far from it, with delight and alarm and wonder.

420. Most of all things on earth I hated pain till God hurt and tortured me; then it was revealed to me that pain is only a perverse and recalcitrant shape of excessive delight.

421. There are four stages in the pain God gives to us; when it is only pain; when it is pain that causes pleasure; when it is pain that is pleasure; and when it is purely a fiercer form of delight.

422. Even when one has climbed up into those levels of bliss where pain vanishes, it still survives disguised as intolerable ecstasy.

423. When I was mounting upon ever higher crests of His joy, I asked myself whether there was no limit to the increase of bliss and almost I grew afraid of God's embraces.

424. The next greatest rapture to the love of God, is the love of God in men; there, too, one has the joy of multiplicity.

425. For monogamy may be the best for the body, but the soul that loves God in men dwells here always as the boundless & ecstatic polygamist; yet all the time — that is the secret — it is in love with only one being.

426. The whole world is my seraglio and every living being and inanimate existence in it is the instrument of my rapture.

427. I did not know for some time whether I loved Krishna best or Kali; when I loved Kali, it was loving myself, but when I loved Krishna, I loved another, and still it was my Self with whom I was in love. Therefore I came to love Krishna better even than Kali.

428. What is the use of admiring Nature or worshipping her as a Power, a Presence and a goddess? What is the use, either, of appreciating her aesthetically or artistically? The secret is to enjoy her with the soul as one enjoys a woman with the body.

429. When one has the vision in the heart, everything, Nature and Thought and Action, ideas and occupations and tastes and objects become the Beloved and are a source of ecstasy.

430. The philosophers who reject the world as Maya, are very wise and austere and holy; but I cannot help thinking sometimes that they are also just a little stupid and allow God to cheat them too easily.

431. For my part, I think I have a right to insist on God giving Himself to me in the world as well as out of it. Why did He make it at all, if He wanted to escape that obligation?

432. The Mayavadin talks of my Personal God as a dream and prefers to dream of Impersonal Being; the Buddhist puts that

aside too as a fiction and prefers to dream of Nirvana and the bliss of nothingness. Thus all the dreamers are busy reviling each other's visions and parading their own as the panacea. What the soul utterly rejoices in, is for thought the ultimate reality.

433. Beyond Personality the Mayavadin sees indefinable Existence; I followed him there and found my Krishna beyond in indefinable Personality.

434. When I first met Krishna, I loved Him as a friend and playmate till He deceived me; then I was indignant and could not forgive Him. Afterwards I loved Him as a lover and He still deceived me; I was again and much more indignant, but this time I had to pardon.

435. After offending, He forced me to pardon Him not by reparation, but by committing fresh offences.

436. So long as God tried to repair His offences against me, we went on periodically quarrelling; but when He found out His mistake, the quarrelling stopped, for I had to submit to Him entirely.

437. When I saw others than Krishna and myself in the world, I kept secret God's doings with me; but since I began to see Him and myself everywhere, I have become shameless and garrulous.

438. All that my Lover has, belongs to me. Why do you abuse me for showing off the ornaments He has given to me?

439. My Lover took His crown and royal necklace from His head and neck and clothed me with them; but the disciples of the saints and the prophets abused me and said, "He is hunting after siddhis."

440. I did my Lover's commands in the world & the will of my Captor; but they cried, "Who is this corruptor of youth, this disturber of morals?"

441. If I cared even for your praise, O ye saints, if I cherished my reputation, O ye prophets, my Lover would never have taken me into His bosom and given me the freedom of His secret chambers.

442. I was intoxicated with the rapture of my Lover and I threw the robe of the world from me even in the world's highways. Why should I care that the worldlings mock and the Pharisees turn their faces?

443. To thy lover, O Lord, the railing of the world is wild honey and the pelting of stones by the mob is summer rain on the body. For is it not Thou that railest and peltest, and is it not Thou in the stones that strikest and hurtest me?

444. There are two things in God which men call evil, that which they cannot understand at all and that which they misunderstand and, possessing, misuse; it is only what they grope after half-vainly and dimly understand that they call good and holy. But to me all things in Him are lovable.

445. They say, O my God, that I am mad because I see no fault in Thee; but if I am indeed mad with Thy love, I do not wish to recover my sanity.

446. "Errors, falsehoods, stumblings!" they cry. How bright and beautiful are Thy errors, O Lord! Thy falsehoods save Truth alive; by Thy stumblings the world is perfected.

447. Life, Life, Life, I hear the passions cry; God, God, God, is the soul's answer. Unless thou seest and lovest Life as God only, then is Life itself a sealed joy to thee.

448. "He loves her", the senses say; but the soul says "God God God". That is the all-embracing formula of existence.

449. If thou canst not love the vilest worm and the foulest of

criminals, how canst thou believe that thou hast accepted God in thy spirit?

450. To love God, excluding the world, is to give Him an intense but imperfect adoration.

451. Is love only a daughter or handmaid of jealousy? If Krishna loves Chandrabali, why should I not love her also?

452. Because thou lovest God only, thou art apt to claim that He should love thee rather than others; but this is a false claim contrary to right & the nature of things. For He is the One but thou art of the many. Rather become one in heart & soul with all beings, then there will be none in the world but thou alone for Him to love.

453. My quarrel is with those who are foolish enough not to love my Lover, not with those who share His love with me.

454. In those whom God loves, have delight; on those whom He pretends not to love, take pity.

455. Dost thou hate the atheist because he does love not God? Then shouldst thou be disliked because thou dost not love God perfectly.

456. There is one thing especially in which creeds and churches surrender themselves to the devil, and that is in their anathemas. When the priest chants Anathema Maranatha, then I see a devil worshipper praying.

457. No doubt, when the priest curses, he is crying to God; but it is the God of anger and darkness to whom he devotes himself along with his enemy; for as he approaches God, so shall God receive him.

458. I was much plagued by Satan, until I found that it was

God who was tempting me; then the anguish of him passed out of my soul for ever.

459. I hated the devil and was sick with his temptations and tortures; and I could not tell why the voice in his departing words was so sweet that when he returned often and offered himself to me, it was with sorrow I refused him. Then I discovered it was Krishna at His tricks and my hate was changed into laughter.

460. They explained the evil in the world by saying that Satan had prevailed against God; but I think more proudly of my Beloved. I believe that nothing is done but by His will in heaven or hell, on earth or on the waters.

461. In our ignorance we are like children proud of our success in walking erect and unaided and too eager to be aware of the mother's steadying touch on the shoulder. When we wake, we look back and see that God was leading and upholding us always.

462. At first whenever I fell back into sin, I used to weep and rage against myself and against God for having suffered it. Afterwards it was as much as I could dare to ask, "Why hast thou rolled me again in the mud, O my playfellow?" Then even that came to my mind to seem too bold and presumptuous; I could only get up in silence, look at him out of the corner of my eyes — and clean myself.

463. God has so arranged life that the world is the soul's husband; Krishna its divine paramour. We owe a debt of service to the world and are bound to it by a law, a compelling opinion, and a common experience of pain and pleasure, but our heart's worship and our free and secret joy are for our Lover.

464. The joy of God is secret and wonderful; it is a mystery and a rapture at which common sense makes mouths of mockery;

but the soul that has once tasted it, can never renounce, whatever worldly disrepute, torture and affliction it may bring us.

465. God, the world Guru, is wiser than thy mind; trust Him and not that eternal self-seeker & arrogant sceptic.

466. The sceptic mind doubts always because it cannot understand, but the faith of the God-lover persists in knowing although it cannot understand. Both are necessary to our darkness, but there can be no doubt which is the mightier. What I cannot understand now, I shall some day master, but if I lose faith & love, I fall utterly from the goal which God has set before me.

467. I may question God, my guide & teacher, & ask Him, "Am I right or hast Thou in thy love & wisdom suffered my mind to deceive me?" Doubt thy mind, if thou wilt, but doubt not that God leads thee.

468. Because thou wert given at first imperfect conceptions about God, now thou ragest and deniest Him. Man, dost thou doubt thy teacher because he gave not thee the whole of knowledge at the beginning? Study rather that imperfect truth & put it in its place, so that thou mayst pass on safely to the wider knowledge that is now opening before thee.

469. This is how God in His love teaches the child soul & the weakling, taking them step by step and withholding the vision of His ultimate & yet unattainable mountaintops. And have we not all some weakness? Are we not all in His sight but as little children?

470. This I have seen that whatever God has withheld from me, He withheld in His love & wisdom. Had I grasped it then, I would have turned some great good into a great poison. Yet sometimes when we insist, He gives us poison to drink that we

may learn to turn from it and taste with knowledge His ambrosia & His nectar.

471. Even the atheist ought now to be able to see that creation marches towards some infinite & mighty purpose which evolution in its very nature supposes. But infinite purpose & fulfilment presupposes an infinite wisdom that prepares, guides, shapes, protects & justifies. Revere then that Wisdom & worship it with thoughts in thy soul if not with incense in a temple, and even though thou deny it the heart of infinite Love and the mind of infinite self-effulgence. Then though thou know it not it is still Krishna whom thou reverest & worshippest.

472. The Lord of Love has said, "They who follow after the Unknowable & Indefinable, follow after Me and I accept them." He has justified by His word the Illusionist & the Agnostic. Why then, O devotee, dost thou rail at him whom thy Master has accepted?

473. Calvin who justified eternal Hell, knew not God but made one terrible mask of Him His eternal reality. If there were an unending Hell, it could only be a seat of unending rapture; for God is Ananda and than the eternity of His bliss there is no other eternity.

474. Dante, when he said that God's perfect love created eternal Hell, wrote perhaps wiselier than he knew; for from stray glimpses I have sometimes thought there is a Hell where our souls suffer aeons of intolerable ecstasy & wallow as if for ever in the utter embrace of Rudra, the sweet & terrible.

475. Discipleship to God the Teacher, sonship to God the Father, tenderness of God the Mother, clasp of the hand of the divine Friend, laughter and sport with our Comrade and boy Playfellow, blissful servitude to God the Master, rapturous love of our divine Paramour, these are the seven beatitudes of life in the human body. Canst thou unite all these in a single supreme &

rainbow-hued relation? Then hast thou no need of any heaven and thou exceedest the emancipation of the Adwaitin.

476. When will the world change into the model of heaven? When all mankind becomes boys & girls together with God revealed as Krishna & Kali, the happiest boy & strongest girl of the crowd, playing together in the gardens of Paradise. The Semitic Eden was well enough, but Adam & Eve were too grown up and its God himself too old & stern & solemn for the offer of the Serpent to be resisted.

477. The Semites have afflicted mankind with the conception of a God who is a stern & dignified king & solemn judge & knows not mirth. But we who have seen Krishna, know Him for a boy fond of play and a child full of mischief & happy laughter.

478. A God who cannot smile, could not have created this humorous universe.

479. God took a child to fondle him in His bosom of delight; but the mother wept & would not be consoled because her child no longer existed.

480. When I suffer from pain or grief or mischance, I say "So, my old Playfellow, thou hast taken again to bullying me," and I sit down to possess the pleasure of the pain, the joy of the grief, the good fortune of the mischance; then He sees He is found out and takes His ghosts & bugbears away from me.

481. The seeker after divine knowledge finds in the description of Krishna stealing the robes of the Gopis one of the deepest parables of God's ways with the soul, the devotee a perfect rendering in divine act of his heart's mystic experiences, the prurient & the Puritan (two faces of one temperament) only a lustful story. Men bring what they have in themselves and see it reflected in the Scripture.

482. My lover took away my robe of sin and I let it fall, rejoicing; then he plucked at my robe of virtue, but I was ashamed and alarmed and prevented him. It was not till he wrested it from me by force that I saw how my soul had been hidden from me.

483. Sin is a trick & a disguise of Krishna to conceal Himself from the gaze of the virtuous. Behold, O Pharisee, God in the sinner, sin in thy self purifying thy heart; clasp thy brother.

484. Love of God, charity towards men is the first step towards perfect wisdom.

485. He who condemns failure & imperfection, is condemning God; he limits his own soul and cheats his own vision. Condemn not, but observe Nature, help & heal thy brothers and strengthen by sympathy their capacities & their courage.

486. Love of man, love of woman, love of things, love of thy neighbour, love of thy country, love of animals, love of humanity are all the love of God reflected in these living images. So love & grow mighty to enjoy all, to help all and to love for ever.

487. If there are things that absolutely refuse to be transformed or remedied into God's more perfect image, they may be destroyed with tenderness in the heart, but ruthlessness in the smiting. But make sure first that God has given thee thy sword and thy mission.

488. I should love my neighbour not because he is neighbourhood, — for what is there in neighbourhood and distance? nor because the religions tell me he is my brother, — for where is the root of that brotherhood? but because he is myself. Neighbourhood and distance affect the body, the heart goes beyond them. Brotherhood is of blood or country or religion or humanity, but when self-interest clamours what becomes of this brotherhood? It is only by living in God & turning mind and heart & body

into the image of his universal unity that that deep, disinterested and unassailable love becomes possible.

489. When I live in Krishna, then ego & self-interest vanish and only God himself can qualify my love bottomless & illimitable.

490. Living in Krishna, even enmity becomes a play of love and the wrestling of brothers.

491. To the soul that has hold of the highest beatitude, life cannot be an evil or a sorrowful illusion; rather all life becomes the rippling love and laughter of a divine Lover & Playfellow.

492. Canst thou see God as the bodiless Infinite & yet love Him as a man loves his mistress? Then has the highest truth of the Infinite been revealed to thee. Canst thou also clothe the Infinite in one secret embraceable body and see Him seated in each & all of these bodies that are visible & sensible? Then has its widest & profoundest truth come also into thy possession.

493. Divine Love has simultaneously a double play, an universal movement, deep, calm & bottomless like the nether Ocean, which broods upon the whole world and each thing that is in it as upon a level bed with an equal pressure, and a personal movement, forceful, intense & ecstatic like the dancing surface of the same Ocean, which varies the height & force of its billows and chooses the objects it shall fall upon with the kiss of its foam & spray and the clasp of its engulfing waters.

494. I used to hate and avoid pain and resent its infliction; but now I find that had I not so suffered, I would not now possess, trained and perfected, this infinitely & multitudinously sensible capacity of delight in my mind, heart and body. God justifies himself in the end even when He has masked Himself as a bully and a tyrant.

495. I swore that I would not suffer from the world's grief and the world's stupidity and cruelty & injustice and I made my

heart as hard in endurance as the nether millstone and my mind as a polished surface of steel. I no longer suffered, but enjoyment had passed away from me. Then God broke my heart and ploughed up my mind. I rose through cruel & incessant anguish to a blissful painlessness and through sorrow and indignation & revolt to an infinite knowledge and a settled peace.

496. When I found that pain was the reverse side & the training of delight, I sought to heap blows on myself & multiply suffering in all my members; for even God's tortures seemed to me slow & slight & inefficient. Then my Lover had to stay my hand & cry, "Cease; for my stripes are enough for thee."

497. The self-torture of the old monks & penitents was perverse & stupid; yet was there a secret soul of knowledge behind their perversities.

498. God is our wise & perfect Friend; because he knows when to smite as well as when to fondle, when to slay us no less than when to save & to succour.

499. The divine Friend of all creatures conceals His friendliness in the mask of an enemy till He has made us ready for the highest heavens; then, as in Kurukshetra, the terrible form of the Master of strife, suffering & destruction is withdrawn & the sweet face, the tender arm, the oft-clasped body of Krishna shine out on the shaken soul & purified eyes of his eternal comrade & playmate.

500. Suffering makes us capable of the full force of the Master of Delight; it makes us capable also to bear the utter play of the Master of Power. Pain is the key that opens the gates of strength; it is the high-road that leads to the city of beatitude.

501. Yet, O soul of man, seek not after pain, for that is not His will, seek after His joy only; as for suffering, it will come to thee surely in His providence as often and as much as is needed for

thee. Then bear it that thou mayst find out at last its heart of rapture.

502. Neither do thou inflict pain, O man, on thy fellow; God alone has the right to inflict pain; or those have it whom He has commissioned. But deem not fanatically, as did Torquemada, that thou art one of these.

503. In former times there was a noble form of asseveration for souls compact merely of force and action, "As surely as God liveth." But for our modern needs another asseveration would suit better, "As surely as God loveth."

504. Science is chiefly useful to the God-lover & the God-knower because it enables him to understand in detail and admire the curious wonders of His material workmanship. The one learns & cries, "Behold how the Spirit has manifested itself in matter"; the other, "Behold, the touch of my Lover & Master, the perfect Artist, the hand omnipotent."

505. O Aristophanes of the universe, thou who watchest thy world and laughest sweetly to thyself, wilt thou not let me too see with divine eyes and share in thy worldwide laughters?

506. Kalidasa says in a daring image that the snow-rocks of Kailasa are Shiva's loud world-laughters piled up in utter whiteness & pureness on the mountaintops. It is true; and when their image falls on the heart, then the world's cares melt away like the clouds below into their real nothingness.

507. The strangest of the soul's experiences is this, that it finds, when it ceases to care for the image & threat of troubles, then the troubles themselves are nowhere to be found in one's neighbourhood. It is then that we hear from behind those unreal clouds God laughing at us.

508. Has thy effort succeeded, O thou Titan? Dost thou sit, like Ravana and Hiranyakashipou, served by the gods and the

world's master? But that which thy soul was really hunting after, has escaped from thee.

509. Ravana's mind thought it was hungering after universal sovereignty and victory over Rama; but the aim his soul kept its vision fixed upon all the time was to get back to its heaven as soon as possible & be again God's menial. Therefore, as the shortest way, it hurled itself against God in a furious clasp of enmity.

510. The greatest of joys is to be, like Naraka, the slave of God; the worst of Hells, being abandoned of God, to be the world's master. That which seems nearest to the ignorant conception of God, is the farthest from him.

511. God's servant is something; God's slave is greater.

512. To be master of the world would indeed be supreme felicity, if one were universally loved; but for that one would have to be at the same time the slave of all humanity.

513. After all when thou countest up thy long service to God, thou wilt find thy supreme work was the flawed & little good thou didst in love for humanity.

514. There are two works that are perfectly pleasing to God in his servant; to sweep in silent adoration His temple-floors and to fight in the world's battlefield for His divine consummation in humanity.

515. He who has done even a little good to human beings, though he be the worst of sinners, is accepted by God in the ranks of His lovers and servants. He shall look upon the face of the Eternal.

516. O fool of thy weakness, cover not God's face from thyself by a veil of awe, approach Him not with a suppliant weakness.

Look! thou wilt see on His face not the solemnity of the King & Judge, but the smile of the Lover.

517. Until thou canst learn to grapple with God as a wrestler with his comrade, thy soul's strength shall always be hid from thee.

518. Sumbha first loved Kali with his heart & body, then was furious with her and fought her, at last prevailed against her, seized her by the hair & whirled her thrice round him in the heavens; the next moment he was slain by her. These are the Titan's four strides to immortality and of them all the last is the longest and mightiest.

519. Kali is Krishna revealed as dreadful Power & wrathful Love. She slays with her furious blows the self in body, life & mind in order to liberate it as spirit eternal.

520. Our parents fell, in the deep Semitic apologue, because they tasted the fruit of the tree of good and evil. Had they taken at once of the tree of eternal life, they would have escaped the immediate consequence; but God's purpose in humanity would have been defeated. His wrath is our eternal advantage.

521. If Hell were possible, it would be the shortest cut to the highest heaven. For verily God loveth.

522. God drives us out [of] every Eden that we may be forced to travel through the desert to a diviner Paradise. If thou wonder why should that parched & fierce transit be necessary, then art thou befooled by thy mind and hast not studied thy soul behind and its dim desires and secret raptures.

523. A healthy mind hates pain; for the desire of pain that men sometimes develop in their minds is morbid and contrary to Nature. But the soul cares not for the mind & its sufferings any more than the iron-master for the pain of the ore in the furnace; it follows its own necessities and its own hunger.

524. Pity is sometimes a good substitute for love; but it is always no more than a substitute.

525. Self-pity is always born of self-love; but pity for others is not always born of love for its object. It is sometimes a self-regarding shrinking from the sight of pain; sometimes the rich man's contemptuous dole to the pauper. Develop rather God's divine compassion than human pity.

526. Not pity that bites the heart and weakens the inner members, but a divine masterful & untroubled compassion and helpfulness is the virtue that we should encourage.

527. To find that saving a man's body or mind from suffering is not always for the good of either soul, mind or body, is one of the bitterest of experiences for the humanly compassionate.

528. Human pity is born of ignorance & weakness; it is the slave of emotional impressions. Divine compassion understands, discerns & saves.

529. Indiscriminate compassion is the noblest gift of temperament, not to do even the least hurt to one living thing is the highest of all human virtues; but God practises neither. Is man therefore nobler and better than the All-loving?

530. Love and serve men, but beware lest thou desire their approbation. Obey rather God within thee.

531. Not to have heard the voice of God and His angels is the world's idea of sanity.

532. See God everywhere and be not frightened by masks. Believe that all falsehood is truth in the making or truth in the breaking, all failure an effectuality concealed, all weakness strength hiding itself from its own vision, all pain a secret & violent ecstasy. If thou believest firmly & unweariedly, in the end thou wilt see & experience the All-true, Almighty & All-blissful.

533. Human love fails by its own ecstasy, human strength is exhausted by its own effort, human knowledge throws a shadow that conceals half the globe of truth from its own sunlight; but divine knowledge embraces opposite truths & reconciles them, divine strength grows by the prodigality of its self-expenditure, divine love can squander itself utterly, yet never waste or diminish.

534. The rejection of falsehood by the mind seeking after truth is one of the chief causes why mind cannot attain to the settled, rounded & perfect truth; not to escape falsehood is the effort of divine mind, but to seize the truth which lies masked behind even the most grotesque or far-wandering error.

535. The whole truth about any object is a rounded & all-embracing globe which for ever circles around, but never touches the one & only subject & object of knowledge, God.

536. There are many profound truths which are like weapons dangerous to the unpractised wielder. Rightly handled, they are the most precious & potent in God's armoury.

537. The obstinate pertinacity with which we cling to our meagre, fragmentary, night-besieged & grief-besieged individual existence even while the unbroken bliss of our universal life calls to us, is one of the most amazing of God's mysteries. It is only equalled by the infinite blindness with which we cast a shadow of our ego over the whole world & call that the universal being. These two darknesses are the very essence & potency of Maya.

538. Atheism is the shadow or dark side of the highest perception of God. Every formula we frame about God, though always true as a symbol, becomes false when we accept it as a sufficient formula. The Atheist & Agnostic come to remind us of our error.

539. God's negations are as useful to us as His affirmations. It is He who as the Atheist denies His own existence for the better

perfecting of human knowledge. It is not enough to see God in Christ & Ramakrishna & hear His words, we must see Him and hear Him also in Huxley & Haeckel.

540. Canst thou see God in thy torturer & slayer even in thy moment of death or thy hours of torture? Canst thou see Him in that which thou art slaying, see & love even while thou slayest? Thou hast thy hand on the supreme knowledge. How shall he attain to Krishna who has never worshipped Kali?

Additional Aphorisms

541. I know that the opposite of what I say is true, but for the present what I say is still truer.

542. I believe with you, my friends, that God, if He exists, is a demon and an ogre. But after all what are you going to do about it?

*

543. God is the supreme Jesuit Father. He is ever doing evil that good may come of it; ever misleads for a greater leading; ever oppresses our will that it may arrive at last at an infinite freedom.

544. Our Evil is to God not evil, but ignorance and imperfection, our good a lesser imperfection.

545. The religionist speaks a truth, though too violently, when he tells us that even our greatest and purest virtue is as vileness before the divine nature of God.

546. To be beyond good and evil is not to act sin or virtue indifferently, but to arrive at a high and universal good.

547. That good is not our ethical virtue which is a relative and erring light in the world; it is supra-ethical and divine.

Note on the Texts

Note on the Texts

ESSAYS DIVINE AND HUMAN consists of short prose pieces written by Sri Aurobindo between 1910 and the late 1940s and not published before his passing in 1950. Most prose works written prior to 1910 on subjects other than politics are published in *Early Cultural Writings*, volume 1 of THE COMPLETE WORKS OF SRI AUROBINDO. Most short prose works written after 1910 and published during his lifetime are included in *Essays in Philosophy and Yoga*, volume 13 of THE COMPLETE WORKS. Short writings on the Vedas, the Upanishads and other specialised subjects are included in the volumes devoted to those subjects. Most of the writings in the present volume deal with philosophy, yoga, and yogic psychology. The contents have been divided into four parts:

Part One. *Essays Divine and Human*. More or less complete essays, most of which were given titles and revised to some extent by the author. They have been grouped by period in five sections.

Part Two. *From Man to Superman*. Notes, drafts and fragments on yoga and yogic philosophy and psychology. Few of these pieces were revised; most are incomplete, several quite fragmentary. The editors have arranged them by subject on lines explained below.

Part Three. *Notes and Fragments on Various Subjects*. Miscellaneous pieces that received little or no revision by the author. They differ from the pieces in Part Two in dealing with subjects not directly related to yoga, philosophy or psychology.

Part Four. *Thoughts and Aphorisms*. A series of aphorisms, revised but never prepared for publication by the author.

PART ONE: ESSAYS DIVINE AND HUMAN

The pieces in this part have been arranged by the editors in five chronological sections. Many of the sections or subsections correspond to organic divisions in the author's work.

Section One (circa 1911)

All but the first piece in this section were written in a single notebook, probably in 1911. "Certitudes" belongs roughly to the same period. Above "Man" Sri Aurobindo wrote a collective title: "Essays — ".

Certitudes. Circa 1911–13. The Sanskrit phrase at the end, a citation from the Bhagavad Gita (4.11), means "as men approach me, so I accept them to my love".
Moksha. Circa 1911.
Man. Circa 1911. The Sanskrit phrase in the second paragraph, an altered citation from the Aitareya Upanishad (I.2.3), means "well-built, indeed".
Philosophy. Circa 1911.
The Siddhis. Circa 1911.
The Psychology of Yoga. Circa 1911. Sri Aurobindo used this title again for a piece in Section Two that was written independently a year or two later and yet again as the general title of the first group of essays in Section Three.

Section Two (1910–1913)

Manuscripts of six of these essays — "The Sources of Poetry", "The Interpretation of Scripture", "On Original Thinking", "The Balance of Justice", "Social Reform" and "The Claims of Theosophy" — were typed in or around 1912 using the same typewriter and the same sort of paper. The other seven essays are related to the typed ones by subject or date or both.

Na Kinchidapi Chintayet. Possibly early 1910. The title is a quotation from the Bhagavad Gita (6.25): "One should not think of anything at all."
The Sources of Poetry. Circa 1912.
The Interpretation of Scripture. Circa 1912.
On Original Thinking. Circa 1912. After the text of the principal version, the editors have placed the draft opening of another version, entitled in the manuscript "On the Importance of Original Thinking". Above this title Sri Aurobindo wrote: "Essays — Human and Divine".

The editors have used a variant of this (see "The Silence behind Life" below) as the title of this part and of the volume as a whole.

The Balance of Justice. Circa 1912. This is a revised and enlarged version of "European Justice" (published in *Early Cultural Writings*), which probably was written in 1910.

Social Reform. Circa 1912. The first nine paragraphs were typewritten. Sri Aurobindo subsequently added five handwritten paragraphs to the last typed sheet. (These paragraphs are difficult to read and parts have been lost through mutilation of the manuscript.) The passage beginning "We are Hindus" was written separately and headed "For 'Social Reform'". Sri Aurobindo left no indication where he wanted it inserted. The editors have placed it at the end, separating it from the main text by a white space.

Hinduism and the Mission of India. Circa 1912. Editorial title. The first pages of the manuscript have been lost; the first surviving sentence lacks its beginning.

The Psychology of Yoga (regarding the title, see the note on "The Psychology of Yoga" in Section One). Circa 1912 (written around the same time as the pieces on Theosophy that follow).

The Claims of Theosophy. Circa 1910–12 (certainly written after January 1908, when Sri Aurobindo met V. B. Lele, the "member of the Theosophical Society who [gave] me spiritual help" mentioned in paragraph six). This article, like the others on Theosophy, was never published by Sri Aurobindo. However much he disagreed with some of the methods or doctrines of the Theosophical Society, he was well aware of the pioneering work done by this movement, which "with its comprehensive combinations of old and new beliefs and its appeal to ancient spiritual and psychic systems, has everywhere exercised an influence far beyond the circle of its professed adherents" (*The Renaissance in India*, CWSA vol. 20, p. 70). He assured a disciple who had been associated with the Theosophists: "I have nothing against it [the Theosophical Society] nor against any of the Theosophists, to all of whom I wish the best. I am not against them" (Talk with a disciple, 11 January 1926).

Science & Religion in Theosophy. Circa 1910–12. Heading in the manuscript: "Papers on Theosophy / II / Science & Religion in Theosophy". (Although not so identified, "The Claims of Theosophy" evidently is the first of the papers.)

Sat. Circa 1912.
Sachchidananda. Circa 1912–13.
The Silence behind Life. Circa 1912. Above the title Sri Aurobindo wrote: "Essays Divine and Human". The editors have used this as the title of this part and of the volume as a whole.

Section Three (circa 1913)

The essays in this section form three groups, which were written in three notebooks in or around 1913. The titles of the first and third groups were given by Sri Aurobindo.

The Psychology of Yoga. Sri Aurobindo wrote this title inside the cover of the notebook used. On the front of the cover he wrote, and then cancelled, "Hints on Yoga".
    Initial Definitions and Descriptions. Circa 1913. Before the first paragraph Sri Aurobindo wrote the numeral "1".
    The Object of Our Yoga. Circa 1913. This essay is found in the notebook containing the pieces that make up the next group, but seems to go better here. It has no title in the manuscript.
Purna Yoga. Editorial title. The three pieces are headed I, II, III in the manuscript.
    I. The Entire Purpose of Yoga. Circa 1913.
    II. Parabrahman, Mukti & Human Thought-Systems. Circa 1913.
    III. Parabrahman and Parapurusha. Circa 1913. Editorial title.
Natural and Supernatural Man. This title is written on the cover of the notebook that contains all the pieces in this group.
    The Evolutionary Aim in Yoga. Circa 1913.
    The Fullness of Yoga — In Condition. Circa 1913. A draft of this and the preceding essay is published as piece 127 of Part Two. The second part of the draft, from the phrase "Yoga in its practice may be either perfect or partial" to the end, was rewritten as "The Fullness of Yoga — In Condition". This essay follows the draft rather closely for two and a half paragraphs; from this point the two are developed on different lines. The significance of the phrase "in condition" in the title is not made clear in the essay; but it is brought out sufficiently well in the draft.

Nature. Circa 1913. This essay was at one point to be entitled "Maya, Lila, Prakriti, Chit-Shakti". Individual pieces on each of these aspects of the force called Nature were apparently planned, but only "Maya" was written.

Maya. Circa 1913. In the second paragraph Sri Aurobindo writes of his intention to "look at the Cosmos from ... the standpoint ... of ... Lila". Although never able to complete an essay on this theme, he did sketch his view of the subject in two sentences written on the back cover of the notebook. These sentences are given as a footnote.

Section Four (1914–1919)

The four essays making up this section were written independently during the period of publication of the monthly journal *Arya* (1914–21). They may have been meant for the journal, but were not published there. They have no relationship with each other except that of date.

The Beginning and the End. Circa 1915. Editorial title. In the manuscript this passage is followed by one that was published in the *Arya* in May 1915 under the title "Thoughts and Glimpses". Subsequently this second passage was reproduced as three parts of the booklet *Thoughts and Glimpses* (published in *Essays in Philosophy and Yoga*).
The Hour of God. Circa 1918.
Beyond Good and Evil. Circa 1918. Editorial title.
The Divine Superman. Circa 1918.

Section Five (1927 and after)

The second, third and fourth essays in this section were written in the same notebook around 1930. The other two were written at roughly the same time.

The Law of the Way. Circa 1927. The manuscript is untitled; the editors have used a phrase from the last sentence as heading.
Man and the Supermind. Circa 1930. Sri Aurobindo returned to the theme "Man is a transitional being" again and again. See pieces 46,

47, 53, 54, 77, 80, 81 and 82 of Part Two. The present essay is the last of several drafts.

The Involved and Evolving Godhead. Circa 1930. Written immediately after the preceding essay in the same notebook. An earlier draft, written around 1927, is published as piece 51 of Part Two.

The Evolution of Consciousness. Circa 1930. Untitled in the manuscript. The Greek sentence at the end of the third paragraph means "God is not but becomes."

The Path. Circa 1930. This essay is one of several pieces written around 1930 on the supramental yoga. Three others are published as pieces 18, 157 and 159 of Part Two.

PART TWO: FROM MAN TO SUPERMAN

The 171 notes, drafts and fragments that make up this part were written by Sri Aurobindo over the course of thirty-five years, from around 1912 to 1947, when failing eyesight obliged him to stop writing by hand.

None of the pieces were revised for publication by the author. It has sometimes been necessary for the editors to make judgments as to what his intentions were. In addition, some of the pieces, particularly those from the 1940s, are quite difficult to read. The editors have been able to decipher all but a few words; doubtful readings and illegible words are indicated in accordance with the Guide to Editorial Notation. Special problems are discussed in the reference volume.

These 171 pieces were never intended to form a single work. The compilation, arrangement and numbering is the responsibility of the editors. They have chosen to arrange the pieces by subject rather than date because a strict chronological arrangement, even if possible, would have resulted in thematic incoherence. A table in the reference volume shows the approximate chronological sequence of the pieces.

The material falls into three broad categories, which have been made the main sections of the compilation: philosophy (the principles of things), psychology (the study of consciousness), and yoga. The pieces in each section have been divided into subsections and sub-subsections.

A number of the pieces have headings in the manuscript. Some apparently were intended to be the titles of the essays or books that the pieces would have introduced. Since Sri Aurobindo frequently abandoned the pieces before the subject given in the title was reached, all headings have been omitted from the texts. They are given in the notes on individual pieces below. Some headings have been made the titles of subdivisions. One heading used twice by Sri Aurobindo, "From Man to Superman", has been used as the title of this part.

Sri Aurobindo usually placed some sort of sign (asterisk, group of asterisks, bar, etc.) to mark his own division of pieces into sections. The editors have represented his sign uniformly by a single asterisk.

Notes on Individual Pieces in Part Two

1. Circa 1927. Heading: "God, Nature and Man" (used as the subtitle of this section; cf. the heading of piece 14). The text of the piece is cancelled in the manuscript.
2. Circa 1936.
3. Late 1920s to early 1930s. Heading: "The Divine".
4. Late 1920s to early 1930s.
5. Circa 1912. Heading: "Ishavasyam". On the next two pages of the same notebook is written a fragmentary commentary on the Isha Upanishad. The present piece clearly is related to that commentary.
6. *Arya* period (1914–21).
7. Circa 1928–29.
8. Late 1920s to early 1930s. Pieces 8–15 are fragmentary treatments of a theme taken up by Sri Aurobindo recurrently over a period of ten to twenty years. Pieces 8–11 all were written in the same notebook. Cf. also piece 55 and piece 128.
9. Late 1920s to early 1930s.
10. Late 1920s to early 1930s.
11. Late 1920s to early 1930s.
12. Circa 1942. The phrase "Ekam evadvitiyam" was written at the end of the first paragraph, then cancelled.
13. 1930s.
14. Circa 1945. Heading: "God, Nature and Soul. / God / I" (cf. the subtitle of this section).

15. 1930s.
16. Circa 1927.
17. Circa 1927. This piece was not included in the 1994 edition of *Essays Divine and Human.*
18. Circa 1930. Heading: "2. The Fundamental Knowledge". Preceded in the same notebook by "The Path" (Part One, Section Five).
19. Circa 1927. The piece clearly is a fragment.
20. 17 June 1914. Heading: "The Tablet of Vedanta." The opening sentence was written above the title in the manuscript, evidently after some or all of the rest had been written.
21. 1930s.
22. Circa 1913.
23. Circa 1942. Heading: "Note on a criticism in the Modern Review". Written in or shortly after August 1942, when *The Modern Review* (Calcutta) published an adverse review of a Sanskrit-Bengali edition of the Gita edited by Anilbaran Roy, a disciple of Sri Aurobindo. The reviewer charged that the Sanskrit phrase *parā prakṛtir jīvabhūtā* (cf. Gita 7.5), translated by Anilbaran according to Sri Aurobindo's interpretation as presented in *Essays on the Gita* (see CWSA vol. 19, pp. 266, 269 and 519), could not bear the meaning given it, viz., the supreme Nature which has become the *jīva* (individual soul). Sri Aurobindo never published his note. His disciple Kapali Shastri answered the reviewer from a purely grammatical point of view in an article published in the *Sri Aurobindo Mandir Annual* of 1943 (no. 2, pp. 236–42).
24. Circa 1913.
25. Late 1920s to early 1930s. Headed "(2)"; the unmarked "(1)" presumably is one of the "Ekam evadvitiyam" pieces written in the same notebook (cf. pieces 8–11), probably piece 10. Cf. also piece 92.
26. Circa 1940.
27. June 1914 (probably between 3 and 17 June).
28. Circa 1927.
29. Circa 1927. This piece is the third of three drafts, written within a short time of one another, of the opening of the revised version of *The Synthesis of Yoga*, Part I, Chapter 11. The first of

these drafts bears an obvious relation to the printed version, the second an obvious relation to the first, and the third to the second; but almost nothing of the third draft appears in the printed version. It has therefore been printed here as a separate piece.
30. Early 1913.
31. Circa 1942. Heading: "Psychology".
32. Circa 1942. In the manuscript this piece comes after a passage consisting of quotations from a book dealing with Bergson's "philosophy of change", and two sentences written by Sri Aurobindo that are reproduced as piece 71.
33. Late 1920s to early 1930s. Written at the top of a page used otherwise for what is printed as the second footnote to piece 56. The present piece seems to have some textual relation to pieces 56 and 57.
34. *Arya* period (1914–21). The edge of the manuscript is damaged and several words partly or wholly lost. The piece may have been intended for the *Arya*, but was never published there.
35. Circa 1912. Heading: "Life".
36. Circa 1912. Heading: "Vedantic Suggestions / The Secret of Life — Ananda".
37. Middle to late 1940s.
38. Circa 1929.
39. Circa 1927.
40. Circa 1942.
41. Circa 1929.
42. Circa 1918. Possibly intended for the *Arya*, perhaps as part of a chapter of *The Life Divine*, but not used even in a modified form in any *Arya* article.
43. Middle to late 1940s. The piece is the second section of a fragment headed "Man and Superman"; the first section is printed as piece 80. In the manuscript three asterisks divide the two sections; the editors have treated them as separate pieces.
44. Circa 1927. The manuscript of the piece occurs amid drafts of "Man and the Supermind" (Part One, Section Five).
45. Circa 1927.
46. Late 1920s to early 1930s.

47. Circa 1947. Heading: "From Man to Superman" (used as the title of this part, cf. piece 53).
48. Circa 1917–18.
49. Circa 1928–29.
50. 1930s.
51. Circa 1927. The piece is a partial draft of "The Involved and Evolving Godhead" (Part One, Section Five).
52. Circa 1942.
53. Middle to late 1940s. Heading: "From Man to Superman / I" (used as the title of this part, cf. piece 47).
54. Middle to late 1940s. Heading: "Superman".
55. Circa 1942. Heading: "The Secret of Consciousness". Note the phrase "Ekam evadvitiyam" (cf. pieces 8–15).
56. Late 1920s to early 1930s.
57. Late 1920s to early 1930s.
58. Late 1920s to early 1930s.
59. Circa 1927.
60. Middle to late 1940s. Heading: "Mat[t]er".
61. Circa 1927. Heading: "Jottings".
62. Circa 1913.
63. Circa 1927.
64. Circa 1927.
65. 1930s, probably 1934.
66. Circa 1927. Written as part of a draft of "Man and the Supermind" (Part One, Section Five).
67. Circa 1927.
68. Circa 1927.
69. Late 1920s to early 1930s.
70. Circa 1927.
71. Circa 1942. Written below the quotations from a book on Bergson mentioned in the note to piece 32. The present piece is headed by the numeral 2, which separates it from the notes. Unlike the notes, the piece is not enclosed in inverted commas and so has been considered to be a writing of Sri Aurobindo's.
72. Late 1930s to early 1940s. Heading: "Intuition".
73. Circa 1927–29.
74. Circa 1928–29.

75. Circa 1928–29. Heading: "On the Supermind."
76. *Arya* period (1914–21), probably towards the end of the period. Pieces 76–82, as well as pieces 46, 47 and 53 are treatments of a single theme taken up by Sri Aurobindo recurrently over a period of more than twenty-five years (or thirty-five if Aphorism 162 in Part Four is taken into consideration). Pieces 64, 66 and 68 are on a related theme. Sri Aurobindo's most complete essay on the subject is "Man and the Supermind" (Part One, Section Five).
77. Circa 1928–29.
78. Circa 1928–29.
79. Circa 1928–29.
80. Middle to late 1940s. Heading: "Man and Superman". This piece was written along with what is published as piece 43.
81. Circa 1942. Heading: "Man and Superman".
82. 1940–42.
83. 1940–42.
84. 1940–42.
85. Late 1930s to early 1940s. Heading: "Consciousness".
86. Middle to late 1940s. Heading: "Is Consciousness Real".
87. 1940–42.
88. Late 1930s to early 1940s.
89. Circa 1927. Heading "Prolegomena".
90. Circa 1937.
91. Middle to late 1940s.
92. Late 1920s to early 1930s.
93. Late 1920s to early 1930s. The piece is the incomplete second part of an untitled essay, the first part of which is published as "The Evolution of Consciousness" (Part One, Section Five). Sri Aurobindo abandoned the piece without examining the question from the second of the two "vision-bases" spoken of in the first sentence.
94. Middle to late 1940s. Heading: "The Conscient in unconscious things".
95. Middle to late 1940s (written immediately after piece 94). Heading: "The Consciousness below the Surface".
96. Middle to late 1940s.
97. Middle to late 1940s.

98. Circa 1942. Heading: "1 The Inconscient Energy".
99. Circa 1942.
100. 1940–42.
101. Circa 1928–29.
102. Circa 1917–18. A half-page blank separates the present piece from piece 103. Heading: "Psychological Maxims".
103. Circa 1917–18. A half-page blank separates the present piece from piece 104.
104. Circa 1917–18.
105. Early 1917. Heading: "The Psychology of Social Development / VII"; this is the title under which the book later published as *The Human Cycle* appeared in the *Arya*; the seventh instalment of the work, unrelated to the present piece, was published in the issue of February 1917.
106. 1912–13.
107. 1912–13. Faces piece 106 in the manuscript.
108. Circa 1927.
109. Late 1940s. Heading: "The Psychology of Integral Yoga".
110. Circa 1942. Heading: "Notes on Consciousness"; the piece is preceded by "1." (no further notes were written).
111. 1 September 1947. Heading: "Consciousness".
112. Circa 1936.
113. 1930s.
114. Circa 1928–29.
115. Late 1940s.
116. Middle to late 1940s.
117. Late 1920s to early 1930s.
118. Late 1920s to early 1930s.
119. Circa 1942. Heading: "*Yoga*".
120. Circa 1930.
121. Circa 1917–18.
122. Circa 1913.
123. Circa 1917–18. Heading: "The Web of Yoga."
124. Circa 1913. Heading: "The Evolutionary Aim of Yoga." The piece apparently is related to "The Evolutionary Aim in Yoga" (Part One, Section Three), and so to piece 127.
125. 1930s.

126. Circa 1920. Heading: "An Introduction to Yoga. / 1 / The Meaning of Yoga".
127. Circa 1913. This long piece can be considered a draft of what, differently developed, became two essays, "The Evolutionary Aim in Yoga" and "The Fullness of Yoga — In Condition" (Part One, Section Three). The sense of the second of these titles is explained better in the last two paragraphs of the present piece than in the revised essay.
128. Late 1920s to early 1930s.
129. Circa 1915. Heading: "Essays in Yoga. / The Seeds of Yoga."
130. Circa 1915.
131. Circa 1927.
132. 1930s.
133. Circa 1927.
134. Circa 1928–29. This piece and piece 135 were written in the same notebook; it is possible that they are passages intended for insertion in a larger work, perhaps the revised version of *The Synthesis of Yoga*. (Note, in the first sentence of both pieces, the antecedentless "this".)
135. Circa 1928–29.
136. Middle to late 1940s. Heading: "Yoga of Devotion".
137. Circa 1945. Heading: "The Yoga of Devotion".
138. 1930s.
139. Circa 1926–27. Heading: "The Way of Works".
140. Circa 1927.
141. Circa 1927.
142. Circa 1927. The manuscript of this piece comes between two drafts of "The Law of the Way" (Part One, Section Five), and parts of the present piece are reminiscent of that essay.
143. Circa 1927.
144. Circa 1912.
145. Circa 1938.
146. Late 1920s to early 1930s.
147. 1930s. Pieces 147–51 were written in this order in a single notebook.
148. 1930s.
149. 1930s.

150. 1930s.
151. 1930s. This piece includes what was published as piece 17 in the 1994 edition of *Essays Divine and Human*.
152. Circa 1928–29. Heading: "The Aim of the Integral Yoga".
153. Circa 1913. The piece breaks off abruptly; it is likely that Sri Aurobindo intended to write about more than two aims of the sadhana (cf. piece 154).
154. Circa 1930.
155. Circa 1930.
156. Late 1930s to early 1940s.
157. Circa 1930. Closely related to "The Path" (Part One, Section Five).
158. Circa 1930.
159. Circa 1930. Heading: "The Path". This piece is the first draft of what is published in Part One, Section Five as "The Path" (the heading of the present piece is used as the title of that essay).
160. Circa 1928–29.
161. Circa 1928–29.
162. Circa 1928–29.
163. 1930s. The piece evidently is incomplete; only one of the four elements mentioned in the first paragraph was taken up.
164. Late 1930s to early 1940s. The piece evidently is incomplete; only one of the three transformations mentioned was taken up.
165. Late 1920s to early 1930s.
166. Late 1930s to early 1940s.
167. Circa 1936.
168. Circa 1927.
169. Circa 1927.
170. Circa 1927. These lines were written (and later bracketed) at the top of an incomplete draft of what is published in Part One, Section Five as "The Law of the Way".
171. Circa 1926–27.

PART THREE: NOTES AND FRAGMENTS ON VARIOUS SUBJECTS

The pieces in this part were written between 1910 and the late 1940s. They have been arranged by subject.

The Marbles of Time. 1910–14. Editorial title. Cancelled heading: "Marbles".
A Theory of the Human Being. 1912–14.
A Cyclical Theory of Evolution. 1910–13. This piece probably was written around the same time as the preceding one. The opening page or pages (and so also the title) are missing.
A Misunderstanding of Continents. Circa 1918.
Towards Unification. Circa 1912. In the manuscript written beneath the heading: "Studies in the Mahabharat — / The Book of the Woman." Evidently the passage printed here was meant to be an introduction to a discussion of the eleventh book of the Mahabharata, the *Stri-Parva* or Book of the Woman. Sri Aurobindo broke off work on the piece without reaching the proposed subject. The title has been supplied by the editors.
China, Japan and India. Circa 1912.
Renascent India. 1916–18. Editorial title.
Where We Stand in Literature. Circa 1916–18. Draft B was written after Draft A in the same notebook.
The Origin of Genius. 1910–14.
Poetic Genius. Circa 1912. Editorial title. In the manuscript the heading is "The Genius of Valmekie" (see the next piece).
The Voices of the Poets. Circa 1912. Editorial title. The text of this piece, like the preceding one, was written under the heading "The Genius of Valmekie". There is no explicit mention of Valmiki in either piece.
Pensées. Circa 1912.
A Dream. 1910–14. Editorial title. Written under the heading "Srevian [?Srevina] / A Tale of Prehistoric Times — Preface." This introductory fragment is all that exists of a proposed story.
The Beauty of a Crow's Wings. 1910–12. Editorial title.
Science. 1914–21. Editorial title.
Religion. Circa 1927. Editorial title.
Reason and Society. Late 1930s or 1940s. Editorial title. The piece seems to be related to *The Human Cycle*. Published here for the first time.
Justice. Late 1940s. Editorial title.

PART FOUR: THOUGHTS AND APHORISMS

Thoughts and Aphorisms. In or around 1913, Sri Aurobindo wrote 552 aphorisms in a single notebook. In May 1915 and May 1916 he published ten of them in the monthly review *Arya*. (These ten have not been reproduced here. They form part of *Thoughts and Glimpses*, included in *Essays in Philosophy and Yoga*.) Of the 542 aphorisms that remain, two have been classed with the "Additional Aphorisms" (see below). This leaves 540 aphorisms forming the main series of *Thoughts and Aphorisms*.

In the notebook, the aphorisms were written in nine groupings, three of which are headed Jnana, three Karma and three Bhakti. The groupings occur in this order: Jnana, Karma, Bhakti, Karma, Jnana, Bhakti, Karma, Bhakti, Jnana. The editors have placed the three groupings of Jnana, the three groupings of Karma and the three groupings of Bhakti together. Sri Aurobindo numbered all the aphorisms in Jnana and Karma, none of those in Bhakti. Since it appears that he intended the numbers to form part of the text, the editors have placed a number before each aphorism. These numbers do not correspond to those in the manuscript because the three groupings of each section have been placed together and the unnumbered Bhakti section included.

Sri Aurobindo left indications in the manuscript that certain aphorisms were to be moved to a different part or position. For example, he seems to have wanted present aphorisms 240 and 241 to be placed after present aphorism 98. But since some of these manuscript indications are not clear, the editors have followed the original notebook order.

The manuscript, entirely handwritten, was revised once or twice by Sri Aurobindo. The original writing is mostly clear, but the revision is sometimes cramped and difficult to read.

"Additional Aphorisms". The last two aphorisms (541–42) in the notebook containing the main series were not clearly intended for inclusion in the Karma, Jnana or Bhakti sections. The editors have placed them in a separate section along with five other aphorisms (543–47) that were written in a different notebook. The handwriting of these last five indicates that they were written somewhat later than 1913 — possibly as late as 1919.

Publishing History

Some of the material published in this volume was brought out in *The Hour of God* (Pondicherry, Sri Aurobindo Ashram) in 1959. This booklet was reprinted in 1964, 1970 and 1973. In 1982 a new, reorganised edition was published. This was reprinted in 1986, 1991 and 1993.

Thoughts and Aphorisms was first published by the Sri Aurobindo Ashram in 1958. A second impression of the first edition was issued the next year. New editions textually identical to the first came out in 1968 and 1971. The texts of the fourth (1977) and fifth (1982) editions each contained corrections of transcription errors. The fifth edition was reprinted in 1988, 1992 and 1996.

In 1971 the contents of the original edition of *The Hour of God*, along with *Thoughts and Aphorisms* and other material, were brought out as *The Hour of God and Other Writings*, volume 17 of the Sri Aurobindo Birth Centenary Library.

In 1994 those parts of *The Hour of God and Other Writings* that had not been published during Sri Aurobindo's lifetime, along with other material of the same nature that had not yet been published in a book, were brought out as *Essays Divine and Human*. The texts of all the pieces were checked against the manuscripts. The present volume is for the most part a reprint of that edition.